263

territorial more (21)
by changing territory,
changes its admin.

223
but made & further
borders
aligne applied by
But 1903,
disposed 1920
223
234
these rules
235

GOVERNMENT
IN
ZAZZAU
1800–1950

GOVERNMENT
IN
ZAZZAU
1800–1950

M. G. SMITH

Published for the
INTERNATIONAL AFRICAN INSTITUTE
by the
OXFORD UNIVERSITY PRESS
LONDON   NEW YORK   TORONTO

Oxford University Press, Amen House, London E.C.4

GLASGOW NEW YORK TORONTO MELBOURNE WELLINGTON
BOMBAY CALCUTTA MADRAS KARACHI LAHORE DACCA
CAPE TOWN SALISBURY NAIROBI IBADAN ACCRA
KUALA LUMPUR HONG KONG

First edition 1960
Reprinted 1964

The publication of this volume was made possible by funds granted by the Carnegie Corporation of New York. The Corporation is not, however, to be understood as approving any statements made or views expressed therein.

Printed in Great Britain

PREFACE

THIS book grew slowly out of a short essay which I wrote in 1952, on the principal changes which had taken place in the government of Zaria since the Fulani conquest. The essay was stimulated by the publication of two Hausa documents dealing with the history of the Habe government of Zaria.

I showed it to Professor Daryll Forde for his comments, and found that further material had to be included in the redraft. The essay was duly rewritten a number of times, expanding progressively without, however, losing its essay character. At this stage it lacked a theoretical viewpoint and a detailed history of the process of change; only the well-remembered salient factors and events were dealt with, and the relevant field materials remained unanalysed. But as the description of the differing governmental systems gradually filled out, I began to feel the need for some conceptual framework on which to base their analysis and comparison. The first draft of Chapter 2—a theory of government—was the result. Then, when the whole manuscript was lost shortly after, I found that I had either to abandon the work or to think of it afresh as a monograph on governmental change.

By this time I had become too involved with the subject to abandon it, and so I started afresh, indexing my notebooks and writing up all the data relevant to my theme. In this new version I included a detailed chronicle of the history of Zaria from 1804 to 1950, and equally systematic accounts of the alternative governmental forms. When this was done, I found that I had set out the materials for a study of governmental change, but had no theory or method of analysis for dealing with it. In Chapter 8, which was my solution of these problems, I was able to test the theory of government set out in Chapter 2 by application. From this history of the manuscript it will be seen that the two theoretical chapters with which it begins and ends arose at different times out of the problems presented by the materials when these had been set forth.

Hitherto, social anthropologists have tended to avoid historical studies, yet without this it is hard to see how an adequate theory of social change can be developed. As social anthropologists, however, we differ from the historians in certain important ways. The two theoretical chapters and the general organization of this study illustrate my view of an anthropological approach to history, and the account of the growth of this book shows how this approach and the theories associated with it have developed.

To Professor Daryll Forde I owe far more than I can acknowledge for his tireless interest and careful criticism of all the drafts of this book. He has always insisted on clarification and fullness of detail, and even when disagreeing with my interpretations, has given generous constructive criticism. It is not too much to say that without his interest the manuscript might not have got much further than the first draft.

Dr. Esther Goldfrank and her husband, Professor Karl A. Wittfogel, have also criticized the manuscript at different stages, and I have drawn much encouragement from their stimulating comments.

To Mallam Hassan and his brother Mallam Shu'aibu, whose books on the Habe of Abuja initially made this endeavour possible, I owe the warmest appreciation and thanks. Mallam Hassan taught me Hausa at the School of Oriental and African Studies, and I had the good fortune to meet Mallam Shu'aibu in Katsina Province, Nigeria, where he was Provincial Education Officer, in February 1959. We discussed his text in detail, and he gladly answered certain critical questions about the patterns of recruitment to Abuja offices which my further experience in Nigeria had raised. A paragraph in the text summarizes this new information.

My Fulani informants are too many to name individually. The chief of them were the Madaki Sa'idu, son of the Emir Aliyu, the Galadima Hayatu, the Madauci Ibrahim, the Fagaci Muhammadu, Mallam Abdulkadiri of Tukur-Tukur, and especially Mallam Ibrahim Mijiniya, who has since died. To these and all others who taught me the cultural significance of their history, I am most sincerely indebted. I also drew on District Notebooks and other administrative records.

The fieldwork on which this study is based was carried out in 1949–50 on a Fellowship of the Colonial Social Science Research Council. Since completing work on this manuscript, I have also had the opportunity to return to Northern Nigeria to carry out comparable studies of political history in the emirates of Kano, Katsina, Daura, and Sokoto as a member of the staff of the

Nigerian Institute of Social and Economic Research. I am most grateful to Professor R. H. Barback and the Institute for providing me with this opportunity, and to the University College of the West Indies for granting an extension of leave for this purpose. My object in returning to Northern Nigeria and studying the history of these states was simply to test those generalizations about the process of governmental change with which this book concludes against new bodies of data. For if, to the social anthropologist, history may permit or require theories of change, these theories must be stated explicitly and must be subject to comparative tests.

M. G. SMITH.

LONDON, *September* 1959.

CONTENTS

CONTENTS   xi

CONTENTS

I

INTRODUCTION

1. THE CONTEXT

THE kingdom whose fortunes we shall be studying is situated in the centre of Northern Nigeria, and has a present area of approximately 13,000 square miles, lying between latitudes 9 and 12 degrees North, and longitude 7 to 9 degrees East. It is a country of many names, Zazzau, Zakzak, Zegzeg, or Zaria, the last being also the name of the capital city. Founded by a legendary warrior queen called Zaria in the sixteenth or seventeenth centuries, the capital had a population of c. 50,000 in 1950, excluding its suburbs.[1]

The land of Zazzau is rolling orchard bush country at a general elevation of 2,000 feet, intersected by thickly wooded watercourses infested with tsetse fly, and broken by clusters of rocky outcrops, particularly in its southern half. Climate, and especially rainfall, varies in a north–south direction, and so to a lesser extent does temperature also; but throughout the area there is a common agricultural cycle falling into two clearly marked seasons: a short rainy period from mid-May to September, and a long dry spell which begins with the harvest, October to December, and is followed by two cold months, finishing with the hot dry months of the harmattan, February to May. Rainfall in Northern Zaria averages about 40 inches a year, but is nearly 60 inches in the south of the state. Vegetation is denser in the south, and the profitable savannah cash crops, such as cotton and groundnuts or tobacco, do not flourish there. Intensive farming is limited to the rainy season; and although some marsh cultivation is carried on in the rainless months, the dry season is traditionally the period of concentrated craft production, long-term trading expeditions, marriage celebrations, hunting, bush clearing for new farms, and, formerly, slave raids and war.

In 1950 Zazzau had a population of approximately 800,000 with

[1] For a fuller account of life in modern Zaria, see Mary F. Smith, 1954, and M. G. Smith, 1955.

an average density of 60 per square mile, but this density varied widely throughout the area. However, with such a relatively low over-all population density, arable land has little commercial value, except on the immediate outskirts of the large settlements. With this low population density we find a system of land tenure under which rights of use and occupancy now have priority over other rights of ownership.[1] In pre-British days the rulers of Zaria sought to increase this population by acquiring slaves for farm production. Of the present population of the Kingdom, about 60 per cent. are Muhammadan Hausa and Fulani, while the rest are members of some thirty or more tribes who are distinguished as 'pagans' (*arna*) from the surrounding Muslims and Christians. Excluding the few settlements of non-Islamized Hausa known as Maguzawa in Northern Zaria, the entire pagan population occupies areas in the southern and western half of the territory which has heavier rainfall and denser woodland than the more open and closely settled north peopled by Muhammadans. Throughout this area of predominantly pagan population the Hausa are found in enclaves, walled towns, or open villages, which are the foci of economic, political, and administrative life in their respective areas. Some of these Hausa enclaves are centuries old, others are of recent foundation. Throughout the territory one also encounters cattle-camps in the bush where the nomad Fulani pastoralists tend their large-horned herds in the course of migratory cycles which follow the movement of the seasons and seek to avoid the tsetse fly.[2]

This large area and variegated population is now administered as a single unit under the Fulani Sarkin Zazzau (ruler of Zaria, or Emir, in the language of the Nigerian Government). Until 1950 he was directly responsible to the Government of Nigeria through the senior local officers of the British Administration, the Resident, and the Divisional Officer.

Before the British established their rule in Northern Nigeria at the beginning of this century, the Fulani had ruled Zaria by right of conquest for almost a hundred years; and before the Fulani conquest Zaria was a Habe kingdom, the southernmost of seven independent but closely related Hausa states, whose origins are lost in antiquity.

For present purposes three critical events may be regarded as

---

[1] See Cole, 1949.   [2] See Stenning, 1957 and 1959.

marking eras in the development of Zazzau: (1) the introduction
of Islam, *c.* 1456[1]; (2) the conquest of Zaria by the Fulani in 1804;
(3) the incorporation of Zaria into the Protectorate of Northern
Nigeria by Lugard in 1900. A fourth era began in 1951 with the
promulgation of the Macpherson constitution for the federation of
Nigeria, and with the development of responsible government
based on elections. However, as our study will not be concerned
with developments after 1950, no discussion of this new constitution and its consequences will be attempted here.

Islamic influences reached Zaria, the capital of Zazzau, from the
north by way of the Habe states of Kano and Katsina, to which
also came camel caravans with salt and other products from the
Sahara and beyond, returning with grain, slaves, leather, cloth,
etc. In view of the number of pagan Habe kings who ruled at
Zaria between 1486 and 1804, when the Fulani expelled the Habe
dynasty, it seems that Islamic proselytization at first made slow
headway in Zazzau. At this period the principal bonds between the
seven Habe kingdoms, including Zazzau, and the more thoroughly
Islamized populations of the Western Sudan, were commercial
and political rather than religious. But eventually, in the early
nineteenth century, peaceful proselytization gave way to force.
Nomadic, semi-nomadic, and settled Fulani groups differing
sharply from the sedentary Hausa in physical and cultural features,
and led by a group of militant Fulani *mallams* (religious leaders
and Islamic scholars), then conquered all the Hausa states in
turn, beginning with Daura, the oldest; these Habe kingdoms
were then incorporated into an expanding Fulani empire under
the leadership and control of Othman Dan Fodio, the Fulani leader
who was thereafter known as the Sarkin Musulmi (Chief of the
Muslims).

When the Fulani attacked Zazzau in 1804, the reigning Habe
king, Makau, fled southwards with certain followers to Zuba, and
managed to resist Fulani attacks from that place. Makau's successors consolidated their position and established an independent
Habe state later known as Abuja in this area, the population of
which had previously owed allegiance to them as rulers of Zazzau.
This Habe kingdom survived until the arrival of the British,
despite severe Fulani attacks, and the kings of Abuja to this day
style themselves 'rulers of Zazzau', adhering to the distinctive

[1] Arnett, 1909.

institutions of their former home as far as new conditions have permitted. There are thus at present two Zazzaus, Habe Zazzau with its capital at Abuja, and Fulani Zazzau with its capital at Zaria.

The Fulani invasion was by no means the first occasion on which the Hausa states had suffered individual defeat or even temporary subjugation. In the fifteenth and sixteenth centuries the seven kingdoms were all tributary provinces of the Songhai Empire. The ancient Muslim kingdom of Bornu near Lake Chad had conquered Zazzau and Kano on different occasions; so had the Jukun or Kororofa to the south-east. For the Hausa, the novel features of the Fulani *jihad* (holy war) were twofold; firstly, it led to the conquest of almost all the Hausa states by an ethnic group which had a single leadership and no other political base in the region; secondly, that conquest was consolidated by a form of direct administration which radically transformed the pre-existing Habe state organization. When Lugard incorporated this Sokoto empire into the Protectorate of Northern Nigeria, it was administered under 'indirect rule', the essential feature of which was officially accorded recognition of traditional chiefs and their administrations.

Unlike their Fulani conquerors, who stemmed from and at first remained closely linked with nomadic pastoralists, the Habe were a sedentary people principally engaged in farming grains, such as millet, sorghum, and maize, with a wide range of subsidiary crops. The Hausa manipulated a comparatively high and varied technology and operated a well-developed economy which, although pre-capitalistic, is particularly interesting for its range of crafts, institutionalized markets, cowrie and other currencies, and long-distance two-way caravan trade (*fatauci*). Even to-day, after several decades of British rule, the traditional settlement pattern of compact walled towns ringed around by bush hamlets is universal in Hausa Zaria. The walled town and its hamlets, now as in the last century, forms the typical unit of territorial administration under the community chief, who is ultimately responsible through his superiors to the head of the state. In Hausa government, chieftainship is essential.

Though originally of different ethnic stock, the Habe and their Fulani rulers are now normally referred to as *en masse* as Hausa. Hausa was originally the name of the Habe language, which is now the native tongue of the conquerors also. After 1804 the Fulani rulers of Hausa states progressively adopted the sedentary habits of the subject population, together with language and other cultural elements. By interbreeding with the Habe, these Fulani conquerors came to form a group quite distinct from the pastoral nomadic Fulani, who have no share in the government of the conquered states. 'Settled Fulani' or 'Town Fulani' are the terms used to distinguish this ruling aristocracy from the 'Bush' or nomad Fulani of the cattle-camps. In the following pages the terms 'Fulani' or 'Hausa-Fulani' are applied to the kingdoms conquered and administered by the Fulani aristocracy, and the term 'Habe' is reserved for such states and populations during the period of their independence of the Fulani. As an ethnic term, 'Hausa' will refer primarily to the subject population of a Fulani state.

Islam simultaneously links and divides the Habe and Fulani within the conquered kingdoms and those which remained independent. It supplies common and closely identified religious and legal systems, a common framework of theory and technique for government. It further invests the Fulani conquest of Hausaland with the religious sanction of Allah's will and so provides religious and moral support for Fulani rule. During the *jihad* religious ideals and forms imposed restrictions on the rapacity of the conquerors who had the responsibility for demonstrating their religious fervour; and this initial Fulani self-restraint may have influenced the Habe towards acceptance of this conquest and its consolidation. In these ways Islam has helped to define the roles of the Fulani as the guardians and teachers of the Faith on the one hand, and the Habe as the wards and pupils on the other.

There is evidence that throughout pre-Fulani Hausaland non-Islamic rituals figured prominently in state organization and ceremonies. Even to-day, after a century of Fulani rule, the *bori* cult, which Greenberg has shown to be organized on a lineage basis among the pagan Hausa, flourishes in the Islamic capitals.[1] But since the *jihad* of 1804, the distinction between Muslims and non-Muslims has been far deeper than that between the Habe and the Fulani. Among the non-Muslims we must now include the British, together with Ibo and Yoruba immigrants from southern Nigeria. However, these immigrants are distinguished as Christians

[1] Greenberg, 1946.

from the pagan tribes of southern and western Zazzau, who have traditionally formed the legitimate target for slave-raiding, the exaction of tribute, and so forth, and whose inferior technology, smaller settlements, and peculiar modes of organization have left them relatively defenceless. Traditionally, these pagan groups sought security by recognizing the suzerainty of Zazzau and by the payment of tribute or tax. On the whole, the closer the pagan group to the limits of Hausa settlement, the more complete was its subjection to Zaria, and the same also held for those tribes surrounding the outlying Hausa enclaves. Subject pagan communities within the territory of Zazzau were administered through their own elders or headmen under the supervision of the king's officers.

Government in these kingdoms is conducted through a system of ranked and titled offices known as *sarautu* (sing. *sarauta*, literally title, rank, office), each of which can be regarded as an exclusive permanent unit, a corporation sole. These titled offices are characterized by such attributes as fiefs, clients, praise-songs, allocated farmlands, compounds and other possessions, and are grouped differently in the various structures we shall be studying, into orders of rank. Relations between offices of subordinate and superordinate rank-orders are highly formalized, while those between offices of co-ordinate status are not clearly laid down.

In Habe and Fulani Zazzau alike, very few of these offices were hereditary. In nineteenth-century Abuja, apart from the vassal chieftainships and royal offices, the only title filled on hereditary grounds was that of the Magajin Mallam, who was the ruler of Bornu's deputy, charged with supervision of Abuja affairs.[1]

In Fulani Zaria, the continual increase in the number of subordinate royal titles itself ruled out the possibility of their distribution among client lineages having hereditary rights to them. Even such Fulani offices as Chikum, Wan'ya, or Katuka, which most nearly approximated to the conditions of hereditary tenure, were held conditionally, and Fulani rulers did not hesitate to distribute these offices among clients lacking all hereditary claims to them. It is perhaps in this feature that the governmental system at Zaria, under both the Habe and the Fulani, shows greatest evidence of continuity and is most unique among these Hausa-Fulani states. In

---

[1] This information was supplied by Mallam Shu'aibu Na'ibi, one of the co-authors of the text on Abuja, when I had the great good fortune of discussing the account of Abuja with him in Katsina in February 1959, some time after this book had been completed.

Daura and Katsina, under both Habe and Fulani, hereditary office was the norm. In Kano and Sokoto also, the Fulani administration was based on hereditary offices. To my knowledge, only in Zazzau, under Habe and Fulani, were the majority of the important offices of the state free of hereditary lineage restrictions, and perhaps only in Zaria were the royal slaves never a dominant political influence. Given these peculiarities of the Zaria government, and its multidynastic character under the Fulani, it would be highly misleading to base generalizations about the Hausa kingdoms on these Zaria data, and it is necessary to undertake comparative studies on the organization and development of these allied states.[1]

Changes which have occurred or are occurring in the functions of particular *sarauta* do not constitute any break in the continuity of the individual corporations concerned, but represent wide readjustments consequent on changes in the system of relations of which these *sarauta* are the fixed points. For example, an important characteristic of *sarauta* in nineteenth-century Fulani Zazzau was the power to appoint a subordinate administrative staff and to invest them with titled offices, but this does not seem to have been a typical feature of *sarauta* in Zazzau before the Fulani conquest.[2] Changes in the function of *sarauta* under the Fulani developed as adjustments to prior changes in the relations holding between the throne and all subordinate offices of the government.

In the central state system, appointive offices were held by freemen, by members of the royal family, eunuchs, and slaves, and the important differences of status among these office-holders found some expression in the differentiation by rank-orders of offices for which different categories of persons were eligible, and also in distinctions between the levels and types of authority attaching to these different offices. As can be gathered from the incomplete list of legally and politically significant statuses just given, differences of social status figured prominently in the social

[1] I undertook such studies as a member of the staff of the Nigerian Institute of Social and Economic Research of the University College of Nigeria at Ibadan. This paragraph summarizes some observations in Katsina, Daura, Kano and Sokoto.

[2] Certain references in the accounts of Habe government at Abuja during the last century indicate that a few Abuja *sarauta* did head series of subordinate titles. I cannot say whether this was an imitation of Fulani patterns, or the persistence of an ancient practice, or a case of convergence. See Heath, 1952, pp. 7, 20, 21, 22, 27.

organization of Zazzau, even before the Fulani conquest. After the conquest, clientage provided the principal mode for the political integration of these markedly different status-groups.

Force was also important in sanctioning and maintaining the state, and the army was drawn from territorial units of the subject population under the leadership of officials who administered these as fiefs. Under such conditions the system depended for its stability on a type of organization which limited the power of fief-holders and controlled their political ambitions while stressing their loyalty and obedience to the king. Clientage within a context of political competition contributed substantially to the development of this solidarity between the king and his officials in ways to be described later.

In its most general and abstract features, clientage is an exclusive relation of mutual benefit which holds between two persons defined as socially and politically unequal, and which stresses their solidarity. There are a wide variety of types and situations of clientage, perhaps most easily classifiable in terms of the statuses of the parties relative to one another and to the community at large. The dependence of the client on his patron increases in proportion to the social distance which separates them, but this dependence is also affected by the position and prospects of the superior within the society at large.

We can illustrate certain features of political clientage most conveniently here by considering the two most senior of the subordinate grades in the hierarchy of government, namely, the appointive officials of state, and vassal-chiefs. Both these groups styled themselves 'clients' (*barori*) of the king, in the same way as the king of Zaria even today styles himself the client (*bara*) of the Sultan of Sokoto. But vassal-chieftainship differed from the freely appointive offices of state in that the hereditary character of the former office set definite limits to the freedom of choice exercisable by the suzerain. Nevertheless, in theory at least, the successful competitor for vassal-chieftainship depended for the retention of his office as well as for his initial appointment on the goodwill of his overlord, and hence the vassal's relation to his suzerain was conceived in terms of clientage. On his accession to office the vassal chief was ritually installed by the suzerain in the latter's capital or by the suzerain's emissary in his own, and in the course of this ceremony he made formal oaths of allegiance which specified the mutual rights and obligations holding between vassal and over-lord. Transgression of these prescriptions could give rise to conflict, and if the vassal resisted successfully, the powers he appropriated from this suzerain would be legitimized as rights.

Unlike vassal chieftains, officials of Fulani Zaria were appointed, promoted, transferred, and dismissed at the king's pleasure, and without any formal restrictions, hereditary or otherwise, limiting the ruler's freedom of action. These appointive offices lacked legislative power and, apart from the judiciary, they exercised no formal judicial authority even within their fiefs, although they could and did intervene in the courts held by the village chiefs of their administrative areas to secure the decisions they wished. Similarly the appointed officers of state lacked independent military authority, and in theory could only levy such military forces, supplies, or tax, as the king directed, keeping a set portion (*ushira*) of the tax as reward; they also took part in the council of state as the king required, acted as captains in war and slave raids, and remained in the capital at the court, administering the communities allotted to them as fiefs through a staff of officials whom they were themselves free to appoint and control.

There were quite significant differences in the rights, obligations, and statuses of vassals and state officials. Yet both were bound to the overlord by relations phrased in terms of clientage, and in these relations contractual elements, even if not always fully explicit, figured prominently. However, the vassal was head of a political unit which was highly discrete and internally autonomous, although subordinate, and his relation with the suzerain laid stress on the community of status elements which they shared at the expense of the formally contractual ones; in contrast the bond between the king and his subordinate state official, although not fully capable of explicit formulation as a contract, has a pre-eminently contractual content and form and emphasizes reciprocal solidarity and interdependence within a context in which the formal differences of status of client and king are maximized.

2. THE DATA

It is now necessary to examine the credentials of our data. Hitherto social anthropologists have not often controlled the kinds of data which allow them to trace and analyse over a sufficient period of time and with sufficient accuracy the development of an institutional complex within a single society. The criticisms of unreliability which have been levelled at unrecorded historical data are especially pertinent to the present study, since data on past political relations and administrative systems must be verbal, and verbalizations about political administration form a large part of the very stuff and technique of that activity. As a rule, general statements about political and administrative practice and organization can hardly be regarded as satisfactory evidence in the absence of fairly detailed and systematic checks. This means that it is inadmissible to use traditions which do not check one another systematically or in sufficient detail even though they may be collected from several sources; likewise, traditions which correspond systematically and in detail but which are drawn from related sources, cannot provide an acceptable basis for sound reconstructions. In the present case, however, a combination of happy circumstances has by good fortune greatly reduced these difficulties.

On the Fulani invasion of Zaria in 1804, the Habe ruler fled southward to Zuba, and, as mentioned above, he and his descendants there established a state known as Abuja, from which they successfully resisted the Fulani until the British arrived. In two recent publications, Mallam Hassan, then Sarkin Ruwa of Abuja, and himself a younger brother of M. Suleimanu Barau, the present Emir of Abuja, has given an account of the customs and history of that kingdom from Makau's reign down to the year 1944, when the present Emir succeeded to the throne and suggested that these traditions should be recorded.[1] M. Hassan's account, interesting and valuable in itself, is especially useful in that it extends our historical knowledge of the *sarauta* institutions of Zazzau, and hence of the system of government of which they were the key institutions, backwards for over 150 years, thereby enabling us to study changes to which these institutions of government have been subject in Zaria since the Fulani conquest.

---

[1] M. Hassan, Sarkin Ruwa, Abuja, and Shu'aibu, Mukaddamin Makaranta, Bida, *Makau, Sarkin Zazzau na Habe* (hereafter referred to as (1), and *Tarihi da Al'adun Habe na Abuja* (hereafter referred to as (2)) published by Gaskiya Corporation, Zaria, 1952. A translation of both books by Frank Heath has since been published by the Ibadan University Press for the Abuja Native Administration, under the title, *A Chronicle of Abuja*, 1952. Mr. Heath's translation is sometimes too free for our purpose and may be compared with that of Appendix A; cf. Heath, *op. cit.*, pp. 72–84.

Such use of M. Hassan's material involves certain assumptions which must be made explicit at the outset. Our first assumption is that M. Hassan's account is substantially correct for Abuja as far as it goes. Its author's membership of the royal family and high official rank suggest that all relevant information on the affairs and history of the state has been available to him freely over a period of many years, while the fact that the compilation was undertaken at the Emir of Abuja's request suggests that all reliable sources of local information were also freely accessible. It is thus of special interest that, whatever may be the bias in the narrative of past wars, the account of political and administrative customs and institutions which M. Hassan gives is almost wholly free from value terms and assumptions as may be seen by examining the appendix. It is perhaps of even greater importance to us that M. Hassan has simply presented a list of the offices of the traditional Abuja government, and has detailed their principal characteristics without indulging in any speculations or reconstruction himself (see Appendix A).

Our second assumption is that the Habe of Abuja continued to adhere to the institutions which were typical of Zazzau before the Fulani conquest; in effect, this means that we can treat M. Hassan's description of nineteenth-century government organization at Abuja as a provisional account of the government of Habe Zazzau in the previous century. No general categorical statement of equation is made by M. Hassan in the publications referred to, and it is clear from a critical study that his compilation was made without reference to these problems. None the less, these accounts contain numerous references to customs which obtained both at Zaria and Abuja, while certain differences were also noted. Such references suggest that, unless otherwise qualified, the institutions described are regarded by the author as common to both historical periods, and this view is borne out by a letter to the present writer after the first draft of this study was completed, in which M. Hassan says simply that 'nothing was changed in the political system of the Habe when they moved to Abuja'.

It is reasonable to assume that the Habe who fled from Zaria to Abuja continued to practise their traditional institutions as far as the new conditions permitted, if only because the unity so essential to the success of their continued resistance to the Fulani would probably have required such conservatism in their government, and also more prosaically because these were the institutions best known to them. Granted this, it would follow that an account of pre-British Abuja will be largely valid for pre-Fulani Zazzau also. We shall later test this assumption of institutional continuity in nineteenth-century Abuja by making a detailed comparison of the *sarautu* (offices) of Abuja and Fulani Zazzau during the last century, concentrating naturally on reported differences between these systems. It may also be pointed out here that the Habe who settled in Abuja, far from copying the political institutions of their subject Gwari, Koro, and Bassa populations, have supplied these tribes with models which have been extensively copied, even if poorly understood.

Finally, we assume that omissions from the data on Abuja and Zaria are not critical for the present analysis. In fact the adequacy of M. Hassan's data will be tested in the course of the analysis, but it goes without saying that no attempt to use either body of data would have been made if they did not seem both useful and challenging. Here again their detailed and systematic correspond-ence provides the decisive test of their adequacy, utility, and reliability alike. In this regard we are particularly fortunate in our Habe source, both in that its author's privileged position permitted thorough acquaintance with all the locally available information, and especially in that his particular interests led him to give a highly detailed and systematic account of government, in contrast with his more cursory and general treatment of such equally interesting fields as kinship or economics. Furthermore, after this study was first drafted, I was able to put to M. Hassan certain questions which the analysis of his published material had shown to be critical, and his replies, in the letter already referred to, have considerably increased the value of his account.

The rare advantage of possessing, through M. Hassan's syste-matic account of nineteenth-century Abuja, an approximate description of the state organization in eighteenth-century Habe Zaria, great though it is, does not exhaust our good fortune, which is the greater when it is remembered that the Fulani conquerors of Zaria systematically destroyed all the written Habe records on which they could lay hands. If we could not bring a systematic set of detailed checks to bear on this account of Abuja, or if we could not show in sufficient detail how nineteenth-century Fulani government at Zaria developed to replace this Abuja system which

forms our base-line, then the data given by M. Hassan might have
a primarily antiquarian interest. However, during the course of a
socio-economic survey of Hausa-Fulani Zazzau in 1949–50, and
before I was aware of M. Hassan's materials, I decided to make as
exhaustive and detailed a study of the historical background and
development of the present system as possible to clear up certain
puzzles and obscurities.

The material on which the following accounts of Fulani Zazzau
in the nineteenth and twentieth centuries are based was thus collected in the course of fieldwork with rather different interests and
problems in mind from those of the present study. In particular
when these data on the development of Fulani rule in Zaria were
being collected, I had no idea of tracing connections between the
government organization of Zazzau before and since the Fulani
conquest, as none of my informants at Zaria was able to discuss
pre-Fulani organization in sufficient detail, and I did not then
know that information on these matters was otherwise obtainable.
During my field enquiries, Fulani Zazzau was therefore treated as
a self-contained system, the development of which could be
studied in isolation to determine continuities of governmental
form and process from the Fulani conquest until the present day.[1]

For much of my data on the history of Fulani Zazzau I am particularly indebted to Malam Ibrahim Mijiniya, who was 84 years
of age at the time of our discussions and was himself a grandson of
Malam Musa, the Fulani conqueror of Zazzau. Mallam Ibrahim,
together with several other elders of high rank in Zaria city and the
rural areas, discussed the history of the Fulani state, and especially
its political and administrative organization and development, with
great patience, interest and scrupulous attention to concrete
particulars. The reliability and detail of the information given to
me first became apparent when accounts collected from the same
individuals on different occasions and in different contexts were
checked against one another, and later when the accounts collected
from different individuals showed an impressive correspondence.
But it was not until the resulting composite account of nineteenth-
century Fulani Zazzau was checked against the record of nineteenth-

---

[1] See Smith, M. G., 1955, Ch. 4, 'The Historical Background,' which illustrates this point. The chapter referred to, and the Report of which it is part,
was completed and prepared for publication before I began the present study,
and also before the Hausa texts of M. Hassan's account of Abuja were published
by the Gaskiya Corporation.

century Abuja unexpectedly made available by M. Hassan, with the special purpose of ascertaining correspondences of detail and the equally unanticipated problem of explaining any differences in terms of particular historical developments, that I fully realized how meticulous my informants had been. The accuracy and detail with which these elders of Zaria discussed the development and organization of their state will be later apparent. Although my data on the historical development of Fulani Zaria were collected without reference to the Habe state system, they leave no unsolved problems of the correspondence or differences between Abuja and Fulani Zazzau. This validates the assumption that M. Hassan's account of nineteenth-century Abuja can be regarded as a description of government organization in eighteenth-century Habe Zaria. That two bodies of data collected independently in such detail and in mutual ignorance should correspond in the degree that these do when checked against each other, with all their differences economically explicable in terms of particular historical events, strongly suggests that each account separately, and both conjointly, have an adequate degree of fidelity and completeness for the study of continuity and change. It is also relevant to note that in comparative work of the present kind, which proceeds by an analysis and comparison of structural principles, an account is more or less adequate to the degree that it defines and specifies clearly the essential characters which differentiate one system from other systems as a unit of particular structural type.

2

THE NATURE OF GOVERNMENT

(a) Politics and Administration

GOVERNMENT is the management, direction, and control of the public affairs of a given social group or unit. It is at once a process, a structure, and an idea. The essential components of the structure and process of government are political and administrative activities. By political action, decisions are taken about the ways in which public business shall be regulated and carried on, and about the modes, functions, and aims of government. Action to conduct this public business and co-ordinate the various activities of government is administrative in character. Political decisions having been made, their execution or translation into effect proceeds by administrative action. Thus political and administrative systems are the analytically distinctive and essential components and aspects of government as a structure and as a process.

The system of political action through which government is directed is a system of power relations, involving competition, coalition, compromise, and similar activities. The system of administrative action through which the business of government is carried on is a system of authority and authorized relations, order, obligations, and rights. Thus power characterizes political action, authority characterizes administrative action. Whether it is regarded as a process or structure, government is simply the political administration of public affairs, and is thus a system constituted by relations of power and authority.

Political administration differs from such other forms of administration as military, economic, legal, or religious administration in its focus and sphere of interest. The subject-matter of political administration is the public affairs of the social unit, its focus is the control and regulation of these affairs, the exercise or maintenance of decisive power to direct their management. Neither of these characteristics is typical of the power or authority exercised by military, legal, religious, economic, or other organizations when these act within their legitimate capacities. Nor are these characteristics realized by such organizations acting outside their legitimate capacities; for in such cases these units are either competitors for power to control the public administration, that is to say, they are political but not governmental units; or else they are themselves the government; in which case their original religious, military or other operations, interests, and organization and spheres are widened to include the control of public affairs by the acquisition of controlling power. In such situations the authority which the leaders of such units exercise as heads of government administration is different in range and character from that which attaches to them within the organizations by means of which they first came to power.

Controlling power within a unit is therefore prerequisite for its political administration or government: the diacritical characteristic of governmental administration is its superior authoritativeness within the area of its exercise. No population can for any length of time remain subject to two governments which claim to exercise an equal authority over it. Such competing authority claims themselves connote a political contest between the two governments which make them for control of the population. Despite their equal significance for government, political and administrative relations and actions are essentially different, and the differences between them correspond to differences between the power and authority which are their respective elements. Throughout the following discussion we shall therefore be concerned with these differences between political and administrative action and their implications for empirical systems of government; but first we must define these concepts more fully.

Administration may be usefully defined as the authorized processes by which public affairs and activities are organized and conducted. A process of organization is one which effects the co-ordination of action. The organization of a process, activity, or group refers to the orderly arrangement of its parts. Thus an organizational component enters into all groupings and co-ordinated activities, and it is useful to consider the administrative status and aspect of this component, paying special regard to its formality or informality, its authoritative or non-authoritative basis, and to the level or type of grouping at which it is found. By the organizational function of an administration, we mean its responsibility for co-ordinating governmental action.

The content of the concept of political action can best be derived from the substantive term, 'policy'. A policy is a plan or course of action, i.e. a particular organizational process, adopted or proposed for adoption by a government, ruler, individual, party, or other group. Action is thus political when it focuses on the adoption, pursuit, or reversal of policy. Thus the focus of political action lies in policy decisions, the subsequent implementation and execution of which forms the task of administration. We can therefore usefully speak of the policy of entities of varying scale, e.g. a government, a ruler, or ruling group, a political party, or lesser groups.

Political groups or units are defined by their active interest in the determination of policy, and hence they normally assume definition in a context of contraposition. This is so because effective decisions on policy are made for any population by the most powerful groups within it. Since by definition policy decisions affect the lives of the population on whose behalf they are taken, groups interested in their formulation and content compete with one another for power to take these decisions, and this competition is inherently segmentary in form and process. Moreover, as competition for power requires power in order to compete, a political group or unit is a unit of power competing for further power in a system of like units, and is itself by definition an organization of roles, activities and positions co-ordinated within this field of competition for policy-making power. Hence the idea of complete monopoly of power, which implicitly provides one extreme of the centralization continuum in many theories of political organization, is fallacious and illusory, and such a concept is based on misapprehension of the specifically political mode of action.

Purely political action characteristically involves a competition for power over the policy-making process, and such competition is itself inconsistent with monopoly conditions. Thus any situation characterized by an apparently complete concentration of power over these policy-making processes really turns out to be one in which competition oriented about policy formation is confined to the cadre or group which exercises governmental control behind a mask of unanimity. Moreover, in so far as unanimity about policy persists within the controlling group over any period of time, there is then either a corresponding absence of political action and process within the society, as for instance is theoretically possible if there is absolutely no content to the term 'public affairs', or else the operative system of political action consists in relations between the controlling and controlled groups. These conclusions follow from the fact that political action and process are defined by the relativity of power relations among the competing components, and such relativism is neither consistent with an exhaustive concentration of power, nor with the cessation of political competition. What one does find historically are situations in which an overriding power is entrenched under conditions which permit autocracy or absolutism, but even in such conditions the component units of this overriding power compete among themselves for supremacy. Since political action is characteristically defined by and expressed through competition for power, it is in the final analysis, competition for the supreme power which is diacritical, that is, for the capacity to make decisions on policy affecting the total population of the unit concerned.

In contrast with this inherently segmentary mode of political relations and activities, administrative action is overtly characterized by lack of formal contraposition at any level, having on the contrary an inherently hierarchic mode of organization. This contrast between political and administrative relations and actions merely reflects their contrary preoccupation with different values, forms, aspects, and problems of social control, namely, with power and authority, in terms of which these two structures and processes are distinguished and defined. Just as political action is based and focused on the appropriation of power, so administrative action derives from, and remains preoccupied with, authority and its problems. Thus the legality of new administrative procedures is conferred by virtue of the policy decisions these are intended to execute, and for which in some theories the administration is not ultimately responsible.[1]

(b) Power and Authority

The distinction between political and administrative action set out above derives from the distinction between power and authority. Authority is, in the abstract, the right to make a particular decision and to command obedience, since the act of command always involves at least one such decision. Power, in the abstract, is the ability to act effectively on persons or things, to take

---

[1] This seems to have been one of the points at issue in the Nuremberg trials, 1945–7.

or secure favourable decisions which are not of right allocated to the individuals or their roles.[1] The modes of action by which power is expressed range from coercion and force through persuasion, influence, manipulations of various sorts and factors, bargaining, to simple suggestion or bluff. Substantively, authority is a derived or delegated right, while power is the possession of manifest or latent control or influence over the actions of persons including oneself. We frequently speak of authority as delegated 'powers' when what we mean is a delegated right, as for instance when we talk of judicial or military powers, all of which are derived and delegated rights, in contrast to political power. Similarly, we often describe politically dominant groups or persons as authorities, for instance, when African rulers and chiefs are described as 'Native Authorities'. Whereas legitimacy in the sense of legality is crucial to the constitution and definition of authority or 'power', power itself is not subject to such limitations.

The confusions which result from imprecise conceptions and the improper use of terms may be deliberate or accidental; but they are certainly numerous and important. If the essentials of government are power and authority, their initial confusion severely limits the chances of systematic analysis in this field. To sharpen the distinction between these principles, and point up the consequences of their confusion, a simple illustration will suffice. The command which an army officer issues to his subordinate is legally enforceable only if it is issued in accordance with the rules defining and governing the exercise and scope of the officer's authority. Should the command be *ultra vires* and none the less obeyed, the response reflects the officer's power, that is, his ability to control the subordinate and to influence him to make a favourable decision to carry out an order beyond the officer's scope of authority conferred.

If we focus attention on the formal aspects of the differences be-

---

[1] It will be remembered that we defined authority as the right to take certain decisions, whereas power is the ability to effect or secure such decisions as one wishes, although these decisions are either not allocated as rights, or are the rights of other persons. Concretely this means that if A has authority to decide an issue involving B's interests and does so independently of B, A exercises an authority which appears to B as power. If on the other hand B is able to secure from A the decision that B desires, then B has displayed power through A's authority. In many situations decisions have to be taken although there is no clear allocation of authority to make them. These decisions reveal the play of power, but they are not the only sorts of decisions governed by power. Cases like that of B influencing A may well be far more important and usual.

tween power and authority, it appears that authority is circumscribed by rules which define its scope and sanctions, and which also specify the positive modes of its exercise. In contrast there are no legal rules which sanction power, or positively specify its modes of exercise, although there is a considerable body of law which carefully defines the conditions of illegality in its operation. The converse is equally important. The administrative officer authorized to do certain things is required to discharge these duties, and can be legally punished for failure to do so. The politically dominant individual or group is neither committed by any rules or person to take any specific actions of this character, nor, during this period of supremacy, can the ruling group be punished for refusal to take such action.[1]

(c) Legitimacy and Legality

These points direct attention to the important distinction between legitimacy and legality. This distinction has practical importance in the analysis of war, rebellion, or revolution, but is also critical for the differentiation of political and administrative action. Legality connotes conformity to the law, the quality of lawfulness; while legitimacy refers to a wider order of norms and principles, and ultimately to the traditional moral system, not all the elements of which are adequately represented in the law. That which is legal is normally legitimate also, but all that is regarded as legitimate may not have legal sanction. Whereas law circumscribes legality, legitimacy is often invoked to sanction and justify actions contrary to existing law. Such processes suggest that where these two sets of norms conflict, certain principles or values are on occasion held by different groups to possess a moral authority superior to that of the law; and it is in terms of this superior moral authority that legal codes and procedures are evaluated and judged to be more or less satisfactory according to their correspondence with the system of values and rules which together form the basis of legitimacy within the society. The repeal, desuetude and revisions of laws reflect their subordination to this order of legitimacy; but the condition of legitimacy also provides a powerful sanction for the system of laws. Yet, although it provides a set of reference points in terms of which the adequacy of legal codes may be estimated, this condition of legitimacy is neither as a rule completely distinguished from the

[1] Cf. the history of indictment in western politics.

law, nor are its bases always clearly defined, except in reference to and criticism of particular laws or practices, such as during the movement to abolish British Colonial slavery. Thus, despite their considerable overlap and intimate connections, legitimacy and legality are analytically distinct. Their distinctness can be illustrated by the contrast between legality which in any society has a uniform definition and content, and legitimacy, of which many different definitions and conceptions may obtain among social segments which adhere to differing systems of belief or value.

The legality and the legitimacy of a social order and a government are also different. When a political group seizes command of a state by *coup*, its rule may or may not at first lack legitimacy, depending on whether the repudiation of allegiance to the former government is regarded as morally justifiable or obligatory. If the *coup* ended a régime which lacked popular support and concensus, even although its methods were unconstitutional, its legitimacy could be claimed and perhaps established on these grounds. On the other hand, whatever may be the moral justification of such a *coup*, its adherents cannot initially claim legality for their behaviour; although so long as they enforce the laws, including those of their own manufacture, the new régime may gradually acquire a 'legal' status. Thus the entire corpus of law, including constitutional law, is in part dependent on and in part independent of legitimacy. For the continuity or perpetuity of a governmental system, both legality and legitimacy are important preconditions.

When referring to the *coup d'état*, we habitually speak of the rebel or revolutionary group as seizing power, but never authority; yet, in consequence of their appropriation of power, the leaders of such movements exercise and enjoy administrative authority as well. But popular idiom of speech may also connote unspecified distinctions between that type of authority which is defined and allocated to administrative agents, and the moral authority of legitimacy which is the ultimate sanction of a régime, and which itself includes the specific conditions of competition for power to direct public affairs through policy-making processes consistent with that régime. In like manner the authority exercised by the occupation forces of a nation victorious in war is consequent on their proven superiority of power and is limited by the rules of international law applicable to such contexts.

(d) The Interrelations of Political and Administrative Systems

This discussion raises certain points of considerable significance for our later analysis. Firstly, the analytic distinction between administrative and political action must not be taken to exclude varying degrees of overlap in their personnel and structures. Every political unit, or power-oriented group, has its own administrative structure, and the greater the permanence and complexity of the unit, the greater are the tasks and responsibilities allotted to its own administration. The converse is equally true. Every administrative structure has its own internal political system, that is a system of groups and individuals competing for power to decide certain matters; and the more extensive and less precisely defined the authority content and roles of the administrative personnel, the more developed will be its internal system of political competition. Where the administration is charged simply with ruling, this internal political competition is indistinguishable from the political system of government, and it may be the source or object of rebellions, palace revolts, and the like. In controlled administrative systems, the units of such internal political competition may be kinship groups, cliques, patron-client teams, religious, economic, or other interest groups, or simply individual competitors for promotion, prize, office, etc. In both these contexts the policy decisions are contested by units defined by administrative position.

The multiplicity of political objectives with which an administrative structure presents its staff is closely related to the hierarchic devolution of authority which defines that structure. In systems of hierarchic authority, superordinate authority is conceived as power by the subordinate, and is sought after as such. This conception of superior authority reflects its capacity to act effectively in circumstances outside the subordinate's control, notably of course on the subordinate himself. The superior's ability to make decisions which intimately affect his inferior is therefore regarded by the latter as an index of the power attaching to the superior office, and is desired by the subordinate for its own sake as well as for protective or other instrumental ends. This inescapable byproduct of their hierarchical organization partly explains the tendency of complex governmental administrations to give priority to their own internal problems as a prerequisite for their efficient operation, and indeed for the maintenance of the structure itself.

Administrative action embodies the authority from which it derives, while political action embodies the power which is its focus and source. But relations between the political and administrative systems may also themselves form part of the content of policy. Hence differences of policy with regard to the treatment of official authority structures involve political competition and conflict, and, may promote revolutionary action. Whether the power which informs policy is or is not constitutional, policies which involve extreme departures from the prevailing systems of administration are correspondingly revolutionary in content: similarly policies which maintain these administrative systems and structures are to that extent conservative, whatever the constitutional character of the power behind them.

In this context it is also necessary to distinguish between the objects or ends of policy and the means. An extreme departure from prevailing policy normally involves fundamental changes of objectives or ends. Changes of means are usually instrumental, although on occasion they form objectives in their own right; where such instrumental changes develop without any revolutionary changes of policy aims, then although revolutionary intentions may be lacking, the consequences may be revolutionary none the less. The close interdependence of political and administrative relations within a governmental system implies that a change in either system will normally promote changes within the other, and in this way 'chain reactions' may sometimes develop through which the system of government as a whole may be radically transformed. For this reason, revolution is not the only process by which governmental systems are transformed, nor is it necessarily the most significant. The normal forms of political competition may themselves produce a different system, and without rebellion or revolution, unforeseen developments may occur despite efforts to prevent it. On the other hand, where the ends and the means of political administration are identical with preceding practice, it would be a serious error to suppose that there is no policy and hence no political action. On general grounds it can be expected that the maintenance of a completely static order, that is, a literally perpetual identity, is both a frequent object of policy, and one that cannot be realized except by continuous and highly diversified political action.

A rebellion seeks to change the ruling personnel while maintaining the system of government. A process by which a system of government is transformed unintentionally may develop through the political actions by which its ruling personnel seek to maintain their rule. Alternatively social change may itself promote changes of the governmental system. A revolution seeks to remove both the ruling personnel and the extant authority structure, and may also be intended to revise relations between the government and the society in some radical fashion.

Although expressing themselves in apparently conservative policies marked by continuity with preceding administrations, rebellions are instrumentally radical movements, characterized by significant changes in the modes of appropriating and exercising power, as well as by changes in the holders of power and the top administrative personnel. The fact that a programme or policy may persist in the face of such intense and disruptive competition for power simply illustrates the truism that supreme power, defined as the power of defining and directing policy, is itself the ultimate end of political competition. In consequence of this, the appropriation of controlling power is at once the goal of political competition and the policy of the competing units, and is desired as much for the enjoyment of its exercise as for the utilities to which it may be put.

In many governmental systems the control of administrative staffs is among the most immediate rewards which follow on appropriation of supreme power. In others, administrative prominence itself suggests and permits appropriation of supremacy by virtue of the independent power which it wields. Systems of government vary widely in the extent to which they differentiate and isolate their administrative and political components, and also in the types of relations which hold between them. In some instances the differentiation of political from administrative roles is so rudimentary that the one implies the other. In such situations the mutual insulation of political and administrative functions is correspondingly rudimentary. At the other end of the scale are those governmental systems which are based on rigorous distinctions between political and administrative activity, and which stress their mutual exclusiveness and erect safeguards against their combination. The degree and type of structural differentiation of their political and administrative components provides a useful basis for the comparative analysis of all forms of governmental systems.

Karl Wittfogel's distinction between a ruling bureaucracy and a controlled bureaucracy is relevant here.[1] As its name implies, the ruling bureaucracy is a ruling group which uses bureaucratic methods and has a bureaucratic organization. The controlled bureaucracy is simply an administrative structure subordinate to the holders of power, and is not itself a system of power but its instrument. To distinguish between ruling and controlled bureaucracies, distinctions between explicit power and authority are necessary.

In theory an administration might be able to eliminate its external political system by assimilating to itself the system of power relations through which policy is decided. Yet this would not in fact produce a monocracy, but would simply transform the administration into a political system, the political system *par excellence* of the society in which it obtains. In other words, the more closely administrative systems are identified with political power, the more intense and continuous the operation of political factors within the administration itself, at the expense of its purely administrative status, and to the detriment of its instrumental administrative functions. In brief, administrative identification with and monopoly of political power have direct implications of segmentation for the administrative structure itself. Hence the internal instability of ruling bureaucracies.

Thus the relations between the strictly administrative and the strictly political sectors of government correspond to the relations between power and authority indicated above. In so far as the administration is strictly administrative, it remains circumscribed by defined *powers* and charged with the performance of specific tasks, and is subordinate to the policy decisions which reflect the current distributions of power. In so far as the administrative structure is itself free to make decisions of policy, then it exercises political power and forms a political unit of a special type. The control of an administration by politically specialized units is expressed in its extreme form through dismissals from and appointments to administrative office by the policy-makers, and by enactments redefining, abolishing, or constituting administrative office and structures of various kinds. The control of a political system by an administrative structure is expressed in its extreme form through the forcible suppression of political action outside the administrative structure itself, and this may also involve new

[1] Wittfogel, 1953.

rules to redefine, abolish, or reconstitute the former political system, as well as the simple replacement of personnel. Either of these alternatives may endanger the stability of the pre-existing system, and either of these developments is likely in proportion to the overlap of administrative and political functions within the system. Hence the importance which is attached to the explicit differentiation and mutual insulation of these activities within certain systems of government, as a precondition of the continuity of these systems: and hence also the critical analytic value of these differentiations, and of the relations between the administrative and political systems in the comparative study of government.

As indicated above, administrative authority and structures are differentiated from political action by rules and procedures which govern and detail the conditions of administrative action, its functions and tasks. No comparable framework of rules positively defines or limits the scope and functions of political activity. In English law, this point is expressed in the principle that the Crown cannot bind itself. In effect this means that Parliament cannot act *ultra vires*, whereas administrative agents obviously can, frequently do, and are often reprimanded for such action. The British rule against civil servants indulging in political action is a simple corollary of the preceding principle.

To point this up, let us consider briefly conditions such as conquest, rebellion, or revolution. In any of these situations governing power is appropriated on the basis of force. In all such situations, the appropriation of power is illegitimate, in the sense that it is inconsistent with the conditions of legitimacy which define the system of government overthrown. In the case of conquest, the governing power is appropriated by an external group, whose rights to govern if previously admitted would have made the conquest unnecessary. In the case of rebellion or revolution, the same point holds, although the appropriators are themselves members of the unit. In either of these events, governments are constituted on bases which do not adhere to previous conditions of legitimacy, but do reflect the distributions of power. In either of these events, the pre-existing authority structure may be retained or revised or replaced. These situations show clearly how self-defeating it is to conceive of government either in terms of authority or in terms of legitimate power solely.

Such consequences follow from the fact that all political action and any political system is, by its very nature as a mode of competition, inherently segmentary in process and form. Scgmentation as the characteristic way in which political relations are expressed and develop is implicit in the definition of these relations by the competition for power, and also in the definition of a political system as a system of such competition. Competition of this sort necessarily involves the contraposition of co-ordinate units at any level, and units are defined as co-ordinate by virtue of their competition.

The composition of competing political units varies widely from one society to another, and this variation provides an important reference point in the comparative study of governmental systems, as we shall see. Moreover, within any society, the composition of co-ordinate political units will vary as a function of the issue, occasion, and situation with respect to which they are mobilized, in much the same way as happens in lineage systems where segmentary organization and processes were first studied in detail directly. As a general rule the more variable the constitution of segmentary political units, the greater the degree of social differentiation, and the more complex the system of government.

(e) Centralization and Decentralization

Political action has been defined in terms of policy-making processes, and these are further defined by the fact that they involve decisions which can neither be subject to authority nor allocated as simple rights. Such processes provide a field within which administrative and political systems often overlap. Under certain conditions initially administrative functions may come to have a primarily political significance in consequence of their policy-making capacities. No code of administrative procedure can be devised which will lay down in advance rules governing the actions of its agents under all possible circumstances; and no administrative code can of itself guarantee faithful reports from subordinates, or vigilant and impartial supervision by superiors. Inevitably, administration is confronted by situations in which the administrator must either act first and seek authority after, or enjoys opportunities for *ultra vires* action which his superior may never know fully about.[1] Inevitably, also, at any level of an administrative

---

[1] This includes the opportunity for administrative officers to influence the decisions taken by those who hold power. Indeed, the senior echelons of an expanding bureaucracy may sometimes openly claim that their functions include the formation and guidance of policy.

structure the decisions made may have some implications for policy. Such conditions are of critical significance in the comparative analyses of administrative structures within governments of different type, and they provide indices of the measure to which authority is effectively centralized and controlled, and of the degree to which political responsibility and authority have common foci. We can, in these terms, readily distinguish between 'tight' and 'loose' administrative structures, on the one hand according to the completeness and effectiveness of their administrative supervision, and on the other, according to the scope which staff of any level enjoy for action *ultra vires* or for influencing policy decisions.

Ultra vires action by administrative staff is *ipso facto* political action, since to the extent that it exceeds authority, it involves the exercise of power; and often indeed this exercise of power is stimulated by the authority already attaching to office, and owes its efficacy to that. Under systems of loose administrative control, such *ultra vires* actions by administrative staff may develop with sufficient frequency and impunity for attitudes of normality to surround them. If unchecked, these processes ultimately saturate the administrative structure with illegitimacy, and convert administrative office into political prize, thereby stimulating rebellious sentiments and providing such political movements with some claim to legitimacy. Under such conditions, if the holders of power postpone attempts to control their subordinate administrative staff unduly, they may find that the subordinate is influenced to repudiate his allegiance, partly for fear of expropriation and punishment and partly due to confidence in the power already appropriated. History shows that decentralization of an administrative structure often develops in this way, the recalcitrant subordinate resisting successfully, and consolidating his power on a territorial basis. In such a context, decentralization really connotes a reduction in the scope of the central authority consequent on a shift or transfer of power to the former subordinate. In fact, as pointed out before, unlike authority, power is not subject to centralization.

Under loose administrative systems therefore, the prominent political aspects of administrative office may convert it into a prime object of political competition. Such conditions are generally to be found when there are overwhelming temporary concentrations of political power associated with extreme identification of the administrative and political systems. Under such conditions, the subject population is frequently hostile, although incapable of resisting effectively. None the less, monopolies of power are ruled out by the competition for supremacy which develops within the ruling bureaucracy or ruling group.

Moreover, when administrative office becomes a political prize, the control which the superior exercises over subordinates is correspondingly shifted from the administrative aspect of their relations, which is defined in terms of authority and is focused on the execution of specific tasks, towards the purely political aspect, which is defined in terms of relative power, and is focused on solidarity or opposition. Under such conditions, subordinate staff may formally appropriate decisive power by successful opposition to the superior. This is the familiar phenomenon of the break-up of empires and other states, the exact reverse of conquest.

The political significance of administrative relationships and actions tends to increase in proportion to the looseness of the administrative structure and supervision. This 'looseness' in turn reflects three related components:

(1) Insufficiently rigorous supervision.

(2) Impotence of the population affected to protest against *ultra vires* administrative action.

(3) Administrative participation in policy-making processes.

Where these conditions occur together, we inevitably find that political solidarity among the administrative staff is significant not only for appointment, retention of office, and promotion, but for the maintenance and development of the governmental system itself. Some substance will be given to these abstractions later, when a developmental and structural analysis of one such system is presented.

The point to note here is that developments of the kind we have just been discussing are both logical and empirical consequences of the distinction between power and authority, which are found, at least implicitly, to characterize governments of any sort. By its very nature, authority consists in a specific nexus of rights and obligations focused on the performance of one or more defined tasks, whereas, equally by its very nature, power can never be positively circumscribed. To define 'power' in specific terms is to transform it into authority. This summarizes the history of the British monarchy. Similarly, to the extent that the scope and nature of authority is incompletely or imprecisely defined, or is extended beyond its defined limits, power is exercised, and the structure or office concerned has political characteristics and significance. This proposition in turn summarizes the development of the British Parliament. Just as there can be no such thing as unconstituted authority, so there can be no such thing as an exhaustive constitution of power.

(f) The Problem of Force

Power has been defined as the ability to act effectively on persons or things, authority as a delegated and limited right to do so. Force differs from power and authority which are both abstract conditions and capacities in the concreteness of its reference. Force denotes physical effort or strength, and in the sociological context, human, especially masculine, strength. The abstract use of this term, force, is a reification of this physical capacity to inflict physical harm. The concrete use of the terms authority and power is an instance of the opposite sort of reification.

Authority and power may both be associated with the control or application of force, but these relations will differentiate authority and power, and in any society, their associations with force will differ by degrees and contexts and possibly also by organs or types of force. Thus force is in part legally constituted and administered, but never entirely so. In its legally constituted form, force is applied within the society through the agency of administration to provide the population with certain essential conditions of physical security, to prevent the use of violence in political competition, and to protect the unit from external attack. Under régimes characterized by overlapping political and administrative systems, force may also be applied authoritatively by political leaders to eliminate their rivals and disperse opposition. Normally, however, such use of force is more or less political, and its authorization in terms of the prevailing conceptions of legitimacy depends largely on the extent to which identification of political and administrative functions has been accepted as itself legitimate. In its external aspect and application, as in war, the administration of force proceeds under authority, while decisions to employ it are political in content and form. In terms of its source, therefore, the force used in war is normally constitutional, although in terms of its target it is normally illegitimate.

To regard force as the source of power is to reverse the order of their relation. Power, defined as the capacity to act effectively on persons or things, has many components or forms of expression, and force is one of these. In the abstract, force is the capacity to inflict harm, and for its exercise clearly presupposes the power to accumulate, co-ordinate, and direct support; less abstractly, force is the manifest infliction of harm, and as such is a concrete demonstration of the power which it presupposes. The crucial feature of centralized administrative systems is never the simple concentration of force within them, but their monopoly of constitutional force; this is in essence a monopoly of the rights to authorize the use of force and to restrain its use by others through the employment of a greater concentration of legitimate force. This monopoly of authorized force in turn depends on public consensus about the legitimacy of the governmental system. In other words, it is not the means of exercising force as such which forms the direct content of the monopoly held by centralized systems of government, but the *right* to control and employ force within the unit concerned. The degree and character of the centralization of an administrative system corresponds therefore to the consensus prevailing about its monopoly rights to control force within the area, and these rights express its authority. Thus the term 'centralization' properly refers to the administrative aspect of a governmental system or structure, since governmental action defined in terms of authority is administrative in character and form. Consequently in centralized systems rules define the conditions under which force may be legitimately employed, and particular branches of administration, such as the judiciary, police, army, intelligence service, etc., are more or less concerned with the application and administration of force.

Since force is the ultimate expression of power in conflict, supremacy of power implies supremacy of force, and is thus locally uncontrollable. For this reason, no set of rules can perpetually guarantee, control, or define the exercise of supreme power. The incalculability of such power ultimately corresponds to its freedom to exercise force outside of the strictly authorized framework. Such possibilities are inherent in all political systems and therefore in all governments, since the political components of government are relations based on, expressed, and mediated in terms of power, and since the government as a unit is related to other governments in a similar fashion. Thus no government can ever enjoy unconditional and perpetual consensus, since power can never be completely monopolized. Even in war, when a society may be threatened with perils which invest its government with an unconditional support, this support is temporary and limited to the situation of conflict, and it is also conditional on military success by the government concerned.

In short, organized force has only two modes or aspects of operation; in its positively delimited and authorized form, it is at once a sanction and an object of administration; in its undefined mode it is an ultimate expression of political power to control the administration. But though an important element in the systems of power and authority, force is coterminous with neither. Firstly, since it is an element of both these systems it cannot be coterminous with either of them; secondly, as each of these systems contains elements and sanctions other than force, they cannot be defined solely in terms of force.

(g) Differentiation and Integration

Ultimately, the popular consensus which authorizes government monopoly of force rests on doubts about the capacities of other methods or institutions to maintain social equilibrium. Generally, the ideal which legitimates such government rights to monopolize force is that of a static equilibrium; but under conditions of increasing complexity, where this static ideal is patently unrealizable, the idea of a controllable moving equilibrium may increase the value of centralized force as a prerequisite for the control and co-ordination of changes consistent with the maintenance of the unit. The type of administrative structure charged with such organizational tasks is then typically bureaucratic, and the society it administers generally shows marked differentiation between its moral, religious, and legal systems as well as great internal differentiation; in short, the political value of force, and hence its administrative centralization, varies according to its significance for the equilibrium or co-ordination of the society as a whole, and this significance increases proportionally with the increase in the number and range of principles which differentiate the population internally, and which thereby serve as bases for segmentary organizations within the unit.

These conclusions indicate the general applicability of the concept of government developed here in terms of power and authority components. Thus in lineage societies, where political and administrative units are identical in composition and structure, segmentation is normally based on two principles only, localization and descent. In such societies, moral-religious values predominate and restrict the internal use of force, the legal system is relatively undifferentiated, the span of administrative co-ordination is typically narrow, the degrees of internal equilibrium and integration are typically high, and there is little conscious concern for change. At the other extreme, in modern Western society there are numerous bases of segmentation, a high degree of social differentiation, low levels of integration and the ideal of a moving equilibrium; the legal systems are extremely differentiated, the administrative and political structures are separately specialized, and force is a prominent aspect of relations within governmental systems as well as between them. In the wide range between these extremes, there are a host of differing types of empirical governments, and it may only be possible to make a detailed comparative study of these along lines similar to those presented here.

The analysis and comparison of governmental systems which are historically successive and which form a single developmental series can contribute much to the general study of governments, and in the following chapters we shall attempt to analyse a case of this sort. This examination provides a searching test of the utility of the theory and conceptions just presented. We shall see whether the definitions and distinctions laid down here can bring the governmental changes which took place in Zazzau during a period of 150 years within a single framework, and help us to analyse the process of change itself.

3

GOVERNMENT IN
NINETEENTH-CENTURY ABUJA

I. INTRODUCTION

(a) Some Preliminaries

THE government of Abuja is complex and unfamiliar, and I therefore summarize its essentials here as an introduction to the analysis which follows.[1] But before plunging into this synopsis certain points must be mentioned briefly.[2]

Kingship is a focal-point of the Abuja government. Succession to kingship at Abuja was based on patrilineal descent, but the king was selected by certain high officials of the state.[3] The kingship and succession of Habe rulers of Abuja since Makau's flight from Zaria city are represented in the following diagram:

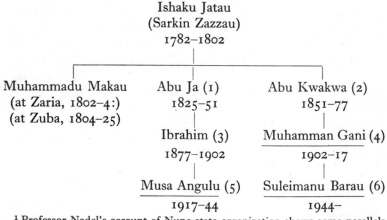

Ishaku Jatau
(Sarkin Zazzau)
1782–1802

Muhammadu Makau
(at Zaria, 1802–4:)
(at Zuba, 1804–25)

Abu Ja (1)
1825–51

Abu Kwakwa (2)
1851–77

Ibrahim (3)
1877–1902

Muhamman Gani (4)
1902–17

Musa Angulu (5)
1917–44

Suleimanu Barau (6)
1944–

[1] Professor Nadel's account of Nupe state organization shows some parallels to these Abuja data; cf. Nadel, 1942, pp. 93–114.

[2] Masterton-Smith, n.d. paras. 13–18. I have prepared a chart of the offices of the Abuja government using the data provided by Mallam Hassan and Mr. Masterton-Smith. This chart should be consulted during the following discussion. Further information on the system of government is presented in Appendix A.

[3] M. Hassan refers to the traditions of former ruling queens of Habe Zaria in his booklet, *Makau, Sarkin Zazzau na Habe*. Whether succession was then patrilineal cannot be determined on the evidence now available.

Notes:

(1), (2), (3) = Order of succession.

————— = Appointments under British Rule.

From the data available we cannot determine the rules which governed eligibility for succession within the royal patrilineage at Abuja, nor the degree to which the succession patterns at Abuja followed those of Habe Zazzau. Succession at Abuja was clearly patrilineal, and a royal descent-group of lineage-type is indicated, internally differentiated by lines descended from successive rulers. Under the British, the Abuja succession has passed alternately between two houses of the royal lineage, descended from Abu Ja and Abu Kwakwa respectively. Whether this is a new development, an instance of continuity, or the fulfilment of a tendency inherent within the former practice of succession, it is not possible to say. The exclusion of Makau's issue from the succession indicates that the local electors exercised great influence on the succession, and that succession itself could modify the structure of the royal descent-group. Whether the electors were able to exercise this influence because the royal lineage was divided by rivalry for the succession, we do not know.

M. Hassan mentions a small group of royal officials, two of whom were females, the Iya (mother), the Sarauniya who was the king's eldest daughter, and the Dan Galadima, the king's chosen successor. Masterton-Smith adds to these the Magajin Dangi (head of the—royal?—lineage) who was a member of the order of mallams. M. Hassan says that the title of Iya was held by 'one of the wives of the previous chief, but not necessarily the mother of the ruling chief'.[1] He notes that despite the king's choice, 'only one Dan Galadima succeeded to the chieftainship' at Abuja.[2] In other words, apart from the king, most of the royal officials were women who were ineligible for succession, and the king's chosen successor was systematically set aside.

The present territory of Abuja, and the area over which the Sarkin Abuja claimed suzerainty at the time of the British arrival in 1900, are shown on the accompanying map.[3] Certain parts of this area were administered as vassal states. According to Master-

[1] M. Hassan, 1952, (2), p. 34.
[2] *Ibid.*, and footnote.
[3] According to Masterton-Smith (op. cit., para. 29) the Emirate was 2239 square miles in the 1940's.

ton-Smith, before the Fulani conquest of Zaria in 1804, 'the Zazzau dynasty used four Koro chiefs to look after their southern domains and exact yearly "tax" (*gandu* — tribute), mainly in the form of slaves. The four were Izom, Kawu, Jiwa, Zuba. The first three chiefs had a large drum (*tambari*) as their insignia of office, handed to them by the Zazzau chief, whilst the last had the title of Barden Yamma, warden of the West.[1] Tambari are the insignia of hereditary chieftainship and vassal status throughout Zaria, Masterton-Smith's information therefore means that Izom, Kawu and Jiwa were vassal states of eighteenth-century Zazzau, just as Kagarko, Jere, Keffi, Nassarawan Kwoto, etc., were vassals of the Fulani state of Zaria in the nineteenth century. Accordingly, in the chart of Abuja state organization, I have grouped these hereditary vassal chieftainships together with office-holders drawn from the royal line of Abuja, on the basis of their status similarities and hereditary claims.

(*b*) *A Synopsis of the Abuja Constitution*

Following the practice of Abuja as recorded by Mallam Hassan, I classify the offices of the Abuja state in eight orders of rank; namely, the kingship, the officials of the inner chamber, the order of household officials, the senior and junior orders of public officials, the order of royal officials and vassal chiefs, the order of mallams, and the order of slave-officials. The official composition of these orders is presented in Chart A. Each of these rank-orders forms a distinct unit, differentiated from the remaining orders in terms of its status or function. Thus the order of royal officials and hereditary chiefs is distinguished in terms of descent, sex, royalty, and claims to succession; the order of chamber officials

---

[1] Masterton-Smith, *op. cit.*, paragraph 14. M. Hassan relates that Muhamman Gani, the ruler of Abuja, 1902–17, feared to claim certain areas traditionally subject to Abuja when Lugard held a conference in 1905 to settle the boundaries of states in that region. During this and subsequent boundary adjustments by Temple in 1910, M. Hassan says that the area of the Abuja Kingdom was reduced by the loss of Kafin, Kuta, Paiko, Jere, and Jajalla. In view of their inclusion in the account of territorial administration at Abuja during the last century, and present exclusion, Koton Karfe, Gusoro, Kagarko, and Tawari should probably be added to this list. Some comments on these 'lost' areas are necessary. In the latter nineteenth century, Kagarko and Jere were ruled by Fulani vassal chiefs of Zaria. Possibly Abuja again laid some claim to these areas after heavily defeating the attack of the Zaria Fulani under Yero in 1893. Other evidence suggests that Abuja exercised authority over the Gwari-Koro settlements of Abuji, Koton Karfe, Tawari, Um'aisha, Gusoro, Paiko, Kuta, and Fuka.

THE KING

Chamber Eunuchs	Officials of the Royal Household *(head)*	Public Officials		Vassal Chiefs	Slave Officials *(servants of king)*
		Senior (Rukuni)	Junior (Rawuna)		
MAKAMA KARAMI	SARKIN FADA - head	GALADIMA*φ	IYAN KASUWA	KAWU	**(a) Police**
SARKIN RUWA	CINCINA	WOMBAI*	BARWA†	GAWU	DOGARAI ⎫ Under GALA-
FAGACI	JAGABA	DALLATU*	DANKEKASAU	JIWA	YAN DOKA ⎭ DIMA
TURAKI	BAKON BARNO†		WAN DIYA	KUJE	
MA'AJI	GWABARE		SARKIN PAWA	ABUCI	**(b) Military**
SARKIN ZANA	MAGAYAKI		SARKIN GAYEN	KUTA	BANAGA
		MADAWAKIφ *(aput of head)*		GWAZUNU	SARKIN KARMA
	HAUNI		KUYAMBANA	IZOM *(office holders)*	SARKIN BINDIGA
	MADAKIN HAUNI		GARKUWA BABBA		SARKIN BAKA
	BARDEN HAUNI		MAKAMA BABBA	*Royal Officials*	KUNKELI
			LIFIDI	DANGALADIMA	
	BARDE		SHENAGU	SARAUNIYA O	**(c) Civil Services**
	DURUMI		SATA†	IYA O	SIRDI
	KANGIWA		WAGU†		SHAMAKI
	BARDE KANKANE			*Order of Mallams*	MADAKIN GABAS
	GARKUWA KANKANE			MAGAJIN MALLAMφ	MAGAJIN KWA
	MADAKIN BARDE			MAGAJIN DANGI	SARKIN NOMA
				SALENKEφ	MAGAJIN NAGABA
	JARMAI			LIMAMIN JUMA'Aφ	BIKON TAMBARI
	CIRITAWA			MAGATAKARDA	BOROKA O
	MADAKIN JARMAI				

ABUJA STATE ORGANIZATION IN THE NINETEENTH CENTURY

O = female
† = slaves
* = eunuchs
φ = royal electors
    For communication and control see text.

consisted entirely of eunuchs; the order of mallams consisted entirely of Islamic scholars; the order of household officials, which contained some slaves as well as freemen, were specially charged with supervision of the king's household, and formed a royal council of their own; the two orders of public officials were responsible for territorial, civil, and military administration; and the remaining order consisted of royal slave-officials.

For lack of any more satisfactory terms, I shall refer to these groupings as orders of rank, and to their component units as titles or offices. Offices were associated with titles, and title connoted rank or membership in a particular order. This use of the term 'rank' distinguishes it sharply from the more general term 'status'. In the present terminology, a member of the king's lineage who lacked office would have royal status but would lack royal or other rank. As used here, the term 'status' denotes position in a series of differentiated positions. Thus royal status is distinguished from non-royal statuses, slave status from free, etc. In the context of state organization, the status of an office is its position within the system. Such position consists in the last analysis of specific relations to other units, but these relations also carried prestige. By status condition we mean position within a series of differentiated status-groups. Groups of persons differentiated by status are referred to as status-groups. With these definitions and background data in mind, the constitution of nineteenth-century Abuja can be summarized as follows:

Among the titled officials of Abuja, four basic statuses were recognized: royals, who were members of the king's lineage or family, or hereditary chiefs in their own right; freemen, who were eligible to receive fiefs; eunuchs, who were recruited by the king from certain villages; and slaves. A fifth status-group consisted of mallams, who were freemen, but as religious leaders could not hold fiefs. Mallams were therefore a special group of freemen.

Titles were divided into different rank-orders, and there was an official order of precedence among title-holders; but this official order of precedence did not correspond exactly with the grading of title-holders according to their social status. Promotional opportunities as well as appointments were defined in terms of social status. Thus a minor slave-official was eligible for promotion to a more important office reserved for persons of slave status, and eunuchs could seek promotion to offices reserved for eunuchs, but eunuchs could not hold slave offices, nor vice versa. Each such status-qualified hierarchy of office formed a separate promotional series; and offices of the same rank-order frequently belonged to different promotional series. Thus the order of senior public officials contained three offices open to eunuchs only, and one office reserved for freemen.

Relations between officials of the various rank-orders and the king were quite distinctive, politically and economically. Fief-holders drew their economic reward directly from their fiefs, and formed a relatively independent aristocracy. The king's chamber officials were remunerated by benefices, in the form of portions of the tribute and tax which they gathered from vassal chiefs and the appointive officials of state; but these chamber eunuchs were also members of the king's household. The household officials, all of whom lacked territorial fiefs, were dependent on the king for support. The order of mallams were recompensed purely by benefice, receiving fees and donations for the performance of their various religious duties.

The king's intimate advisers and agents, his chamber officials, were a staff of eunuchs who were partly dependent on him for maintenance, and who were also his official channels of communication to the other officials of state, as well as to the vassal chiefs. The household officials were mostly freemen, and were eligible for promotion to fief-holding office. For administration outside the palace, the king had a staff of titled slaves, who were jointly supervised by an agent of the head of the household officials, the Sarkin Fada, and by an agent of the head of the Public Officials, the Madawaki. The senior eunuch public official, the Galadima, directly supervised the police, who were also royal slaves. Thus both the eunuchs and the free officials participated in supervision of the slaves, and so could guard against these slave-officials acquiring political significance. Similarly, joint supervision of the royal slaves by the senior public and household officials also prevented either of these supervisors from using the royal slaves unconstitutionally.

The offices of certain rank-orders, such as the orders of chamber officials, the household order, and the orders of public officials, were organized internally on hierarchic lines and in certain cases they were also formally segmented. Thus the Makama Karami was in charge of the chamber eunuchs; the Sarkin Fada was head of the household officials, and this order was further segmented; the two public orders, senior and junior, were subdivided into two groups, under the two most senior officials of state, the Madawaki and the Galadima. Each of these two officials controlled a section of the order of junior public officials. In contrast with the elaborate internal organization of these three rank-orders, the order of mallams and the order of royal officials lacked both hierarchic and internal segmentary organization. The order of slave-officials also lacked internal hierarchic grouping, although they were divided functionally into three groups, corresponding to their police, war, and civil duties.

The offices directly responsible for public order and administration were the two public orders. They were responsible for tax-collections, execution of justice, and territorial administration. Offices of those two orders were grouped into two contraposed units, each of which contained offices belonging to two different ranks, namely, the *rukuni* or senior order, and the *rawuna* (turbans) or junior order. The territorial administration for which these rank-orders were responsible, took the form of fiefs; but one section, under a freeman, the Madawaki, had special military functions and contained freemen, while the other, under a eunuch, the Galadima, who was assisted by two other senior (*rukuni*) eunuchs, was specially responsible for civil administration, including police, prisons, markets, and supplies to the capital and to the army. The Galadima had no direct military powers. The Madawaki was commander of the army, and he himself was head of the cavalry, its most important arm; Madawaki supervised the distribution of booty and shared the captives equally with the king, rewarding the other public officials from the half allotted to him.

Heads of vassal states were required to provide annual tribute, and to assist with contingents in war; but they had no office within the state of Abuja itself. On the other hand, they held authority within their own chiefdoms, succession to which was on a hereditary basis. With the exception of these semi-autonomous vassal chiefs, all other offices of the Abuja government, and ultimately even the kingship, were appointive, although the status qualifications governing eligibility for any office severely restricted the number of candidates. Vassal chiefs and other hereditary officials received the king's requests and instructions from his eunuchs, either the *rukuni* eunuchs, or those of the inner chamber.

On any major issue, the king was by custom obliged first to consult his senior household officials, and next, the *rukuni* or senior order of the public officials, that is, the Madawaki, and the three eunuch *rukuni*, Galadima, Wombai, and Dallatu. If all these were agreed on the course to be pursued, the king could not resist their advice and in fact the power of the state would be against him if he did. On the other hand, proposals initiated by the Madawaki and the orders of public officials could be vetoed by the order of household officials under the Sarkin Fada (chief of the Palace). Where these two groups disagreed, the king was free to act independently as he thought fit. Sarkin Fada and the other household officials could influence the composition of the public orders by using their veto on proposed appointments, and by becoming public officials themselves. In this way also they could influence policy. But such promotion of household officials to the public orders required the co-operation of Madawaki and his group of senior public officials, and also the support of the king. Thus the household officials could not control policy decisions or appointments if the king and the Madawaki's group combined against them. At the same time, while the king had great administrative authority, he could not act politically against the combined will of the public and household orders.

The household officials had no administrative authority or responsibility, but they enjoyed considerable political influence, as measured by their effect on appointments and policy. The public officials had great administrative responsibilities and authority, individually within their separate fiefs, and as a group within the kingdom as a whole; but they had little power of independent political action in view of the veto power of the household officials. The chamber officials who were eunuchs were creatures of the king with no political power or independent administrative authority; but three of the most senior offices of state were reserved for them in the *rukuni* order, and from this position eunuchs could influence policy decisions and appointments.

The process by which appointments were made to office makes it unlikely that personal clientage offered a simple or direct basis for recruitment to office or for promotion. The Madawaki's clients could be kept out of office by the veto of household officials; and the Madawaki's group could oppose nominees of the Sarkin Fada; the king's personal clients would also have to be supported either by the public or the household officials before he could appoint them. Considering the delicacy of the distribution, as shown by the conditions governing appointment, it is unlikely that any single official, including the king, would have enjoyed sufficient support to ensure the automatic appointment of personal clients.

Although there was a formal heir apparent, the Dan Galadima, the royal succession was not determined either by the king or by the royal lineage, but by certain traditional electors. These electors were all officials, and apart from the two most senior *rukuni*, the Madawaki, who held the highest office open to freemen, and the Galadima, who held the highest office open to eunuchs, the electoral council included three Koranic scholars or mallams; thus the mallams had a majority on the royal electoral council, and were able to hold a balance among the public officials in this one context, and also to decide the succession in a way which prevented dynastic struggle. On his accession, the new ruler found that the officials of state were not easily dismissable, individually or as a group, and that his own power of appointment to office was limited by them.

Titled office was associated with specific functions and tasks, but as indicated earlier, titles do not form a single continuous series. Titles were grouped into several orders of rank, they were also arranged according to specialized functions, and there were only very limited possibilities for the transfer of persons from one of these series to another. Thus the series of military offices was headed by the Madawaki, of the *rukuni* order, with certain junior public officials, *rawuna*, under him; but this military segment also contained half of the household officials, who formed another order, and half of the slave-officials. The series of offices specially associated with civil administration, such as roads, ferries, police, supplies and the like, was headed by the Galadima, and his two eunuch assistants of *rukuni* rank, with certain junior public officials of *rawuna* rank under him, the majority of these being persons of free status; this series also included half of the order of household officials, under their chief, the Sarkin Fada, together with numerous slave-officials and the police who were directly under Galadima's control. The vassal chiefs did not belong to either of these complex series, but they were individually responsible to the king through his chamber officials, who formed the king's lines of communication to the heads of the various orders of rank, the various official mallams, and to the royal fief-holding officials. It is noteworthy that communication proceeded between the king and his vassal chiefs, royal officials, or titled mallams individually; but that the king's communications with the civil or military officials was addressed to the senior title of each rank-order separately. These modes of communication may be related to the different political and administrative significance of the offices concerned, and may have been linked with the hierarchic arrangement of offices within some but not all orders of rank. The control which senior offices exercised over their immediate sub-. ordinates is expressed in the organization of communication.

The order of mallams or Koranic scholars, was separated from the offices just discussed by their special religious and legal func-tions. As freemen, the official mallams were eligible for promotion out of their order into positions reserved for free persons; but while remaining mallams, they could neither administer fiefs, nor execute the secular religious and civil duties associated with such offices.

Of the two royal councils, one was headed by an official with special interests in civil administration, although lacking territorial fiefs; the other was headed by an official with special military interests and territorial fiefs. Both these officials, the Sarkin Fada and the Madawaki, were freemen; and the former was eligible for promotion to the latter's office. But the Sarkin Fada, whose council was able to veto the proposals of Madawaki's council, had no duties of civil administration beyond the supervision of slave-officials which he exercised jointly with Madawaki. On the other hand, the three *rukuni* eunuchs whose duties lay in the sphere of civil administration, were members of the Madawaki's council. This arrangement may have served to prevent the permanent division of the officials of state into two contraposed groups, the one, free, the other, eunuchs, differentiated also in terms of military and civil interests.

2. POLITICS AND ADMINISTRATION AT ABUJA

(a) Differentiation by Function and Rank

Offices which constitute the various orders of rank are indicated together with these rank-orders in the chart of Abuja state organization, but no attempt is made to present the ranks in an ascending scale there. The chart also shows the functional grouping of offices within the various rank-orders, the traditional electoral offices and the statuses eligible for offices within the different orders, but not the lines of communication between the king and his officials, nor between officials of the same order. External connections between Abuja and the superordinate state of Bornu are omitted, and lines of communication with the subordinate vassal chiefdoms are not shown. Fiefs proper, such as those administered by the king, the Madawaki, Galadima, or Iya, are also excluded from the chart, which is only intended to summarize certain structurally significant features of the Abuja government organization, and to clarify the summary just given.

The chart also indicates the separate groupings of offices which formed closed series for promotional purposes at Abuja. A brief discussion of this point is in order. There were four major status divisions among the population of Abuja, and each of these found expression in the official system as a condition of eligibility for particular offices. These status conditions were royalty, slavery, freedom, and eunuchhood. The offices reserved for members of these status-groups belonged to various orders of rank, and their scope, significance, and prestige increased in an ascending scale up to the *rukuni* order. Slaves formed the lowest official order, but were eligible for promotion to special positions in superior orders. Thus the title of Bakon Bornu (messenger to Bornu) in the household order was a slave office, and the offices of Barwa, Wagu, and Sata in the *rawuna* order of junior public officials were also reserved for slaves. These slave-titles formed a closed promotional series. The series of eunuch titles were headed by the Galadima with his two eunuch *rukuni* assistants, the Wombai and Dallatu, and included the order of chamber officials under Makama Karami. The offices reserved for freemen formed another promotional series headed by the senior *rukuni*, the Madawaki, with several junior public officials of *rawuna* rank under him, and this series also included the majority of the household officials. Mallams who were freemen were distinguished from other groups of free officials by their religious calling, and formed an order which was also a self-contained promotional series; if a mallam was appointed to an office outside this order of mallams, he had first to abandon his status as a mallam. In theory another promotional series linked the offices of Dan Galadima and the throne. Only the mallam's order formed a self-contained promotional series. Apart from the order of mallams, there were only two other orders entirely staffed by persons of the same status condition. These were the order of chamber officials and the order of slave-officials. Both these orders of chamber officials and titled slaves were of instrumental rather than political significance for the system of government.

Another point mentioned in the preceding summary which requires further discussion concerns the functional groupings of office of various orders of rank, taken separately or together. The Madawaki (or Madaki as he is called in Fulani Zazzau, both forms being abbreviations of Mai-dawaki, the 'owner of the horses', that is, commander of cavalry) acted as commander-in-chief, receiving half the booty of war or slave-raids for distribution to the public officials. All free title-holders of Madawaki's group, namely, the Kuyambana, Garkuwa Babba, Makama Babba, Lifidi, and Shenagu, had military duties, and were prominently concerned with the direction of war. But the Madawaki also had two subordinate slave *rawuna*, the Wagu and the Sata. Wagu was the title of the royal sexton, and his position directly under the Madawaki is explained by the latter's role as head of the electoral council, as well as his duty as commander-in-chief, responsible for the care of the royal mausoleum. The other slave subordinate of the Madawaki, the Sata, had the function of supervising the order of slave-officials, a duty which was shared by Hauni, who acted on behalf of the household officials under Sarkin Fada, Madawaki's principal opponent in council. Duplication of this supervision of slave-officials, and the division of these duties between the Madawaki and the Sarkin Fada, was clearly a protective political device. It simultaneously ensured that the order of official slaves would be closely controlled and also that neither the public nor the household officials would be able to subvert these titled slaves, or bring them into the arena of political competition. This division of supervisory functions which neutralized the slave order politically thereby defined it as a purely administrative staff.

The Galadima's duties in the field of civil administration contrast directly with those of the Madawaki, and this contrast was further underlined by their differences in social status, the Madawaki being a freeman, the Galadima a eunuch. The principal subordinates of Galadima controlled markets, the supply of meat, exercised jurisdiction over unmarried mothers, and officiated at royal weddings. The Galadima himself was in charge of the state police, and his compound served as the place for punishment of offenders. In the war camp, the Galadima's deputy was the Dallatu, another eunuch of *rukuni* rank, who acted as head of the army's civil administration, while the Barwa, a slave-official of *rawuna* rank, subordinate to the Galadima, was in charge of the royal encampment itself. The Galadima did not proceed with the army on its campaigns, but remained in Abuja town, as the king's deputy, and was head of the civil administration during wartime. The capital was divided between the Galadima and the Madawaki for administration, each ruling one-half as a fief. This served to neutralize it politically, just as division of control over the slave-officials neutralized that order politically. Division of the capital between Galadima and Madawaki denied either the chance to seize power by *coup* without the other's consent; and as the Galadima was a eunuch, already enjoying a high authority but unable to perpetuate personal power, this meant in effect that the Galadima could be relied on to side with the king against the Madawaki's personal ambitions. In so far as the Madawaki's aims were less personal, but reflected matters of general policy, then the Galadima was free to support him in council, in association with or in opposition to the Sarkin Fada. An instance which is discussed later illustrates neatly how valuable was this administrative division of the capital at Abuja between the civil and military chiefs. This is the story of a non-eunuch Galadima of Fulani Zaria who enjoyed undivided administrative control of the capital at a period when the king and the Madaki were mutually opposed, and who was tempted by these circumstances to rebellion.

Four of the Abuja rank-orders contain functional divisions of offices in terms of their special military or civil interests and duties. Within each of these rank-orders, the relations between these functionally differentiated official groups have a similar structure, and this pattern is also duplicated for the system of rank-orders as a whole. Each of these functionally differentiated segments has an internal hierarchy of its own, these hierarchies expressing authority relations among their component offices; and each of these functional hierarchies is in contraposition with the other as administrative, political, and promotional units. In a state known historically to have been almost continuously engaged in military action, whether in the form of slave-raids or war, since the days of its foundation, this contraposition of military and civil officials and activities was perhaps inevitable if these competing interests were to be harmonized and integrated with a system of limited monarchy. However, this contraposition also had direct political significance as a factor governing the process of policy decision. In this respect it is noteworthy that the Madawaki's following was internally divided in more ways than was that of the Sarkin Fada whose position made him the principal free spokesman for the civil interest.

The more obvious characteristics of the Abuja system of government can now be stated succinctly. The various titled offices of this system were associated with specific tasks, and the orders of rank were also differentiated according to the sphere and importance of these official tasks, e.g. public administration and war, affairs of the royal household, religious and legal matters, etc. Differences of status condition were institutionalized prerequisites of eligibility for different offices, and the offices reserved for persons of identical status formed a closed promotional series, the units of which belonged to different orders of rank. Within most rank-orders there was a functional division between offices of military and civil kinds, and these two series of functionally differentiated titles correspond also to separate promotional series, the offices within these series being distributed among persons of different status conditions as is shown in the following Table. There were marked dispersals of power and authority among the offices of these functionally differentiated groups and between the various rank-orders, and the kingship was limited by this context. However, on occasions when his councillors could not agree, the king was free to take such decision and action as he chose. Within the council, the Sarkin Fada, a civil administrator and head of the household order, whose rank was much below that of the Madawaki, exercised the essentially political power of veto over the latter's proposals, although the Madawaki was the commander-in-chief, the senior elector, and the head of the territorial administration. Mallams, vassal chiefs, royal officials, the order of titled slaves, and the order of chamber eunuchs had no part in the councils of state, but mallams were represented on the electoral council which controlled the succession.

Such a system of offices, differentiated functionally and in other

TABLE I

OFFICES OF THE ABUJA GOVERNMENT CLASSIFIED BY FUNCTION,
RANK-ORDER, AND STATUS CONDITION

Public orders	Household officials	Slave officials
(a) Military offices		
Madawaki	*Barde*	Banaga
Kuyambana	Durumi	Sarkin Karma
Garkuwa Babba	Kangiwa	Sarkin Bindiga
Makama Babba	Barde Kankane	Sarkin Baka
Lifidi	Garkuwa Kankane	Kunkeli
Shenagu	Barden Maidaki	
Wagu[1]	Madakin Barde	
Sata[1]	*Jarmai*	
	Ciritawa	
	Madakin Jarmai	
	Kacalla	
(b) Civil offices		
Galadima[2]	*S. Fada*	Sirdi
Wombai[2]	Cincina	Shamaki
Dallatu[2]	Jagaba	Madakin Gabas
Iyan Kasuwa	Gwabare	Magajin Kwa
Wandiya	Magayaki	Sarkin Noma
Dankekasau	Bakon Barno[1]	Magajin Nagaba
Sarkin Pawa	*Hauni*	Bikon Tambari
Sarkin Gayen	Madakin Hauni	Boroka (f.)
Barwa[1]	Barden Hauni	

Notes: [1] = Slave   [2] = Eunuch   (f.) = Female.
Senior officials in each order are italicised.

ways, contained various structural checks and balances which were of value in promoting and maintaining the equilibrium of the system; and thereby in ensuring its continuity. Apart from their functional differentiation in terms of military and civil interest, offices were also differentiated in terms of their political and administrative significance at Abuja, and this differentiation was related to the variable composition of segmentary political groupings. The interest and constitution of these contraposed groupings altered according to the context or issue, while the segments themselves reflected certain pervasive principles, namely, the rank-ordering of offices, the distribution of office according to status conditions, their promotional organization, economic differentiation, and the like. The presence of administrative agencies specialized to co-ordinate these contraposed units and to maintain the minimal conditions essential for the order and unity of the system as a whole is correlated with this variability of political segmentation at Abuja. Whether the operation of multiple principles of alignment and contraposition precedes the development of specialized administrative agencies cannot be stated, either for Abuja or in general. Probably, the two developments are functionally related, and probably the multiplication of principles of alignment is initially associated with the growth of politically significant differences of status, especially hereditary differences.

(b) *The System of Political Relations*

In the general discussion of government, political action was defined by its focus on policy, and by its segmentary process and form. These segmentary processes were further defined by conditions of variability in the composition of contraposed units; and this variability is limited on the one hand by the range of issues, and on the other by the basic principles of the particular social structure. From this, it follows that the operation of segmentary principles defines the field of political relations, and also that the differentiation of administrative action is associated with the operation of an increasing number of segmentary principles as criteria for the composition of contraposed political groups. This increase in the number of segmentary principles considerably increases the variability of political groupings, with the consequence that specialized agencies committed to maintain the minimal conditions of order and unity are necessary if the system is to persist. These general ideas can be applied usefully to the organization of government at Abuja.

At Abuja, the principal field of political relations was constituted by the king, the household officials, and the two orders of public officials, namely the *rukuni* and the *rawuna*. The chamber officials were marginal to this structure, although they were indirectly linked to it, as they supplied holders of the offices of Galadima, Wambai, and Dallatu. On the information at our disposal, it is difficult to see how either the mallams, the dynasty, the royal officials or the order of titled slaves could enter into contraposition with one another, or with either of these previously mentioned groups. The chamber officials, despite their prospects of promotion to *rukuni* eunuch offices, must also be regarded as a subordinate administrative staff, the main functions of which were communications, care of the treasury, the insignia, the royal harem, and the king. The king was head of both the political and the administrative systems, controlling the latter directly, but not the former; and he was probably preoccupied with problems of co-ordination and equilibrium, rather than with the personal direction of the government as a whole. In other words, the monarchy was limited in its power, simply by virtue of its participation in a system of segmentary political relations with the orders of public and household officials. In this situation, neither the king nor his political partners had the decisive voice in selecting his successor.

Although political issues mobilized political groups at Abuja, the variety of segmentary principles at work in the official orders ensured that the composition of these groupings would vary according to the issue. One reason for such variability lay in the fact that the principles in terms of which contraposed groups were organized were not all of the same order. For example, together the *rukuni* and the *rawuna* formed a single inclusive group of public officials which was distinguished structurally and functionally from the inclusive group of palace personnel, namely, the household officials and chamber eunuchs. Unlike these two latter orders, the *rukuni* and *rawuna* administered territorial fiefs. The household officials were dependent on the king for reward; and the chamber eunuchs were also partly dependent on the king, although, in their capacity as messengers to the vassal chiefs and the other official orders, they enjoyed certain benefices. Their lack of salary or any specified means of official reward distinguished the order of household officials by emphasizing their identity of interest with the kingship on which they were economically dependent. This identity of interest between the king and his household officials may have been the ultimate basis for their power to veto proposals made by the public orders, and their economic dependence on the king was probably expressed by their actions on various occasions.

Of the *rukuni* offices, the most important position, that of Madawaki, was only open to freemen, whose training was primarily military, and who were already holding office of *rawuna* rank. Promotion into these military *rawuna* offices, reserved for freemen. was in turn open only to free nobles in the household order. It is quite conceivable that from time to time, this rigorously defined promotional system may not have been fully observed, either due to the desire of a Sarkin Fada to regain his power, or due to influences of personal clientage on appointments and promotion. For example, M. Hassan mentions that a slave of the Fulani king of Zaria who fled to Abuja in 1879 with 700 men was given the office of Dallatu and later became Galadima.[1] None the less, a careful study of M. Hassan's history of Abuja in the last century suggests that such departures from the patterns of promotion were rare, and this agrees with our preceding analysis of the influences governing appointment and promotion.

The civil offices of Galadima, Wombai, and Dallatu were normally filled by eunuchs who had been trained in affairs of state as officials of the inner chamber. Other civil offices of the public order were reserved for freemen trained as household officials, but these civil offices were of junior or *rawuna* rank. It is thus possible to distinguish more limited and extensive groupings within the official organization by such criteria as differences of promotional series, status eligibilities, rank-order and precedence, functional specialization, i.e. military or civil interests, economic status, or control of territorial fiefs. That these conditions were expressed variably in the segmentary organization of political groupings seems highly likely; and it is also probable that on occasion, conflicts of interest may have developed within each of these different groupings according to the character of the issue.

Equally significant is the division of officials in terms of their

[1] Hassan and Shu'aibu, 1952. *A Chronicle of Abuja.* Translated by Frank Heath, p. 17.

economic interests. On the one hand, there were those officials whose economic interests were closely identified with those of the king, and on the other there were the public orders which derived their economic reward from the administration of fiefs and the prosecution of war. Thus apart from the formal contraposition of rank-orders, different issues may have mobilized a wide variety of differently composed political groupings.

To illustrate certain readily conceivable possibilities, the following contrapositions may be sufficient: (1) *Rukuni* and *rawuna* vs. the household officials, with or without the king's support; (2) Madawaki and his subordinates together with Jarmai, Barde, and their subordinates, vs. Galadima and his subordinates, Sarkin Fada and his subordinates, with or without the king's support; (3) Madawaki and his subordinates, together with Sarkin Fada and his subordinates, vs. Galadima, Wambai and Dallatu, with or without the support of the chamber eunuchs. These alignments merely illustrate certain discernible possibilities, and by no means exhaust them.

Thus apart from the formal differentiation of subordinate orders of rank, there were a variety of principles capable of providing bases for politically contraposed groupings of differing composition. The variety of interests which operated within the political orders of the Abuja government thus provided for a variety of politically contraposed groupings corresponding to the variety of issues and contexts. The simultaneous operation of several segmentary principles in this way ensured a greater freedom and variety of political alignments. Granted the existence of the administrative agencies functionally necessary to a structure of this type, the operation of these diverse segmentary principles provided for a greater flexibility and adaptability of the total system than could have been developed if their number or range of operation were less. However, the relative complexity of governmental systems is not measurable solely in terms of the segmentary principles which they incorporate, nor even by the degrees to which their administrative and political components are differentiated; the complexity of governmental organization consists in its internal diversity and the interrelation of its parts and also reflects the type and degree of differentiation typical of the society of which the government is part. Nor can this be otherwise, since both the administrative and the political personnel are recruited from that society, and in their hierarchies and relations they mirror the composition and values of the wider unit.

(c) Social Status and the Official System

In view of this, it is necessary to consider the nature of the basic status differences and conditions current in Habe society. Apart from the king, his family, and other members of the royal lineage, there were hereditary vassal chiefs, and freemen who were divisible into officials, aristocrats not holding office, mallams or religious leaders, manumitted slaves, and freeborn commoners. The society also contained slaves and eunuchs, together with subordinate pagan populations which were culturally and linguistically distinct. Of the major status-groups, the category of free persons showed the highest degree of internal differentiation. Thus, to consider only office-holders, among free persons, the Sarkin Gayen, a former Habe village chief, was noble by descent as well as office, while all others, although holding important titles such as Madawaki or Sarkin Fada, might have risen from the commoner class (*talakawa*). The religious order of mallams, who were all freemen, embodied another principle of differentiation within the status-group of free persons. Moreover, as M. Hassan's ethnography of Abuja indicates, occupational differences had significant status implications for the free commoners. Butchers, for example, were accorded very low status.

These statuses differ significantly according to their social implications, mutability, and modes of differentiation. Thus slavery was a legal status, terminable for both sexes by manumission, purchase of freedom, or death, and also, for females, by bearing a child for their master as his concubine. Freedom was also a mutable legal status, since capture normally led to death or enslavement in another society. In contrast, the status of eunuch was immutable, wherever the individual might be, and irrespective of captivity. The eunuch's condition rendered the question of his freedom or slavery meaningless, since he was unable to marry or beget issue, and so had no family to succeed or inherit from him. The eunuch's dependence on his master was thus variable, according to the facilities which he enjoyed.

Among free officials also, it seems clear that very few titles were held on a life-tenure basis, while none were hereditary, except for the royal offices, the vassal chieftainships and the title of Sarkin

Gayen. Officials were in theory subject to dismissal as well as promotion after their appointments. There were also occasions on which persons of a particular status exercised rights and powers typically the privilege of other statuses. Thus the religious order of mallams, which enjoyed high prestige as a non-political group, was charged with the political function of selecting the successor to the throne.

Within the royal lineage, and even within the king's family, individual status remained alterable through death and succession, and varied according to the specific relation holding between the king and different persons. Significantly, the Dan Galadima or heir apparent rarely succeeded to the throne; and the administrative responsibilities or authority of the various royal officials further differentiated between them; thus neither the heir presumptive nor the Magajin Dangi (head of the—royal?—lineage) are reported to have controlled fiefs, although the king's eldest daughter, the Sarauniya, is said to have done so. Whether this reflects an omission in the account or corresponds to the original allocation of duties cannot be said.

The precise definitions of rank-orders, their peculiar compositions, interrelations, hierarchic structure and arrangement in a variety of closed promotional series gain new significance by relation to this background of social differentiation. Only by some such system of precise and predictable relations was it possible to organize the participation of persons of such varied statuses smoothly and continuously within the system of government; and only through the participation of persons of these different status-groups could the personnel of government sufficiently reflect the differentiation of the society, to evoke popular consensus and support. The differentiation of official roles within the government, and the particular allocations of office to different status-groups were functionally related, and between them ensured that the social composition and structure of government corresponded to that of the society.

Allocation of three out of the four *rukuni* offices to eunuchs is noteworthy in two respects. Firstly eunuchs were the only group whose status was immutable. Secondly such allocations served to protect the system of government against change. These two features are closely related. As eunuchs, such high officials could not entertain personal ambitions of a type inconsistent with the current system, and they were thus best fitted, by virtue of their physical incapacities, to be given a large share of administrative responsibilities. Lacking issue, the eunuch could have no ambition extending beyond his lifetime, and was therefore no threat to a government based on hereditary chieftainship. The allocation of three *rukuni* offices to eunuchs who had already been trained in government procedure as members of the king's chamber staff, thereby strengthened the position of the king *vis-a-vis* both his household and public officials, whose principals were of free status, capable of developing lineage or dynastic ambitions. Had the four *rukuni* offices been regularly allotted to free persons, it is unlikely that this constitution would have persisted without further changes in its other elements.

The motivation of these different groups of government officials also merits attention. Within the Abuja government motivation of officials was linked to their promotion. Thus slave-officials could seek promotion to the position of Bakon Bornu in the household order, or to the three *rawuna* offices reserved for them. They might also secure manumission, and might then be eligible to compete for the titles of freemen.[1] Free men enjoyed prospects of promotion from the household order to the junior public order (*rawuna*), and thence to the supreme position of Madawaki. Even the mallams could be promoted to administrative or political office, if they were willing to surrender their religious status. But the eunuchs were by their physical disability for ever excluded from these offices reserved for physically complete persons, and they were also by this same disability the most trustworthy candidates for senior positions. This was the logic of a limited monarchy in which three of the four highest offices were allocated to eunuchs. At the same time, the system of government included for officials of different status opportunities which sought to stimulate their loyalty by prospects of increased authority, prestige and economic independence which were bound up with promotion. As status though varied was except for eunuchs alterable, and, as the prospect of promotion was necessary to ensure the efficient co-operation of officials of such diverse status conditions in the process of government, the definition of offices in terms of their special authority

---

[1] This is not certain. Possibly these free titles were reserved for persons born free. If this was so, the manumission of a slave-official spelt the end of his official career.

and the allocation of offices of different ranks to different status-groups were both logically unavoidable and implicit developments.

(d) Specialized Administrative Staffs

Special interest attaches to the lesser order of eunuchs, those of the king's inner chamber, who were his closest dependants, and who may well have served him as spies reporting on officials of the other orders. These officials formed the first group to be consulted by the king; but apparently he could take no constitutional action in matters of public importance on their advice only, having also to consult the household officials and the public orders. The chamber eunuchs thus lacked the capacity of councillors. As a group they also differed from the orders of household and public officials in lacking any internal segmentary organization. Whereas between them Madawaki and Galadima divided the ranks of public officials, while the household officials were also subdivided under Sarkin Fada, Jarmai, Barde, and Hauni, all chamber officials were supervised directly by Makama Karami (Makama the lesser). Such lack of internal segmentation itself suggests that the order of chamber eunuchs lacked political functions, and this suggestion corresponds with their incapacity to initiate action or to participate in the decision of policy, although they could discuss issues of state with the king informally when he chose to consult them.

These chamber eunuchs served the king in two principal fashions. Four were messengers to particular officials, three of these being messengers to vassal chieftains also. All four messengers enjoyed benefices as rewards. The remaining two chamber officials, Ma'aji and Sarkin Zana, were respectively entrusted with the care and custody of the king's treasury, including the royal insignia, and the harem, and these two were entirely dependent on the king for their support. All these types of service required constant attention, availability, specialized knowledge, and the precise execution of orders. As a precondition of regularity and efficiency in the execution of these tasks, they were therefore assigned to a special staff with the permanent physical and status disabilities of eunuchs, and this group was further insulated against political influence by its constitutional incapacity for participation in the process of policy formation on the one hand, and by the conditions of entrance to the order on the other. Thus the order of chamber eunuchs constituted a quite distinct and specialized administrative staff, and in consequence of this they lacked internal or external segmentary relations.

Our data indicate the existence of two other specialized administrative orders; firstly, the king's slaves, among whom were groups distinguished in terms of military, civil, and police duties; and secondly, the religious order of mallams, who officiated at rituals and who advised technically on the content and application of Muhammadan law. Significantly also, both these orders, the mallams and the slaves, lacked any internal segmentation or external contraposition with other groups, and were distinguished by particular lines of communication with the king. Thus the king communicated with each mallam individually through his chamber eunuchs, while the supervision of military and civil groups of slaves was carried out for the Madawaki by the Sata, himself a promoted slave, and for the Sarkin Fada, by the Hauni, with consequent political neutralization of this order, while the police and town-guard were separately controlled by the Galadima.

Positively, in the specification of their duties and in the allocation of means and authority for their execution, and negatively, by their exclusion from the processes of policy formation, these two orders, the slaves and the mallams, and the various offices which separately constitute them, exhibit a purely administrative character. Their exclusion from the system of political action is evident in two ways: firstly, by the incompatibility of their roles with political office, from which the slaves and the mallams were by definition excluded so long as they remained slaves and mallams; secondly, by their insulation from political influence and appointments due to the status requisites applying in either case. Furthermore, as pointed out above, these orders exhibit no internal or external segmentary relations. Thus, although the order of slave-officials was internally divided into functional groups, none of these divisions had a head or hierarchic internal organization.

The order of mallams is of special interest, as it furnished the majority of the electoral council entrusted with the selection of the king's successor. This function might suggest that this order had a political character; but on this point, fortunately, the data are very clear. Together with the Madawaki and the senior eunuch, Galadima, three mallams were authorized and required to select the new king; but, unlike the two public officials with whom they were associated, after deciding the succession, the authority and responsibility of these mallams was exhausted, and they retired from the political scene, back to their religious duties. It is thus quite clear that the electoral mallams, though authorized to select the ruler, were otherwise excluded from the policy-making process, and that in selecting the ruler they were held to be carrying out an authorized, that is, an administrative task. This indeed explains their presence as the majority group on the electoral council. Mallams were given numerical dominance on this council in order to out-vote its purely political element; to minimize the threat which succession presented to the continuity of the system; by their religious prestige, to legitimize the new ruler's appointment; to frustrate the nomination of persons whose incapacity for the throne would give their political nominators opportunities for the improper exercise and appropriation of power; and to select the most suitable candidate with the minimum of political bargaining.

(e) *The Nature of Office*

An analysis of the segmentary aspects of the Abuja government directs attention to the nature of the units of the system. These units are offices, which were defined as perpetual and exclusive statuses in a system consisting of such statuses and their interrelations. In the definition of any particular office, or of office generally, the relations between each unit and other members of the system forms a very important part. The position of an office within the system really consists in its relations to other parts of the system. But this does not fully describe the office, nor exhaust its meaning. Offices were differentiated politically and administratively, as we have just seen; and those different types of office had different types of relation with the society at large. Although the functions of office were governmental, these functions were not entirely confined to the system of offices itself, and their execution brought offices of this system into contact with the society at large.

The offices of a governmental system and their interrelations together form its structure, while the activities of these units constitute its function. We can therefore distinguish between the structure of the system of government on the one hand, and the functions of the system or its constituent offices on the other. We must also distinguish between administrative relations by which government controls the society and conducts its affairs, and political relations by which the actions of government are controlled. Political and administrative relations are distinguished by their functions within a system of government, as well as their form. Thus the political and administrative relations of its components are the critical formal elements in the structure of a governmental system. Moreover, the interdependence of these relations suggests that changes of structure and function within the governmental system may be closely related. Such changes, although they would naturally affect the offices through which they are expressed, would not necessarily change their character. This capacity of office to persist in the face of functional and structural change emphasizes its ultimately ideological character, as a corporate unit, a perpetual status especially appropriate for the organization of a governmental system, the essential precondition of which is its presumption of perpetuity.

On these data from Abuja, the Habe concept of *sarauta* (ranked and titled office) involved the following elements: title, specified tasks, authority, and means of execution; supra-individual continuity; membership in a system of similar units, which was itself hierarchically ranked and organized in closed promotional series; political and administrative differentiation; differentiation according to the status conditions of eligible candidates; and appointment by selection, rather than on a hereditary basis. The material attributes of these Habe *sarautu* varied according to the particular office. It is likely that offices of all kinds had appropriate modes of installation, regalia, praise-songs, and perhaps farm lands. The more important offices also had compounds attached to them, wards, fiefs, benefices, rights and powers, set positions of precedence in the council and court, and on campaigns. The difference between various *sarautu* only illustrates the plasticity and ideological character of the concept of office; it does not mean that the differentiated positions to which these roles attached were different kinds of unit.

In Max Weber's terminology, each Habe *sarauta* was 'an administrative organ' of some kind.[1] This was their functional aspect. Structurally, each *sarauta* was a corporation sole, and each order of *sarautu* was a grouping of such corporate units, which may or may not have formed a corporate group.[2] In the councils of state, the orders of household officials and public administrators each

[1] Weber, 1947, p. 303.   [2] *Ibid.*, pp. 133–6.

had a corporate character and organization; but, as pointed out above, these formal features were consistent with wide variability of political groupings among them. On the other hand, the order of chamber eunuchs, which lacked political functions, was clearly a corporate group, the constituent offices of which were also distinct corporations.

The Abuja *sarautu* are discrete corporations, in that each *sarauta* appears to be an indivisible and perpetual member of the system, independent in some degrees of the relations in which its membership in the system involves it. Indeed, without the *sarautu*, the system could not exist, as it would then reduce simply to a set of relations between non-existent units or points. *Sarautu* owe their unique· perpetual character to the fact that it is easier to conceptualize units of a system of relations as fixed and perpetual, than to conceptualize in this way the relation or complex of relations, especially perhaps since such relations can only be expressed through individual persons, and are thus likely to be obscured by personal factors.

Among the *sarautu* of Abuja, hierarchic relations of precedence, promotion, and authority were carefully patterned and fixed—for example, the relation of Kuyambana to Madawaki; but relations between offices of parallel status in the different segments were not so clearly defined. Moreover, relations between the various rank-orders were carefully defined, and these were usually expressed through the most senior offices of the separate orders; but the order of slave offices was controlled by junior members of the household and public orders. It is this persisting framework of fixed and patterned relations which ultimately constitutes the system of government at Abuja, and which also expresses the Abuja conception of governmental office.

(f) The Conditions of Office

In this system of government, the degree of independent authority allocated to any office varied inversely with its closeness to the throne; and this was expressed, firstly in terms of its intimate association with and continuity of access to the king, and secondly, in terms of identification of economic interests with those of the king. These two conditions were closely related. For example, after the king, the greatest authority was exercised by the public officials. The eunuchs of the inner chamber who were in most intimate and continuous association with the king had purely instrumental functions as messengers; and the household officials, whose relations to the king were closer than those of any orders except that of the chamber eunuchs, lacked territorial jurisdiction and economic independence together. This tendency to separate specific administrative office from the area of the king's personal influence may have been a precondition of the differentiation of political and administrative functions within the official system; or it may have resulted from efforts to preserve the system as a whole against the direct exercise of royal power.

This dissociation of specific administrative authority from the throne is also a feature of relations between the king and the royal lineage. Two women of the royal family held titles, the Sarauniya and Iya; but, being women, both were ineligible for succession. The Dan Galadima, who was the king's chosen successor, apparently lacked administrative fiefs, but we are told that he 'followed', that is, was subordinate to, the Galadima, and was therefore administratively junior to the *rukuni*. The Magajin Dangi, who may have acted as head of the royal lineage, was classified with the order of mallams, and communicated with the king through the agency of Fagaci, a chamber eunuch. These rules which simultaneously limited the number of men of the royal house who could hold office, and specified the offices which they could hold, were especially important in protecting the system of government against royal nepotism, and against disruptive competition for the succession between royal officials. For, as we shall see, such developments could transform the system of government into a type of familistic autocracy. Such changes seem to have developed at Abuja, after the British reorganized its government. Thus Mallam Hassan has himself held the titles of Sarkin Ruwa and Makama Karami, which were formerly reserved for eunuchs. Likewise, the present emir was promoted to the throne from the office of Iyan Bakin Kasuwa, and his immediate successor from the title of Madawaki.[1] This recent increase in the number of royal officials contrasts with the traditions and practice of Abuja in the last cen-

---

[1] Hassan and Shu'aibu, 1952, *A Chronicle of Abuja*, pp. 32, 34, 57. See also Masterton-Smith, *op. cit.*, para. 30: 'The Emirate is divided into 3 districts containing 16 village areas. . . . All the village areas except Abuja Town . . . are ruled through chiefs selected by the local elders themselves. The only appointments made direct by the Emir are the 3 District Heads and Abuja Town head. These are members of the Abuja ruling family.'

tury. The history of Abuja, as recorded by M. Hassan, reveals that the rules which limited the distribution of office among the king's family and lineage, were actually observed between 1804 and 1900. Exclusion of the dynasty from office implies that this group were either economically independent through inheritance, or that they were dependent on the king for support. Probably, they were in part independent, and in part supported by the king; and the dynasty was internally differentiated. Officials of various orders discharged a variety of duties on behalf of the royal lineage. Normally the officials charged with such duties were either eunuchs or slaves, or were themselves members of the royal group.[1]

As mentioned above, it was the function of the electoral council to eliminate conflicts over succession to the throne by legitimately mobilizing the total structure in support of their choice. In this process, the order of mallams exercised great influence. The Limamin Juma'a, the Salanke, and the Magajin Mallam, took part in the electoral council, together with the Madawaki and the Galadima; or, if a eunuch did not hold the latter office, at the time, with the Madawaki and the Kuyumbana. Nowadays, consequent on the elimination of eunuchs from official positions, the composition of the electoral council has changed also.[2]

In this context, the menial duties of certain important offices, such as those of the eunuch *rukuni*, Galadima and Wombai, are also worthy of note. The Galadima officiated at the marriages and naming ceremonies of the king's children (Appendix A). The Wombai 'was responsible for the cesspits, and for the urinals of the king and of the women of the palace' (Appendix A). This distribution of menial and non-menial tasks carried out on behalf of the royal household underlined differences of social status between various categories of officials. It is also possible that formal retention by offices of these palace functions also results from continuity of this government with the past, and so marks the processes of its development into a limited monarchy of the type described by M. Hassan. Several customs reported in his account suggest that this Habe chieftainship was originally of a sacred or semi-sacred character; if so, the retention by certain offices of these menial

---

[1] See Appendix A, *re* duties of Galadima, Wambai, Wagu, Sarkin Zana, Sarauniya, Iya.

[2] Hassan and Shu'aibu, *op. cit.*, p. 13.

palace functions could be interpreted as survivals of these earlier phases of the governmental system.[1]

It also seems clear from his account that the care of the royal family and lineage provided an important focus of government action and solidarity. Whether this was initially the principal function of office, and whether the system of government at Abuja had its origins in the administration of a royal menage, cannot be stated. History records certain suggestive parallels, in which elaborate official systems gradually developed from the administration of humble tasks in royal households.[2] But in nineteenth-century Abuja, while the royal family and lineage for whom these trivial duties were performed were excluded from office and power, the officials who discharged or supervised such tasks enjoyed effective control of the state administration.

In comparing the economic status and independence of the various official orders, their relation to the throne is specially important. In this comparison of official orders, the vassal chiefs must be included initially, since they were subordinate to the king of Abuja, and also constituted one of the Abuja rank-orders, despite their semi-autonomous control of hereditary chieftainships, and their exclusion from any of the promotional series open to Abuja officials. As heads of semi-independent subordinate states, these vassal chiefs enjoyed the highest degree of economic independence, but their marginal relation to the Abuja administration, and their non-participation in the internal affairs of the kingdom, differentiates them from other groups of officials.

At first glance, the appointive officials of the Abuja government seem to fall into four economic categories; those who were fully independent by virtue of their official position, such as the two public orders, and some if not all of the royal officials; those whose office provided them with some remuneration, but who were nevertheless partially dependent on the king for support, such as the chamber officials, and probably the mallams; those who had no official sources of income and depended on the king's largesse, such as the household order; and finally, those who were property of the throne, such as the order of slave-officials.

The position of the mallams in this classification is not quite

[1] Cf. Dr. C. K. Meek's account of the Jukun or Kororofa who conquered Habe Zazzau in the seventeenth century for a detailed description of official roles within a system of divine kingship. Meek, C. K., 1931, (1).
[2] Weber, op. cit., pp. 314–17, 337 ff. See also Stenton, 1951, pp. 11–56.

clear on the data available. Each official mallam had definite religious duties allotted to him for which he was paid. These duties included burial of various classes of folk, marriages, etc. Thus the official mallams enjoyed benefices, and were to that degree partially independent of the king for support. Under Hausa Islamic practice, they were also the principal recipients of public alms. In the present classification only those members of the royal line who held official position are of interest, and the royal lineage as a group must be disregarded. The order of slave-officials may also be omitted from further discussion, since their slave status classifies them as property, and rules out the possibility of their independence.

We are therefore left with three economically distinct categories of officials: those who by virtue of office were economically independent, namely, the public orders; those who by virtue of office were fully dependent on the king for support, namely, the order of household officials, and those who by virtue of office were partly dependent on the king for support, and were partly independent through receipt of benefices, namely, the chamber officials and the order of mallams. For reasons apparent later, the order of mallams can also be excluded from further discussion. This classification raises important questions about the ways in which political significance, administrative authority, and economic independence were related to one another and to the structure of offices in this system of government.

(g) The Structure of Official Relations

The chamber eunuchs, the public orders, and the household officials were distinguished systematically from one another by the economic conditions attaching to their different offices. These three orders were also differentiated in terms of their relations to the king; and these relations to the throne were among the most important fixed features of this system of government. To change the conditions of tenure of office would in all probability involve other changes in the structure of the system itself; and the definition and fixity of the different economic conditions which characterizes these official orders may have served to limit the play of economic interests in the formation of *ad hoc* political groupings of officials, and thus to preserve the equilibrium of the total system. In this particularly, relations between the chamber eunuchs, the household officials and the public orders were heavily buttressed by other factors, such as rank-order and precedence, functional differentiation, and especially, perhaps, by the promotional linkages. Through this promotional system, all holders of subordinate office including slaves were motivated to regard their present appointment as a stepping-stone to higher positions in which their economic independence would increase together with their rank and responsibilities, whether these were civil or military in character, or political or administrative in form. Of themselves these promotional arrangements considerably reduced the dangers which faced the governmental structure through the development of an unbridled competition for economic reward among its officials. But the way in which the distribution of political and administrative functions was associated with this economic differentiation of offices was of equal significance for the continuity of the system.

In Abuja, as freemen the king's household officials were eligible for promotion firstly to the *rawuna* rank, and thence to the principal office of Madawaki; but, so long as they remained household officials they were completely dependent on the king for official rewards. None the less, in M. Hassan's words, 'the whole country was theirs, as they appointed the other (i.e. public) officials'.[1] This implies that the household officials shared in the king's official income, and had no need of separate remuneration, since their control of appointments itself guaranteed their income. As noted above, the vote of these household officials was decisive in council, and their leader, the Sarkin Fada, had the power to veto proposals made by the Madawaki on behalf of the public orders. Only in cases of deadlock between his public and household councils was the king free to act summarily; otherwise he was obliged to take counsel first with the household officials, and whether or not agreement was reached, in matters of public interest, with the public orders also. In this way the king could appeal to the public orders under the Madawaki and the Galadima for support against the advice of the household officials under the Sarkin Fada. At the same time, as M. Hassan tells us, the Madawaki and the Sarkin Fada would sometimes arrange privately beforehand to override the king with joint proposals.

The position of the household officials in this political system

[1] M. Hassan, personal communication. See Appendix A.

under their head, the Sarkin Fada, was certainly a strategic and noteworthy one. It cannot be explained simply in terms of a tripartite division of political power. In such a system agreement between two of these three political units would be both necessary and decisive for policy formation. But even within the tripartite political structure of Abuja there was room for a wide variety of alignments, consequent on the multiplicity of segmentary principles which entered into its constitution. Moreover, the Madawaki's council consisted of two orders, the *rukuni* and *rawuna*, whereas the Sarkin Fada's consisted of only one. Yet, apart from the royal succession, we are informed that whatever the issue, the Sarkin Fada, as head of the household officials, had power to veto proposals by the public orders directly, and was indirectly able to thwart the king's policy. This means that the household officials exercised an influence over official appointments and also over promotions and dismissals, which had definite policy implications. Thus although the economic conditions under which they held their offices were apparently unrewarding, the order of household officials, as the dominant political order within the state, had the least need of such economic prescriptions, and may have enjoyed the greatest security of official tenure. None the less, despite their political dominance in ʹcouncil, these household officials were economically dependent on the throne, and the king, by agreement with the public orders under the Madawaki, could promote individual members of this household order out of their strategic position, or simply dismiss them from office. On the other hand, these household officials occupied positions which allowed them to secure their own appointments to higher offices of *rawuna* or *rukuni* rank. These promotions involved a certain loss of political power, but they also carried high rank and prestige, substantial administrative responsibilities, increases in official income and economic independence. To obtain these individual goals, the household officials, especially their leaders, had to maintain good relations with their counterparts in the public administration, and also to keep in favour with the king. In this way, the promotion of these household officials was contingent on restraint in the use of their privileged political position.

Differential political power and administrative responsibilities were linked with this economic differentiation of office in a significant manner. Under the king, those offices which exercised greatest administrative authority and enjoyed the most favourable economic conditions exercised less political power than those with lesser administrative responsibility, lower remuneration and lower degrees of economic independence. Even the kingship itself conformed to this pattern. The king, whose income and economic independence exceeded that of all other officials, and who also enjoyed the highest administrative authority, could only exercise a decisive influence on policy under conditions of stalemate and continuing disagreement between his two councils, those of the household and the public orders. Apparently the leaders of these councils further limited the king's freedom of action by entering into private agreements with one another. In such a system of political relations the household order, which lacked functions of territorial administration, enjoyed the most favourable political position, followed by the public orders under the Madawaki, while the power which the king could exercise independently was very limited indeed.

Although the king initially took counsel with his personal staff of chamber eunuchs, he would have been guilty of action *ultra vires* had he implemented such decisions without first consulting the Sarkin Fada and his group of household officials. Kingship at Abuja was in fact an office with prominent administrative elements and functions, and as such its scope for free action was clearly limited and defined. Furthermore, as the pivotal point of the governmental system, being simultaneously the supreme administrative office and the central office of the political system, the kingship was basic both to the equilibrium and co-ordination of the total system. Hence, though itself involved in segmentary relations with other units of the political system, kingship exercised the least power over policy formation of any of the three units which participated in that process, except, significantly, when the equilibrium of the system was at stake through irreconcilable differences about policy between the public and household orders.

The coexistence of a chosen heir with an electoral council, and the infrequency with which the heir presumptive succeeded to the throne, are now both intelligible. Had the king been able to direct the succession as he wished, or had his chosen heir been given office carrying great latent power, the political structure which we have just described could not have persisted without change; and it is also very unlikely that the administrative system to which this political structure was linked would have persisted without corresponding change. Yet, without constitutional appointment of the king's chosen heir to some official position, the hereditary nature of the kingship would lack sufficient emphasis and expression to ensure that the throne should remain unchallenged within the royal line. In this way the appointment of a chosen heir to office considerably reduced the chances of usurpation or dynastic conflict, and it further safeguarded the state against decentralization brought about through officials appropriating power. The office of Dan Galadima was a symbol which denied the legitimacy of all claims to the throne by persons who were not members of the royal patrilineage. It also served to remind claimants of royal stock of the indeterminacy in succession. In other words, the appointment of an heir apparent whose succession was unlikely was a symbol through which the exclusive right of the royal lineage to the succession was expressed and maintained, and it was by virtue of this symbol that the continuity of the Abuja government as a system of limited monarchy was ensured.

3. THE TYPOLOGICAL CHARACTER OF ABUJA GOVERNMENT

In concluding this discussion of the Abuja government, its position in a general typology of governmental systems is of special interest to us since this Habe government was the original with whose transformations we are concerned.

In the first place, Abuja conforms to the general idea of a 'state', perhaps the most important element of which is the exercise of government through a system of offices. But in Abuja, the king who was the head of the state was neither marginal to the process of policy formation, as were the Jukun or Shilluk kings, nor did he direct policy autocratically, as did the Zulu kings. The political power exercised by the Habe king was distinguished from his authority, and was limited and conditioned by the context of political alignments in which he operated. We cannot therefore classify this Abuja system as either segmentary or centralized since its details reveal the prominence of both these conditions, and their differentiation coincides with the difference between its political and administrative systems.[1]

[1] See Smith, M. G., 1956.

(a) Bureaucracy at Abuja

At first glance, the system of government at Abuja may seem to approximate closely to Max Weber's ideal-type of 'traditional authority'[1]; but here also there are significant differences, and these have certain theoretical implications.

In an especially interesting passage, Weber compares traditional and bureaucratic administrations, and relates them developmentally.

> 'Bureaucracy first developed in patrimonial states with a body of officials recruited from extra-patrimonial sources; but, as will be shown presently, these "officials" have originally been personal followers of the chief. In the pure type of traditional authority, the following features of a bureaucracy are absent: (a) a clearly defined sphere of competence subject to impersonal rules; (b) a rational ordering of relations of superiority and inferiority; (c) a regular system of appointment and promotion on the basis of free contract; (d) technical training as a regular requirement; (e) fixed salaries, in the type case paid in money. In place of a well-defined impersonal sphere of competence, there is (in traditional systems of authority) a shifting series of tasks and powers commissioned and granted by the chief through his arbitrary decision of the moment. An important influence is exerted by competition for sources of income and advantage which are at the disposal of persons acting on behalf of the chief or of the chief himself. It is often in the first instance through these interests that definite functional spheres are marked off, and with them definite administrative organs.'[2]

Several elements of this definition, such as rationality and impersonality, are unsatisfactory because of their imprecision and normative qualities. Such terms imply scales, in terms of which some systems of rules are more 'rational' than others, and some patterns of relations are more 'impersonal'. But as regards the relative rationality of systems of rules, it is surely necessary to have precise criteria; rules which are quite 'rational' or instrumental with respect to one set of objects may be quite irrational or unserviceable with regard to another.[3] Likewise, with regards to the impersonality of relational structures, care must be taken to distinguish and include the informal and the formal aspects of such structures. It is quite conceivable that a formally impersonal system

---

[1] Weber, *op. cit.*, pp. 313–29.   [2] *Ibid.*, p. 315.   [3] *Ibid.*, pp. 332, 312.

MAP A

Abuja and Fulani Zazzau
in the nineteenth and
twentieth centuries.

SOKOTO

Sokoto
200 m.

KANO

o Kano

o Durum

BAUCHI

o Fatika

Zaria o

o Birnin
Gwari

o Kauru

o Lere

Bauchi o

o Kajuru

R. Kaduna

o Kagarko

Jemaa o

KEY

o Bida

Abuja o

Dominions under Filani Zazzau
in the 19th century.

Emirate of Zaria 1950.

Areas ruled by Vassals of Filani
Zazzau in 19th century.

Emirate of Abuja, 1910–50.
Extent of Dominion claimed by
Abuja in 19th century.

Emirate boundaries.

Capital towns.

(All boundaries are only approximate)

o Keffi

R. Niger

Nasarawan
Kwoto

o Doma

o Lafia

Lokoja o

R. Benue

0   50 MILES

SCALE

of relationships may be quite as heavily loaded with personal factors and relations as one which candidly confesses itself to be based on personal solidarities and cleavages.[1] Thus neither rationality nor impersonality can be accorded the diacritical significance for the identification of bureaucracy which Weber attaches to them.

Our data show that administration at Abuja was organized through officially defined spheres of competence and responsibility; that there was a predictable and fairly 'rational' ordering of relations between superior and inferior positions within the system; and that, in so far as this system of relations endured between offices rather than individuals, its character was impersonal. Moreover, state organization at Abuja included regular systems of appointment and promotion, and provided for the empirical training of senior staff through their experience of subordinate office, distinctions being made between military and civil personnel and between various secular skills on the one hand, and the knowledge of Muhammadan religion and law on the other. Officials of this government received various types of economic reward, and one of these forms, the fixed proportions of tax retained by the chamber eunuchs, approaches the concept of salary quite closely, while another, the rewards received by mallams for the religious services which they rendered, can be regarded either as an official benefice or as wage payment on a piecework basis, or as a mixture of both.

The only feature of Weber's ideal type of bureaucracy which is not to be found in the strictly administrative structure of the Abuja government is appointment on a basis of free contract. At Abuja official mallams may have been appointed on free contract, but more probably the appointment consisted simply of selection and installation, since the mallam's 'contract' was already extant in his undertaking to abide by and uphold the principles and laws of Islam, whatever his position. With this possible exception, all the strictly administrative offices of Abuja were filled by compulsory recruitment rather than voluntary contract, the king appointing slaves or eunuchs to such positions. In contrast, wherever an office had political functions, its appointment involved voluntary undertakings. Thus even the eunuchs on promotion to *rukuni* positions, such as Galadima, Wambai, or Dallatu, undertook voluntary obligations; and these allegiances were renewed by both the public and the household officials four times a year at various

[1] *Ibid.*, p. 312.

Muhammadan festivals.[1] Thus the strictly administrative officials of the Abuja government, the titled slaves and the order of mallams and the chamber eunuchs, were not appointed contractually. In contrast, those office-holders whose appointments clearly involved contractual elements, exercised political functions, and participated in the formation of policy. The character of the contractual link between such political officials and the king also varied, and these differences corresponded to their official roles. Thus the public orders whose functions included administration as well as political action governed fiefs under 'feudalistic' contracts. The household officials whose functions were almost purely political were linked to the king by relations which corresponded more closely to the patrimonial norm. However, neither of these categories of political office was held directly on the basis of personal clientage to the king; the obligation of loyalty lay to the system of government as a whole; and the king, so far from controlling appointments to these offices, was indeed subject to control by his officials in selecting persons for appointment.

Recruitment of the strictly administrative staff of the Abuja government on a compulsory rather than a contractual basis does not of itself indicate that their organization was non-bureaucratic. Granted this, the three ranks in question, namely, the mallams, the chamber eunuchs, and the order of slave-officials, must be regarded as bureaucratic organizations. In contrast with these three bureaucratic orders, the two public ranks contain offices which are simultaneously political and administrative in character; and the order of household officials, with its minimal administrative commitments and internal segmentation, diverges furthest from the purely bureaucratic form of organization, and also shows the highest degree of political specialization.

(b) Unity and Diversity

Thus the administrative aspects of Abuja government combined bureaucratic and traditional elements, the latter being both feudal and patrimonial in kind. The heterogeneity of this administrative system corresponds to the heterogeneity of the political system of the government; and this correspondence reflects the variety of factors influencing the equilibrium of the total system, and the corresponding variety of relations pressed into service to maintain

[1] Hassan and Shu'aibu, op. cit., p. 81.

and develop an equilibrium for the system. In a political system constituted on patrimonial and 'feudalistic' bases, co-ordination and equilibrium was achieved by the development of a strictly administrative staff, which was insulated against political action by its status composition of eunuchs, slaves or mallams, and by structural relations of special kinds, such as the joint supervision to which the slave order was subject. It was the function of the strictly administrative staff to discharge duties of co-ordination and organization which were the minimal conditions of government in Abuja, and which were essential to the unity and persistence of the state.

Clearly, for such a complex administrative staff to function efficiently, it had to be under a single direction, and this could be entrusted to no one but the king. However, precisely because the king was head of this specialized administrative staff, he was charged with the maintenance of the unity of the state in its current form, and hence his freedom to initiate political action was correspondingly limited. This limitation was itself implicit in the king's administrative role with its commitment to maintain the state as a stationary equilibrium.

This analysis applies to the various orders of subordinate office at Abuja as well as to the role of the king. The focus of interest here is the differentiation of political and administrative capacities, and the distribution of these among offices of the system. Much of the data bearing on these distributions have already been discussed, and only a brief recapitulation is now necessary. The distinction between the non-contractual character of bureaucratic office and the contractual character of non-bureaucratic office is relevant here. At Abuja, bureaucratic officials, such as the eunuchs and slave-officials, were recruited patrimonially by the king, whereas officials who were recruited extra-patrimonially divided political power with the king. These extra-patrimonial appointments can be further subdivided. On the one hand there were the household retainers, whose relations to the king were assimilated to the forms of patrimonial clientage, especially in their economic dependence; on the other hand there were feudal clients who administered economically rewarding fiefs and had clearly defined military and civil duties. In the light of our preceding discussion of government, it follows that within systems of administrative and political differentiation, the more specialized an office is in the one function, the less it will be in the other. Put another way, within governments based on differentiated political and administrative systems, there is an inverse correlation between the political and administrative significance of office; this follows from the simple fact that the greater the influence which an office exercises over the formation of policy, the less can its authority be defined within strict limits. Conversely, the more precisely is the authority of an office definable, the less is its influence over policy formation and decision.

Applying this admittedly rough criterion to the official rank-orders of the Abuja government, we can place them in a scale of descending political power and specialization as follows: (1) the household officials; (2) the senior public officials; (3) the junior public officials; (4) the king; (5) the mallams; (6) the slave-officials; (7) the chamber eunuchs. Granted the validity of this classification in terms of political specialization, then a corresponding classification in terms of administrative specialization would simply consist in the reversal of this order; as indicated by the discussion of their bureaucratic characteristics, the orders of slave-officials, mallams, and chamber eunuchs are the most strictly administrative units in the Abuja government, followed by the king, the junior public officials, the senior public officials, and lastly, by the almost purely political order of household officials.

The extent to which authority in a unit of government is undefined is the measure of its political element and significance. The clearer is this definition and its observation or enforcement, the more does the resulting system conform to Weber's concept of bureaucracy. But there are important differences between the formality and the fact of control, and also between a bureaucracy which neither formally nor otherwise admits of control, and one which does.

4

GOVERNMENT IN FULANI ZAZZAU
1865

IN this chapter I present an account of the government of Fulani Zaria as it was in 1865 to facilitate its comparison with that of Habe Zazzau. In succeeding chapters we shall trace the history of its development and further growth.

I. VASSALS AND VASSALAGE

(a) Relations with Sokoto

The Fulani *jihad* of 1804–10 established an empire of which Fulani Zazzau was part. This Fulani empire was controlled by the Sultans of Sokoto, who were descended from the leader of the *jihad*, Shehu dan Fodio, of the Toronkawa clan of Fulani. The Sokoto dynasty administered this empire in association with the kings of Gwandu, who were also Toronkawa Fulani, closely related to the family of the Shehu. That part of the empire placed under the supervision of the kings of Gwandu lay to the west; the sultans of Sokoto retained control of the east. Zaria lay in this eastern division and was thus directly under the supervision of Sokoto.

Zaria was a vassal state of the Sokoto empire. But Zaria was one of the five or six most important states of the empire, and had several vassals of its own. There were important differences between the relations of vassalage which bound Zaria to Sokoto and the vassalage of its subordinate units to Zaria. These differences were significant for the development of government in Zaria itself. Whereas Zaria did not directly intervene in the internal affairs of its vassals, and they had no voice in the affairs of Zaria, the sultans of Sokoto could and did intervene in the government of Zazzau, at various times and in various ways, and these interventions often marked changes in the structure or functions of the Zaria government. I shall therefore discuss the relation of Zaria to Sokoto and to its own vassal states separately, beginning with Sokoto.

The Sultan of Sokoto supervised the state of Zaria through his kinsman, the Waziri (Vizier) of Sokoto. This Waziri was the official link between the rulers of Zaria and Sokoto. He was kept informed about local affairs through visits by himself and his agents, and in this way he maintained a continuous contact with the kings of Zaria. The Waziri was responsible for collecting the tribute which Zaria made twice annually to Sokoto, on the occasions of the main Muhammadan festivals of Id-el-Kabir, and Id-el-Fitr (known in Hausa as the Greater and the Lesser Sallah). At such times, the kings of Zaria were expected to visit Sokoto, taking with them tribute in the form of slaves, Zaria cloth, horses, mats, and some cowrie currency. The content of this tribute changed over the century, and its value tended steadily to increase. Apart from the tribute which the rulers of Zaria sent to Sokoto, levies of grain were collected for the Wazirin Sokoto on his annual visits to Zaria. This collection was known as *bani-bani* (give me—give me). By 1860 it had become customary for the king of Zaria to make donations of money and goods to both the Waziri and the Sultan of Sokoto on his appointment to the throne. This *kurdin sarauta* (money of taking office) was introduced in the years between 1835 and 1845, when Sokoto asserted its right to select the rulers of Zaria.

Sokoto chose the rulers of Zaria from one or other of three principal dynasties; the Mallawa, who were descended from Mallam Musa, a Fulani of Malle, who was the deputy appointed by dan Fodio to conquer Zaria; the Bornawa, who were descended from Yamusa, a Fulani of Bornu origin, and Musa's Madaki (*madawaki*, commander of cavalry); and the Katsinawa who were descended from Abdulkerim, a Fulani of Katsina, who helped Musa in the conquest of Zaria, and was then placed in charge of all pastoral Fulani in the state with the title of Sa'i.

In 1860 the Sultan of Sokoto for the first time deposed a ruler of Zaria, and Audussalami of the Suleibawa Fulani, a native of Zaria, the holder of the title Makama, and a distant agnatic kinsman of the royal lineage of Kano, was appointed as ruler of Zazzau. The development of relations between Zaria and Sokoto was thereafter closely linked with this power of the Sultan to depose as well as appoint the rulers of Zaria, and the history of these relations will be related in the following chapter.

By 1863 the process through which the king of Zaria was selected had taken the following form. There was an electoral council at Zaria composed of the chief priest (Limamin Juma'a), the Galadima, and one other official mallam, normally the chief judge (Alkali), but on occasion the Limamin Kona, a priestly office which had persisted at Zaria from Habe times. The official composition of this local electoral council varied little during the century; the rule was that it should not include either of the competing candidates or any members of the ruling lineages. This electoral council considered the leading cómpetitors for the throne and prepared a short list of three candidates ranked in the order of their preference. This list was sent to the Waziri of Sokoto, who, as the *Kofar Zazzau* (the supervisor or intermediary between Zaria and the Sultan), discussed the final choice with the Sultan, and would visit Zaria to announce and instal the new king.

Like so many other elements of the Fulani government, the crowning or installation of the ruler also changed during the last century. It seems that the first two kings were not crowned by Sokoto. It is possible to argue also that Yamusa, the second ruler, was not selected independently by Sokoto. However, the third Fulani ruler, Abdulkerim, was selected by the Sultan of Sokoto on the basis of recommendations by the electoral council of Zaria; and he was crowned by the Waziri of Sokoto in Zaria city at the traditional place for such ceremonies, the compound of the Magajiya. Hamada, the son of Yamusa, who succeeded Abdulkerim, refused to be crowned there, but died after reigning for only fifty-two days. Later kings were appointed by Sokoto and were crowned at the king's palace (*gidan Bakwa Turunku*) in Zaria city. To reduce the chances of civil war developing over the succession after 1880, the Sultans of Sokoto decided to select and crown the king of Zaria at Sokoto. This was done twice; but in 1897 the rule was changed again, and an attempt was made to select and instal the new king in Zaria city, with consequences which will be related in due course.

Sokoto first claimed and exercised the power to depose rulers of Zaria in 1860. Further depositions occurred in 1873, 1881, and 1890. It is thus fair to say that by 1863 the Sultan of Sokoto had appropriated powers to appoint and dethrone the rulers of Zaria. Moreover, beginning with Audusallami's accession in 1860, the rulers of Sokoto also controlled appointments to certain of the principal offices of the Zaria government.

As a vassal of the Sultan of Sokoto, the ruler of Zaria paid tribute and attended the Court at Sokoto annually; he also reported on the affairs of his kingdom, and supplied military or other aid as requested. For example, in 1851 the kingdom of Hadejia repudiated its subordination to Sokoto, and in the secession war which followed, the king of Zaria sent several contingents of local troops to the assistance of Sokoto.

The Sultan of Sokoto had rights to inherit portions of the property left by rulers of vassal states. When a king of Zaria died in office, one-half of his childless concubines and one-third of his slaves and his cattle went to the Sultan, an equal share going to the next king, and the remainder to the late ruler's family. When a king of Zaria was deposed, the Sultan of Sokoto received one-half of his slaves and his cattle. Land, compounds and slaves attached permanently to the throne were not subject to this subdivision or inheritance; nor were the horses, which were used for the cavalry of Zaria, or the large herds of cattle permanently endowed to the throne. This right to a share in the inheritance of the personal estates of vassal chiefs was a source of considerable income to Sokoto. Certain kings of Zaria are said to have had over 6,000 slaves as personal property.

Within his kingdom, the ruler of Zaria exercised power over appointments to office, dismissals, promotions, the creation of new offices, and related matters. However the king of Zaria did not exercise such wide powers over appointments to the chieftainships of states which were his vassals as the Sultan exercised over Zaria itself. Early in the century when a ruler of Zaria sought to reward a supporter with one of these vassal chieftainships, the vassal state protested successfully, receiving support from Sokoto. Thereafter the rulers of Zaria merely confirmed the candidates selected by the local electoral councils, but neither chose nor deposed these vassals.

The king of Zaria was free to make war against non-Muhammadan populations, to levy tax or tribute as he pleased within his dominions, and to administer justice, including capital punishment. He could appeal to Sokoto for military aid when necessary, and it was traditional for the kingdom of Kano to supply Zaria with cavalry reinforcements.

The king of Zaria exercised a supervisory jurisdiction over his vassal states, and several of these lacked powers to pass sentence involving mutilation or death. In addition the ruler of Zaria received one-third of the slaves and cattle, and one-half of the childless concubines of his vassal chiefs who died in office, together with one-sixth of the horses, cattle and slaves of all Zaria officials, and one-half of the property of those who were dismissed from office. On his own accession and their appointment, a king received handsome *gaisuwa* (gifts of greeting) from his officials and vassal chiefs. The king made similar gifts to the Sultan of Sokoto. For example, the king of Zaria, Audullahi, sent Sultan Rufa'i a hundred slaves as a greeting (*gaisuwa*) on the latter's appointment to the throne of Sokoto. Such gifts expressed the subordinate's allegiance and loyalty. To forestall the official division of their estates and to protect their families against impoverishment, kings sometimes gave their children substantial numbers of slaves during their lifetime, and such gifts were not included in the inheritance.

(b) Zaria and its Vassals

The geographical distribution of the vassal states of Fulani Zaria during the last century is presented on the map. The larger vassal states of Jema'an Dororo, Nassarawan Kwotto, and Keffi lay farthest south from Zaria, and each of these chiefdoms was over 3,000 square miles in area. Another small vassal state, called Doma, lying near these to the south, had a mixed population of pagans and Muhammadans and a tradition of sacred chieftainship. Lafia, east of Doma, had been a vassal state of Zaria until 1812, when the king of Zaria transferred it to the ruler of Bauchi, his eastern neighbour. Lapai, another small chiefdom which until 1836 owed allegiance to Zaria, was also transferred on its own request to the kingdom of Nupe, itself a vassal state of the western division of the Fulani empire under the King of Gwandu. The small community of Bagaji was the fifth southern vassal of Zaria.

Two of the three largest southern vassal states of Zaria, Keffi and Jema'a, were founded by Fulani leaders to whom Mallam Musa, the conqueror of Zaria, had given flags (*tuta*) as symbols of leadership over the Faithful in those territories. The rulers of Keffi and Jema'a were selected by local electoral councils, but they were usually crowned at Zaria. These states, like other vassals, paid tribute (*gandu*) to Zaria, rather than tax (*haraji, kurdin kasa*). The amount of the tribute which any one state paid varied slightly from year to year; but Zaria expected a hundred slaves from each of the larger vassal states annually. If tribute had not been paid for three consecutive years, the king of Zaria enforced its collection by military means. Such a forced collection of tribute from Keffi in 1873 led to the deposition of one king of Zaria, who refused to stop his attacks, although instructed by the Sultan of Sokoto to do so. Apart from slaves, gowns, salt, locust-bean, mats, palm-oil, kola-nuts, grain, cowrie currency, and horses were also sent regularly to Zaria as tribute by vassal chiefs.

After 1840 the kings of Zaria lost the power to select or depose the kings of Jema'a, Keffi, and Kwotto, although they retained suzerainty of these states. Jema'a, Keffi, Kwotto, and Doma had powers to make war on pagans or with nearby Abuja, although not on one another. In fact, there was frequent fighting between these states. Some of these campaigns were stopped and punished by the king of Zaria, while others were over before Zaria was able to intervene.

Every vassal had a set of royal drums (*tambari*) as insignia of hereditary chieftainship; rulers of the three larger states had complete jurisdiction within their dominions, being able to pass and enforce sentences involving mutilation or death, to levy tax, and to allocate state offices at their pleasure. Each of these states had its own judiciary with powers to imprison, levy fines, administer floggings, to decree divorce and the like.

Rulers of vassal states nearer to Zaria lacked the powers and relative autonomy of these peripheral southern chiefdoms. These proximate vassal states were Kajuru, Kauru, Fatika, Kagarko, Lere, and Durum. Of these Kajuru, Kauru, and Fatika were already in existence before the Fulani conquered Zaria, while Lere and Kagarko were established at some time during the last century, and Durum, which was given vassal status at the conquest, was later reduced to the position of a fief. Each of these nearby vassal states was ruled by its own hereditary dynasty, and within his dominions each of these vassal chiefs could levy tax or tribute, allocate local offices, and had jurisdiction over minor offences (*karamin shari'a*) and legal issues such as inheritance, divorce, land issues, and debts, and the right to impose fines, imprisonment, and whipping. *Manyan shari'a*, i.e. issues giving rise to heavier punishments such as multilation or death, were referred to Zaria for decision. Appeals lay from the vassal's court to those of Zaria. None of these proximate vassals had power to engage in war or raids without permission from the king of Zaria. During the late nineteenth century, the rulers of Zaria stationed armies at Kacia near the borders of

Kajuru, Kauru, and Kagarko, to keep local tribes in control and to protect caravan routes in the area.

The kings of Zaria exercised powers of selecting and deposing the rulers of these proximate vassal states. Of them, only Kajuru, Lere, Kauru, and Fatika had *tambari* of their own, or could *shiga kokuwa*, i.e. were given the *alkyabba* (robe of chieftainship) on their installation. The *tambari* given to Durum in 1804 were later removed together with its vassal status. There is no record that these closer vassal states either failed to pay tribute promptly, or ever waged war on one another throughout the period of Fulani rule at Zaria. Members of the royal lines of these states were unable to hold office within the government of Zaria, and members of the leading families of Zaria were unable to hold office within these states. Thus, despite differences in the degrees of their subordination and the effectiveness of their control by Zaria, all vassal states were discrete governmental systems in the sense that participation in any of these systems entailed exclusion from all other systems of similar kind, including the government of the sovereign state.

Each of these vassal states was linked to the ruler of Zaria through a *kofa* (door) or intermediary. These intermediaries included titled officials of Zaria, but the king retained direct control over certain vassals, and communicated with them through his own *jekada* (agent, intermediary), who would also be the vassal's *kofa* (door). Kauru and Kajuru were supervised by the Makama Karami, Lere, and Durum by the Turaki Karami; Jema'a was originally placed by Mallam Musa under the Limamin Juma'a, and Keffi was originally allotted to an untitled mallam and pilgrim, Alhaji Musa, whose religious scruples would not allow him to take territorial office. These two states, together with Kwotto, Bagaji, and Fatika, were later supervised by the Madaki, while Doma, Kagarko, Durum, and Lere were supervised directly by the king. Through the appointed intermediaries, these vassal states submitted their tribute to the king, the intermediary keeping one-fifth of the total, just as the Waziri of Sokoto kept some of the tribute sent from Zaria to Sokoto. The intermediaries were also responsible for reporting the legal cases to the Zaria courts, for passing on instructions to the vassal chiefs, and for keeping the king of Zaria informed about developments in their several chiefdoms.

2. SOCIETY IN FULANI ZARIA

The population of Fulani Zaria in the last century was partly slave, partly free. The slaves included captives, few of whom were Muhammadan, but those born into slavery were reared as Muhammadans. Free members of the society were either freedmen or born free. Eunuchs must also be distinguished from the slave and the free, although they suffered many of the legal disabilities of slaves in Fulani Zaria.

The free population of Fulani Zaria were divided firstly by religion into Muhammadan and non-Muhammadan groups. Most of the non-Muhammadans were tribesmen living to the south and west of the state, and slaves were regularly drawn from these populations by raids or tribute. Excluding these non-Hausa-speaking 'pagans', the principal division among the free Muhammadan population of Zaria was between the Fulani and the Habe, the conquerors and the conquered. The conquest reflected this ethnic differentiation and initiated new relations of superordination and subordination which were established in the process of consolidation.

(a) Rank and Lineage among the Fulani

The Fulani of Zaria were divided into Settled and Nomadic groups. The Settled Fulani ruled the state, intermarrying with their Nomadic cousins, who also assisted occasionally in raids and war. The Settled Fulani were internally divided into a number of lineages, and these were stratified according to their position within the system of government. There were four dynasties at Fulani Zaria, the Mallawa, Bornawa, Katsinawa, and Suleibawa. Of these the first three were the most important politically, and had the largest membership. In addition, there were a number of other aristocratic Fulani patrilineages, such as the Katsinawa 'Yan Doto, the 'Yan Doto of Gusau, the Fulanin Wunti, Fulanin Yesqua, Fulanin Joli, Fulanin Gadidi, and the Fulani of Dan Durori; certain other patrilineages such as the Fulanin Bebeji, or the Fulanin Shanono were of Kano origin; the Toronkawa Fulani were descended from Waziri Gidado of Sokoto by the daughter of M. Musa, the baMalle conqueror; and there were also Fulani from various parts of Katsina such as Damfa, the Dokaje, and others. The aristocratic status enjoyed by these lineages was related to their political roles in two ways. Aristocratic status qualified them for political roles and office. It was further established through and enforced by participation in government. This list of noble Fulani lineages reflects in part the heterogeneous composition of the Fulani force which invaded Zaria under Musa; but it also includes some Fulani who were already settled in Zaria at that date.

The status of the ruling lineages was superior to that of other Fulani in Zaria. Members of these dynasties were royals by birth. Their male members were each a *yerima* (prince), their females, a *gimbiya* (princess). Such persons paid no land-tax (*kurdin kasa*), and were also exempt from other annual taxation under the rule of *hurumi*, or perpetual exemption, a right which vested in these dynasties by virtue of their royal status.

The other aristocratic Fulani lineages of Zaria were also internally differentiated through their competition for political office. Successful lineages tended to have higher status and greater wealth than their less successful competitors. Such differentiation was itself a ground for the allocation of office, while the allocation of office further increased these differences. Office provided its holders with opportunities for the accumulation of wealth, booty, and slaves, and slaves were the main sources of farm labour. An owner having sufficient slaves usually established his own settlement. This was called a *rinji* (slave-village or hamlet, pl. *rumada*; alternatives *keffi*,[1] *tunga*). The number and size of the *rumada* which a person or family controlled was evidence of the owner's wealth and power. Merchants and many other non-officials had slaves, but permission was necessary in order to build separate settlements for *rumada*, and this was generally given only to the nobility. In Zaria, the majority of the larger *rumada* belonged to one or other of the dynasties. These *rumada* were the principal forms of capital investment in Zaria, and thus political status was closely related to the distribution of wealth; conversely, the distribution of wealth was related to the distribution of political office. The relations between noble status, political office, and wealth tended to be circular, in the sense that each of these factors reinforced the other. However, this circle was neither closed nor complete for the following reasons.

Firstly, commoners were never completely excluded from

---

[1] The southern vassal state called by this name was often regarded as a slave reserve.

political office. Even slaves held office, and they often amassed wealth. Thus the Turaki Ba'idu, a slave-official of Mallam Musa, himself had over 1,200 slaves, and was one of the wealthiest men in Zaria at that time. Although manumitted by Musa and renamed Abdullahi, the Mallawa inherited the Turaki's property as he was a eunuch.

Secondly, the duties levied on the estates of officials on their death or dismissal also tended to reduce the rate at which these lineages accumulated property through political appointments. The throne received substantial portions of the estate of its officials.

Thirdly, the membership of these dominant lineages increased with unusual speed due to the opportunities for acquiring concubines which were provided by political office. This population growth promoted the progressive differentiation of descent-lines within these lineages, and this differentiation was further accelerated by frequent re-distributions of office. Since the number of political offices was limited while the population descended from aristocrats was not, the number of noblemen holding office formed a continually diminishing proportion of the number of noblemen eligible for and interested in such office. The differentiation of descent-lines within the Fulani patrilineages corresponded to the relative political success of lineage males and expressed these conditions of intense competition for office. The extreme case of intra-lineage differentiation is provided by the dynasties, and its form can be seen from a glance at the skeleton genealogies attached.

Finally, towards the end of the century the security of slave property tended to diminish, partly due to attacks from external enemies, such as Kontagora, the Habe of Maradi, and the Ningi; partly due to increased local kidnapping by 'Yan Kwanta; partly to the effects of political competition within the state itself. These were the most important factors which prevented the development of a rigid and caste-like stratification in Zaria through changeless coincident distributions of wealth, office, and status. Under these conditions the system of stratification permitted both downward and upward social mobility, and although the opportunities for social movement were greater for the Fulani than the Habe, the latter also enjoyed chances of limited mobility.

Certain aristocratic lineages were also differentiated by functional specialization. Thus the Katsinawa 'Yan Doto were a

Fulani lineage taking a special pride in their knowledge of Islam and Muhammadan law (*shari'a*). As such they provided the state with persons specially fitted to hold judicial positions or priestly offices. The office of Limamin Kona was traditionally reserved for a Habe family originally from Bornu. Particular offices of state were allocated to certain other Fulani lineages such as the Wuntawa, and such lineages would only compete for the reserved offices, gradually establishing quasi-hereditary interests therein. Other aristocratic lineages were linked to the ruling groups of neighbouring states, and competed for a wide variety of local offices.

Competition for office took a variety of forms. Of these clientage was perhaps the most important. Individuals might become clients of particular persons, such as office-holders eligible for promotion to the throne; or they might enter into a looser association with an important family or branch of a family; or one family or descent-line could be clients of another or of an office. The most effective form of clientage was usually based on individual relations; but the association of descent-lines for purposes of political competition was also significant. Such familial clientage was often expressed in marriage alliances, since the heads of descent-lines who sought to preserve their solidarity and perpetuate their association over the following generations would frequently arrange for the children of their more important members to marry one another. Although official appointments and relations to which such familial clientage gave rise would be expressed through individuals, these individuals would represent the continuing association of their descent-lines. Thus Mallam Musa established a close bond between his lineage and that of the Wazirin Sokoto, the Toronkawa, by giving his daughter in marriage to the Waziri. The children of this union were in due course returned to Zaria, and have since been appointed to numerous offices by the Bornawa as well as by their Mallawa kin.

Under Muhammadan law, the child of a slave concubine by her master is a free member of the master's family, inheriting with other issue on its father's death. This rule, coupled with extensive opportunities for recruiting concubines from their own slaves, allowed the ruling Fulani to increase more rapidly than any other part of the population; and this together with their increasing number of slaves meant that as time passed their overthrow became correspondingly more difficult.

Fulani patrilineages were not exogamous. The Settled Fulani followed Islamic practice under which the preferred form of marriage is that between two brothers' children. Among the subject Habe, matrilateral cross-cousin marriage was the preferred form. This Fulani preference for marriage between agnatic kin, including first-cousins, enabled the different descent-lines within a lineage or dynasty, as well as different lineages or dynasties, to intermarry for political reasons. This pattern of political marriages was an important method of associating family-lines, within and between lineages; but although it helped to weld the numerous Fulani lineages and their politically differentiated segments into a ruling group the parts of which were bound to one another by kinship and marriage as well as by lineage and clientage, it also expressed and promoted their internal rivalry.

Within lineages differentiation was especially important in the contest for political office and at inheritance. This differentiation developed through units known as *dakuna* (huts; s. *daki*). Under Muslim law a man may have four wives, and as many concubines as he can afford. Aristocratic Fulani males of sufficient means normally had four wives each, and they usually divided their fertile concubines among the 'huts' of these wives. Thus the wife's 'hut' would include her own children, together with the concubines placed under her control and their children. On the death of the common husband (*mai-gida*, head of the household) his property would then be divided among the four 'huts' distinguished by reference to his wives. The eldest son of each wife took charge of the portion allotted to her hut. Under Muhammadan law all male issue were entitled to equal portions of the inheritance, while daughters received half the portions allotted to sons except for land. If these legal principles were observed exactly in the division by *dakuna*, then the portions allotted to each *daki* would correspond to the number and sex of the heirs within them. Alternatively, the estate would be divided into four equal portions, one for each hut. In either case, subdivision of an inheritance applied to land, slaves, cattle, and other movables, and inheritance implied subdivision. The net effect was that the principal type of corporate property held by politically successful descent-lines were the *rumada* which had originally been allotted to separate *dakuna*. Such 'family' *rumada* would be administered formally by the eldest surviving son of the descent-line and were supervised by one or other of the

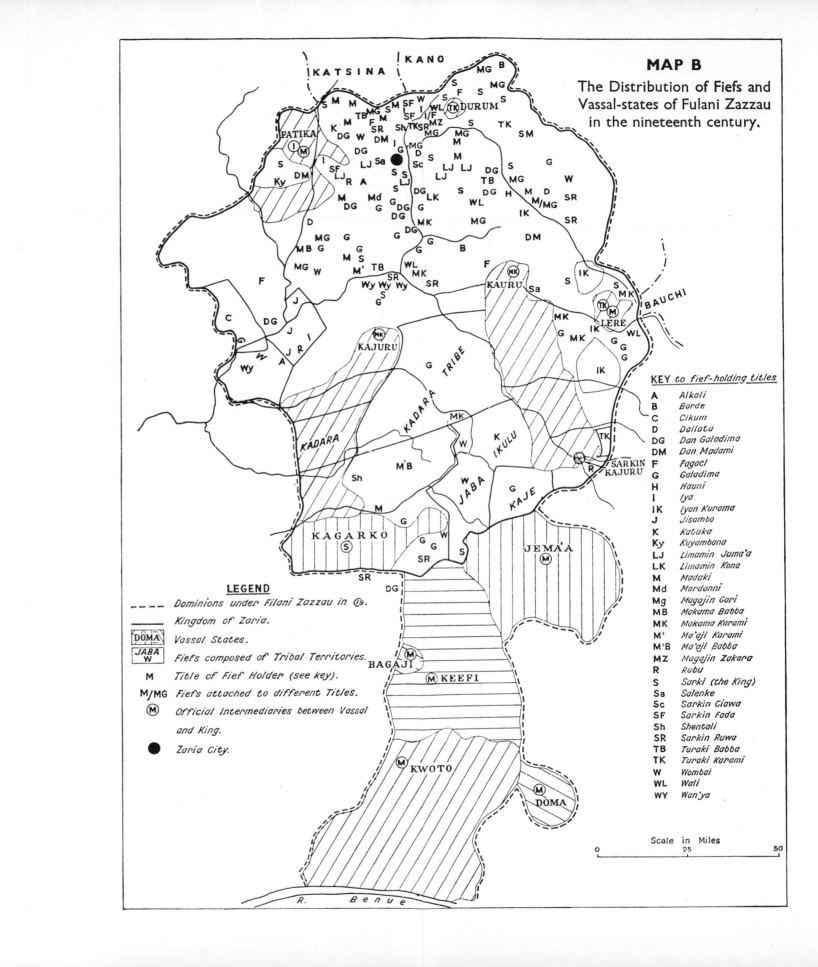

MAP B

The Distribution of Fiefs and
Vassal-states of Fulani Zazzau
in the nineteenth century.

KEY to fief-holding titles

A	Alkali
B	Barde
C	Cikum
D	Dallatu
DG	Dan Galadima
DM	Dan Madami
F	Fagaci
G	Galadima
H	Hauni
I	Iya
IK	Iyan Kurama
J	Jisambo
K	Katuka
Ky	Kuyambana
LJ	Limamin Juma'a
LK	Limamin Kona
M	Madaki
Md	Mardanni
Mg	Magajin Gari
MB	Makama Babba
MK	Makama Karami
M'	Ma'aji Karami
M'B	Ma'aji Babba
MZ	Magajin Zakara
R	Rubu
S	Sarki (the King)
Sa	Salenke
Sc	Sarkin Ciawa
SF	Sarkin Fada
Sh	Shentali
SR	Sarkin Ruwa
TB	Turaki Babba
TK	Turaki Karami
W	Wombai
WL	Wali
WY	Wan'ya

LEGEND

- - - Dominions under Filani Zazzau in C19.

——— Kingdom of Zaria.

DOMA   Vassal States.

JABA
W   Fiefs composed of Tribal Territories.

M   Title of Fief Holder (see key).

M/MG   Fiefs attached to different Titles.

Ⓜ   Official Intermediaries between Vassal
      and King.

●   Zaria City.

Scale in Miles

0   25   50

heirs (*iyayen giji*), who would distribute portions of its yield annually to others.

Subdivision of estates on inheritance meant that the accumulation of property by families was accompanied by its dispersal. The subdivision at inheritance defined separate *dakuna* as segments within agnatic lines, at the same time that the preference for marriage between ortho-cousins or cross-cousins permitted the selective association of individuals of the same or different *dakuna* by the intermarriage of their children. As a rule, full brothers supported one another in this intra-lineage competition, whereas paternal half-brothers were traditional rivals. The genealogical structure of the politically important lineages was such that this contraposition of *dakuna* and agnatic descent could be combined and varied according to the context. The net effect is that descent-lines within lineages are differentiated by reference to the rank of their founders and senior males, by the distribution of differing sibling relations, by marriage alliances within and outside the lineage, and by property, especially corporately owned herds of cattle and *rumada*. The room for manoeuvre with which these variables presented political competitors was fully exploited by the Fulani of Zaria, and such manoeuvres were important to their form of government.

(b) The Subject Population

Habe whose ancestors had not held political office lack lineage ties completely. For such commoners, the system of kinship and descent is bilateral, although inheritance, residence, and various other conditions of kinship emphasize agnatic ties. During the last century, Habe mainly participated in the government of Zaria as subordinate officials charged with tax-collection. The majority of these offices were defined by relation to occupational groups. For example there was a Sarkin Makeran Zazzau (Chief of the Blacksmiths of Zaria) appointed to collect an industrial tax from the blacksmiths of the kingdom. In turn, he appointed other blacksmiths to assist him, gave them appropriate titles, and allocated them to stated districts from which each would collect the blacksmiths' tax. This system of occupational taxation was developed during the century to embrace most of the craftsmen of Zaria, with corresponding increases in the number of occupational tax-collecting officials. These occupational officials, being normally recruited from the craft for whose tax they were responsible, were almost all of Habe origin, since the Habe were the craftsmen of Zaria from pre-Fulani days.[1] Among themselves, Habe observed a 'class' system emphasizing hereditary occupation in the male line. A special feature of this system was its caste-like depreciation of butchers, hunters, tanners, and blacksmiths. These four occupational groups had the lowest ranking, and descent from any of them was regarded by other groups as a valid barrier to marriage.

In the years immediately following the conquest, political office was equally open to Habe and Fulani; but by the mid-nineteenth century almost all important offices were reserved for royal or noble Fulani. In part this exclusion of Habe from important office reflected the increasing pressure of the expanding Fulani population on the limited number of offices; in part, it may have been an unavoidable implication of the conquest, which placed the Fulani in a superior position to the Habe.

Among the slaves of Fulani Zaria the important distinction was between the native-born and the captives. Native-born slaves were Muhammadans by training, and were morally not alienable. They were often employed on important business of a confidential nature, being specially suited by their status and upbringing for such roles. Their slave status made them completely dependent on the owner; their membership in his family since birth provided ground for identification of interests; and their training provided them with the necessary cultural skills. These *dimajai* (native-born slaves) also formed an important part of the armed force of Zaria, especially the bowmen and infantry. They were also employed as *jakadu* (intermediaries), and as household servants, and were occasionally put in charge of military detachments or territorial fiefs. Despite their inferior status, such *dimajai* shared many interests with their owners and with the free population, and were often more reliable than free agents. It is notable that throughout the last century, despite the fact that there were considerable opportunities for a successful slave rebellion in Zaria, there was never any danger or fear of such a development. Judging from accounts of Hausa-Fulani kingdoms given by Barth and other travellers who visited these areas during the last century, perhaps one-

---

[1] A list of the principal occupational officials is given in the chart of State organization in nineteenth-century Zaria, and a catalogue of their taxes is to be found in Appendix D. For further details of these and other taxes of Fulani Zaria, see Arnett, 1920, p. 16; or Smith, M. G., 1955, pp. 96–7.

third or one-half of the population in the densely settled Muham-madan areas of some Fulani states were slaves.[1]

Eunuchs occupied few important offices in the latter half of the last century at Fulani Zaria, and consequently we know little about them. In 1890 the last of the offices traditionally reserved for eunuchs from Habe days was given to a free man at the same time that this office was invested with territorial fiefs. This was the office of Sarkin Zana (Chief of the Harem). However, while the old Habe offices for eunuchs were passing into the hands of free men, new eunuch titles were being created to discharge certain essential tasks within the royal household. These new eunuch offices were strictly menial, and their functions were strictly limited to the royal household.

3. STATE FUNCTIONS AND ORGANIZATION

(a) Integrative Principles

The total area over which the king of Zaria exercised suzerainty during the last century may have exceeded 20,000 square miles. Of this, the kingdom and its nearer vassal states had an area of about 13,000 square miles. The state was a conquest state, the unity and control of which was a Fulani responsibility. It was also part of an empire, on the one hand exercising suzerainty over tributary vassal states, on the other itself a vassal state of Sokoto.

Its intermediate position within the imperial hierarchy affected the government of Zaria in several ways. This intermediate status considerably reduced the opportunities for successful military rebellion by Zaria or elements within it, for such a revolt would meet with opposition from the armed forces of the Fulani empire as a whole. Yet this very condition paradoxically increased the value of force in the competition for the throne. Since civil war among the ruling Fulani would endanger the stability of the local state and the Fulani empire, threats to use force were common in this competition and the compromise arrangements by which they were disarmed only served to condone them. Its tributary position also stimulated the rulers of Zaria to develop machinery for the collection of tax within the state and for the collection of tribute from its vassals. Its imperial situation gave Zaria great security from external enemies, and also sanctioned the local kingship and

[1] See Barth, 1857, or Denham and Clapperton, 1826.

government in terms of *imama*, that is, leadership of the Faithful within a province of the *dar-es-Islam*. Thus Islam sanctioned Fulani rule which was initially established to enforce its observance; and at the same time it sanctioned the claims of local dynasties to the throne.

In the prevalent ideology the organization of government was justified so long as it provided conditions essential to the maintenance and expansion of the Muhammadan religion. Such an ideology initially weakened the opposition of the Muhammadan Habe to Fulani rule, and this threat to the conquerors from the native Habe of Zaria was progressively reduced by the prolific expansion of ruling Fulani groups through the combination of patrilineal descent and extensive concubinage, and also through the increasing number of slaves under Fulani control. Moreover, as free Muhammadans, the Fulani and Habe were committed by their common interests to try to maintain the current social and political order; numerically also they were together strong enough to prevent a successful revolt of their internally divided slave populations. Within the system of competing patrilineages, clientage served to bring Fulani and Habe into close political association, thereby reducing the separateness and unity of these conquered groups. Solidary political relations of clientage were the usual basis of Habe appointments to office; and although offices allocated to Habe were generally subordinate to those filled by Fulani of noble lineage or royal descent, they provided their holders with opportunities for the accumulation of wealth, for upward social mobility, and for the exercise of power. Finally, the system of multidynastic competition increased the urgency and span of political competition, thereby increasing the numbers who participated within this system. Since the distribution of most subordinate offices of the state, such as village-chieftainships or occupational titles, depended on the distribution of the senior offices and proceeded on similar lines, the political competition and its integrative functions were equally extensive, and the institutions through which these political relations developed were just as solidary in function as they were differentiating in form.

These integrative elements in the government were usually latent and were clearly unplanned. They developed as it were accidentally, almost in spite of the form of the state. But the Fulani were not content to rely on such accidental integration for the maintenance of their government. They actively sought to assure its continuity through their organization of territorial administration, law, taxation, tribute, and military force. The principles of organization which the Fulani developed for the recurrent discharge of these governmental functions fell within the permissive framework of Islamic political ideas, and served both to motivate the necessary loyalties and to ensure the free flow of recruits for office.

(b) Territorial Organization: Fiefs, Estates, and Communities

The territorial organization of Fulani Zaria was based on the local chieftainship of community units. Settlement patterns emphasized defensive values and were based on the compact distribution of population within walled towns, strung out along the principal caravan routes. Each of these towns had a few smaller settlements near it which owed allegiance to the village chief of the area in which they were sited. Many but not all of these hamlets were slave-villages (*rumada*); other *rumada* large enough to form towns of their own, would have the walls and other fortifications typical of a town (*gari*). Most of the large *rumada* with their own fortifications belong to one or other of the dynasties, and several of them were established by kings whose permission was always necessary before settlements could be walled. In his court the ruler of Zaria settled any boundary disputes between neighbouring townships. Rivers, streams, and flood-water courses were widely used to mark such boundaries. It was common to bury charcoal within shallow trenches cut along the boundary for later reference.

Within each community, the village chief administered its population through a hierarchy of ward-heads, whom he was free to appoint to office, to promote or dismiss. Occupational officials of the area were chosen by the local community chief from each occupational order separately. The subordinate officials of the community formed the instrument through which the local chief gave his orders to the people of his area; the orders he gave were executive, and the community chief had no legislative power, but since refusal to obey his orders led to punishment for *kin umurci* (disobedience), the main restriction on the *de facto* legislative power of the community or village chief was the supervision exercised by his superior, which gave the villagers chances to appeal or complain. Normally the orders issued by community chiefs related to such matters as repair of the town walls, mosques, or other public buildings, including the chief's residence, or work on the overlord's farm, the arrest of runaway slaves or criminals, assistance for caravans, or service on military expeditions as required by the overlord. The collection of tax and tribute was another responsibility of the local chief, who also informed his overlord about local developments, supervised the markets and caravan routes within his area, allocated land to strangers, adjudicated minor issues relating to land, inheritance, divorce, illegitimacy, apprehended runaway slaves, and enforced the observance of Islam within his territory. There being no formally constituted court or judge in these villages, serious charges (*manyan shari'a*) such as theft or assault, which gave rise to such punishments as mutilation, were properly referred to Zaria by the village chief.

These local communities were administered as fiefs by the state officials, who resided at the capital, Zaria, and owed their office to the king. These *hakimai* (s. *hakimi*, overlords, territorial administrators, fief-holding officials) supervised their distant fiefs through staffs of titled subordinates, some of whom were appointed *jekadu* (s. *jekada*, intermediaries) to one or more of the overlord's fiefs. On his appointment as intermediary between the lord and a fief, the *jekada* was usually but not always given a title. Such titles established the *jakada's* official position as agent for the lord. The titled subordinates of a *hakimi* were his official staff, whom he appointed, promoted or dismissed as he willed. The office to which these subordinate titles attached was therefore an administrative organ in Weber's sense and these titled *jekadu* formed the administrative staff of the office.[1] The titles of these subordinates expressed their relation to the principal office explicitly. Thus the senior subordinate of the Fagaci or the Makama would be the Madakin Fagaci or Madakin Makama.

The *jekada* dealt directly with the community chief, passing on his superior's instructions, and receiving the local tax or supplies for his lord. Since the overlord (*hakimi*) controlled appointments to the village chieftainship, his *jekada* was highly influential in the political affairs of the community. The *jekada's* duties involved keeping his lord informed about the character and conduct of the local chief and his rivals, and he was charged with collecting the

[1] Weber, *op. cit.*, pp. 303 ff.

gaisuwa (gifts of greeting) by which the community chief expressed loyalty and official clientage to his superior. In battle, the *jekada* fought alongside contingents from the village under his supervision. Of the tax, tribute, materials, and other collections for which he was responsible, the *jekada* was allowed by his lord to retain a set portion—usually one-tenth—as remuneration, but it is clear that the *jekada* also enjoyed ample scope for the over-collection of tax and supplies.

The fief-holder was responsible to the king for the maintenance of good order within his fiefs, for its observance of Muhammadan law, religion, and custom, for the collection of tax, tribute, labour, materials, and military forces as required, for the maintenance of the public buildings, town walls, mosque, market, caravan routes, etc., within the area, and for ensuring that the local chief did not exceed his authority. This last duty involved the reference of all local cases classified as *Manyan Shari'a* (crime and certain torts) to the courts of the capital. The majority of these cases would then be heard within the court of the *Alkali*, the senior judge; but the king presided over boundary disputes and such administrative issues as were referred to him in his own court. Although the *hakimi* had no officially constituted court, he frequently settled cases of *tsafi* (magic, non-Islamic cult practice), *zalunci* (tyranny, including *ultra vires* action), and matters relating to lands and farms. In practice, the most usual and effective means by which the *hakimi* controlled his community was through the dismissal of local chiefs who were not his clients. Frequent dismissal of local chiefs by fief-holders stimulated political competition within the community, but it also served to limit the opportunities of those local chiefs who were not bound to their overlords by ties of clientage to indulge in *ultra vires* actions with impunity.

Besides these rural communities with their officially recognized local chiefs, there were numerous *rumada*, some independent, while others were under the immediate jurisdiction of these community chieftainships. Before anyone could build a *rinji* or slave-settlement as an independent township, the king's permission was necessary. Before a separate slave-settlement could be built within any community, the *hakimi's* permission was necessary, as well as the village chief's. An independent *rinji* which belonged to one or other of the royal lineages was exempt from tax or tribute, under the rule of *hurumi*. Otherwise its owner would pay *gaisuwa* (tribute) to the king. If the owner of a *rinji* was not of royal status, he paid tax on his free dependants;[1] but slaves were not subject to taxation in Zaria, except for the tax levied when they changed hands in the slave-market. *Rumada* which formed separate walled settlements were administratively independent of the community chieftainships on their boundaries. Their establishment by permission of the king was itself title to the land on which they farmed. The owner and his family (*iyayen giji*, s. *ubangiji*) would co-operate with the local chief, but were not under the latter's authority. If the owner was a man of prominent lineage, his power and status often exceeded that of the community chief, and his descendants would sometimes hold nearby local chieftainships.

(c) State Revenue and its Collection

The king retained direct control of certain local communities. The throne also had certain herds of cattle which the king administered through his own staff or *jekada*. Besides these royal domains there were certain *rumada* which belonged to the throne in perpetuity, and these were independent settlements peopled mainly by royal slaves. The bulk of a ruler's personal property consisted of the slave-settlements inherited from his father, and those which he had established himself. The ruler's income from his personal property was added to his income from his royal domains and from the throne's *rumada*, without any further distinction. In addition the king received a large share of the state tax, a half-share of military booty, tribute from vassal states and certain pagan tribes, death duties of office-holders, and that portion of his predecessor's estate which was due to him as successor. Part of this huge annual income went into the maintenance of the royal household, part to the support and enrichment of the

---

[1] In Zaria this was a curious form of poll-tax, levied on the hoes used in farming. Hausa distinguish two main sorts of hoe, the hand-plough (*galma*) which is a spurred hoe, used for heavy work; and the light hoe (*fartanya*) used for weeding, reaping groundnuts and top-soil work. This hoe-tax is referred to in Zaria, alternatively as *kurdin galma* (a tax levied on each *galma*), and *kurdin fartanya*, a tax on each light hoe. Since women can manage the light hoe but not the *galma*, as tax-units these different hoes would have different references, in one case to men only, in the other to women also. However, free Hausa-Fulani women took no active part in farming at this time, although slave-women did. Since no tax was paid on slaves, this really meant that *kurdin galma* was largely the same as *kurdin fartanya*. For this reason these terms are used interchangeably. Barth discusses this peculiar Zaria tax in his journals. See Barth, *op. cit.*, vol. i, p. 309.

royal lineage, part to the king's personal clients in office and out of office, part to the Waziri and Sultan of Sokoto, and part to the maintenance of state property or military stores, such as horses for the cavalry; part went in obligatory distributions, such as alms to mallams and paupers, but much of the king's surplus income went into the formation of new slave-settlements, which once founded became his personal property, although on the king's death his successor and the Sultan would each receive a portion of his estate. The king was at once the wealthiest and most powerful man in the kingdom.

The way in which tax-collection was grafted on to the system of territorial administration simultaneously remunerated the administrative officials, and kept their numbers from increasing. The community or vassal chiefs who acted as local collectors kept a portion of the tax or tribute due from their areas and handed the rest over to the *jekada* for their lord. The *jekada* kept another portion, and the lord kept rather more. The remainder went to the king who forwarded the tribute due to Sokoto through the Waziri, the latter keeping a portion for himself. But the official hierarchy remunerated through this tax-collecting process was responsible for territorial administration, and were also important in the military and judicial systems. Thus the remuneration of officials by stated portions (*ushira*) of the tax which passed through their hands may have been economical to the state.

The incidence and form of taxation in Zaria changed several times during the last century. Apart from the establishment and expansion of the order of occupational tax-gatherers, these changes had little effect on the structure of tax-collection itself. This is one instance in which changing elements of the government, or redefinitions of previous functions, had no significance for the structure of the system itself.

The first two Fulani rulers collected a grain tithe called *zakka*, which was due to them as mallams or Koranic scholars; in addition they collected a hoe-tax of 500 cowries, and taxes from blacksmiths and dyers, the latter being levied on dye-pits. All nomad Fulani herdsmen with more than thirty cattle paid an annual tax of one in every ten cattle to the ruler through the official called Sa'i, who was charged to collect this *jangali* (cattle-tax) and to administer the nomad Fulani, confirming the appointment of their headmen (*ardo*), settling disputes, supervising their movements, etc. Neither of these first two Fulani rulers levied tolls on caravans, canoemen, or market transactions; they neither paid nor received *kurdin sarauta* (the money of taking office). By 1860 the system of taxation included annual occupational taxes, a land-tax levied on each householder amounting to 2,000 cowries per family,[1] taxes on caravans, canoemen, market-sales of slaves, *kurdin sarauta*, and death-duties levied on the estate of office-holders. It is said that local taxation was increased in response to the orders of the Sultan of Sokoto, Aliyu Babba, who reigned from 1842 to 1859. The tendency for taxation to increase continued throughout the rest of the century, and in 1892, the range and rate of occupational taxation levied in Zaria was further increased. The official tribute due. to the Sultan remained fixed throughout this period, but the Waziri's personal demands steadily increased.

(d) Legal Administration

The Fulani empire had been established by a *jihad* or Holy War for the local purification and expansion of Islam. This objective and origin committed the future governments to observe Islamic practice regarding religion, law, and war on the infidel. Religion was accordingly strengthened by the early establishment of an official Fulani priesthood, the Limamin Juma'a, whose holder held a seat on the conqueror's council and extensive fiefs. The new official, Limamin Juma'a, was also given a seat on the electoral council of Zaria. Within the rural communities, each walled town (*gari*) also had its own *limam* (*imam*, priest); and the administrative officials were directly responsible for seeing to the observance of Muhammadan religious practices.

In conformity with Islamic patterns of legal administration, the Fulani conquerors established at the capital a new court under a qualified Muhammadan legal scholar. The new judge had the title of Alkali (judge) and heard appeals from the court of the Salenke, a judicial office established under the Habe. The Alkali was the senior of these two judges. The new Alkali's court also dealt with *manyan shari'a* (issues giving rise to mutilation or capital punishment), both those referred to it by local chieftains, and those sent on to the capital by the nearer vassal states. As regards land issues,

---

[1] Barth who visited Kano in 1851–3 reports that the hoe-tax in Zaria was then levied at the rate of 500 cowries per hoe. By 1900 the average rate of hoe-tax (*kurdin galma*) in Zaria was 6000 cowries. See Barth, *op. cit.* vol. 1, p. 309. See also, Arnett, 1920, p. 16.

there appears to have been some overlap of jurisdiction. The village chiefs certainly heard land issues within their communities; and these were also sometimes decided by the *hakimai* of the fiefs. The king presided over boundary disputes, and over such conflicts of pagan· custom and Islamic law as were reported to him. He also acted as the executive arm of the legal administration, sending offenders to trial and enforcing the Alkali's sentences through his police (*dogarai*), who were slaves of the throne under a slave police chief. His executive role gave the king opportunities for pardoning offenders, or for otherwise influencing the execution of sentences. The king's mother, who held no official position but was known as the Mama or Uwar Sarki (mother of the king), was frequently asked to intercede on behalf of condemned persons. This informal intercession is said to have been often effective; it was entirely outside the framework of Muhammadan law.

In theory the king was responsible for the suppression of *zalunci*, which means the improper and oppressive exercise of political or administrative power.[1] The Fulani created a new office, called Wali, and its holder was commissioned to adjudicate on administrative issues, especially with regard to the abuse of their power by members of the royal lineages. The Wali's court was also commissioned to deal with administrative malpractice and with religious activities contrary to Islam. In addition there was the court of the Salenke, which had been established in Zaria before the Fulani conquest. The Salenke was judge of the encampment, accompanied the army on campaigns, and decided all issues which arose there. Between campaigns, the Salenke also held court in Zaria city, and may occasionally have visited rural areas. The Salenke dealt with a similar range of offences to that of the Alkali's court, but appeal lay from the court of the Salenke to that of the Alkali, and from the Alkali's court to that of the king. In his court the king relied on the advice of certain assessors who were mallams learned in the *Shari'a* and Islamic lore.

[1] Despite its permissive pragmatism, Islamic political theory lends itself to an interpretive application which is forthrightly puritanical. This argument runs somewhat as follows: 'The purpose of the state is to provide proper conditions for the good life (*ibada*) of its citizens. Maladministration militates against this good life in various ways. Therefore it is opposed to Islam and must be rooted out.' The concept of the good life basic to Islamic political thought is that enunciated in the Koran, the Traditions, the Law and the Commentaries. Naturally this concept is somewhat ambiguous, even at Law; and consequently reformism is inherent in Muhammadan politics. The Fulani *jihad* was itself one such reformist movement. See Von Grunebaum, 1955, pp. 127–40.

(e) The Military Organization

To the Muhammadan Fulani, war was politically and economically advantageous and also a religious obligation. The *jihad* was annually renewed in dry-season raids and campaigns designed to extend the Fulani dominions or to intensify the subjugation of non-Muhammadan populations already within them. Slavery was the usual fate of captives, and the collection of captives was a major object of these military adventures. For the fifty years following their conquest of Zaria, the Fulani were engaged in somewhat indiscriminate offensive war. Towards the end of the century they were thrown on the defensive; but the Fulani military organization and strategy which had been developed mainly for aggression was ill suited for defence. The Fulani army was mobilized as the king required from his subjects through the agency of his fief-holders and their subordinates. Thus, when urgently required for defensive purposes, the army was often non-existent. On the other hand, for a raid or an attack, this mode of recruitment had obvious advantages. By this organization the burdens or benefits of campaigns were distributed more widely and variably than may otherwise have been possible. It also relieved the state of the economic burden which a standing army involved. The king provided equipment for his own bodyguard, and for certain units of the army. The Madaki provided horses for selected cavalrymen, and through the organization of craftsmen such as blacksmiths, the king and his officials saw to the preparation of military stores and supplies.

The army being organized for offensive war, its typical formation was an attacking one, even on the march. Pathfinders under a nomad Fulani leader with the title of Kato preceded the army; they were followed by scouts (*gonau*) under officers, such as the Sata (theft), or the Baraya (robber). A little behind with the main force of heavy cavalry (*barade*, s. *barde*) came the Madaki, slightly ahead of the infantry and the bowmen. As the century wore on, musketeers (*'yan bindiga*) were attached to this division and its flanks were protected by light cavalry (*'yan Kworbai*). Some distance behind came the king, with a smaller force of cavalry (*lifidi*), clad in leather helmets, chain-mail, and quilted cotton armour, and a reserve of heavy infantry. The king's entourage included various officials who acted as liaison with the Madaki's detachments. Bringing up the rear was the Wombai with a reserve of horses, and the Rubu with medical supplies and a complement of barber-doctors to take care of the wounded. Camp-builders and administrators were usually stationed with this rearguard. The main force under the Madaki bore the brunt of the fighting, and was the most specialized division of the army. It included detachments of musketeers, bowmen, archers who fired incendiaries into the thatch-roofs of the village under attack, and heavy infantry under their captain, the Sarkin Karma. Military equipment included javelins, small round shields (*kunkeli*), spears, swords, daggers, poisoned arrows, incendiaries (*sango*), muskets, and a variety of defensive armour.

The general pattern for the disposition of officials on campaigns were as follows:

(*a*) Pathfinders under Kato.

(*b*) Scouts under the Sata and the Baraya.

(*c*) Forward Force. Barde and cavalry. Sarkin Karma and infantry (*dakaru*). Sarkin Baka and bowmen. Sarkin Bindiga and musketeers. Kwaramaza and light horsemen ('*yan Kwarbai*).[1]

(*d*) Main force. Madaki with Karfe,[2] Wali, Fagaci, Iyan Kurama, Makama the lesser, Turaki the lesser, Dangaladima, Iya, Magayaki, Sarkin Fatika the vassal chief, Madakin Galadima and his warriors, Madakin Makama Babba and his warriors, Madakin Turaki Babba and his warriors, Madakin Sarkin Yaki and his warriors.

(*e*) The king with Sarkin Yaki, Makama Babba,[3] Galadima, Katuka, Jisambo, Salenke. Also Sarkin Garkuwa, Barwa, Hauni, Wagu, Sarkin Dakaru, Sarkin Zana, Bajimin Gabas, heavy cavalry (*lifidi*) and some light cavalry under the Kuyambana.

(*f*) Rearguard; Wombai with Sarkin Kauru, Sarkin Kajuru, reserve of horses, Rubu and medical staff, followed by Sarkin Fada in charge of rearguard warriors.

Certain territorial officials, such as the Wan'ya, the Mardanni, and the Magajin Gari, did not take part in campaigns. Neither did the Alkali, nor the two Limams of Juma'a and Kona, nor such slave-officials as the Madauci who was responsible for organizing

---

[1] Kwaramaza, sometimes said to be captain of *lifidi* (heavy armoured cavalry), sometimes said to be captain of the '*yan Kwarbai*. Subordinate to Kuyambana.

[2] Karfe, the Madaki's chief lieutenant and administrative assistant, was usually the Madaki's eldest son. This office also bore the title Kaura, and was really the Madaki's Madaki.

[3] Makama Babba (the big weapon) was the senior military office of state under the Madaki, and was the latter's second in command in battle. Hence his position with the king's forces as liaison.

and forwarding necessary supplies. Unfortunately I failed to ascertain the exact battle positions of the Dallatu, the Magajin Zakara, and the Danmadami. The king was responsible for providing military equipment for the followers of the Barde, Kuyambana, Sarkin Yaki, Sarkin Garkuwa, Sarkin Karma, Rubu, and Magayaki. The Sarkin Yaki (chief of battle) acted as captain of the forces actually grouped about the king; in between campaigns he acted as the chief of the king's bodyguard. Of the king's entourage, the Galadima, Makama Babba, and Turaki Babba had none of their own troops with them, while the Sarkin Zana (chief of the harem) was the king's personal attendant, and until the last decade of the century this office was held by eunuchs.

The king's war-council was composed of the Madaki, Galadima, Wombai, Dallatu, and Magajin Gari. The latter remained at the capital and acted as the king's deputy in charge of the government, during the king's absence on campaigns. I do not know whether the Dallatu always accompanied the king to battle, but some holders of the Dallatu title died in action during the last century.

Detachments mobilized by fief-holders were usually separated from their *hakimai* and fought as units under the captaincy of the fief-holder's chief lieutenant, who was his Madaki. Most fief-holders remained with the Madaki and relayed the Madaki's orders to their several detachments by messengers. In the crude arrowhead formation which was usual, the commanders were stationed behind the centre on the march, and directed battle from a rise in the ground.

The military organization and dispositions just described were intended to secure the most efficient use of the troops. To this end, not only were formerly civil offices invested with military duties, but the traditional Habe division of military command between the king and his Madaki were supplanted by new functional groupings, which were themselves subject to change according to the situation. For this reason the actual dispositions of officials and troops may often have deviated from the model just described. Similarly, the command exercised by Madaki over other fief-holders and officials on campaigns lapsed during peacetime, although Madaki's precedence remained.

Division of the booty and slaves captured during the campaign took place on the battlefield and was regulated by conventions. The Makama Babba, as representative of the Madaki, and the

Sarkin Yaki as representative of the king, divided the spoils between them, with the Fagaci presiding to ensure fair play. The king was given half of the captives and the Madaki took the remainder. The Madaki rewarded the officials and troops who fought directly under his command from his half-share while the king rewarded his entourage from his portion. In 1862 Audusallami, the baSuleibe king, attempted to postpone this division of booty until the army had returned to Zaria, planning to reward the infantry and the cavalry differently. This innovation was suggested by Sokoto, but Audusallami died before he was able to give it effect.

Hakimai had no power to levy troops or make war independently. Occasionally kings would place an army under the command of close relatives, who held office, for a specific campaign. Thus S.Z. Yero[1] authorized his full brother, Makama Ja'afaru, to attack the Kadara of Shara. The leader of such an expedition would receive a portion of the *humushi* (one-fifth of the booty), from the king. Fief-holders eagerly sought authority to lead expeditions because of the larger rewards which it gave them. The Madaki was the only official regularly despatched by the king with armies under his sole command. Military leadership was the distinctive feature of the Madaki's role.

Although almost all territorial officials had military roles, some officers were specially entrusted with military functions. These officials included the captain of the bodyguard, captains of cavalry, infantry, and the like. The cavalry were mainly freemen, but infantry and bowmen included native-born slaves. In the latter years of the nineteenth century, slave-generals with large forces were stationed in the centre of southern Zaria to protect the local caravan routes and control the nearby pagans. This disposition weakened the kingdom's northern defences and represented the development of a standing army.

When tribute or tax was overdue, the king could collect it by force; sometimes he went in person, or he might send the Madaki. Muhammadan Hausa-Fulani fiefdoms never invited such treatment. The collections of overdue payments from pagan tribes normally involved the burning of a few towns and the enslavement or execution of considerable numbers of people. The Jaba tribe, defeated by Mamman Sani in the 1840s, were loath to pay tribute

[1] S.Z.—Sarkin Zazzau, the king of (Fulani) Zazzau or Zaria.

in slaves, and suffered heavily, although preserving their independence. The slave-general stationed at Kacia *c.* 1885 was charged with the collection of annual tribute from the Kaje, Kamantan, Ikulu, and neighbouring tribes, if necessary by force.

The extensive participation of Habe and Fulani in slave-raiding and war was achieved by mobilizing contingents from the fiefs; and military action offered such troops rewards in the form of booty, appointments, and promotion. The frequency and success of these military adventures may have persuaded many people to support the system of government. Since political and administrative office provided the principal means of enrichment and social mobility together, and had clear military commitments, the recruitment of officials for these expeditions presented no problem.

(*f*) *Instability and Force*

The territorial organization with which these legal, fiscal, and military systems were integrated can be summarized as a systematic dispersal of fiefs allocated to any single office, which deprived fiefs of military importance and reduced the opportunities for independent military adventures by individual fief-holders or groups. Further, the number, size, and distribution of the fiefs allocated to different offices expressed differences in the seniority of these offices and in the social status of persons eligible for these differing offices. Persons appointed to fief-holding office would normally have received some training in this political and administrative organization as subordinates or clients of senior officials. Dynastic personnel who were acquainted from youth with political competition and administration had less need for such training than others, and were occasionally given office at an early age.

The real difficulty which faced the Fulani system of government was that its system of political competition would stimulate rebellions or other attempts to appropriate the throne by force. The first Fulani ruler, Mallam Musa, had to suppress an attempted palace revolt led by another Fulani, Mallam Bagozeki. Musa thereafter remained in the capital and sent out his Madaki on campaigns. The second ruler, Yamusa, was openly threatened with war by a candidate for the position of Madaki. In 1860 the second Mallawa king, Sidi Abdulkadiri, was deposed after his half-brother, Muhammadu Baki, had marched on Zaria with a force of cavalry. In 1863 the only baSuleibe king of Zaria was assassinated at Ridi on his

THE KING

Royal Officials	Vassals	Client Offices	Order of Mallams	The Order of Occupational Offices	Slave Officials
(a) Yan Sarki*	(a) Supervised by Madaki	(a) Freely appointive	LIMAMIN JUMA'A*	S. PAWA (Butchers)	(a) Without Fiefs
MADAKI	FATIKA	GALADIMA*	LIMAMIN KONA*	S. MAKERA (Blacksmiths)	(i) Eunuchs
WOMBAI	KEFFI	SARKIN FADA		S. MAKERAN FARI (Silversmiths)	SARKIN ZANA
DAN GALADIMA	JEMA'A	FAGACI		S. RINI (Dyers)	KASHEKA
IYA	KWOTTO	(WAZIRI)		S. DUKAWA (Leather workers)	KILISHI
MAGAJIN GARI		MAKAMA BABBA	ALKALI*	S. SAKA (Weavers)	
MAKAMA KARAMI	(b) Supervised by Makama Karami	TURAKI BABBA	SALENKE	S. DILLALAI (Brokers)	(ii) Military
	KAURU	KUYAMBANA	MAGATAKARDA		BAKON BARNO
(b) Jikokin Sarki**	KAJURU	BARDE	S. MALLAMAI	S. AWO (Grain sellers)	GARKUWA II
DALLATU		SARKIN MAI			WAGU
WALI	(c) Supervised by the King	MA'AJI BABBA	Free Household Officials	S. TUKUNYA (Pot makers)	KWARAMAZA
MARDANNI	KAGARKO	MA'AJI KARAMI	MAJIDADI		S. LIFIDI
SA'I	DOMA	HAUNI		S. MAKADA (Drummers)	S. KARMA
SARKIN RUWA	DURUM (till 1860)		S. YAKI	S. MAGINA (Builders)	S. BAKA
TURAKI KARAMI	LERE	(b) Quasi-hereditary***	S. GARKUWA	S. BUGU (Dye beaters)	S. BINDIGA
		DAN MADAMI	S. FIGINI	MAGAJIYA O (Prostitutes)	BAJIMIN GABAS
* Sons of kings, eligible for promotion to the throne.		IYAN KURAMA	MAHARI	MAGAJIN KASUWA (Markets)	S. DUKARU
** Grandsons of kings, not eligible for promotion to the throne.		RUBU	BARWA	SANKIRA (Eulogists)	
		KATUKA	MAGAYAKI		(iii) Civil Services
		MAGAJIN ZAKARA	JAGABA		S. NOMA
		WANYA			S. TAMBARI
		MAGAJI			S. ZAGI
		JISAMBO			SHAMAKI
		CIKUM			MADAUCI
		*** See Chapter 4, section 5(c).			(iv) Police
					DOGARAI
					YAN DOKA
					(b) With Fiefs
					S. YAMMA
					S. YARRA
					S. CIYAWA
					SHENTALI
					S. DOGARAI

ZARIA STATE ORGANIZATION IN THE LATE NINETEENTH CENTURY

* = electors
S = Sarki = Chief (of)
o = female

return from a campaign against Kugwaru and Munku. In 1873 Audusallami's successor, Abdullahi of the Bornu dynasty, was deposed by Sokoto for attempting to collect tribute from the vassal state of Keffi by force, and for refusing to halt his attacks despite instructions by Sokoto. When Abdullahi was reinstated by Sokoto in 1876, the acting Madaki and a former Galadima of Zaria joined together in rebellion, and the Sultan had to ask the king of Kano to arrange a compromise. In the 1880s another Galadima, a Habe called Suleimanu, with the assistance of Ningi invaders sought to seize the throne by force. In 1897 the Madaki Kwassau did seize the throne by force, and compelled the Wazirin Sokoto, who was then visiting Zaria, to appoint and install him as king. In the preceding reign when Yero, Kwassau's father, was ruling, the king's slave-musketeers (*'yan bindiga*) terrorized the population with the king's compliance and protection, removing or destroying the property of rivals and others without redress. Not until the ruler possessed guns was he able to overawe the population in this fashion; but after the Royal Niger Company established its trading station on the Niger, the king of Zaria monopolized the available supplies of these weapons and thus acquired an overriding force. This abruptly altered the balance of power within Zaria, and enabled the Madaki Kwassau who retained control of these rifle-squads after his father's death to overawe the Wazirin Sokoto and seize the throne.

This summary of the outbreaks of violence in Zaria during the nineteenth century indicates the intensity of political competition within the state. Relations between Zaria on the one hand and its vassal states and its suzerain, the Sultan of Sokoto, on the other, were also in continuous development. There was an inherent instability in these hierarchical relationships, since they were defined in terms of authority, but really reflected distributions of power. Flanked by Sokoto, Kano, Bauchi, and Katsina, the largest states of the Fulani empire, Zaria was less able to resist the Sultan than the smaller but more distant territories such as Hadejia or Jema'are on the frontiers of Bornu. Keffi, Kwotto, and Doma lay so far to the south of Zaria that they were able to pursue fairly independent courses of action despite the wishes of their suzerain. Thus, despite their administrative form, relations between vassal and suzerain were often political; these relations corresponded to distributions of power as well as authority, and were therefore variable in time as well as space. They accordingly involved cleavages, compromises, and other characteristic processes of political competition, together with the simple command and obedience which expressed authority. In the external context of the nineteenth-century Fulani state of Zaria, these external relationships of vassalage and suzerainty loomed large, and they will be analysed in due course; but in discussing the system of political administration within Zaria itself, they must be treated as given facts.

In the preceding pages we have discussed the functions of government in Fulani Zazzau and the organization of activities by which these functions were discharged. The brief history of violence and appeals to force which characterized this government illustrates its instability, and thereby indicates the incompleteness of accounts which deal purely with these administrative arrangements and activities. A satisfactory description of the overt or manifest functions of government, and a catalogue of governmental methods and activities designed to fulfil these functions, need scarcely mention the system of political activity through which governmental office and power are distributed, directed, and controlled. Our description of the administrative system of Fulani Zazzau therefore illustrates the distinction already made between the administrative and political aspects of government. In describing the administrative organization of Fulani Zazzau I have simply discussed those activities by which the manifest functions of government were discharged. In the following section I shall attempt to describe the political system to which this administrative organization was linked.

4. THE POLITICAL SYSTEM

(a) The Elements of Dynastic Organization

The basic units of the system of political competition were the four dynasties. Of these the Suleibawa were the last to acquire the throne (1860), and they were also the weakest. The three powerful dynasties were the Mallawa, Bornawa, and Katsinawa; and of these, the first two were the more important. Membership in these dynasties were based on patrilineal descent, but non-equivalence of siblings seems to have been the rule within them, and all were marked by extreme internal differentiation.

In part this differentiation of siblings was based on differences of maternal descent and kinship, and this was formalized by inheritance. The children of two brothers were further differentiated according to the rank and wealth of their fathers. Between less closely related lineage kin, governmental rank also provided ground for further differentiation, and the different relations of marriage or clientage established by these individuals within the lineage or outside it, further increased their political individuation. Through this combination of clientage, marriage, paternal and individual rank, and differences of matri-kinship, the dynasties, like other Fulani lineages of noble status, were highly complex units.

Although these units were corporate and solidary in their competition with one another, by its internal organization, a dynasty encouraged its members to pursue individualistic political careers, and through these careers its component lines were progressively differentiated in terms of size and wealth as well as uterine and agnatic kinship and differences of past and present rank. In these conditions, dynasties and noble lineages lacked continuous unitary leadership and rigid rules for succession to leadership, other than those provided by the distribution of political rank and prospects within the system of competition with other units of similar status and structure. Thus within dynasties and other politically significant unilineal groups, leadership reflected the present seniority and promotional prospects of male members. For example, if three members of a certain dynasty held office, but one of these offices was clearly pre-eminent and entailed greater likelihood of promotion to the throne, the dynasty would normally recognize its incumbent as their main leader, and would support him as their candidate for the kingship, expecting that he would then appoint other of his lineage kin to territorial office, if successful. Office-holders normally appointed their closer kin, such as sons or full brothers, to positions under their control; but such appointments themselves furthered the processes of differentiation within their lineage, and thus the differences of status, numbers and wealth between the component descent-lines tended to increase with each generation.

By 1865 the system of political competition in Fulani Zaria centred on the relations within and between the four dynasties, and included other Fulani lineages of noble rank. A great many families and persons of varied status, free Fulani and Habe, native-born slaves and captives, were linked to one or other of these political principals directly or otherwise by ties of clientage, marriage, kinship, ownership, or the like. Participation within the political system was expressed by direct or indirect relationships of solidarity with one of its principals and opposition to their rivals. Leadership implied subordination, and only dynastic males could become independent competitors.

(b) The Nature and Implications of Dynastic Competition

The principal object of dynastic competition was the kingship. This position gave a temporary control over the subordinate offices of state, and these offices were normally distributed among the kinsmen, clients, and slaves of the king. By thus rewarding his supporters the king simultaneously discharged his obligations of patronage and kinship and increased his followers. Moreover, to administer the state the king needed loyal subordinates, and he could not exercise the necessary control if its senior offices were held by his rivals or their supporters.

Thus competition for the kingship between the various dynasties converted administrative office into a political instrument as well as a political prize. Briefly, the rule was for a new king to dismiss his predecessor's kin and supporters from important office, and to appoint people of his own. His successor repeated the process. Thus office circulated rapidly among an expanding population of competitors and this circulation of official positions carried with it increased prospects of appointment for the numerous competing candidates. It thereby stimulated the development of clientage by the hopes of political reward, and it also enjoined persons of noble status to participate in this system of political competition as the sole alternative to political impotence and loss of status.

The accession of a new king was never followed by a total turnover of offices. Various factors limited the number of replacements a king was actually able to make. In theory he was free to dismiss and appoint whom he liked. This theoretically unrestricted royal control of administrative appointments had no formal ideological basis apart from the Islamic dread of schism and the concept of *imama* (leadership). However, the interpretation of these appointments which actually obtains in Zaria pays no heed to

Islamic ideas. We can illustrate the local interpretation by the following comments:

(a) 'Between us (the Mallawa and the Bornawa dynasties) there is no hatred, but rivalry.'

(b) 'Why did Sarkin Zazzau Sambo (1881–90) dismiss the Turaki Karami Dan Manga from office?'

'*Ap*! aren't they enemies? When you become king, you appoint your own people, dismiss your opponents, appoint your supporters.'

'Yes, but what was his offence?'

'*Ap*! Is there any need for offence? When you become king, offence is not necessary. You simply dismiss your opponents, and appoint your supporters. That is why there are so many titles.'[1]

The first statement expresses the desire of rivals for continuity of the system and indicates the basis of this desire. The speaker, a baMalle prince, distinguishes hatred from rivalry. Hatred seeks the elimination of its object; rivalry is competition within a framework, the persistence of which is itself prerequisite for continuity of the competition. Hatred, expressed as the attempt to eliminate dynastic rivals, would have entailed civil war in which all parties would suffer and could lose their rights to the throne.

The Turaki Dan Manga, who is mentioned in the second quotation, was a member of the Bornawa dynasty, and as such was a rival of Sambo, a Katsinawa king. Sambo therefore dismissed the Turaki from office as unreliable, and appointed his own kin instead. Such dismissals served two functions: they freed the king of untrustworthy and politically hostile officials, and they freed offices for allocation to one or other of the king's supporters. In this system of multi-dynastic competition, these dualisms made it politically imperative that the king should control appointments. Without this control of administrative appointments, the king could not ensure that his officials would be loyal to him, and thus he could not govern effectively. In this way multi-dynastic competition for the throne compelled the king to seek complete control of appointments to office. Since the principal offices of state were distributed among nobles on a political basis, and not by an impartial body such as a civil service commission, this was unavoidable. In other words, since the political and administrative systems

---

[1] *Ap*, a Hausa exclamation expressing astonished surprise.

were integrated through the hierarchy of offices, and since the constitutive units of this political system were dynastic groups, an autocratic administrative structure was inevitable. To paraphrase my informant, 'administrative offence is not necessary for dismissal'. Neither was administrative offence a sufficient ground for dismissal, nor administrative merit a sufficient ground for appointment. Political offence, defined by the system as attachment to the king's political rival, was the principal ground for dismissal; and political solidarity with the king and opposition to his rivals was the principal ground for appointment.

Under such a system, maladministration was defined as disloyal or ineffective administration and there was little hope that a rigorous supervision of strictly administrative activities would develop. To retain office its holder had two major commitments: the first was loyalty to the king, and this allegiance was demonstrated by gifts and obedience; secondly, the official had to execute the king's instructions effectively and promptly, to collect the required tax, tribute, supplies, or military detachments, and to discharge the various routine tasks already described. Throughout this system the great administrative sin was the sin of omission, the failure to execute promptly the order of one's immediate superior. Unless political disaffection was thereby expressed, actions beyond the strict authority of an individual's office were quite irrelevant; and in any event, sins of commission were difficult to define, since the office-holder derived his appointment from the king, and since the official derived his power from political solidarity with his superior. Thus administrative office was political in its allocation and exercise, its basis, and its orientation. In this situation the strict tasks of administration were loosely supervised by the king, but the political loyalties of officials were decisive for their retention of administrative office; thus administrative offence was neither a sufficient nor necessary reason for dismissal, just as administrative excellence was not a sufficient reason for appointment to office.

In consequence, courts established to control maladministration (zalunci), and especially maladministration by senior officials of royal status, failed to discharge the function for which they were formed. Nor could it be otherwise, since dismissal from and appointments to administrative office were governed alike by political considerations, and since administrative office had impor-

tant political aspects and functions. Where 'offence is not necessary' for dismissal from office, law can neither apply nor develop;
when political solidarities are protection against dismissal and
political opposition is inexcusable, law becomes void. This is a
characteristic condition of absolutist régimes. In Zaria, although
courts were established by the government specifically to decide
administrative issues, they were prevented from fulfilling their
formal functions by the structure of the governmental system itself.

(c) The Political Varieties of Office

The Fulani state was a monocracy in which the king exercised
absolute powers of rule, i.e. authority through his control of
appointments to the offices of state. Despite important qualifications, this description is broadly valid. The administration was
centralized, and the king's authority was formally supreme within
the administrative hierarchy, although by virtue of his political
context and political relations with his officials, the king could not
effectively suppress maladministration. His freedom of action was
limited, on the one hand, by the law, on the other by the structure
and context of the government. As leader of the Faithful, the king
was required to uphold and enforce Muhammadan law (shari'a);
he could not legitimately act against it, although he could refrain
from enforcing it. His political context also qualified the absolute
authority vested in the king, principally because the security of his
throne, his lineage, and his family were all conditional on his observance of the constitutional conventions which governed political
competition. Kingship therefore conferred a temporary absolutism,
under the supervision of Sokoto, within the context of competition
for the succession. The king's power and authority were thus at
best time-limited. However, whereas his authority was absolute
within its demarcated spheres, his power was conditional; and the
king's power was neither absolute nor unrestricted; the conventions
which protected his political rivals and appointed officials against
his power were essential conditions of the structural context in which
he ruled. Thus, even within this monocratic administration, the
king's power was conditional rather than absolute. The dispersal
of power among the administrative staff corresponded to the
ruler's essential dependence on them for loyalty and support, and
this conditional power of the king's appointees was expressed by
their impunity as administrators. To rule effectively, the king

needed loyal subordinates in office. The fruits of office ensured
that these positions were sought after by many, but the candidates
for office sought office as much for its fruits as for itself, and the
king perforce had to allow them to enjoy those fruits of office
which were politically neutral. In this way the king had to condone
certain improper uses of office, and although rulers occasionally
dismissed their own appointees from office, in general they strove
to avoid this.

Administrative positions varied widely in their significance. The
order of mallams' offices included the judiciary and were peripheral to the system of political control; consequently the holders
of these offices enjoyed a high degree of security in their tenure.
Of the religious and legal offices, the Habe title of Limamin Kona
continued to be inherited within a Habe lineage; the office of
Limamin Juma'a was usually given to members of the Katsinawa
'yan Doto Fulani; and the judicial position of Salenke was often
held by one descent-line of the Fulanin Shanono, a family learned
in Islamic lore.

There were also certain territorial offices, the competition for
which was restricted to particular lineages. Such quasi-hereditary
titles were responsible for the administration of fiefs which were
situated at some distance from the capital and contained non-
Muhammadan populations. Thus different areas inhabited by the
Gwari tribe were administered by the fief-holding titles of Chikum,
Magaji Jisambo, and Wan'ya. The lineage of Yegwamawa Fulani
held the title of Chikum, the Fulanin Wunti held the title of
Jisambo, and the Fulanin Gadidi held the title of Wan'ya. Other
territorial titles which normally drew their holders from a restricted number of lineages during the last century include the
offices of Iyan Kurama, Rubu, Magajin Zakara, Katuka, and
Dan Madami. In all cases the fiefs administered by these offices
were tribal territories lying at a considerable distance from the
capital. To control these tribes a well-informed local administration was necessary, and this presumed an unusual stability in the
tenure of office. Accordingly such distant tribal areas were administered through offices tied to particular lineages. Of these
officials, Chikum and Magaji Jisambo were permanently stationed
in their fiefs; the remainder resided at Zaria, visiting their fiefs
once annually to collect the tax, and otherwise at such times as the
local administration required.

The association of particular titles with particular lineages gives the appearance of hereditary succession, but lacks the reality. The king could and often did appoint people whose family had no previous connections with these titles. However, where an effective administration required continuity of knowledge and contact, successive appointments would be made from the same lineage and accordingly such titles tended to be allocated among particular family lines. The Yesquamawa Fulani of Kagarko present a somewhat different case. They first established a small chieftainship at Kagarko in the extreme south of Zaria, and then recognized the suzerainty of Zazzau. However, they were not given *tambari* or other insignia of full vassalship. This case can be regarded with equal validity as illustrating trends towards centralization or decentralization alike.

Continuous allocation of particular titles to particular lineages had another important implication. Lineages holding these titles regularly were virtually excluded from other titles of state. Thus all other offices were closed to lineages having quasi-hereditary claims to particular titles. This condition parallels the separation of vassal and suzerain states expressed in the rule against dual participation in them. Continuous recruitment of these officials on a lineage basis and their high security of official tenure also parallels conditions of vassalship; the holders of these quasi-hereditary positions were regarded as clients of the throne rather than as personal clients of the king. On the other hand, these quasi-hereditary titles differed from vassalship since the king could ignore lineage affiliations in filling them. Moreover, although members of lineages with special interests in these titles could not compete for other offices in Zazzau, there was nothing to stop the candidates for office in Zaria from seeking appointment to these special titles. In the present century when the number of territorial titles was being reduced, several of these peripheral offices were allowed to lapse, while those which persisted were filled thereafter on the same conditions as other offices; but these recent changes have neither abolished vassal chieftainships, nor converted them into freely appointive office.

(d) The Royal Succession

Office-holders of royal status were distinguished from others; there were also degrees of royalty. Differences of royal status developed together with the rules which defined the conditions of eligibility for the throne. The conditions governing eligibility were not explicitly formulated at any single instant. They developed historically within the context of the royal succession as this was administered by Sokoto. The history of this development will be related later, but by 1865 the main conditions governing the succession were clear. Succession to the throne was governed by a system of rules which can be summarized as follows:

(*a*) Successive kings should not be chosen from the same 'dynasty'.[1]

(*b*) Only the sons of kings were eligible for promotion to the throne.

(*c*) Only those princes who had held or were holding territorial office were eligible for promotion.

These principles have been abstracted from the details of the succession to kingship in Zaria, and summarize the norms current in Fulani Zaria. Although they may never have existed as a coherent system of formulae, their validity and importance cannot be doubted. Such a system of rules developed slowly in contexts of political competition among the Fulani of Zaria, and between these Fulani and the rulers of Sokoto. Sokoto's appropriation of rights to appoint and dethrone the kings of Zazzau was itself gradual and strongly contested; but once effective, this control was not easily repudiated. Moreover, the type of multidynastic political competition which emerged among the Fulani of Zaria made Sokoto's supervision welcome to competitors and non-competitors alike, since this overlordship was an assurance against both civil war and unilineal absolutism.

The rule that successive kings should not be drawn from the same dynasty set a time limit of one reign on the monopoly of office by any one dynasty.[2] This ensured that the kingship rotated

---

[1] In 1846 Hamada, the Bornawa candidate for the throne, died after a reign of 52 days. He was succeeded by his half-brother, Mommon Sani, who ruled until 1860. This was the only case in which Sokoto freely consented to appoint two consecutive rulers from the same dynasty. On Hamada's death the electoral council of Zaria recommended Mommon Sani's succession. In this way the Fulani of Sokoto and Zaria indicated their awareness of the distinctions between an accession and a reign, and between kingship as an individual and a lineage role. In their view, Hamada's untimely death justified his brother's succession, since it was still the Bornawa's turn to rule, and thus to 'inherit' the kingship from Hamada. The parallel with the levirate which Muslim Fulani abhor is obvious.

[2] See preceding footnote for the meaning attached to the concept of a 'reign'.

among the dynasties with sufficient regularity to maintain them as viable units in a competition further defined by rules limiting candidacy for the throne to those sons of kings who had themselves held territorial office.

This rotation of kingship prevented rulers from indirectly selecting their successors by the gradual transfer of governing power and functions to a selected heir appointed as their deputy (*mukkadas*). Although it was usual in Fulani Zaria for kings to single out one of their sons for special distinction and leadership, this neither involved a transfer of governing power, nor the perpetuation of a unilineal monocracy.[1]

The rule by which sons of former kings must have held territorial office in order to succeed to the throne imposed severe restrictions on the number of persons eligible for the succession, and intensified the differentiation of descent-lines within the dynasties by giving an hereditary significance to the difference in the ranks of their members. In consequence, lineage males whose fathers were kings were thereby distinguished sharply from those whose fathers had not ruled Zaria, although their grandfathers or great-grandfathers had done so. Royalty was thus a general category of status, within which there was a wide range of status conditions having differing implications. Sons of kings were political royals in the sense that they could qualify for the succession through tenure of a fief-holding title. Their ortho-cousins who were not descended from past rulers but from former officials were thus not eligible for kingship, and precisely because of this and because of lineage ties they were valuable allies in the competition for kingship, and were also therefore effective competitors for subordinate offices. In contrast, members of dynasties whose fathers and grandfathers had not held territorial office were royals only in name. Such persons had no chance of enjoying or appropriating the power to rule which was the substance and expression of royalty. Every generation further increased this internal differentiation of the dynasties by rank; the process was progressive and could neither be halted nor reversed, although the

---

[1] Kwassau's seizure of the throne on the death of his father S.Z. Yero in 1897 is no exception to this rule, although Kwassau was his father's Madaki, and controlled the squads of slaves and rifle men ('*yan bindiga*) which Yero had established. Kwassau's *coup* owed even more to certain exceptional circumstances which unified the Fulani of Zaria behind him against Sokoto than to the forces at his command. These developments are discussed in later chapters.

practice of intra-lineage marriages allowed those descent-lines which could compete for the throne to attach to themselves the ineligible segments of the dynasty, and thus at the same time to integrate the dynasty in support of their claims, and to divide it further by intra-dynastic competition for support.

(e) Categories of Royal Officials

The rule that only those sons of the king who had held office were eligible for the royal succession stimulated and sanctioned the king's allocation of office to his children. By appointing his sons to office the king provided his dynasty with eligible candidates for future successions. Kings tried to distribute office among the sons of their various wives equitably. Offices were thus distributed among the king's issue by 'huts' (*dakuna*). The rule was for at least one son of each wife to be appointed to office. But the king had other kinsmen with claims on office. Of these, his full brothers received preferential treatment, but *jikoki* (grandchildren of former rulers who were members of the dynasty) were also appointed. The king was also expected to appoint some kinsfolk related to him by cognatic kingship, for instance, a mother's brother, a sister's son, or more rarely a daughter's son. The last category of his relatives to be appointed by the king were his *surukai* or affinal kinsmen. This group consisted mainly of the husbands of the king's daughters or sisters, and the brothers or fathers of the king's wives. These royal affines and cognatic kin were eligible for appointment to some of the offices to which the king's agnatic kin were not usually appointed.

Offices filled by the king's agnatic kin were classifiable according to the status of their holders. Thus there were *sarautun 'yan Sarki* (titles held by the sons of kings), whose holders became eligible for the throne by virtue of these appointments. There were also offices allocated to *jikokin Sarki* (s. *jikan sarki*, patrilineal grandchildren of kings) who were not themselves eligible for promotion to the throne. Offices allotted to *surukai* (affines) or *dangi wajen mace* (kinsfolk connected through women) formed a small group of more variable composition.

By appointing some of their agnatic kinsmen who were not eligible for promotion to the throne, kings sought to preserve the lineage constitution and solidarity of their competing dynasties. Allocation of offices among those dynastic descent-lines which were ineligible for the royal succession preserved the dynasties as units in this political competition by integrating their differentiated segments, and by reducing their differentiation of interest conditionally. But for such distributions of office the kingship would belong to individuals rather than lineages, and the king would be correspondingly isolated; under such hypothetical conditions, allocations of office to the king's sons would isolate them from lineage kin completely. The lineage principle would thus disappear in dynastic relations; and the conventions by which competition for the throne was controlled would lose their force, with corresponding increases of political instability. All these possibilities were prevented by the appointments of *jikokin Sarki* to office. By these appointments several important segments of the dynasty were linked directly to the throne and interests in the kingship were spread to various branches of each dynasty. Thus appointments of *jikokin Sarki* perpetuated the dynastic political system as a competition between royal lineages of corporate character.

Appointments of *jikokin Sarki* to office served to keep those segments of royal lineages whose members were not themselves eligible for the throne actively interested in the competition for kingship. Such appointments increased the number of the king's agnatic kin who held office, and brought the distinctions between *'yan Sarki* (s. *dan sarki*, son of a king), who were eligible by birth for the throne, and *jikokin Sarki* (grandchildren of kings) who were not, into the official system as a basis for the differentiation of offices reserved for the dynasties. In practice, offices normally filled by *jikokin Sarki* were often allotted to their sons by kings, or to other categories of kin, and even occasionally to non-relatives. Similarly offices traditionally reserved for the sons of kings were sometimes allotted to *jikokin Sarki*, or to *dangi wajen mace* (cognatic kinsmen); and in practice there was less uniformity in the distributions of royal ranks among the king's kinsmen than the ideology of allocation would imply. None the less, the history of official appointments shows certain regularities. Such positions as Madaki, Wombai, Dan Galadima, Iya, Makama Karami, Magajin Gari, and Dallatu were normally held by sons of kings, normally appointed by their fathers. The last five of these titles were also occasionally allotted to *jikoki*. The offices of Wali, Turaki Karami, Mardanni, Fagaci, and Dallatu were most frequently allotted to *jikokin Sarki* or to cognatic kin of the ruler. Two early kings,

Yamusa and Abdulkerim, the founders of the Bornawa and Katsinawa dynasties, also appointed their classificatory brothers to office, but such appointments were inconsistent with the developing definition of dynasties as agnatic groups descended from kings, and were consequently abandoned.

The historical distribution of titles among direct descendants of kings, their grandchildren, agnatic or cognatic, and their affinal and other kin does not fall into simple and regular patterns, partly because it was only one of a series of interconnected developments within which the ideology of official appointments was defined. Indeed the progressive definition of succession rules and conditions, to which this distribution of offices among the ruler's different categories of kin was related, was not completed before 1860. Inevitably also kings had more numerous progeny than their brothers, and the progressive increase in the offices allocated to the sons of kings disturbed allocations to other status-groups. Occasionally, even such offices as Galadima or Makama Babba, which were reserved for non-relatives of the king, were given to his kinsmen. The principles which governed the allocation of office among different status-groups developed within contexts of political competition and correlative administrative re-organization, which were themselves linked directly with the history of successive appointments to the throne. In the course of these developments the new patterns which were institutionalized were clearly not traditional, and they were never cut and dried, but always subject to change. None the less the main outlines of these patterns are quite clear, as set out below.

(f) Status Differences and the Allocation of Office

Certain titles were regularly allocated among persons of royal status; two classes of royal officials were distinguished, *'yan sarki* and *jikokin Sarki*, and only the *'yan sarki* could qualify for promotion to the throne by tenure of office. Members of leading Fulani lineages, and some Habe clients (*barori*) of the king, held other titles reserved for freemen. As already shown, some of the titles reserved for free clients were recurrently allocated to particular Fulani lineages; but members of these favoured lineages were not usually eligible for appointment to those *barori* (client) titles filled by open competition. There were also some offices strictly religious or legal in character; although the duties of these offices included administration of fiefs, training in Muhammadan law and lore was their essential qualification; the religious chracter of this technical training distinguished these offices as a group from all other territorial offices, *barori* and royal alike. In addition, there was an order of occupational offices mainly filled by Habe. The main function of these officials was the collection of occupational tax from craftsmen and traders. The king also appointed certain clients to offices in his own household; officers of the royal household lacked fiefs; but in their composition, organization, recruitment, function, and scope, they differed from the Habe order of household officials. Finally came the order of royal titled slaves, and for most of the century these lacked fiefs.

The old Habe division and organization of offices by military or civil functions, by the mode of their remuneration, and by their relation to territorial administration, had lapsed by 1865. So had the general form and particular content of the Habe rank-orders, their status-qualifications for office, promotional arrangements, modes of selection and appointment, and distributions of power or authority in terms of contractual or compulsory appointments. Under the Fulani, the senior officers of state were *hakimai* (territorial administrators). These *hakimai* offices had both military and civil functions, the former consisting of the recruitment and organization of warriors and of captaincy in war, the latter of territorial administration. All fief-holders, royal or other, were free persons, and they were remunerated in an identical form—by portions of the tax or tribute collected from their fiefs. Despite variability of status and individual relations with the king, the terms and form of these official appointments were always contractual, and emphasized their political solidarity with the ruler in his struggle against his rivals.

During the progressive appropriation of offices for persons of royal status the old Habe rank-orders were inevitably revised and new rank-orders were differentiated as follows: royal titles, territorial titles open to free clients, mallamships, occupational tax-collecting offices, the new household order, and slave-titles. The elimination of women, eunuchs, and slaves from territorial offices had proceeded simultaneously with the allocation of fiefs to many formerly non-territorial offices of the Habe household order. Some of these formerly non-territorial titles were incorporated in the royal ranks, for example, the offices of Wombai, Dallatu, Makama

Karami. Others were allocated to free clients; for example, the offices of Sarkin Fada, Sarkin Ruwa, Barde, Fagaci; but redefinition of those titles formerly reserved for palace eunuchs and officials as fief-holding offices allocated to royals and noblemen did not eliminate the need for household attendants or for a royal bodyguard; and as experience revealed these needs such new titles as Kasheka, Kilishi, or Baba Mai-gaskiya were created for the king's personal eunuchs, and other military titles such as Sarkin Yaki or Jagaba were created for the captains of his bodyguard. However, the household officials of this new order remained economically dependent on the king, and were not entrusted with territorial administration.

(g) Official Promotion and Precedence

Throughout the nineteenth century the number of offices appropriated by the ruling dynasties continued to increase. This increase in the number of royal offices took place at the expense of the number of offices open to free clients; and although there was some multiplication of titles and a considerable number of slave and eunuch offices were transferred to the *barori* rank, increases in the number of royal ranks took place at the expense of *barori* positions. Thus titles were progressively transferred from the *barori* to the royal rank-order. Although this process also was neither simple nor unambiguous, its development and form are shown in the chart of office-holders under the nineteenth-century Fulani kings (see Appendix B). The general effect of this progressive transfer of titles to the royal rank-order was to increase the instability of promotional arrangements within all the orders affected. Not only were office-holders liable to peremptory dismissal on the death of their royal patron, their offices also were liable to be transferred to another rank and given to persons of different status, since the allocation of office was governed by the king's political situation and needs. In consequence, although titles of any rank-order were arranged in scales of precedence, no fixed promotional arrangements developed among them.

A diagram of selected official promotions and demotions is given in Appendix E. In the frequencies with which individuals moved from one office to another, this diagram reveals certain promotional trends, but no regular promotional arrangements are observable. Lack of systematic promotional series was in part due

to the brevity of official tenure, and in part to the frequent transfers of offices between the newly emerging rank-orders; but a
careful study of these individual official careers shows that, within
the Fulani system, holders of the same office were not thereby
politically equivalent. The political importance of two individuals,
X and Y, who held the same office consecutively, differed according to their personal status and prospects, their relationships with
the rulers, and the political contexts of their appointment. One
king might appoint his cognatic kinsman to a particular office
while the next ruler might appoint his own son. Differences in the
political relations and prospects of the cognate and the king's
son would rule out the possibility of their political equivalence.
In other words, the promotional position of offices as well as
their position in the new rank-orders varied with their holders'
status and for this reason also no stable promotional ladders
developed.

In such conditions the king rarely moved his officials from one
position to another, except to free particular offices. Such transfers might seem equally like promotion or demotion to the persons
moved. Sometimes these reallocations represented individual re-
appointments within rank-orders based on differences of birth-
status. Even so, certain Habe promotional relationships persisted
in idea. For example, movement from the office of Sarkin Ruwa
to that of Makama Karami was regarded as promotion. However,
such movements were rare, due to the redistribution of titles
formerly part of the same Habe promotional series among new
rank-orders which were also promotionally closed. For example in
Fulani Zaria the title of Sarkin Ruwa was allotted to free clients,
that of Makama Karami to royal persons.

Under the Fulani, the relative precedence of different offices was
reflected in their relative authority, wealth, and political significance, especially in so far as the number, size, and importance of
their duties and fiefs permitted comparison. Some titles controlled
several fiefs, others only one or two. The more important titles
also supervised vassal states, and these positions were usually given
to close agnatic kin of the king. The fiefs administered by offices
recurrently allocated to selected lineages, such as Jisambo or
Chikum, formed undivided blocks of territory, and such offices
were neither linked to one another promotionally nor were they
included in the promotional organization of state titles. For this

reason these lineage-linked offices were not fully integrated in the prestige scale which applied to other titles.

Distinctions between royal and *barori* titles were expressed in these precedence rankings. The principal royal rank was that of Madaki. The principal client rank was Galadima. As a group, the royal ranks took precedence over client offices, and this was ex-pressed in the distribution of fiefs, wealth, and influence, and their relation to the throne. Within the royal ranks, offices reserved for *'yan Sarki* took precedence over others reserved for *jikoki*, and the king's cognatic and affinal kin were not included. Moreover, among the *'yan Sarki* offices, precedence reflected historical differences in these individual titles as springboards for promotion to the throne. Thus of the Fulani kings of Zazzau in the last cen-tury, five had held the title of Madaki before becoming kings, three others had acted as Wombai, and the titles of Dan Galadima, Sa'i, and Makama Karami had supplied one king each. The two princi-pal royal ranks were therefore Madaki and Wombai in that order of precedence. The title of Sa'i was not usually allotted to the king's kin, and properly belonged among the ranks of clients, although it later became a *sarautar jikan Sarki* (office held by a king's grandsons).

(h) The Councils of State

The absence of firm patterns of official promotion was correlated with the progressive redistributions of offices among the emerging rank-orders. These reorganizations expressed the king's control of official appointments, and revealed the influence of a series of changing political contexts on the exercise of such power. The accompanying transformations of traditional Habe patterns were bound up with changes in the context of kingship and in the rela-tions between the king and his officials. These changes naturally involved reorganization of council and communications pro-cedures. The king dealt as he wished with his officials, individually or through the senior member of their rank-order. Each morning the Galadima and the Madaki visited him together for consultation. Administrative orders might then be relayed to other royal or client title-holders through these senior officials. But territorial officials were themselves responsible for communicating with the king about their fiefs, and other duties. Such individual contacts were politically important. They provided the king and his officials with opportunities for increasing their mutual knowledge and solidarity, and they also emphasized the official's direct responsibility to the king, and his dependence on the latter's favour for the retention of office.

In this system of short-term autocracy, set patterns of council procedure and composition could hardly develop. It was the essence of this system that the king should direct policy personally in the light of his political situation, with its internal inter-dynastic rivalry, and its external context of vassalage and suzerainty. The principal consideration which influenced the king in his formation of policy was the effect which actions of different types could be expected to have on his political position within Zaria itself, that is, on the maintenance and increase of his power. Inevitably rulers adopted that course of action which seemed most likely to increase their power and to benefit them. This being the case, the king, who had the fullest knowledge of his own political situation and acted as leader of his dynasty, was the best judge of his interest; consequently, policy which was governed by the king's interests was properly decided by him as and how he saw fit. Royal councils and councils of state were thus identical and both were informal, their composition changing with the ruler and with the issue involved, according to the types of information or advice which the king wanted.

As the two most important subordinate officials, the Madaki and the Galadima were most frequently consulted by the king; they were also usually the first to be informed about his decisions on matters of public interest. But the king could also consult with his kinsmen including those not holding office, with his own clients, with mallams, with members of nearby states, or with individual officials. Office-holders who were specially trusted for advice by any king would be regarded as his councillors; but in all probability the officials most frequently consulted by his successor would hold other titles; and there was thus little chance of developing a formally constituted council of state with defined powers, procedures and official members within this changing system of government.

The position of the electoral council was different: its composition was fixed, its purpose and powers limited; it met on the death of a king to select the three candidates for the royal succession and to advise the ruler of Sokoto of this selection—but the power of final decision remained with the ruler of Sokoto. The electoral council of Fulani Zazzau consisted of three officials, drawn from the Galadima, the Limamin Juma'a, the Alkali and the Limamin Kona. The council usually selected one member from each of the principal dynasties for the succession, and ranked them in order or preference. Under the succession practice adopted by Sokoto, only those nominees who were not members of the late king's dynasty were really eligible to succeed. But the Sultan also noted all individuals proposed by the electoral council of Zaria as possible future rulers, and Sokoto watched the political careers of these unsuccessful nominees with greater interest than those of other local officials.

(i) Kingship in Fulani Zazzau

Kingship was the pivot of the Fulani government. Its significance for the system of government as a whole increased with its power over the administration; and this in turn increased as the system of dynastic competition developed. As this competition intensified, the kingship which was its object needed and acquired increasingly immediate and autocratic control over the administration. This increasing control was expressed in the king's power of independent policy formation as well as appointment and dismissal. Although tasks and powers of government were distinguished and delegated in stable patterns, these distributions were never final, since the king's freedom to dismiss officials and to redefine official functions and powers qualified the prevailing distribution of roles and duties.

Under the system of discontinuous succession, with its rotation of kingship among several lineages of equal status, autocratic rule by the king was unavoidable. Moreover, once the suzerains of Sokoto had exercised their power to depose the kings of Zazzau as well as to appoint them, insecurity in the tenure of the throne was added to the discontinuity of lineage succession. To protect themselves against their rivals and to further the interests of their own dynasties, kings appropriated autocratic power and tried to wield this power to increase their individual advantage. Moreover, within this context of dynastic competition and supervision by the suzerain at Sokoto, by a paradox the maximum rewards of kingship corresponded closely to its minimum preconditions. Effective kingship included among its rewards the appointment of one's kin and supporters to office, the exclusion of rivals from such positions, and the accumulation of wealth and influence by military action, slave-raiding, taxation, and the like. The administrative structure under the king was simultaneously the instrument for the pursuit of these objectives and for the control of the state. To realize such poliical goals the king needed sufficient power to govern the state at will. Yet unless he realized these political goals the king would lack the minimum of power and authority essential for the government of the state. Thus the increasing absolutism of kingship and its rotation among the rival lineages were mutually implicit in the pattern and context of dynastic competition under Sokoto's control.

Competition for kingship always remained a competition between dynasties rather than individuals, although the kingship was vested in individuals, and although rulers used their opportunities for personal as well as dynastic ends. Kings lacking dynastic support could not rule effectively. In 1860 Sidi Abdulkadiri, the son of Mallam Musa, was dethroned by Sokoto after his own dynasty had complained against actions which threatened to destroy the dynasty as a basic unit of this political system. In 1863 Sidi's successor, Audusallami of the Suleibawa was assassinated with impunity. The Suleibawa had never previously produced a ruler of Zaria, and their lineage had split into segments even before Mallam Musa conquered Zaria. This initial division largely explains their failure in the competition for the throne.

In Fulani Zaria the king received and exercised power as the leader of a competing dynasty. This position carried certain obligations which limited the king's freedom of action. In the first place, his strength depended on the support of his dynasty, and his own dynasty also contained potential rivals and other candidates for the succession. The king sought to win the support of such kinsmen by careful appointments; at the same time he sought to reduce his dependence upon the dynasty by appointing and allocating offices to his personal clients and relatives, especially his *surukai* (affines) or *dangi wajen mace* (cognatic kin), whose personal tenure of office depended on their personal loyalty to him. In distributing office among his clients the king sought to elicit the widest possible support for his régime among the aristocratic Fulani and subject Habe. With the resulting body of picked lieutenants the king was able to execute his will effectively, and to maintain a stable administration. His rivals could not rebel without inviting the disapproval of Sokoto and punishment by the Madaki, who controlled the military force of the state and was usually the king's son. His fief-holders and subordinates were the king's supporters and kinsmen, to whom the idea of rebellion offered little attraction, and who in any event lacked the individual power for such adventures. As the ruler appointed by Sokoto, the king was the ultimate source of authority within the state; and as the leading representative of the ruling dynasty, he also exercised dominant power. But the power of the king was by no means absolute. He depended on his dynasty and on his clients in office or out of office for support. In consequence, although individually they were no match for the king, these officials were quite influential, and their power was expressed in the improper exercise of their authority over the fiefs placed under their control. The king condoned such *ultra vires* actions so long as there was no question about the loyalty of the fief-holders to him. The fief-holder on his part took care to act within the limits of the king's tolerance. These limits were politically narrow, administratively wide.

The situations of successive rulers differed widely. The simple fact of succession presented each monarch with a distribution of power and authority quite different from that which his predecessor enjoyed. In addition the relationship between the state of Zazzau and its suzerain of Sokoto was continually changing; and successive kings were members of different dynasties with differing resources and composition, despite their general similarity of form. Even kings drawn from the same generation of a single dynasty occupied significantly different positions, for example Hamada and Mommon Sani. This was due to the internal differentiation of the dynasties themselves; such internal differentiation virtually ruled out the chance that two monarchs would occupy identical kinship positions; and this difference of their intra-dynastic kinship positions intimately affected the allocations of office which rulers made among their agnatic and other kin. Differences in the dynastic positions of kings were expressed in their different distributions of office among their kin and non-kin. Moreover, as time went by, the differential growth of rival dynasties changed their relative political significance. No two Mallawa rulers had to deal with an opposition of identical character, personal resources, support, wealth, or power. Competition for the throne being a competition between dynasties, and these units being defined by patri-descent and distributions of rank, the political composition or significance of any single dynasty was continually changing, according to its expansion, successful competition for the kingship or for various types of subordinate offices, intermarriage and the like. To these variables must also be added the individual relations of clientage by which its members were linked to other participants in the political system. Given such a highly complex and variable context, each king enjoyed different resources and power on his accession and employed them in a different fashion. Thus the exercise of ruling power aimed at its increase in order to rule the more effectively within the context of increasing dynastic rivalry and increasing insecurity of the throne. The result was increasing autocracy.

(j) Politics and Administration

The absolutism of a king's rule was therefore no index of the centralization or monopoly of power. Ineradicable dispersals of power among the dynasties between which kingship rotated made autocratic administration necessary. Authority was the essential quality centralized in kingship, and this authority was sanctioned by the overriding power which the king wielded *within* the hierarchy of government officials. But the political system of the state was by no means coterminous with its official hierarchy. This system of political relations was constituted by the four dynasties and their respective supporters; its forms and modes of operation were inherently segmentary, its groupings were defined in terms of contraposition. The structure of this system of relations was at the same time evidence of the dispersal of power and of the form in which power was dispersed.

However, although quite distinct, the political and the administrative systems were closely interdependent. Their interdependence was fully evident in the kingship, with its functions, power, authority, and conditions of transmission. The difference between the political and administrative systems was expressed sharply by the exclusion of the king's rivals from the administrative structure. The political system was segmentary in form, and consisted of the competing dynasties and their clients. The administrative system was hierarchic in form, and consisted of the king, and those of his kin or supporters who held office; in theory the officials would be drawn from one dynasty and their adherents only.[1] Within the political system power lay with the dynasties; and between these dynasties there were no authority relations. Within the administrative structure, the king controlled overwhelming authority and power, but some power was also derived from the political interdependence of the ruler and his officials; such conditions of political interdependence enabled the king's kin and agents to administer their fiefs with little interference from their sovereign.

5. THE GOVERNMENTS OF HABE AND FULANI ZAZZAU

(a) The Character and Scope of their Difference

The government of Fulani Zazzau differed from that of the Habe of Zazzau in a number of ways. The Habe system was a limited monarchy with a single dynasty, whereas the Fulani system was an autocratic kingship which rotated among a number of dynasties. Among the Habe, offices were distinguished by their political and administrative capacities and roles; and there was an inverse correlation between the administrative and the political significance of office. Under the Fulani, office was an administrative organ, the king controlled the administrative structure, and the system of political relations was sharply distinguished from the administrative; at the same time, political considerations controlled administrative appointments, which were usually made and terminated on political grounds, and the administrative and political functions of government were closely identified. Within the limitations set by his dynastic context and his vassalage to Sokoto, the Fulani king ruled dictatorially; and although he had the power to decide policy, he consulted his officials on various issues as he saw fit. In the Fulani state officials were expected to execute the king's commands and to remain politically loyal. Although the Fulani kingship was the source of authority, authority was decentralized and delegated to fief-holders whose political relations with the king also gave them power. Effectively, the king and his officials formed a ruling bureaucracy, whose power, although neither total, absolute, nor indefinite in duration, was overwhelming while it lasted, and being legitimated by conditions of appointment, was in part expressed as authority.

[1] For exceptions, their origins and consequences, see Chapter 5.

In the Habe government, there had been a system of checks and balances which limited the appropriation and exercise of power by the king and other administrative staff, and the council organization of Abuja reveals this clearly. But under the Fulani there was no formal council, and during a king's reign the only checks and balances on the exercise of power were those which inhered in the distribution of power itself. This distribution of power had four overlapping sectors with the following constitution: firstly, the king and his officials; secondly, the government and rival dynasties; thirdly, the dynasties and their supporters only; and finally the state of Zaria and its suzerain, Sokoto. In brief, after the Fulani conquest the system of government of Zaria changed from a constitutional monarchy to a qualified absolutism, which grew and persisted as a system, although its personnel changed with each reign as an effect of dynastic rivalry.

This major transformation proceeded through a host of particular innovations or changes, some of which were prerequisites for further changes, while others were effects of prior changes, or were functionally related to other aspects of the general process. In the course of these developments the old Habe rank-orders were replaced by a new classification of offices, which was based on the status of their holders. The Habe differentiation of offices by special military or civil functions was largely abolished. Habe promotional arrangements disappeared, together with Habe distributions of office among different status-groups. In place of the hierarchic communication structure characteristic of Habe government, the Fulani king dealt directly with his fief-holders, and communicated with his vassals through fief-holders, mostly of royal status. The special functions of the Habe order of chamber eunuchs therefore disappeared, together with that order. In Fulani Zaria the king's eunuchs were purely personal attendants with no governmental roles. Under the Habe, offices had also been differentiated by the forms in which they were remunerated, e.g. fiefs, benefices, or patrimonial support. Under the Fulani, fiefs were allocated to all offices held by free persons, and the emergence of a new order of household officials directly dependent on the king for support was gradual and governed by purely functional considerations.

Other changes effected by the Fulani in this general transformation are less immediately obvious. Under the Habe, immediacy of access to the king was inversely related to administrative responsibility; and the important offices of Galadima, Wombai and Dallatu were charged with certain somewhat menial functions. Under the Fulani, administrative responsibilities marched hand in hand with immediacy of access to the king; and important office lacked menial duties.

Again, under the Habe, official orders formed political units, and the councils of state were the arena for policy formation, for the appointment of officials, for decisions about promotions and the like. Under the Fulani, the basic political units were the dynasties, of which at any moment only one exercised governing powers or held office; and in this Fulani system the officials were neither responsible for policy formation, nor was there a formally constituted council having such power. Moreover, within the limitations set by his dynastic context, and by his relation to Sokoto, the king decided official appointments, promotions, and dismissals as he saw fit.

Under the Habe, there were important distinctions between officials according to the character of their relations with the king and the government. Some Habe offices were of a feudal character, while others were held by the ruler's patrimonial clients, and the holders of other offices were recruited compulsorily as eunuchs or slaves. These differences corresponded with the relative importance of these offices in the state administration. The free officials of the Fulani government were all appointed on a contractual basis; formally and informally their appointment stressed their allegiance, solidarity, and loyalty to the king. But in Fulani Zaria there were several categories of free officials. Some free clients were appointed to offices competition for which was open to anyone; there was also an order of occupational tax-collectors, an order of mallams and judicial officials, an order of household officials; and there were several quasi-hereditary titles such as Chikum, Wan'ya, Magaji Jisambo, or Magajin Zakara. Of these various classes of free officials, only those people appointed to offices in open competition were direct political nominees of the king. By their low status and specificity of role, the order of occupational tax-gatherers were excluded from participation in the processes of dynastic competition and control. They formed a strictly subordinate administrative tax-gathering staff of Habe status. The religious and judicial mallams were also marginal to the system of political competition, and they were primarily concerned with the administration of religion and law. The officers of the royal household were excluded from territorial administration, and formed a household staff which was freely changed by successive kings, but which had no political influence. Quasi-hereditary titles, such as Chikum, were territorial offices associated with particular lineages, and their holders enjoyed considerable security of tenure. These quasi-hereditary offices were also marginal to the system of open competition for political offices in Zaria, and lineages attached to these titles were thereby excluded from the competition for other offices of state. Being marginal to the political system of Fulani Zazzau, these quasi-hereditary offices provided their holders with a political security expressed in continuity of tenure, but for this reason they were also strictly administrative. Because they were marginal to the political system of Zaria, such quasi-hereditary titles were linked by ties of clientage to the throne of Zazzau, and their holders were not usually personal clients of individual kings.

In 1860 the slave-officials of Fulani Zazzau were administrative subordinates, charged with purely instrumental tasks. Being slaves, they were of course recruited under compulsion rather than contract. Some of these slave-officials belonged to the ruler personally; in most cases they were hereditarily attached to the throne. Subsequent to this date, certain kings of Zaria placed slaves in command of standing armies stationed in the south of the kingdom. In the following chapter the development and consequences of these innovations will be related. In this place it is only necessary to point out that the slave status of these commanders excluded them from the processes of political competition; and that the king evaluated their official performance in terms of its administrative effectiveness rather than its political implications. The special focus of such supervision itself differentiates these slave-officials from the free fief-holders, whose exercise of office was scrutinized by the king for indications of their political loyalties rather than for its conformity to administrative rules.

(b) *Elements Common to Both Systems*

The extensive and important changes in the Habe system of government which developed after the Fulani conquest raise two major problems, the one related to the measure and type of continuity in this governmental system, and the other to the logic or order of change. We shall postpone the discussion of this second problem until our account of the political history of Zaria is complete. The other problem of continuity in the elements of the system really divides into two: the one historical, the other morphological. There is the strictly historical question, whether the Fulani government of Zaria actually developed from or replaced a system of government of the type which obtained at Abuja during the nineteenth century. The morphological question is one of formal correspondence in the general and particular features of the Habe and Fulani systems of government. The fact that these two systems share certain general features does not demonstrate their historical relations; for acceptable evidence of historical connections we shall have to make a detailed examination of the separate systems. But it is convenient to start by discussing the common general characters of these two governments before considering the particulars of their correspondence, and the problem of their historical relation.

Both Habe and Fulani society consisted of ranked and differentiated statuses. Among the Habe, the principal distinction was between the free and the unfree. The non-free were further divided into slaves and eunuchs. Free persons were differentiated into three major status groups, namely, royalty, mallams, and others, and this last category was further divisible into nobles and commoners. Another basic status differentiation in Habe Abuja was that between the Habe Muhammadans and non-Muhammadan tribesmen over whom they ruled. Membership in the political society of Habe Abuja was confined to Muhammadans. These status divisions persisted in Fulani Zaria, but the difference between the Fulani conquerors and the subject Habe was heavily emphasized. The Fulani conquerors were differentiated into royalty, nobility, and commoner statuses; and there were also certain lineages of mallams devoted to the pursuit of Koranic learning. In Fulani Zaria the eunuch status lost significance when eunuchs lost their official functions. Under Fulani rule, Habe were distinguished by their occupational status and were eligible for occupational titles. In both the Habe and Fulani societies there were thus complex hierarchies of status; and both systems of government recruited officials from all the major status-groups of their respective societies. Thus both systems incorporated the significant status differentiations of their societies by allocations of office to these different categories of personnel.

Besides.this, both the Habe and Fulani governments share concepts of office and of official hierarchies with chieftainship as the supreme office. In both systems the chieftainship was hereditary in character, but the chief was unable to control the succession. In both systems the majority of offices were filled by open appointment; but in each system certain offices were reserved for slaves or were allocated to eunuchs. In either of these systems the administrative and political functions of different offices corresponded with the status differences of the groups eligible to hold them. In both systems the complex official structure staffed by personnel of widely differing status contained separate arrangements for the promotion of these categories of persons and for their motivation and reward.

To summarize, the Habe and Fulani systems of government had the following general features in common; status-differentiation, office, chieftainship and hierarchical relations among offices which corresponded variously with the differentiation of their individual political and administrative functions. The problems of recruitment, remuneration, motivation, and control of officials were common to both these systems and derived from yet more general conditions of state organization. However, although both governments discharged these secondary functions, they did so by different methods.

(c) *The Problem of Historical Succession*

The simplest method of determining the correspondence of particular elements in the two systems of government is to begin by listing their common elements, and then to list and examine the elements peculiar to either system. To establish their historical relation, we shall then have to account for the differences of particulars in the two systems in directly historical terms. Since offices and statuses are the most important general features common to both systems, and since the allocation of office was governed by status conditions in both systems, this comparison of particulars consists in a comparison of the individual offices of the two governments. In making this comparison, it is simplest to begin with the charts of the offices at Abuja, and to discuss them by their rank-orders.

All offices of the inner chamber at Abuja are present in the Fulani system, but at Fulani Zaria these offices were not held by eunuchs. Of the offices of the royal household at Abuja, such titles as Sarkin Fada, Hauni, Barde, and Magayaki persisted at Zaria. The Habe office of Kacalla,[1] which owed its existence to the suzerainty exercised by the Shehu of Bornu over Habe Zazzau, lapsed at Fulani Zaria which was not subordinate to Bornu. Such other household offices as Cincina, Gwabare, Durumi, Kangiwa, and Ciritawa are also missing from the Fulani list, together with the military title of Jarmai, who was in charge of the Abuja household infantry. The four *rukuni* offices of Abuja are all present in Fulani Zazzau, together with all the *rawuna* offices of Abuja, except the Dankekasau, the Shenagu, and the Sarkin Gayen. The Iyan Bakin Kasuwa of Abuja is recognizable as the Magajin Kasuwa of Fulani Zazzau, and the Abuja slave-office of Barwa was revived by the Fulani of Zaria as the title of a free household official of the king. The Wan'diya of Abuja is the Wan'ya of Fulani Zazzau; the Garkuwa Babba (bigger shield) of Abuja is the Sarkin Garkuwa (chief shield) of Fulani Zazzau. The Lifidi of Abuja is the Sarkin Lifidi of Fulani Zazzau. The Sarkin Gayen of Abuja was a village chief of Zaria who fled with Makau to Juba and was given a territorial fief there.[2] The Abuja title of Sata was given to nomad Fulani scouts at Zazzau. The Abuja title of Sarkin Pawa (chief butcher) appears among the occupational offices of Fulani Zaria, but was filled under Mallam Musa by a Habe supporter of the Fulani who administered territorial fiefs.

The different vassal chiefs of Abuja and Fulani Zazzau simply reflect the separate territorial boundaries and constitution of the two states. Vassalage being an exclusive relation, vassal chiefs appearing in the one chart must be excluded from the other.

The royal titles of Abuja persisted at Zaria. The first Fulani king, Musa, appointed three of his daughters to the titles reserved under the Habe for the king's daughters; these were the offices of Iya, Magajiya, and Mardanni. The Magajiya of Zazzau is the Sarauniya of Abuja. The evidence for this equation is that Ajuma, sister of the Habe king of Zazzau Aliyu IV (1767-73), who founded the town of Kumbada in Niger province, held the Habe title of

---

[1] Kacalla is an official status in the government of Bornu, and the term is of Kanuri (Bornu) origin. See Temple, 1919, p. 437. See also M. Hassan (1), p. 5.
[2] See Appendix A.

Magajiya at Zazzau. Mallam Hassan also related that the Sarauniya Zainabu, who fled with Makau from Zaria, later built a ward in the town of Abuja known as the Magajiya ward.[1] Although my enquiries in Zaria were not directed at this present problem of historical relations with Habe Zazzau, my Fulani informants at Zaria asserted confidently that the Mardanni title was taken over by Mallam Musa from the Habe government as an office held by the king's daughters. It is quite possible that this title lapsed at Abuja following the Habe flight. The royal office of Magajiya was abolished at Fulani Zaria by Yamusa. It has since reappeared as the title for the head of the prostitutes. The position of Sarauniya persisted at a purely titular level in Fulani Zaria, being held by the king's mother, who was known as Sarauniya, Mama, or Uwar Sarki. The Magajin Dangi of Abuja became the Magajin Gari of Fulani Zaria.

Of the mallams' order, the Magajin Mallam (head of the Mallams) of Abuja became the Sarkin Mallamai (chief of the Mallams) at Zaria.

Of the slave-offices of Abuja, the following titles lapsed: Banaga, Kunkeli, Magajin Kwa, Sirdi, Magajin Nagaba, Boroka. The Madakin Gabas (Lord of the East) of Abuja is the Bajimin Gabas (Bull of the East) of Zaria. The titles of Garkuwa Kankane, Bakon Barno, and Wagu, formerly belonging to the household and junior public orders of Abuja, are held by royal slaves of Fulani Zaria. The Bikon Tambari (Royal Drummer) of Abuja is the Sarkin Tambari (chief of the Royal Drums) of Fulani Zaria.

(d) Offices Peculiar to Fulani Zaria

We now have to list and account for titles present at Fulani Zaria but absent from Abuja. Titles designating vassal states have already been dealt with. By virtue of conquest, the Fulani of Zazzau became overlords of Kauru, Kajuru, Fatika, Durum, and Lere. Keffi, Jema'a, and Doma were conquered by Fulani agents under Mallam Musa's direction. Kwotto, Lere, and Kagarko were established as vassal states during the early years of Fulani rule.

The order of free household retainers at Fulani Zaria contained such titles as, Sarkin Yaki, Sarkin Figini, Mahari, and Majidadi, which are missing from the Abuja list. The Sarkin Yaki was the king's war chief, commanding the reserve stationed with the king

[1] Hassan and Shu'aibu, 1952 (1), p. 10.

in battle. He administered no fiefs, and the office was created on purely technical grounds. Sarkin Figini (chief of the Fence) had charge of the king's bodyguard. Mahari was a scout attached to the king's war chief, the Sarkin Yaki. Majidadi was the king's favourite and companion. After the Fulani had eliminated the Habe order of household officials and had invested them with territorial fiefs, there were few remaining officers of the royal household at Zaria and their functions were non-governmental; but during the following years, various kings realized the necessity for such officials, and a new order was accordingly created to ad-minister the king's household and defend him.

The following fief-holding offices were peculiar to Fulani Zazzau: Magajin Zakara, Magaji Jisambo, Cikum, and Mardanni, the last of which has already been discussed. The first Wali was appointed by Yamusa, the second Fulani king, supposedly in imi-tation of the Walin Sokoto. The Walin Zazzau was a royal rank, and was charged with jurisdiction over the administrative malpractices of office-holders, particularly the king's kin. Yamusa appointed his eldest son, Hamada, Wali, with these functions. The first Sa'i was appointed by Mallam Musa. The office was entrusted with supervision and control of the nomad Fulani throughout the province, and was given to Abdulkerim, who later became the king of Zaria and founder of the Katsinawa dynasty. The Fulani conquerors created this office to collect *jangali* (cattle-tax), to supervise their nomad Fulani cousins, and to provide them with direct access to the king. Sarkin Mai was an official in charge of the pagan Habe or Maguzawa, who are scattered throughout northern Zaria. There being no Maguzawa in Abuja, it is understandable that there is no Sarkin Mai there. The office of Rubu was in charge of all uncultivated land throughout the kingdom of Zaria, under the Muhammadan doctrine of *Wakf*, which governs rights in the uncultivated land of a state conquered during a *jihad*. The condi-tion of conquest which accounts for this office of Rubu in Fulani Zaria also explains its absence from Habe Abuja. Such Fulani offices as Danmadami, Iyan Kurama, Katuka, Magajin Zakara, Jisambo, Cikum, and Wan'ya were all territorially specialized; Iyan Kurama, as the name implies, was the governor of the Kurama tribe in eastern Zaria; Katuka controlled the Katab tribe; Wan'ya, Jisambo, and Cikum were specially concerned with administration of the large Gwari population. Their territories bounded on each other. Danmadami and Magajin Zakara were other offices by which the ruler of Zaria administered large pagan populations of the kingdom. All the tribal areas administered by these lineage-linked titles of Fulani Zaria lay outside the boundaries of Abuja; consequently these offices are not to be found in the Abuja government. In Fulani Zaria, it must be remembered, such offices as Danmadami, Iyan Kurama, Rubu, Katuka, and the like were allocated to particular families who were specially knowledgeable about the problems and conditions presented by their special administrative areas. It must also be borne in mind that whereas the kingdom of Zaria itself had an area of about 13,000 square miles in the last century, Abuja was then only about 3,000 square miles. Consequently the specialized territorial offices of Zaria outnumber those of Abuja. Territorial offices common to both systems were those entrusted with the administration of the Muhammadan population in either state. Offices administering non-Muhammadan populations in Zaria and Abuja differed in title, number, and administrative area.

Of the official Mallams of Zaria, the Fulani titles of Alkali, Waziri, and Limamin Kona are lacking from Abuja. The Limamin Kona was a Habe priestship antedating the Fulani invasion, and has traditionally been held by one Habe lineage of Zaria.[1] The Limamin Kona of Zaria in 1950 was a member of this family and related that his ancestors, having refused to flee with Makau at the conquest, were confirmed in their position by Mallam Musa, who also appointed the first Alkali, or Chief Judge of Zaria, and the first Waziri or Vizier, the latter being a non-territorial office, held by the king's principal adviser. As the Fulani system of monocratic government developed at Zaria after Musa's death, this new office of Waziri became redundant, and only one other appointment to this position was made during the nineteenth century, that by Mallam Musa's son Sidi in 1860. None the less, the creation of this office is evidence of the initial Fulani intention to imitate hallowed Muhammadan political practice.

The official system of Fulani Zazzau contained an order of occupational offices which is entirely lacking from Habe Abuja. The Fulani system of occupational taxation was developed under the Sultan of Sokoto, Aliyu Babba, 1842–59, and was instituted in Zaria under the Bornawa king, Mamman Sani, 1846–60. The de-

---

[1] Zaria city contains an ancient ward of the Limamin Kona.

velopment of this occupational order in Zaria after the Fulani conquest accounts for its absence from Habe Abuja.

Concerning the king's slave-officials there is no need for dilation. Kasheka and Kilishi were eunuch offices created by Fulani rulers who experienced the need for eunuchs within the royal household, after the original Habe eunuch titles had been allocated to freemen. In 1860 S.Z. Sidi Abdulkadiri appointed freemen to the eunuch titles of Fagaci, leaving only the Habe office of Sarkin Zana of the old eunuch order. Later, in the 1890s, S.Z. Yero appointed a free client, Amshe, to the office of Sarkin Zana, and placed him in charge of certain fiefs. The office of Madauci at Zaria was a slave-title from pre-Fulani days, traditionally allocated to one lineage of royal slaves, and it remained so after the conquest. Sarkin Zagi had responsibility for the king's horses and safety on the march. Under the Fulani, positions such as Kwaramaza and Wagu were occasionally allocated to freemen, but were as a rule reserved for slaves.

The extensive list of military slave-officials indicates that the Fulani king relied heavily on royal slaves in his armed force. Such titles as Sarkin Yamma and Sarkin Yara or Sarkin Ciyawa were late creations which gave an extreme expression to this principle. The Sarkin Yamma, who was a slave appointed in charge of the standing army at Kacia, exercised administrative powers around his encampment; Sarkin Yara and Sarkin Ciyawa were slave-captains appointed by S.Z. Yero to command his new squads of slave-musketeers. The office of Shentali is the most interesting of these slave-titles. On certain occasions this office had been filled by members of the dynasties; on other occasions by free clients, and only rarely by slaves. Until 1860 the king supervised his slave-officials through the Hauni, a free official who at this time was a member of the king's household order, and held no fiefs. By 1870 the office of Hauni had also become a fief-holding title, though it continued to be responsible for the supervision of all slave-officials, except the king's eunuchs. Thus, under the Fulani, the office of Hauni retained the function of slave supervision which it had discharged under the Habe.

(e) Conclusion

We have now examined in detail all offices of the Abuja and Fulani systems. We have found that these details overlap considerably, and that their differences are easily explained in terms of particular historical developments, most of which are quite well known at Zaria. My informants at Fulani Zaria spontaneously listed all the Habe eunuch offices, and distinguished between those offices which were Fulani creations and others which the Fulani had taken away from eunuchs and had given to freemen. They were also quite clear about such duplication of titles as Turaki the Greater (Turaki Babba) and Turaki the Lesser (Turaki Karam). This duplication developed when Turaki the Greater was still a eunuch title; actually it represents a play on words, *Babba* meaning 'greater' or 'a eunuch', according to the intonation. Similarly, the Ma'aji title became distinguished as Ma'aji Babba, an office filled initially by eunuchs, and Ma'aji Karami, in charge of Kacia. The Habe precedent for this is clear in cases such as Makama Babba[1] and Makama Karami, Garkuwa Babba, Garkuwa Kankane (Garkuwa the Lesser) Barde and Barde Kankane. Such titles as Madakin Hauni, Barden Hauni, Madakin Barde, and the like, are subordinates created by the principal office. Thus the Madakin Hauni is the Madaki of Hauni—Hauni's chief assistant. All important Fulani offices discharged their duties through certain subordinate staff appointed by the office-holder, with titles belonging to the office itself. Thus, provided the principal title persists, its subordinates will also persist. The relations between administrative superiors and subordinates in Fulani Zaria differ from the old Abuja pattern, as represented by the Madawaki's control of the Kuyambana and other junior public officials whom the Habe Madawaki did not directly appoint to office, and who formed a group quite distinct from the subordinate staff which he did appoint unilaterally. Except for the Hauni who supervised the royal slaves, under the Fulani no office-holder supervised any others except his own subordinates.

To list the titles common to both Habe and Fulani systems of government is the simplest method of testing or demonstrating their historical relatedness. Abuja titles persisting without change of name at Fulani Zaria include Madaki, Wombai, Makama Karami, Dangaladima, Iya, Barwa, Magayaki, Jagaba, Galadima, Dallatu, Sarkin Fada, Sarkin Ruwa, Fagaci, Hauni, Sata, Makama Babba, Limamin Juma'a, Salenke, Magatakarda, Sarkin Pawa,

---

[1] Note that Makama Karami was the Habe eunuch office, Makama Babba was a title held by freemen at Abuja and is translated 'the Bigger Weapon'.

Sarkin Zana, Sarkin Noma, Shamaki, Bakon Barno, Garkuwa Kankane, Wagu, Sarkin Karma, Sarkin Baka, Sarkin Bindiga, and Sarkin Dogarai. Titles which persisted and were duplicated at Zaria are Turaki and Ma'aji. Habe titles persisting at Fulani Zaria with slight changes of name are Sarkin Garkuwa, Magajin Gari, Sarkin Mallamai, Magajin Kasuwa, Sarkin Tambari, and Bajimin Gabas.

Even if we had not been able to account for all the differences between Abuja and Fulani Zaria which have just been discussed by concrete historical developments, the number and variety of elements having identical forms at Abuja and Fulani Zaria could not possibly be explained in any other terms than the historical relatedness of these two systems. Moreover, given the facts of Fulani conquest and Habe flight, such historical relation could only have one form, namely, the development of the Fulani government from the Habe system by transformation of the latter. This in turn means that the system of government at Abuja described by Mallam Hassan was substantially the same system as that which the Habe operated at Zaria before the Fulani conquest.

When one group which has conquered another with a developed government seeks to consolidate this conquest by direct administration of the conquered population, it must make use of many elements of the pre-existing governmental system in order to start its own administration. Yet such consolidation itself entails changes in the structure and function of those elements which have been retained, and this implies that new administrative and political organs will be developed, and that the system as a whole will undergo further changes. This happened in Zaria after the conquest; and in this way the Habe model described for Abuja by Mallam Hassan was transformed into the Fulani government we have just described.

5

A CHRONICLE OF FULANI ZARIA
1804–1900

(a) The Conquest

THERE were Fulani in Zaria before the Fulani conquered it under Mallam Musa. It is said that when the Habe of Zazzau moved from Turunku to the present site of Zaria city, they found Fulani herding their cattle there. This may be a myth, rationalizing or justifying the Fulani conquest as a resumption of ancient rights based on initial occupancy; but, even under Habe rule, the Fulani chiefs of Fatika to the west of Zaria were recognized vassals of Zazzau; and when the Madakin Kankarro planned to assassinate the Habe king and seize the throne, the Fulani chief of Fatika warned his liege and received as reward a fief within the city of Zaria itself called the ward of Fatika.

During the years immediately preceding the Fulani invasion the Habe king of Zazzau also exercised suzerainty over two southern vassal states, Kajuru and Kauru, whose rulers were of Habe origin. At this date the Gwari at Lapai and Kusheriki were also ruled by Habe vassal chiefs of Zazzau, and it is probable that the chiefs of Karigi, an old Maguzawa (pagan Hausa) town in the north, at that time had a status approaching vassalage.

By 1804 there were several Fulani lineages settled at Zaria. Some of these Fulani were Islamic teachers and priests, one of whom, the Limam Dan Madami, reared a considerable number of horses and was in touch with Mallam Musa for seven years preceding the invasion. These horses later provided mounts for the invading Fulani. Nearly fifty miles to the south of Zaria city, close by the present site of Kaduna, there were two Fulani lineages, the Bornawa, led by Yamusa and his brother, Bapaiyo, and the Suleibawa, led by Mallam Kilba and his son, Audusallami. Midway between Kaduna and Zaria city there was another lineage of Suleibawa Fulani, under Jaye, and at Kwassallo and Ricifa, to the north-east of the capital, there were yet other Suleibawa families, who joined in the assault on Kano when the *jihad* began and later became its rulers. The Suleibawa of Zaria were thus split into three segments before Musa's invasion. Of these, the Suleibawan Igabi were closely linked to the Bornawa, Yamusa having married M. Kilba's daughter. Some Suleibawa of Kwassallo under Jaye refused to await the arrival of the deputy appointed by Dan Fodio, and had initiated a revolt of their own against the Habe king shortly before Musa's arrival. This was repulsed by the Habe forces, and Jaye was driven back to Ricifa, near Kwassallo. Jaye's independent attempt to seize the throne is evidence of Fulani unrest on the eve of the *jihad*.

Mallam Musa had visited Zazzau some years before his invasion. On that occasion he taught the Koran at Zaria city, and had travelled as far south as Igabi. He knew Yamusa and the family of Mallam Kilba, as well as the Fulani of Zaria city, including the Limam with the horses. Musa was a Fulani from Malle, an ancient town in the region of Timbuctoo, and he was well known to Dan Fodio and other Toronkawa Fulani, having himself been a student of the Shehu.[1] At the start of the *jihad*, Dan Fodio gave Musa a flag (*tuta*) of leadership, with authority to conquer Zazzau and reform Islam within it. Strict Muhammadans were expected to obey these chosen leaders of the Shehu; to assist the *jihad* was a religious duty for them. Not all of the flag-holders appointed by the Shehu were Fulani. Yakubu who was sent to conquer Bauchi was not a Fulani; the Shehu selected his deputies for their religious sincerity and knowledge of Islam, as well as for their ability and strength.

There are several legends about the Shehu's relations with the Fulani leaders in Zaria, and these versions are not inconsistent. In one version the Bornawa and Suleibawa, under Yamusa's leadership, protested to the Shehu that they were the Fulani native to Zaria, and needed no leaders from elsewhere. It is said that Yamusa sought to be appointed as the Shehu's deputy for Zazzau as a whole, or at the least to be given the southern half of the kingdom, and that it was only with difficulty that he was persuaded to act as Musa's chief lieutenant. Another story tells how the Shehu instructed Musa to associate himself with Yamusa, with Audusal-

---

[1] Usuman, or Othman, Dan Fodio, leader of the Fulani in the *jihad* of 1804, is also known as Shehu or the Shehu. He was the founder and first ruler of the Fulani empire with the title of Sarkin Musulmi (Chief of the Muhammadans).

lami of the Suleibawa, and with Abdulkerim, another Fulani pupil of the Shehu, from Katsina state. These instructions may have been given either before or after Yamusa's protest to Dan Fodio, or before or after the conquest. It is further possible that this ruling attributed to the Shehu may be a myth developed later to legitimate and sanction the multidynastic system, while denying legitimacy to other lineages with royal ambitions. These legends reveal the heterogeneous composition of the Fulani force which conquered Zaria, and the competition of its principal elements for command. These conditions partially explain the political system which later developed.

Musa was with the Shehu when he defeated the Habe king of Gobir, Yunfa. In one legend Musa also took part in the invasion of Kano before being appointed to conquer Zaria. He is said to have crossed into Zaria from Kano with seventy-four horsemen and some infantry, and first met with opposition at the old Maguzawa town of Kudan near the Kano–Zaria border. The near-by village of Zabi, which had a Muhammadan population, came to his assistance and Kudan was captured and burnt. Makau, the Habe king, on receiving news of the invasion had despatched his Madaki with the main force of cavalry to Hunkuyi, another Habe town near Kudan. According to one version M. Musa routed the force under Makau's Madaki at Hunkuyi; in another he was warned that the Habe were at Hunkuyi in strength, and accordingly moved from Kudan over to Durum. The village-chief of Durum is said to have put all his cavalry and men at Musa's disposal, and he was later rewarded with the gift of vassal status. At Durum also, Musa received other supporters led by the Habe Sarkin Pawa (Chief of the Butchers) of Likoro, another large town nearby. Either Musa defeated the Habe cavalry at Likoro or he avoided them; but he proceeded directly to Zaria city and, according to M. Hassan, entered the capital from the north-west while the Habe king and his supporters were celebrating the Greater Sallah at the prayer-ground outside the city.[1] Fulani simply say Musa's men overpowered Makau's, and then Makau fled.

Musa pursued Makau to Kajuru, after the defeated Habe king had been driven from his halting-place at Gwanda by the Fulani chief of Fatika. At Kajuru, Makau received aid from his vassal, and for several weeks the Fulani were held at bay. Eventually, by

[1] Hassan and Shu'aibu, 1952, *A Chronicle of Abuja*, p. 5.

strategem, Musa seized the women and children of the townsmen, including the family of the Kajuru chief, and threatened to enslave them unless the Kajuru forces submitted. Makau and his Habe followers from Zaria then moved farther south. Musa then deposed the chief of Kajuru and appointed Jaye of Ricifa, the baSuleibe who had joined the invaders, to the Kajuru chieftainship as a vassal, resident at Kajuru. In this way Musa simultaneously sought to rid himself of Jaye and to control the Habe of Kajuru. Musa also rewarded the Sarkin Pawa of Likoro who had assisted him at Durum with the title of Sarkin Pawa of Zazzau, and appointed him to rule the fief of Hunkuyi.[1]

Musa sent detachments to Zuba after Makau, but the main Fulani forces were kept busy in the northern part of the kingdom, suppressing opposition in such towns as Haskiya, Gadas, Girku, Karigi, and among the Gwari of Kusheriki, who lost their vassal status at this time. Lapai surrendered and retained its vassal status. Meanwhile, Musa appointed deputies with flags of their own to extend the Fulani dominion southwards, and in this way the vassal states of Keffi, Jema'a, Doma, and later Kwotto were established. Under Musa, the Fulani of Zaria carried their attacks as far south as Wukari and the Tiv country. The Fulani of Kano sometimes sent cavalry to accompany these expeditions. Subjugation and conquest rather than enslavement was the object of these expeditions. When vassal chiefdoms had been established in these southern regions, the Fulani of Zaria ceased their incursions. The Fulani of Zaria were occupied next with expansion to east and west. The Gwari of Kuriga in the west were attacked, and in the east the vassal chieitainship of Lere was founded.

From the beginning relations between the Fulani of Zazzau and their southernmost vassals were somewhat strained. The leading Fulani of Jema'a and Keffi had set out to visit the Shehu at Sokoto, and to ask for flags of their own; they were turned back at Zaria by Mallam Musa who informed them that the Shehu had already given him these southern regions, and Musa then gave them flags of his own. Subsequently, when the Fulani chief of Keffi died, the

---

[1] Hunkuyi, Likoro, and Kudan were ancient Maguzawa (pagan Hausa) towns. It is possible that Durum also contained Maguzawa. Relations between these pagan Habe and their Muhammadan cousins have generally been strained. It is possible that the Maguzawa supported Musa in this northern district to square accounts with the Muhammadan Habe of Zaria, and that Musa did not receive much aid from the Muhammadan Habe themselves.

then king of Zaria sent his client, Makama Dogo, a Habe who had helped in the conquest of Karigi, Gadas, and Haskiya, to rule over Keffi. The Fulani of Keffi rejected Makama Dogo on two grounds: firstly, they claimed that the vassal chieftainship was hereditary, and that the succession had already been decided at Keffi by the local electors; secondly, as Fulani they bluntly refused to accept a Habe chief. The ruler of Zaria then told Makama to establish another vassal state at Kwotto, south-east of Keffi. Hostilities between Kwotto and Keffi occurred sporadically throughout the century, despite their common vassalage under Zazzau.

Initially, the Fulani of Zazzau also ruled over two southern vassals at Lapai and Lafia. Lafia lay to the north-east of Doma and near to Bagaji, another very minor vassal state of Zaria. Musa transferred Lafia to his neighbour Yakubu, the deputy of Dan Fodio who ruled Bauchi, as an act of solidarity.[1] Lapai sought its own transfer and requested the Fulani ruler of Bida to act as its overlord. The ruler of Bida informed his liege, the king of Gwandu, who was suzerain of the western states of the empire, and the king of Gwandu and the Sultan of Sokoto between them arranged for Lapai to be transferred from Zazzau to the Fulani of Bida as a vassal state.

These transfers show that Sokoto, Bauchi, and Zaria exercised coeval powers of redistributing vassal dependencies. Transfers of Lapai and Lafia to Bida and Bauchi did not alter their vassal status. Transfers changed relations between particular units without affecting the relative statuses of the units themselves. However, the duality of powers involved in these redispositions is revealing. An intermediate vassal such as Zazzau supervised his vassal chieftains and was supervised by his overlord. Under the terms of his own vassalship, the powers over his vassals which he exercised could also be exercised over them by his own suzerain. These ambiguities continued to affect relations between Zazzau and Sokoto throughout the century.

(b) Mallam Musa, 1804–21

Makau was accompanied by certain officials on his flight to Zuba. Among these were the Madawaki, the Galadima, the Wambai, the Chief Imam (Limamin Juma'a), the Salenke, Jarmai, Barde,

---

[1] It is possible that Musa received Lere in return. Bauchi legends attribute the conquest of Lere on the eastern border of Zazzau to Yakubu.

Magaji, Kuyambana, Magajin Mallam, the village chief of Gayen, the Kacalla, Iya, Sarauniya, Dangaladima, and certain other members of the king's family. It is also probable that the king's chamber eunuchs fled with him. Other Habe officials remained behind. Accordingly M. Musa on his arrival in Zaria found several Habe officials and native Fulani who were well acquainted with traditional patterns of government.

Musa's administration shows that he was well informed about this Habe system of government and its rules for the allocation of office; where traditional principles did not conflict with political or religious necessity he followed and maintained them. Thus Musa appointed his three daughters to the offices reserved by the Habe for the king's womenfolk; and he gave office to only two of his sons, Sidi Abdulkadiri being appointed Dangaladima, the traditional office of the chosen heir, and Zakari being installed as Magajin Gari, the traditional office of Magajin Dangi (head of the dynasty) being redundant, as there were no dynasties in Musa's reign. These were the only members of his kin appointed to office by Musa.

Excluding the new vassal states established during or after the *jihad*, Musa's departures from Habe principles of appointment to office were intended to bring the government more into line with Islamic norms as conceived by the Fulani reformers. Thus eunuchs were eliminated from certain offices such as Wombai, Galadima, Dallatu, Makama Karami, and Ma'aji. Musa also reduced the number and power of the household officials severely, transferring many of these offices to the territorial, fief-holding order, and allotting military duties to them while allowing other household offices to lapse. He also left several eunuch offices unfilled, and the few new offices which he instituted bear witness to his zeal for reform. Thus he established the office of the Alkali or Senior Judge, and separated judicial from administrative functions; he created the position of Waziri without territorial fiefs or military duties, and gave it to a mallam, Cafudu, whose role was to advise the king; he also established the new office of Sa'i to administer the nomad Fulani, to arrange for their help in war, to settle their disputes and collect the cattle-tax (*jangali*); finally, after an unsuccessful attempt at a palace revolt by a Fulani, Mallam Bagozeki, Musa established the new office of Sarkin Yaki, with control of the royal bodyguard. Otherwise, Musa was content to rule by means of the Habe official system, although he changed the principles governing official tenure and appointment, and redefined official roles.

Musa is credited with the order that *hakimai* should remain at the capital, thus separating them residentially from their fiefs. It is said that by this means he sought to reduce their opportunities for both rebellion and oppressive administration, but it is possible that he was merely following Habe practice. Musa's appointments to office included several Habe, mainly from Kano. It is possible that he preferred to reward important supporters who were born in Zaria by the grant of vassal status rather than fiefs. Thus the village chief of Durum was given vassal status, and Jaye of the Suleibawan Ricifa was appointed Sarkin Kajuru. Mai-gerke of Likoro was installed as Sarkin Pawan Zazzau with drumming on *tambari*, but was not given vassal status.

Musa also retained certain of Makau's eunuchs in office, notably the Turaki Babba, Ba'idu, and the Makama Babba, Sharubutu, who continued to represent the king in dividing the war-booty. Yamusa was appointed Madaki on instructions from the Shehu at Sokoto, Abdulkerim was made Sa'i, and Abdusallami of the Suleibawa was given the office of Makama Karami. In this way Musa sought to reward all his supporters with office, Fulani and Habe alike, and to associate them with him in the government.

Musa's religious interests are reflected in the composition of his council, which differed radically from that of the Habe. Musa had only one council, of which the Madaki, the Limam Juma'a, Iyan Kurama, Katuka, and Rubu were members, together with various mallams, such as M. Sogiji, M. Garba, M. Mamudu, and one Alhaji Musa, a pilgrim whom Musa had appointed as the *kofa* (supervisor, intermediary) between Zaria and the vassal state of Doma. Musa's determination to place the government in the hands of the religious leaders of the Muhammadan community is also evident in many other ways. He gave his daughter, the Iyan Zazzau, Atu, in marriage to the chief priest, Gabdo, a member of the Katsinawa 'yan Doto lineage. The office of Iya controlled many fiefs and the title-holder's husband had effective charge of these. In addition, Musa gave the Limam Juma'a several fiefs of his own and appointed him to supervise the new vassal state of Jema'a. Musa also tried to persuade Koranic scholars to accept territorial office. He was not always successful. Mallam Kilba, the head of the Suleibawa, refused such offers. At this period there were many Fulani mallams who, although quite willing to advise the ruler in council, refused to accept territorial appointments. Partly for this reason, the composition of Musa's council varied during his reign; but its official elements included Fulani and Habe, and no member of the ruler's family was a councillor.

Musa sought to ally himself by marriage with the principal Fulani groups interested in the government of Zaria. He gave his daughters in marriage to such important people as the Waziri of Sokoto, the Limamin Juma'a of Zaria, and to his Galadima, Dokaje, a Fulani from Tofa in Kano. Musa also allied himself by marriage with Abdulkerim, the leader of the Katsinawa. Between the Suleibawa and Bornawa there were already marriage alliances. By linking himself with the rulers of Sokoto, and with the family of Abdulkerim, Musa sought to extend and perpetuate relations of solidarity between his family and other powerful Fulani lines.

Musa also effected a distribution of land rights among the four leading Fulani lineages which took part in the conquest of Zaria. This distribution centred on the capital. The Katsinawa were allocated land to the west of Zaria city, the Bornawa and Suleibawa had the land to the south and east, while Musa's family held rights over land to the north, in the present district of Makarfi. Besides this, Musa allocated farm lands to each title of state. Much of this office-land lay close by the capital, on the site presently occupied by the European reservation and other new suburbs. Moreover, he redistributed the towns and villages of the kingdom as fiefs among his officials, allocating set portions of the tax and tribute collected therein as remuneration. In these ways, Musa rationalized the system of territorial administration and sought to limit the need and opportunities for extortionate rule. He also built the new outer walls of Zaria city, using slave labour. These walls are still impressive although they have not been repaired since 1900.

Musa's distribution of fiefs among titles left a good many rural areas under the king's direct control. Some of these units had formerly been administered by the throne; others had been attached to various offices; yet other of these areas, such as Kusheriki, were being incorporated within the kingdom by Musa's wars and were allocated to various titles later. In this way the throne became responsible for administering unattached settlements and also the fiefs of unfilled titles, during their vacancy. The royal agent who acted as *jekada* during such vacancy had the status of *mukaddashi* or deputy for the title-holder, while the tax or tribute went direct to the king. Subsequent rulers would sometimes keep important titles vacant for several years in order to increase their own income and power.

Musa's distribution of fiefs also established some other important principles. It implied the possibility of some redistribution in the future. However, the bases and forms of Musa's allocation imposed clear limits on the scope and character of future redistributions. Fiefs being attached to the titles, and these latter being appointive, this distribution ruled out the development of a hereditary feudalism, even in such marginal cases as the Magaji Jisambo, who lived at his 'capital', Jaji, and was normally recruited from a single lineage. An even more important implication of Musa's territorial reorganization was that no person who did not hold office could hold fiefs. Another important implication was that no individual could hold more than one title at any one time; this was implicit in the initial distribution of fiefs among the different titles and in the throne's administration of fiefs attached to vacant titles. Future increases in the number of titles governing fiefs thus depended on territorial expansion or on further creations of fiefs from the towns which remained at the king's disposal. This limitation imposed on the number of titles by the number of available fiefs was important later, when the expansion of royal ranks reduced the number of titles available to non-royals. During the Fulani century, some increase in fiefs occurred as a result of the kingdom's territorial expansion. Other increases arose as new towns were built in northern Zaria. Since all townships were fiefs or liable to be allocated as fiefs, the king's permission was necessary for their establishment. The throne's control of fiefs presupposed control over the siting and establishment of new settlements. As numerous slave-settlements were built under the Fulani, and as their establishment on the king's permission entailed continuing relations with the throne, the king's territorial jurisdiction was continually increasing; but when these new settlements outgrew exclusive private ownership they were generally allocated to officials as fiefs.

Musa was never crowned king of Zaria. Neither was his successor, Yamusa of the Bornawa. As deputies of the Shehu, and leaders in the Holy War, they retained the status of mallams throughout their reigns. In those days the ruler was saluted with the greeting appropriate to mallams, '*Allah, ya gafarta, malam*', (May God forgive you, Mallam), and never by the titles *Zaki* (lion), or the stock phrases appropriate for chiefs, '*Ranka ya dade*' (May your life be prolonged), '*Allah ya ba Sarki nasara*' (May God grant the king victory), '*Allah ya bai*', etc. During Musa's reign, therefore, the status of royalty was irrelevant and undefined. To this day the Fulani conqueror is referred to simply as 'Mallam'. The heavy representation of mallams on his council of state and the system of taxation are thus easy to understand.

The principal tax collected by Musa and Yamusa was the tithe of grain (*zakka*) which was due to them as mallams. During their reigns money formed no part of the tribute sent by Zaria to Sokoto. It is said that Sultan Bello of Sokoto, the son and successor of Dan Fodio, refused 5 *keso* of cowrie currency (about 100,000 shells) which was sent to him by Yamusa, commenting that each must be content with his own. This also seems to have been Musa's principle in providing his *hakimai* with farm lands and official compounds at Zaria city, and in allotting them large portions of the tax collected from their fiefs. The tribute which Zaria received from its vassals was divided between the ruler of Zaria and his officials responsible therefor.

This account of Musa's administrative methods and reforms enables us to see why and in what ways he departed from the practice of his Habe predecessors, and it also allows us to see how widely the régimes of his successors differed from his own. On Musa's appointment as his deputy by the Shehu, Yamusa had requested the southern half of Zazzau for his own kingdom, and it was on direct instructions from the Shehu that Musa had appointed the Bornawa leader to the office of Madaki, dismissing his first Madaki, Makaye, who was also the last person of non-royal status to hold that title at Zaria. In the early years of Fulani rule, Musa and Yamusa went on campaigns together; but once when Musa was away from the capital, Mallam Bagozeki tried to seize the throne; thereafter he remained at Zaria, while Yamusa took charge of the campaigns through which the Fulani dominion was extended and consolidated.

Despite Makau's flight, there was no single moment at which Fulani government could have been said to be established throughout the territory of Zazzau. After the capital had surrendered, its environs had to be subdued, and after the resistance in these areas had been overcome, other districts remained hostile. The process of consolidating Fulani dominion was moreover pro- longed and complicated by the territorial expansion of Zazzau itself. Campaigns to subdue outlying districts sometimes pene- trated into new areas and bypassed large populations, which were only subdued years after. Under Musa, Fulani consolidation and territorial expansion went hand in hand, and throughout most of the early years of his reign his rule rested on force and remained open to challenge by force. Later, when the Fulani of Zaria had consolidated their dominion up to the boundaries of its vassal states, the problem of kingship which was inherent in their organization became especially acute. But in the early years the ruler of Zazzau was leader of the Fulani rather than king, and the context of his government was a Holy war rather than a settled administration. If the boundaries, bases, and forms of the state were then fluid and difficult to define, so too was the system of government. Even the concept of royalty was undefined, its place being filled by that of the deputy of the Shehu. This is the type of situation, discussed by Max Weber, in which charisma has yet to be routinized; but in this instance its routinization could not pre- cede subjugation of the territory to which its administration applied.

Apart from Bagozeki, Musa's rivals among his allies included Yamusa and Jaye, both Fulani native to Zazzau supported by numerous kin. Musa had immobilized and isolated Jaye by ap- pointing him to the vassal chieftainship of Kajuru. At first Yamusa was controlled when Musa went on campaigns; but after Musa was forced to remain at the capital, Yamusa had a free hand, and in his successive raids, sieges, and punitive expeditions he amassed an enormous personal booty of slaves and proved himself the ablest general of the Zaria Fulani. In consequence, he acquired a position of overwhelming power within the state. Excluding the ruler himself, Yamusa had no rivals, and even during Musa's lifetime the government was identified with them both. It was the government of Musa and Yamusa rather than Musa alone. As indicated above, this was probably just the sort of government which Musa desired. It is clear from the composition of his council, and from his administrative reforms, that he did not wish an autocracy. His appointment of a Waziri without territorial duties as his principal adviser is one indication of his outlook. Another was the establishment of regular law-courts separate from that over which he presided. By his distribution of lands Musa had tried to assure the future prosperity of his family and those of his rivals. Having appointed his children to offices traditionally reserved for the ruler's family, he showed no further concern about the problem of his successor. Perhaps he regarded the succession as assured for his children. Perhaps he suspected that Sokoto had already promised it to Yamusa. The succession itself could hardly have had a definite meaning, there being then no kingship to succeed to, merely leadership, the character of which was pragmatic rather than formal, and which was specially open to functional evaluation during a period of continuing war and conquest. Whatever Musa's private opinions, his administration and official appointments showed that he expected the Fulani of Zaria to continue living in unity; that the loyal Muhammadan Habe would continue to take part in the government; that the influence of mallams would continue to govern policy formation; and that the Habe governmental forms would persist, with some modification to increase their simplicity, effectiveness, and accordance with Islam.

Musa's death changed the situation radically. It is interesting to speculate what might have followed if Yamusa had died before him; probably, the multi-dynastic system would have developed in any event, whichever of these leaders survived. But after Musa's death, the leading Fulani of Zaria without hesitation supported Yamusa's selection by the Galadima and the Limamin Juma'a who led the electoral council; and Sokoto, without attempting to crown Yamusa, recognized him as the ruler of Zazzau.

(c) Yamusa, 1821–34

Like Musa, Yamusa was never crowned king; he remained a mallam to the end of his days. But with his accession there were now two families of mallams with interests in the chief position of the state, Musa's and Yamusa's. Yamusa's appointments underlined and stimulated this rivalry; but as rivalry was implicit in this context, he may not have had much choice.

The new ruler first abolished the female tenure of such titles as Mardanni, Iya, and Magajiya, dismissing Musa's daughters from these positions and appointing his son Atiku to the title of Iya, and his brother Bapaiyo to the position of Magajin Gari in succession to Musa's son, Zakari, who was also dismissed. By dismissing Zakari from office Yamusa declared his political opposition to the Mallawa.

In imitation of Sokoto he instituted the new office of Wali with jurisdiction over administrative issues to prevent maladministration. Yamusa appointed Hamada, his eldest son, who had formerly been his senior lieutenant, with the title of Karfe, to the new office of Wali. Another son, Umoru, was appointed to the lowly title of Shentali, and another, Awaisu, was given the office of Sarkin Mai and put in charge of the Maguzawa of northern Zaria. Yamusa let lapse the Waziri office and that of the Sarkin Pawa. By these means he placed his kin in a dominant position within the official hierarchy.

These measures involved many important innovations. They were radical departures from the Habe patterns of appointment which Musa had followed. They asserted the ruler's appropriation of autocratic powers of appointment and dismissal. They showed that tenure of office would in future be governed by political considerations. They initiated new patterns by which a number of offices were distributed among the ruler's kin. They also opened the way for dynastic competition by means of official appointments.

Yamusa had no sooner begun to rule than his supremacy was challenged by Jaye, the baSuleibe whom Musa had appointed vassal chief of Kajura. Jaye demanded the key position of Madaki, from which Yamusa had himself succeeded to the throne. He openly threatened to fight if his demand was not granted. Yamusa had no alternative but to appoint Jaye Madaki, although he had intended to give his own son, Hamada, this office.

The broad outlines of the emerging political system were thus laid down by Yamusa. Its principal features at this time were simple: several families now had an interest in the supreme position; and their competition for leadership proceeded by competition for the critical title of Madaki, which carried command of the army. A third element, the progressive increase of offices held by members of the ruler's family, was also emerging. Thus the important administrative changes effected by Mallam Musa were matched by the far-reaching political developments which Yamusa initiated.

Under Yamusa, the administrative structure set up by Musa persisted. It was the political aspect of government which changed most sharply. Yamusa's council was a smaller unit than Musa's, with changing personnel; and there is reason to believe that his kinsmen provided another council, which, although lacking official

status, was politically influential. The trend was towards autocracy, and towards routinization of charisma on a multi-dynastic
basis; Jaye's rivalry for supremacy was itself a factor promoting
this development. By successive raids, sieges, and campaigns, the
kingdom's consolidation continued, the slave-settlements increased and the boundaries of the state hardened. On Jaye's
promotion to the Madakiship, the former ruling house of Kajuru
were reinstated as vassals of Zazzau in charge of Kajuru. Maliki,
another Fulani, at this time established his rule at Kagarko, as a
vassal of the ruler of Zaria. When Jaye died, Yamusa at once appointed his son Hamada to the Madakiship, giving the office of
Wali to a son of Gidado, the former Waziri of Sokoto. Another of
Yamusa's sons was appointed Dallatu, and after the death of
Sodengi, a Habe who was Musa's Wombai, Yamusa appointed
another of his own sons to this office also. Yamusa's sons now held
six major offices, including that of the Madaki. His brother was also
the Magajin Gari, who acted as the ruler's deputy in charge of the
state and remained at the capital during Yamusa's absences on
campaigns or visits to Sokoto. The stage was set for a series of
dramatic developments. Jaye's death during Yamusa's lifetime
had thrown open the issue of succession. Had Yamusa been the
first to die, there is no doubt that if Jaye had not succeeded him,
there would have been civil war. Yamusa kept Sokoto informed
about Jaye's behaviour through the Waziri who represented
Zazzau at the Sultan's court. Jaye's ambitions elicited little direct
support from the Suleibawa of Ibada under Audusallami. In effect,
Jaye was claiming rulership for his own branch of Suleibawa who
were settled at Ricifa; the other branch under Audusallami remained aloof from this competition, just as it had remained passive
when Jaye raised his unsuccessful rebellion against the former
Habe king. Thus Jaye's manoeuvres revealed the cleavages among
the Suleibawa. These internal divisions considerably reduced the
political efficacy of that lineage in the emerging dynastic tussle.
Meanwhile, two sons of Mallam Musa, Sidi Abdulkadiri and
Abubakar, held the offices of Dan Galadima and Iyan Kurama
respectively. This was the position when Yamusa died in 1834.

(d)　Abdulkerim, 1834–46

Yamusa's death posed the succession issue as a simple alternative, should the Bornawa or the Mallawa succeed? Of the Bornawa,

Hamada, Yamusa's eldest son, held the title of Madaki, and was the leading claimant. Of the Mallawa, Sidi Abdulkadiri, Mallam Musa's eldest son, was the Dan Galadima, and had the strongest claim. To appoint the Madaki as his father's successor would have furthered the trend towards unilineal absolutism initiated by Yamusa, by vesting the monarchy in one ruling house through dispossession of Musa's heirs. On the other hand, Sidi's well-known harshness was likely to exacerbate rivalries and tensions among the leading Fulani groups. The 'Limamin Juma'a and the Galadima, Dokaje, faced with these alternatives, decided to seek another way out. They recommended to the Waziri of Sokoto, that the Sa'i Abdulkerim should succeed Yamusa. The Limam and the Galadima knew that Sidi and Hamada were each more powerful than the Sa'i they had selected as king. But this recommendation, which was really an appeal for external power to stabilize the unity and leadership of Zazzau, had far-reaching consequences for the state.

By this decision ultimate powers of appointing the rulers of Zaria were thus transferred to the Sultan of Sokoto; and the way in which this transfer took place left the respective rights of Sokoto and Zaria ill-defined; such ambiguities were especially important for the future government of Zaria. Secondly, it led to the establishment of kingship at Zaria, since the Sultan of Sokoto could only declare his support or legitimate the new ruler by a formal installation at the traditional place for the coronation of Zaria's former Habe rulers. But the coronation of Abdulkerim also made explicit the royal status of his two predecessors in office. In effect this meant that the kingdom now contained three dynasties, the Bornawa, the Mallawa, and Abdulkerim's lineage. Appointment of Abdulkerim also left the door open for the emergence of yet other dynasties, since all of the three first Fulani rulers were drawn from different lineages. This in turn implied the virtual exclusion of Habe from eligibility for succession to the throne. Appeal to the Sultan also reduced the autonomy of Zazzau *vis-à-vis* Sokoto. Abdulkerim's accession further increased the intensity of political competition within the Fulani of Zaria, since the addition of a third dynasty threatened the others with less frequent appointment to office. Abdulkerim's accession also helped to institutionalize Yamusa's policy of appointing kinsmen, although the opposition to this practice had weakened Hamada's claim. The method of

Abdulkerim's appointment also redefined the area of political competition at Zaria to include Sokoto's decisive control of these issues. At the same time the Sultan's role in the selection of future kings greatly reduced the chances of open conflict among the contestants and their supporters, since successful *coups* would challenge the empire, including the neighbouring states of Bauchi, Kano, Katsina, and Sokoto itself; these were hopeless odds, considering Zaria's strategic position.

Finally, Abdulkerim's appointment indirectly emphasized the values of dynastic solidarity in the competition for the throne. Despite Hamada's pre-eminence among Bornawa candidates by virtue of his position as Madaki, Bornawa support was divided among a number of candidates all of whom were sons of Yamusa and had held important office. Likewise, the two principal Mallawa candidates, Sidi and Abubakar, were rivals for nomination. The Suleibawa were even more sharply divided between the kinsmen of Jaye at Ricifa, and those of Audusallami from the south. Of all the leading Fulani lineages, only Abdulkerim's was solidly ranged behind a single candidate.

Selection of Abdulkerim to succeed Yamusa appealed indirectly to the tradition of *mallamci* (religious learning and interests) which had been established at Zaria by Musa and Yamusa. Abdulkerim had been a leader in the conquest, while Sidi and Hamada belonged to a junior generation. Abdulkerim, who was popularly regarded as a *waliyi* (saint), could be relied on to preserve and strengthen the religious interests and elements in government. In fact, he immediately set about building the mosque at Zaria city with Gwari slave labour, and this mosque still stands to-day. His grave near the new town of Giwa in north-western Zaria remains a place of pilgrimage. His reputation as a *waliyi*, his seniority and his knowledge of the nomad Fulani groups in Zaria, helped to justify Abdulkerim's appointment, despite his political weakness.

Abdulkerim was himself quite aware of his weak position *vis-à-vis* the Bornawa and Mallawa. He privately sought advice from the Suleibawa king of Kano, Dabo, whose cavalry were then with the army of Zaria in the south. Dabo discussed the matter with his Galadima Ango, who commented cryptically that Abdulkerim could only remove his weakness by 'taking the left hand to beat back the right'. This advice was relayed to Abdulkerim who acted upon it promptly. He simultaneously dismissed Hamada and Sidi

Abdulkadiri from their offices of Madaki and Dan Galadima, and promoted Sidi's younger brother to the position of Madaki. By this stroke, Abdulkerim intended to set the Mallawa and Bornawa at odds with one another, and further to split the Mallawa between Abubakar and Sidi. By leaving Hamada's brother, Mommon Sani, in office as Wombai, Abdulkerim also hoped to divide Bornawa loyalties between Hamada and Mommon Sani. By eliminating his two rivals for the kingship from their offices, Abdulkerim further strengthened himself and asserted his kingship through the independent control of appointments to subordinate office. He followed up these changes by appointing his own son, Aliyu, to replace Yamusa's son in the office of Iya. The new ruler appointed his brother's son, Jamo, to the two offices of Sa'i and Magajin Gari simultaneously; his sister's son, Mai-Kurna, was made Galadima, and a son of the Sa'i Jamo was put in charge of the king's troops with the title of Sarkin Yaki; the king also appointed his brother, Mamudu, to the office of Salenke, and the office of Mardanni was given to a son of the Galadima Mai-Kurna.

These appointments followed the lines laid down by Yamusa, by which the king's kinsmen were given an undue share of the offices of state. At the same time Abdulkerim's appointments differed from Yamusa's in distributing office more widely among the king's agnatic and cognatic kin, while reducing the number of the king's sons who held titles. Abdulkerim's extension of the kinship range from which royal officials were drawn was perhaps designed to show his opposition to Yamusa's policy of appointments, although the number of the king's kinsmen in office was actually increasing. But perhaps Abdulkerim was unaware of the significance of territorial office in qualifying the sons of a king for future succession. Indeed, he could hardly have foreseen that this condition would limit the number of persons eligible for kingship, since his own accession tended to override precedents and emphasized the unpredictable elements in the succession at Zaria. By these appointments Abdulkerim clearly sought to strengthen himself and to weaken the Bornawa and Mallawa, and to this end he gave his kinsmen strategic positions such as Magajin Gari or Sarkin Yaki.

Hamada and Sidi, dismissed from office, sought to bury their rivalry, and tried to unite their lineages against their Katsinawa rivals. An agreement was reached by which Sidi and Hamada undertook not to compete for the throne against one another, and also to appoint the other's son to the position of Madaki whichever of them first became king. This unique effort to limit political competition for the throne was also intended to preserve the autonomy of Zazzau by reducing the power of Sokoto over the succession. Both Sidi and Hamada were naturally opposed to the Sultan's intervention in the elections of Zazzau. By this agreement they sought to establish the alternate succession of Bornawa and Mallawa monarchs. The agreement also sought to regulate political competition by administrative methods and rules. For this reason it was doomed to failure, despite the excellent intentions and ability of its negotiators. Indeed, for the kingship and the political system of which it was the axis, this remarkable agreement proved to be little short of calamitous, as we shall see.

Abdulkerim's accession represents one of the turning-points in the history of Fulani rule in Zaria. Although the consequences of this event were not fully evident for some years, it marked the end of Zaria's autonomy, as the Fulani of Zazzau were soon to discover. It was during this reign that the Waziri of Sokoto, who was the Sultan's *jekada* to Zaria, first demanded his own tribute, in addition to the *gandu* (tribute) of slaves, locust-bean, cloth, mats, and the like which was annually sent to the Sultan. As a mallam, the Waziri of Sokoto demanded grain, and the collection on his behalf was known ironically as *Bani, Bani* (give me, give me). At the same time, the tribute sent to Sokoto was increased to include money. Abdulkerim's authority over his vassals at Keffi and Kwotto was also reduced, when the Fulani of Keffi refused to accept Makama Dogo, a Habe, whom Abdulkerim had selected as their chief. The Fulani of Keffi had Sokoto's support and Abdulkerim was forced to accept this rebuff, appointing Dogo chief of Kwotto instead. This refusal by the Fulani of Keffi to accept a Habe ruler was part of a general trend to exclude Habe from important positions in the government of these conquest states, and corresponded with current trends in Zaria itself, as shown by the progressive reduction of Habe-filled offices in these reigns.

Abdulkerim himself did not go to war, and in his reign the southern dominions of Zazzau were less adequately controlled than before. During the latter years of Abdulkerim's reign the Sultan of Sokoto, Aliyu Babba, let it be known in Zaria through his Waziri that '*kurdin sarauta*' (money for the taking of office) was expected in future. *Kurdin sarauta* had not been paid under Fulani rule in Zaria before. Its institution opened the door to the use of money in the competition for kingship or other offices. Only at the lowest level were offices ever liable to direct or indirect sale; but officials guilty of maladministration did benefit from their donations (*gaisuwa*) to the king which this institution of *kurdin sarauta* encouraged and legitimized. In short, Sokoto's extension of authority over appointments simultaneously reduced the powers of kingship and saturated the administration with political factors.

(e) Hamada, 1846

Abdulkerim was succeeded by Hamada, the son of Yamusa, whom he had dismissed from the office of Madaki. Hamada reigned for only fifty-two days and then died. He therefore had little time in which to redistribute offices or to fulfil his agreement with Sidi. To reassert the internal autonomy of Zaria *vis-à-vis* Sokoto and symbolize it, Hamada refused to be crowned; and harking back to the context of Abdulkerim's accession, Hamada stressed his selection by the electors of Zazzau as the condition which legitimized his rule. Hamada's election showed that those sons of kings who had formerly held office but no longer did so, were just as eligible for the succession as those holding office when a king died. Hamada's accession also suggested that in future there would be only three dynasties in Zaria. When Hamada was succeeded by his half-brother, it seemed even more certain that competition for the throne would in future be limited to the three dynasties already established.

(f) Mommon Sani, 1846-60

Mommon Sani, Hamada's half-brother, was the son of Yamusa by a concubine. In choosing Sani to succeed Hamada the electors of Zaria again called on Sokoto for support. There is a story that Hamada had foretold his own death shortly after becoming king, and also that Mommon Sani would succeed him. Sani had held the title of Wombai without interruption from the reign of his father Yamusa. At Hamada's death he was the leading Bornawa claimant. His selection by the electors of Zaria reflected their fear of Sidi and local ideas of lineage rights in the throne. It was argued that another Bornawa leader should succeed Hamada, because the latter's reign had been unduly brief, and the Bornawa had not fulfilled their appointment to rule. On the other hand, this second appointment from the Bornawa dynasty was opposed by the Mallawa, and especially by Sidi, his agreement with Hamada having had as its aim the alternate appointment of Bornawa and Mallawa kings. Fearing Sidi's opposition, the electoral council again called on Sokoto, and the Waziri of Sokoto was sent to Zaria to crown Mommon Sani, who raised no objection, being aware of his dependence on Sokoto's support. Sidi remained at his slave-town Bassawa, in anger, but took no action. By Sani's accession Sokoto more than regained the influence it had lost over Zaria under Hamada.

Sani knew the details of Hamada's agreement with Sidi of the Mallawa; in view of Hamada's expectation that Sani would succeed him, it is probable that the two brothers had discussed this matter before Hamada's death. Shortly after his succession Sani began his redistribution of office by dismissing Sidi's half-brother Abubakar from the position of Madaki, and by giving that office to his own son. At the same time he reappointed Sidi Dan Galadima to mollify and neutralize him, and also to deepen the cleavages within the Mallawa dynasty. His own son, Umoru, Sani appointed Dallatu; his brothers, Bagemu and Doko, were made Iya and Wombai respectively, and in due course his agnatic first-cousin, Hamman, the son of Bapaiyo, Yamusa's brother, was reappointed Magajin Gari. First, however, Sani had to reduce the power of the Katsinawa. He dismissed Abdulkerim's son from the position of Iya, and at one stroke deprived Jamo of his dual titles of Magajin Gari and Sa'i. As already shown, under Musa's redefinition of *sarauta* as fief-holding office, it was improper as well as impolitic for one person to hold two offices. Abdulkerim had carefully exploited this element in the definition of office in order to strengthen himself *vis-à-vis* the Bornawa and Mallawa. For precisely this reason Mommon Sani could not allow Jamo to retain these two offices. Jamo's dismissal also evoked wide support for the ruler among the Fulani, being a restoration of original patterns and more in harmony with their political structure. Mommon Sani was the first Fulani ruler to make an appointment to the title Wan'ya which had remained vacant since the conquest; he also recognized the Fulani chief of Lere as a vassal of Zazzau, and created certain eunuch titles, such as Kasheka, for service within the royal household.

The new king busied himself with military campaigns, ravaging the Gwari and other tribes in the present emirate of Kontagora, an area which had not as yet been incorporated in the Fulani empire. He also forced the Kaje tribe in southern Zaria to submit, and render tribute. When his son Abdu, the Madaki, was killed by the Gwari at Gusoro, Sani gave this office to another of his sons. Sani also attacked the Habe of Abuja, whose king, Abu Ja, had just founded the town bearing his name. During these campaigns, the king gathered an immense booty of slaves, with which he established various *rumada*, the largest of which, Taban Sani, is said to have contained over 3,000 slaves.

In 1850 Buhari, a chief in Hadejia, on the eastern frontier of the Fulani empire, repudiated his allegiance to Sokoto, when the Sultan sought to appoint a rival as successor to the throne. Supported by the people of Hadejia, Buhari led the resistance against the forces sent by Sokoto. Together with Kano, Katsina, and Bauchi, Zaria sent several contingents to reconquer Hadejia for the Sultan. But the forces of Sokoto and its vassals failed to overthrow Buhari, their supply-lines being unduly long. None the less, this war with Hadejia demonstrated the strength of the imperial organization to its member states. It also showed that the Sultan's authority could be repudiated only by force.

The major administrative changes which took place during Mommon Sani's reign relate to taxation. The *kurdin kasa* was redefined as a tax on every hoe (*galma*) and was rated at 2,000 cowries.[1] Money was now remitted to Sokoto regularly with the tribute, and the *Bani-Bani* for the Wazirin Sokoto was also increased. In addition, the taxation of occupational groups, which had persisted in a very limited form from Habe times, was developed systematically. Besides the traditional taxes on dyepits and blacksmiths, taxes were levied on tanners, caravans, canoes, butchers, drummers, and other economic categories. The incidence of this taxation now began to increase and continued to do so steadily for the remainder of the century. It is said that the Sultan's pressure was responsible for this increased taxation. In Zaria, Mommon Sani even attempted to collect land-tax (*kurdin kasa*) from descendants of Mallam Musa and Abdulkerim, whose

---

[1] Cf. Barth, *op. cit.*, Vol. 1, p. 309, and footnotes to pp. 92, 94 of Ch. 4 above. Note that Barth reckons the land-tax in Zaria to be 500 cowries per small hoe (*fartanya*). Sani may have increased this tax after Barth visited Kano.

royal status had involved perpetual exemption (*hurumi*) from payment of tax. This innovation provoked hostility and was probably
abandoned. With this increased taxation and tribute, his extensive
slave-raids and slave-farming, and *zakka* (grain-tithe), Mommon
Sani was probably the richest of the Fulani rulers of Zaria. It is
said that the third share of this king's grain which was inherited
by his immediate successors to the throne lasted them for eleven
years; and also that he owned 9,000 slaves at his death, of which
3,000 went to the Sultan, 3,000 to the dead ruler's family, and the
rest to his successor in office. Whatever the element of hyperbole
in these assessments, it seems clear that during the period covered
by Sani's reign at Zaria, and by Aliyu Babba's sultanate at Sokoto,
the Fulani empire lost some of its early religious dedication and
began to be regarded as a source of revenue for its rulers. The
system of occupational taxation introduced in the years between
1846 and 1860 perhaps expresses this change of imperial attitudes
most clearly.

    In the northern kingdom of Kano the effect of this innovation
was immediate. Certain Habe mallams of Tsokuwa in south-
eastern Kano who until then had accepted Fulani rule on religious
grounds, now turned against it bitterly and fled to nearby pagan
areas on the northern borders of Bauchi. There they found pagan
tribesmen eager to avenge the slave-raids they had suffered. Their
superior military knowledge made it easy for these Habe of Kano
to exercise leadership over some of these tribes, and their hostility
to Fulani rule encouraged them to direct these tribal armies against
the two nearby kingdoms of Kano and Zaria. Over the following
thirty years these attacks on Kano and Zaria continued to increase
in their severity and range.

    In Zaria itself, the occupational tax-collectors were almost all
Habe, these being the craftsmen and traders of the kingdom; but
although Habe were incorporated in the government through these
occupational offices, the novelty and scale of the taxation itself,
and the opportunities for exploitation with which it presented the
new officials, alienated many of the Habe, at whom this taxation
was directed. At the same time the establishment of the order of
occupational tax-gatherers concluded the redefinition of Habe-
Fulani status relations. Thereafter the senior offices administering
fiefs were mainly reserved for Fulani, and the Habe could only look
forward to official appointment within this new order of occupa-

tional tax-gatherers. Of course, this rule had exceptions. Some Habe families continued to fill such titles as Katuka, and Habe occasionally held one or two other offices. Some decades later the most powerful man in the kingdom was a Habe official. But being exceptions, these cases only served to underline further the status differences between Fulani and Habe.

(g) Sidi Abdulkadiri, 1860

Mommon Sani's death marked another turning-point in the history of Fulani Zazzau. In Sani's reign the Fulani of Sokoto had considerably increased their influence over affairs at Zaria. Sani's successor was Sidi, who had been made to wait almost forty years before succeeding his father, Mallam Musa, to the throne, and Sidi had therefore little cause to love Sokoto.

Sidi's mother's brother, the Limamin Juma'a, of the Katsinawa 'yan Doto, was his champion in the electoral council of Zazzau. The council had a real choice only between Sidi and his brother Abubakar, since the Bornawa were now ineligible due to the successive appointments of Hamada and Mommon Sani to the throne, while the Katsinawa were weak and leaderless.

There was clearly no chance that the succession could now be confined to one dynasty only; such redefinition of royalty would have been acceptable neither at Zaria nor at Sokoto. At Zaria, it would have meant a monodynastic autocracy, and at this time the ruling dynasty could only have been Bornawa. However, the increasing taxation of Sani's reign had disturbed the people, who were now afraid of overwhelming royal power and its unilineal transmission. The selection of yet another Bornawa to rule Zaria would also provoke the Mallawa and Katsinawa who had equal claims to the throne. Sokoto could be relied on to reject such a nomination; and after the accession of Mommon Sani, Sokoto exercised a decisive influence on the appointment of Zaria kings. It was in this context that the electoral council of Zaria selected Sidi Abdulkadiri to rule, informing the Sultan of Sokoto of their choice.

Sidi's rule was brief but dynamic. His first act was to appoint Abdullahi, the son of Hamada, to the Madakiship, thereby fulfilling his agreement with the dead king, and seeking Bornawa support against his own brother, Abubakar. Next, he appointed another son of Hamada to the title of Dan Galadima made vacant by his own accession. His wife's brother, Aliyu, the son of Abdul-kerim, was reappointed Iya; and after dismissing Hamman, the son of Bapaiyo, Yamusa's brother, from the office of Magajin Gari, Sidi appointed his uncle, Jemari, a Fulani of Joli, whose sister, Aminatu, had been a wife of Mallam Musa. Thus Sidi made no appointment to important office from the members of his own dynasty.

His brothers at once reacted. Abubakar, accompanied by half of the Mallawa lineage, their slaves, and some supporters, withdrew to Sokoto and complained to the Sultan that Sidi intended to destroy his own dynasty, the Mallawa, and preferred his traditional rivals, the Bornawa and the Katsinawa, to his own kin. Another of Sidi's brothers, Muhammadu Baki, collected a force of cavalry and set out to attack the ruler in Zaria city. The Sultan ordered the Waziri to visit Zaria at once.

Meanwhile Sidi was busy on several fronts. He despatched one force under his half-brother Ali to exact allegiance and tribute from all communities between Zaria city and the boundaries of Nupe emirate. Ali held no office on appointment to this command. Sidi next suppressed the revolt led by his brother Muhammadu Baki and duly imprisoned him. He then sent his Makama Audusal-lami, the baSuleibe whom Musa had appointed to that office over forty years before, to raid Kwotto and collect its overdue tribute. He showed his severity by ordering the execution of two men for theft, although one of them was his own client.[1] Another, a slave formerly belonging to Mommon Sani, was executed for having insulted Sidi after his previous dismissal from office. These were minor flourishes.

Shortly after Sidi's accession, the vassal chief of Durum died. It will be recalled that Mallam Musa had created this chieftainship to reward the people of Durum for their aid during his invasion. The dead chief of Durum left several heirs, one of whom the ruler of Zaria had to choose as the new chief. Sidi had other ideas. He removed the *tambari* which were the insignia of Durum's hereditary status of vassal chieftainship, and appointed his son, Nuhu, to administer it as a fief. Nuhu was thus put in charge of a fief, although he held no title; moreover the unit which now formed the

---

[1] In their severity these sentences exceeded the punishment prescribed by the law (*shari'a*) for theft, and thus suggested that Sidi was not always be willing to abide by the law.

fief had formerly been a hereditary vassal chieftainship. Sidi may have been imitating a practice which had grown up at Sokoto under which the Sultan's sons administered fiefs, often without holding office. I am as yet unfamiliar with the details of state organization at Sokoto during this period; but such practice was clearly incompatible with the concept of *sarauta* on which the government of Zaria was based. All offices of Fulani Zaria did not involve administration of fiefs, but all fiefs were administered there through territorial office (*sarautar hakimai*). Thus at Zaria the administration of fiefs by unofficial persons was defined as illegitimate.

Territorial administration through fief-holding office involved a fairly definite organization of official rights, duties, and relations to the fief, to other offices and to the ruler. The addition of unofficial fief-holders was incompatible with this existing official structure, despite the variety of forms such unofficial fief-administration may have taken. If the rights and duties of unofficial fief-holders were identical with those of official appointees, then their relations with the king, the fief, and other fief-holders would also be identical, hence official appointments and the official structure would become indistinguishable from the unofficial system, and with redundancy would lose significance. On the other hand, if the administration of fiefs by unofficial appointees differed from that of officials in any way, this would promote a competition of the differing systems of territorial administration to the disadvantage of either. In either event, therefore, such innovations endangered the unity and form of the state.

It is possible that when Sidi gave Nuhu the fief of Durum, he remembered how Alhaji Musa had acted as *kofa* (intermediary) between Keffi and Sidi's father, Mallam Musa. But apart from the different circumstances of government in 1810 and 1860, the relations involved in these two situations were also quite different. The differences between Zazzau in Musa's and Sidi's day were differences between a conquest in process, and its consolidation as a state. When Musa gave Audu Zanga his flag with instructions to make Keffi know the will of Allah, neither Musa nor Audu Zanga were kings, and neither of them administered governments with settled forms or boundaries. As mallams, it was quite appropriate for them to communicate through a pilgrim, himself a mallam. But the kingdom over which Sidi ruled had long since been established with set governmental forms, procedures, and relations.

In the Fulani government of 1860, differences between the *hakimi* (fief-holder) and the *kofa* or *jekada* were familiar and clear. The *hakimi* administered a fief and controlled appointments within it, could levy what he willed, and could requisition troops therefrom and adjudicated certain issues. The *kofa* (door) was a channel of communication between overlord and vassal, neither of whom could make appointments in the other's domain, nor levy taxes, nor raise forces, nor adjudicate issues of first instance or the like. The *jekada* was a messenger, the agent of the office-holder who employed him to administer particular localities or functions. A *hakimi* administered his fiefs through his *jekada*, and the *jekada* as agent of the *hakimi* exercised an authority sanctioned by the *hakimi*. No authority was inherent in the office of the *kofa*. Alhaji Musa had been merely a channel through whom Mallam Musa and his vassal at Keffi communicated. But Nuhu, on his appointment to Durum, had been given the power of a *hakimi* without any of the limits or responsibilities which *hakimai* were obliged to respect. In short, Sidi's innovation implied or involved radical redefinitions of the concept of office, and foreshadowed the replacement of the current governmental system by *ad hoc* commissions to unofficial agents patrimonially recruited by the ruler.

It is perhaps for this reason that Nuhu's appointment remained unique in the history of Fulani Zazzau.[1] Abdulkerim had appointed one man to hold two offices simultaneously. This was incompatible with the notion of offices as exclusive corporations, and was duly revoked. But Abdulkerim's example was twice repeated in the following decades. That of Sidi Abdulkadiri was not, perhaps because such repetition would have destroyed the concepts and hierarchies of office which were basic to the state organization. Especially in this multidynastic political system would the state and its administration lack firm foundations if the ruler was free to give fiefs to his kin and supporters without

---

[1] As already mentioned, Sidi had sent his kinsman, Ali, with an army southwest to the Niger. Like Nuhu, Ali held no office, but held his authority by an *ad hoc* commission from the ruler. Ali's appointment like Nuhu's conflicted with the current concept of office at Fulani Zaria. By Mallam Musa's reforms, military leadership had been identified with office, and the command of an army or campaign was reserved for senior territorial officials. By giving Ali command of an army before appointing him to office, Sidi indicated that office no longer carried exclusive rights of command. With little modification, the analysis of Nuhu's appointment applies also to Ali's, and for this reason these two appointments may be treated together.

defining their powers or duties and responsibility in the standard terms of an office. Such unofficial administrations would either be challenged or imitated by other dynasties, and in either event conflict and disorganization was likely.[1]

Sidi's treatment of Durum has another lesson. This consists in the power by which Sidi, as ruler of Zazzau, abrogated Durum's vassal status, and terminated its hereditary chieftainship. The resulting redefinition of Durum's position was not a relative but an absolute change from the status of vassal chieftainship to that of a fief, ruled by appointees, official or other. The history of Fulani Zaria provided no precedent for such an action; nor could this action be legitimate by the traditional pattern of relations between vassal and lord, since these relations stressed their mutual solidarity, loyalty, and respect of one another's rights. Sidi's action was as naked a demonstration of superior power as it was a rejection of authority and tradition. It redefined the status and relations of Durum and Zazzau through the exercise of power by defying authority. The lessons of Durum were well learnt by the other vassals of Zaria, whose security and independence were thereby questioned; they were also learnt by the Sultan of Sokoto.

Sidi also revived the office of Waziri, which had remained vacant since Musa's death. It is said that one reason for this revival was to show Sokoto that the government of Zaria had an equal and independent status, by emphasizing its parallel form. Sidi may have remembered the *yakin Buhari* (the war with Buhari) which ended in Sokoto's defeat and Hadejia's independence.

This was the situation in Zaria when the Waziri of Sokoto arrived. Sidi forbade the Waziri to enter Zaria city and ordered him to remain at Gimi, about ten miles away. At this, some of the king's supporters began to express anxiety. Sidi was unperturbed. Like Hamada, he did not intend to allow the Waziri of Sokoto to crown him, and he may also have contemplated repudiating allegiance to Sokoto. He also did not intend to allow the Wazirin

---

[1] It will be recalled that Yamusa refused to make further appointments to the title of Sarkin Pawan Zazzau, to which Mallam Musa had appointed Mai-Gerke with an installation which included the drumming on *tambari*. But Mai-Gerke did not thereby receive vassal status. He ruled Hunkuyi as a fief, and his title, Chief of the Butchers of Zazzau, was an office of the state of Zazzau, not the chieftainship of a separate state. Thus Yamusa's decision to let this title lapse was not strictly comparable with Sidi's treatment of Durum. Fief-holding titles can be kept vacant until they lapse, but vassal chieftainship cannot. It is a continuous office and can only be terminated by abrogation or conquest.

Sokoto to collect his *Bani Bani*. When the Waziri sent, in the Sultan's name, to ask Sidi the reasons for Abubakar's flight and Muhummadu Baki's imprisonment, and for Sidi's attack on Kwotto, he was told these were not Sokoto's affairs. '*Sarauta, na gaje shi*' ('I have inherited my office, i.e. the kingship'). If this was not a repudiation of allegiance to Sokoto, it was certainly a clear declara- tion of Zazzau's internal autonomy, and an equally clear denial of the Sultan's authority in future elections of Zaria's rulers. The Waziri returned post-haste to Sokoto, and the Sultan sent a messenger to summon Sidi. Sidi went, was declared deposed, and was kept at Wurno, the capital of Sokoto, until his death.

It seems clear that Sidi was informed about the Sultan's dis- pleasure before he set out for Sokoto. Yet it is unlikely that he either contemplated his own deposition or could have resisted even if he stayed in Zaria. Until this date, no king of Zaria had ever been deposed. Nor had Zaria ever deposed its own vassals. Even the concept of deposition was unfamiliar. But Sidi had alienated his own lineage, his vassals, and his *hakimai*, by imprisoning Muham- madu Baki, by giving Ali command of the army, and by his treatment of Durum. His unusually harsh sentences in court had also frightened many, and his armies were absent from Zaria, one force being in the west with Ali, his brother, while the other was in the south with Audusallami, his Makama. Thus beside his lack of political support, Sidi was also without military force at the moment. He was therefore in no position to resist openly and in- vite an immediate war. Negotiation may have seemed the prefer- able course. He therefore went to Sokoto.

(h) *Audusallami, 1860–63*

Sidi's deposition emphasized the power of Sokoto over Zaria. Sidi had challenged the Sultan and failed, without even fighting. His deposition created yet another situation in which Sokoto's power was necessary to stabilize the government of Zaria; and in this situation the stabilizing power could be freely exercised. As usual, the succession provided the critical issue. Even had they wished, the Fulani of Zaria could do nothing to prevent Sidi's deposition. His removal to Sokoto left them leaderless, and there could be no resistance to Sokoto without a leader. On the other hand, there could be no new leader without action by Sokoto.

To appoint Abubakar of the Mallawa as Sidi's successor was out of the question; such an appointment would appear to sanction future rivalry within individual dynasties, as well as between them; it would also suggest that deposition would be followed by another appointment from the same dynasty. Thus, both in dismissing Sidi and in refusing to appoint his brother, Sokoto showed that it regarded the dynasties as the basic political organs of Zaria, whose separate unity were essential to the preservation of the state itself. Sokoto was also sensitive to the threats of repudiated allegiance which were implicit in Sidi's actions; and, perhaps remembering the *Yakin Buhari*, the Sultan may have sensed that if the three Zaria dynasties ever joined to challenge Sokoto's control, it would be difficult to overawe or overpower them. On their part too, the dynasties of Zaria had begun to appreciate that the Sultan's suzerainty was essential for the continuity of their political system. There was a genuine fear of unilineal autocracy at Zaria; and Sidi's reign had increased this fear in various ways.

Sidi had reigned for less than a year; and his deposition had occurred in a manner which left Sokoto in control of all his property, his slaves, cattle, and other movables. The ex-king was still alive, and his estate could not therefore be inherited. But the distribution of this estate raised many problems. It could not be left ownerless, since it consisted mainly of slaves for whose behaviour or support none would then be responsible. Moreover, Sidi's estate was then the largest unit of property in Zazzau. It could not be simply turned over to the Bornawa, whose last king, Mommon Sani, had contributed so handsomely to its formation. Nor could it be transferred to Sidi at Sokoto, since this would establish an awkward precedent and may have enabled him to return to Zazzau. Nor could it be turned over to his brother, Abubakar, since this would seem to reward intrigue, and the idea of such rewards for intra-dynastic rivalry might easily destroy the dynasties themselves. The only possible course was to divide the deposed ruler's estate equally between the Sultan of Sokoto as the overlord, and the next king of Zaria.

The problem of Sidi's estate was intimately related to the problem of the succession itself. If Abubakar of the Mallawa was unsuitable as a successor to his brother, Sidi, the Bornawa candidates were even more unsuitable. An immediate resumption of Bornawa dominion could have continued the trend towards a unilineal autocracy, which Sokoto and Zaria sought to avoid. Moreover, in 1860 there was no pre-eminent leader among the Bornawa. It is true that Sidi had appointed Abdullahi, the son of Hamada, to the Madakiship; but Abdullahi was then quite young and Sidi had placed all the troops commanded by Madaki under his own son Ali, for the western campaign. In this way Sidi had tried to empty the Madaki office of its power and meaning, and so to destroy the current structure of government. Thus Abdullahi had been Madaki in name only, and that for less than a year. But apart from Abdullahi, the Bornawa were divided among a number of Yamusa's sons or descendants, such as the Iya Atiku, Dan Galadima Ibiru, and Wombai Doko, all of roughly equal political status. Appointment of either of these men was as likely to split the Bornawa into rival segments as to increase their power. Thus both the Bornawa and the Mallawa candidates were unsuitable for immediate succession. This left only the Katsinawa, whose sole eligible candidate, the acting Iya Aliyu, was married to Sidi's full sister; but Aliyu could not be appointed to succeed Sidi in view of the Katsinawa's political weakness.

Apart from the difficulty of finding a suitable successor, the election of the new king was also a problem. Sidi's deposition had created a situation without precedent in the previous history of Zazzau; and the manner in which it had occurred gave special urgency to his successor's appointment, and also revived the question of the rights of the electoral council of Zazzau and the Sultan of Sokoto in selecting the new king. This simply restated the old problem of the autonomy of the vassal state. Rather than raise this question under conditions which invited opposition from Zaria, Sokoto decided to interpret the situation created by Sidi's deposition in the way most favourable to its own power and interests. Thus Sokoto arrogated to itself the power to select Sidi's successor. To ensure the new king's dependence and increase its own control over Zaria, Sokoto chose as king Audusallami of the Suleibawa of Ibada, who was on his way back to Zaria from Kwotto at the head of an army.

To the Fulani of Zaria, Audusallami's appointment indicated that Sokoto rejected those hereditary restrictions which they themselves accepted as conditions of eligibility for the throne. Audusallami's appointment also indicated that Sokoto would not admit Sidi's claims of internal autonomy for Zazzau. Autonomy was a question which could only be settled on the basis of power; but as we have seen, this power was not reducible to military force. To give the Sultan's suzerainty formal expression, the Waziri of Sokoto installed Audusallami as king by a ceremony in Zaria city. By the time Sidi's brother, Ali, had returned from his expedition, Audusallami was already king, and there was nothing that Ali could do except to hand over his command and booty to the new ruler.

Audusallami's succession is currently rationalized in Zaria in terms of his religious character and age. Of all the officials in 1860, he was the only one then alive who had seen the Shehu face to face and knew him well. Such an interpretation indirectly approves Audusallami's appointment as a return to the lost charisma and moral fervour of the *jihad*. In fact, Audusallami's selection was governed by two factors: Sokoto needed a weak king in Zaria, through whom they could recover the influence lost to Sidi; secondly, in order to suppress the theory of dynastic succession and political autonomy expressed by Sidi, Sokoto wanted a king whose lineage had not yet held the throne. Audusallami fulfilled these conditions.

The Suleibawa of Zaria were divided between the lineage of Jaye at Ricifa, and the segment at Ibada to which Audusallami belonged. Thus the new king lacked support even within his own dynasty. In consequence, he made very few changes in official appointments, other than those suggested by Sokoto. At the Sultan's request, the Bornawa Wombai Doko was replaced by Sidi's brother, Abubakar, and the Mallawa who had fled to Sokoto with Abubakar were sent back to Zaria. On the death of the Galadima, Audusallami appointed Hamman, the son of Yamusa's brother, Bapaiyo and a former Magajin Gari, to this office, to reassure the Bornawa of his neutrality. The Madaki Abdullahi, Hamada's son, continued in office, and Malle, the son of Jaye and leader of the Suleibawan Ricifa, was appointed as Dallatu in an effort to enlist their support. But Audusallami's appointment of Abubakar to the office of Wombai further extended Sokoto's power in Zazzau. This was the first occasion since Musa's reign in which Sokoto directly influenced the allocation of subordinate offices at Zaria. The new precedent was followed later with dire results.

Audusallami's rule was brief, and insignificant in itself. With his accession the number of dynasties in Zaria was increased to four. This was to remain the maximum. Audusallami was killed in action at Munku. According to local tradition he was shot by a client of the acting Sarkin Fada, who desired Abdullahi's succession. Shortly before this assassination, Audusallami had given further indication of his subservience to Sokoto by postponing the division of booty until the army had returned to the capital, on their suggestion.

The most important actions taken by Audusallami were reversals of Sidi's innovations. Thus Durum was taken away from Nuhu; the army under Ali was returned to its legitimate commander, the Madaki; and the office of Waziri was disestablished. Sidi's experimental revision of the government was quite erased. By revoking unofficial allocations of authority, Audusallami sought to preserve the *sarautu* as the only legitimate organs of government. He appointed as chief of Durum a son of the former chief, but did not re-establish Durum as a vassal chieftainship, attaching it to the crown instead as a royal domain, with its own hereditary line of community chiefs. Likewise he disbanded Ali's troops, giving him two-fifths of the booty as was due to the leader of such an expedition. Ali's portion was large enough to enable him to build his own *rinji* at Ifira near Rigachikum, along the route he had travelled. Following its disestablishment by Audusallami the office of Waziri remained vacant until the British arrived.

The reign and assassination of Audusallami brought the formative period of the development of Fulani government at Zaria to an end. The political system of Zaria now contained four competing dynasties, and the state maintained uneasy relations with its vassals on the one hand and its suzerain on the other. Its administrative structure was clearly based on territorial office, and political considerations governed appointments to office and its exercise. The territory of Zazzau had by then reached its furthest limits, and the organs, forms, and content of political and administrative action were definite and familiar. By 1863 the conditions and forms of legitimacy were also well defined; and under Sokoto's supervision, the continuity of the state seemed assured. In the subsequent thirty-seven years of Fulani rule, this framework of government persisted, despite a variety of pressures for changes of one sort or another; but the simple persistence of this system involved its continual development.

(i) Abdullahi, 1863-73

The Mallawa still being discredited by the events of Sidi's reign, and the Katsinawa being as weak in 1863 as they were three years before, only the Bornawa could furnish a successor to Audusallami. Of the Bornawa candidates, the Madaki Audullahi, who was the son of Hamada, and had demonstrated his ability during the preceding reign, was clearly the strongest candidate. The electoral council of Zaria recommended Abdullahi's succession, and the Sultan of Sokoto agreed, sending his Waziri to crown Abdullahi at Zaria. On his appointment the new king was instructed that the Sultan expected the Mallawa candidate Abubakar to retain the office of Wombai. Abdullahi had to accept this; but to nullify and isolate Abubakar he redistributed most of the other important offices among the Bornawa and their closest supporters.

The king promoted his brother Ibiru from the position of Dan Galadima to that of Madaki, which his own accession had made vacant. Ibiru died shortly after, and Abdullahi made his own son, Yero, Madaki. He gave Husseini, another of his sons, the office of Dan Galadima. He removed Sidi's Magajin Gari, Jembari, from that office, appointing his own wife's elder brother, a *suruki*, in his stead. The king appointed his paternal uncle, Dan Kakai, to the position of Wali. Hamman, the son of Yamusa's brother, was still Galadima. The former eunuch office of Fagaci which had long been vacant was given to a Fulani client. Aliyu, a grandson of Hamada, was appointed Mardanni, and Ja'afaru, one of the ruler's sons, was appointed Makama Karami. Abdullahi appointed his mother's brother to the office of Sa'i, and after the latter's death he gave the office to this mother's brother's son, Habu, a joking relation (*abokin wasa*). These appointments gave the ruler undisputed control of the government, and also restored the patterns of appointment initiated by Yamusa and developed by Mommon Sani.

Abdullahi allowed the Katsinawa candidate, Aliyu, to retain the office of Iya, either to enlist their support for his rule or to identify them with that office, and thus indirectly to reduce their claims for the throne. When this Katsinawa Iya Aliyu died shortly after, Abdullahi appointed Aliyu's son, Abdurrahman (also called Abdurrahul), to succeed him. Yaji, another of the Bornawa, who was Abdullahi's grandson by his son, the Makama Ja'afaru, was given

the title of Sarkin Ruwa. This was the first time that any member
of a dynasty had held this office. On the death of the Suleibawa
Dallatu Malle, Abdullahi appointed his own ortho-cousin, Mallam, the son of Iya Atiku, in his place. Abdullahi then dismissed
the Galadima Hamman on grounds of old age, and appointed
Adamu instead. Adamu's father had been Musa's Galadima, and
his brother was married to Abdullahi's daughter.

It will be clear from this summary that Abdullahi used the
king's power of appointment quite deliberately as a political
instrument to strengthen himself. His appointees to administrative
office were bound to him by common political interests and by
ties of kinship or clientage, and were correspondingly opposed to
his rivals and their supporters. With this sort of official structure
under his control, Abdullahi's rule could not easily be challenged
in Zaria. He was thus free to attend to other matters, which he
did, to his own undoing.

Sidi's attack on Kwotto had disturbed the balance of power
among Zaria's southern vassals by reducing the power of Kwotto
relative to that of Keffi. During Audusallami's reign, the Habe of
Abuja, under their king Abu Kwakwa (1851–77) made frequent
incursions into the southernmost districts of Zaria, raiding caravans and slaves. Ningi attacks on the eastern districts of Zaria were
also increasing in strength. Abdullahi sought to strengthen the
eastern vassal state of Lere and restore order in the southern
territories. Taxation within Zaria was increased, and tribute was
demanded from Keffi, which had fallen behind in its payments.
The Kaje, Chawai, Katab, and Gwari of southern Zaria were controlled by the appointment of Tatumare, an Ikulu convert to
Islam, to the military office of Kuyambana, which commanded
the *lifidi* (heavy-armed cavalry). Tatumare knew these districts
intimately from boyhood, and with the help of Sarkin Kauru and
Sarkin Kajuru, whose dominions bordered on the Ikulu and
Kamantan, was able to secure more regular payment of tribute
from these southern tribes.

Abdullahi next turned his attention to Keffi, and himself led an
army to subdue its vassal chief and exact the overdue tribute.
Yamusa, the chief of Keffi, asked the Sultan to call off Abdullahi's
army. Abdullahi was unable to fight a decisive engagement with the
forces of Keffi. Although Sokoto sent thrice ordering him to
withdraw, Abdullahi still continued his attacks on Keffi, and re-

plied to the Sultan that Zaria's dealings with its vassals were not Sokoto's affair. None the less, Abdullahi set out to visit the Sultan during the dry season of 1873, when the rulers of the principal kingdoms habitually went to Sokoto to deliver tribute, render homage, and to consult with the Sultan on matters of common concern. On a previous visit Abdullahi had been asked by the Sultan to secure the return to Sokoto of one of the Sultan's sons who had fled to Doma, the vassal state of Zaria, south-east of Keffi. Another matter of some general interest at this time was the establishment of the kingdom of Kontagora in the dominions under Gwandu by another member of the Sultan's lineage. Kontagora kingdom was then expanding by conquest and devastation in the Gwari lands west of Zaria and north of Nupe. Abdullahi may have intended to discuss these or similar matters at the Sultan's court.

However, at Sokoto Abdullahi was told that the Sultan had deposed him for refusing to obey his instructions regarding Keffi. Abdullahi's revival of Sidi's claim for autonomy may have been another ground for his deposition. Abdullahi was deposed without any formal indictment or trial, perhaps because the issue of autonomy was not one which could profitably be argued at law, although the issue of disobedience (*kin umurci*) may have been. It is Sokoto's refusal to depose Abdullahi by legal process which suggests that his claim for autonomy was an important reason for his deposition as well as his disobedience.

(j) Abubakar, 1873–76

Sokoto followed the precedent created on Sidi's deposition, and itself decided the succession of Zaria without consulting the local electoral council. Abubakar of the Mallawa was selected to succeed Abdullahi. Abubakar's experience at the hands of Sidi seemed to give him a claim for compensatory treatment. Since his return to Zaria, with the Sultan's support, Abubakar had retained the important office of Wombai under both Audusallami and Abdullahi, and it is even possible that he may have been promised the succession by Sokoto years before. Abubakar was the leading Mallawa candidate, and the deposition of their kinsman made the Bornawa candidates ineligible to succeed him. The leading Katsinawa candidate was then Iya Abdurrahul, whose father had not been king. It is possible that the rulers of Sokoto were first led to formulate the rule of immediate descent from previous kings as a condition of eligibility for the throne by consideration of Iya Abdurrahul's claims. The Suleibawa, consequent on their long exclusion from office, also lacked candidates qualified by tenure of territorial office as well as direct descent from a king. Abubakar was perhaps the only available choice.

As one of the Mallawa, Abubakar was free to share in Abdullahi's estate without this inheritance disrupting his dynasty and without precedent created in the transmission of Sidi's estate being upset. Half of Abdullahi's estate went to the Sultan and the new king received the remainder. Abdullahi's childless concubines were likewise distributed. Ali, the half-brother of Sidi, acquired some of Abdullahi's concubines from Abubakar. The new king also distributed some of his predecessor's estate to the ex-Galadima, Hamman. The legitimacy of these distributions was challenged later on the grounds that Abdullahi had been deposed without due process of law.

The Mallawa have never recovered from the clash between Abubakar and Sidi, the two most powerful of Mallam Musa's sons. To this day, Mallawa lands and slave-estates are divided. Sidi's portion has been administered as a unit first by his son, Muhammadu, then by Muhammadu's brother, Aliyu, and most recently by the latter's son, Sa'idu, while Abubakar's portion has passed as a separate unit from his son, Yaro, to its present administrator. In this way the two major Mallawa segments each held their own property of land, cattle, and slaves as separate corporate units, while personal estates of individuals in either segment continued to be subdivided at inheritance among the owner's lineal issue. Thus even after Sidi's death and Abubakar's resumption of Mallawa kingship, the Mallawa were disunited. This condition, and the shortness of Abubakar's reign, partly explains the rapidity with which their Bornawa rivals were subsequently able to resume leadership.

On Abubakar's accession, the Sultan instructed him to appoint Sambo, a son of the Katsinawa ruler, Abdulkerim, to the office of Wombai, which had now been made vacant. By this appointment Sokoto sought to qualify Katsinawa candidates for the succession, in order to maintain the tridynastic system. At the same time Sokoto wished to weaken the kingship at Zaria and to discourage further claims for autonomy.

Abubakar's reallocations of office reflected Mallawa disunity. Given the Mallawa division into two segments, and the history of his relations with Sidi, the new king could not rely heavily on support from Sidi's segment, nor could he afford to alienate them further by giving many offices to his own children. Sidi, in his distribution of office, had carefully eschewed nepotism and dynastism alike. Abubakar now had the task of replacing the Bornawa office-holders without appearing to favour his own segment of the Mallawa unduly.

He dismissed Abdullahi's son, Yero, from the office of Madaki; but instead of appointing his own son, as was usual, he gave the office to his brother, Ali, whom Sidi had formerly placed in charge of a force and sent to conquer the country since incorporated into the expanding new kingdom of Kontagora. Ali's military prowess, direct descent from Mallam Musa and former solidarity with Sidi, served to show the Mallawa that Abubakar was prepared to let bygones be bygones and to distribute office among them as fairly as he could. Ali's son, Sadauki, was also appointed Turaki Karami, and Sidi's son, Nuhu, who had been allocated the fief of Durum unofficially by his father, was appointed Dan Galadima and placed formally in charge of Durum. Thus Abubakar tried to make peace with his kinsmen; but he dared not reveal too obvious a preference for his own close kin.

He sought simultaneously to retain Sokoto's support and to keep loyal persons in office, by allowing the offices of Wali and Makama Karami to remain with the Toronkawa Gidadawa, who were descended from Mallam Musa's daughter by the Wazirin Sokoto Gidado. Shehu, Hamada's son, was dismissed from the office of Mardanni, and this was given to Yelwa of the Katsinawa. Abubakar also allowed the Katsinawa Iya to continue in office, perhaps in the hope of winning Katsinawa support for Mallawa rule. He dismissed Abdullahi's kinsman, Mallam, from the office of Dallatu, and appointed his own son, Karfe. On Nuhu's death, another grandson of Mallam Musa, Bamurna, whose father had held the office of Magajin Gari, was appointed Dan Galadima. Adamu, Abdullahi's Galadima, was replaced by Abubakar's son, Yaro Muhammadu. Apart from this, Abubakar contented himself with eliminating Abdullahi's clients from office and appointing his own. Sirajo was dismissed from the office of Fagaci, and was replaced by the village chief of Giwa, whose title was Danfangi.

Lineages which had had Bornawa support in developing quasi-hereditary claims on such positions as Katuka, or Dan Madami, were temporarily replaced by appointments from other families loyal to the Mallawa cause; but other lineages with quasi-hereditary rights to such positions as Rubu, Chikum, or Magajin Zakara were retained in these offices by Abubakar, being linked to the Mallawa by marriage and other ties.

The principal innovation attributed to Abubakar is the creation of a second Ma'aji title, with responsibility for south central Zaria, especially the district around Kacia, among the Ikulu, Kamantan, Jaba, and nearby tribes. Abubakar is said to have created a Ma'ajin Kacia since the Sarkin Kajuru was unable to police Kacia satisfactorily; and in this he tended to follow the precedent created by Tatumare's appointment as Kuyambana, with special responsibility for the Ikulu and Kamantan tribute. Abubakar made only one raid during his reign, attacking Gwodo near Jema'a, and died in 1876.

(k) Abdullahi, 1876–81

Shortly after Abdullahi's deposition a new Sultan, who disagreed with the ground and method of Abdullahi's dethronement, had been appointed at Sokoto. On Abubakar's death this Sultan decided to make amends to Abdullahi and reappointed him king of Zaria. The reappointment proved to be an error of judgement, but the manner in which it was done was rash indeed. The electoral council of Zaria were not even consulted, and while they were busy considering the problem of succession, they received the news that the Sultan had reappointed Abdullahi king of Zaria and had crowned him at Sokoto. In its confidence, Sokoto had overplayed its hand.

As mentioned above, the estate of a deposed king was divided between his successor and his suzerain. Abubakar had distributed among his senior officials portions from that half of Abdullahi's estate which had been alloted to him. Abdullahi, reinstated, may not have had the power to demand restitution from the Sultan, but as king of Zaria he could seek to recover those portions of his former estate which had been distributed at Zaria; and this included his concubines. Until recently the deposition of a ruler had been an unprecedented event. Precedents regularizing these situations had been rapidly developed, but there were institutional limits to the variety of possible precedents. An already deposed king could only be reappointed without regard to the wishes of the local electoral council, or in opposition to them. The reappointment of a deposed ruler was one thing no electoral council could recommend, and it created a situation for which workable precedents could not be easily developed.

On hearing of Abdullahi's reappointment, the Madaki Ali, who had received some of Abdullahi's concubines from Abubakar, gathered his slaves and supporters and withdrew from his *rinji* at Magada to Ifira, another slave-settlement near Rigachikum, on the route to Bida. The former Galadima Hamman, who had also benefited from the distribution of Abdullahi's estate, supported Madaki Ali; and other officials also wished Ali success in his rebellion. Ali had taken with him some of the cavalry he controlled as Madaki, and at Ifira he raised the flag of revolt. Abdullahi despatched a slave, Maigoto, ordering Ali's return. Maigoto was killed by Ali's men, and the king then sent a force to reduce Ifira. This proved difficult, and Abdullahi then appealed to the Sultan to intervene. Thus Sokoto's initial intervention promptly led to a request from the king for further intervention.

The Sultan asked the ruler of Kano, who controlled a powerful force of cavalry, to visit the Madaki and negotiate his surrender. Since his own intervention might have led to a war between Kano and Zazzau, and since he was in sympathy with Ali and the claim of Zaria for internal autonomy, the king of Kano decided to send the Madakin Kano, to find out why Ali had revolted. Ali said bluntly that Sokoto's reappointment of Abdullahi without even consulting the Zaria electors was the cause. "Even the Shehu, before he appointed Mallam Musa, discussed the leadership of Zaria with its people." The Madakin Kano was then commissioned to offer Ali the throne after Abdullahi, if he called off the revolt. Ali accepted, and went with the king and Madaki of Kano to the Sultan's court to present his case formally, to renew allegiance and conclude the negotiations. Thus Sokoto's intervention in Zaria's affairs led to Kano's also; and to enforce its reappointment of Abdullahi without consulting the electoral council of Zaria, Sokoto had to make further illegitimate arrangements about the succession. Ironically, the Madaki Ali, who had been moved to rebel through Sokoto's illegitimate and impolitic interventions in the affairs of Zaria, was also persuaded to desist by an equally illegitimate scheme of which he was the principal beneficiary. The tridynastic political system of Zaria enabled Sokoto to win local support for its successive interventions, however illegitimate, by aiding one faction against others. At the same time political dis-equilibrium, which had led to the Sultan's renewed intervention, increased in proportion to Sokoto's control. The remedy was here as unhappy as that which it sought to cure.

Abdullahi found himself in an awkward position. As Sokoto's nominee he was unwelcome to the Zaria Fulani, and, apart from the Sultan, he could only rely for support on his Bornawa kins-men. Of his opponents the Mallawa were the strongest. The Katsinawa and Suleibawa had both refrained from actively taking sides in the recent dispute, since such action may have put their dynastic status at stake. But Madaki Ali had temporarily reunited the Mallawa by reviving Sidi's claims for local autonomy, and by his spirited opposition to the resumption of Bornawa rule. More-over, Ali was the half-brother of both Abubakar and Sidi, and had also served under both of them, without becoming committed to either side of their dispute.

Abdullahi's reallocations of office reflect his dependence on Sokoto for support, his need to win local support among the Fulani, and his need to reduce Mallawa power. Under instructions from Sokoto, Abdullahi retained the Mallawa Dan Galadima Bamurna and the Katsinawa Wombai Sambo in their offices. He dismissed the Katsinawa Abdurrahman, who sympathized with Ali, from the office of Iya, and left this title vacant; but the Kat-sinawa Yelwa retained the office of Mardanni, and another Katsinawa, Sule, was appointed Sarkin Yaki. A member of the Suleibawa was given the title of Magaji Jisambo, and one of the king's kin, Dan Manga, was appointed Turaki Karami in place of the Mallawa title-holder. Adamu, who had formerly held office as Galadima under Abdullahi, was restored on the dismissal of the Mallawa holder, Yaro Muhammadu. Abdullahi's son, Yero, was reinstated as Madaki. The Toronkawa Gidadawa lineage of Zaria, who were the kinsmen of the rulers of Sokoto, now held the offices of Wali, Makama Karami, and Fagaci—the last being a new appointment by Abdullahi. Other titles such as Sa'i, Shentali, and Sarkin Ruwa were given to the king's kinsmen. Finally, to control the administration of law, Abdullahi appointed Sada, a Fulani client from the Suleibawa of Katsina, to hold the two offices of

Alkali and Salenke. Possibly by combining these judicial offices under Sada, Abdullahi intended to facilitate the recovery of his own distributed estate. Abdullahi completed his redistributions of office by reappointing those lineages whose quasi-hereditary tenure of special offices had been interrupted by Abubakar. Abdullahi also took the unusual step of appointing one of his slaves, Yawa, to the title of Sarkin Yamma, with command of a small force stationed at Kacia. This was done to police the caravan routes of the area and to ensure the rapid collection of tribute from pagan tribes near Kacia. The innovation aroused little opposition at the time, but had important consequences in the following reign.

Abdullahi was unable to recover his former estate from its principal local beneficiaries, such as the ex-Madaki Ali. Ali had discussed this problem in his negotiations with Sokoto, and he returned to Zaria with the understanding that Abdullahi would not be able to proceed against him for rebellion or for this estate. In addition Ali knew he was to succeed Abdullahi. He therefore retired to his *rinji* and waited. But Abdullahi's inability to recover his former property weakened his loyalty to Sokoto, and excited his son and Madaki, Yero, whose inheritance was at stake.

During his earlier reign, Abdullahi had led military expeditions against the Kagoma near Kagoro, the Gwari of Dan Bunu, the Katab at Sabon Kaura near Malagum, and Keffi. But after his return the king took no part in campaigns, being old and unwell; nor could he afford to send his son, the Madaki, away from the capital with the army, for fear of his rivals and the threat of Ningi attacks. Another slave, the Bajimin Gabas, was stationed with a small force at Kudaru near Lere in the path of the Ningi invaders. Taxes were raised to support these standing forces and to maintain the defence.

Abdullahi's relations with Sokoto worsened quickly. Like Sidi he had already experienced the dangers of visiting the Sultan's court. Despite reinstallation and his neat legal provisions, he was unable to recover his former property or to allocate offices freely. He held the kingship without kingly power. He showed his annoyance with Sokoto by refusing to make the annual visit of homage to the Sultan's court, although the tribute was forwarded promptly. He knew from his sojourn at Sokoto that the imperial lineage had split over his initial deposition; one section held that such action was illegitimate and reflected a purely personal pique by the

Sultan; the other that no form of law was required, since Sokoto exercised suzerainty over Zaria. The decision to prohibit Abdullahi from recovering his distributed estate was a compromise between these conflicting views, given his reappointment. However, in 1881 the Sultan who had reappointed Abdullahi died, and his successor, who had advocated the earlier deposition, was also personally hostile to Abdu. On the ground that Abdullahi's continued non-attendance at the Sultan's court implied disloyalty, he was peremptorily summoned to Sokoto and again deposed. To fulfil their agreement with the Mallawa leader, Ali, the Sultan sent him a letter appointing him to rule Zaria, but when this letter arrived the ex-Madaki was on his deathbed. He thanked the Sultan for honouring the agreement, but declined the offer. For the Mallawa, Ali's illness and death at this time was most unfortunate, but it gave Sokoto the chance to reconsider its policy toward succession and control of Zazzau, and led to a novel agreement.

On this occasion the Sultan instructed the electoral council of Zaria, the two Limans, the Galadima, and the Alkali, to send their three candidates for the succession in person to Sokoto, rating them in order of preference. In this way the new Sultan sought to combine the elector's approval with his own freedom of choice, and to demonstrate to the Fulani of Zaria that consultation had in fact taken place, while keeping the final power of decision in his own hands. Moreover, while at Sokoto, the three candidates would be separated from their supporters, and could not then use force to contest the decision. And before they received permission to return to Zaria they would each have to accept the Sultan's decision. Finally, the Sultan's choice would also have to accept coronation at Sokoto on the Sultan's conditions. From every point of view the new arrangement suited Sokoto admirably, and it was especially welcome because of the alternative which had accidentally been avoided.

(l) Sambo, 1881–90

In the opinion of the Zaria electoral council the three leading candidates for the throne at this time were Yero, Abdullahi's son and Madaki; Sambo, the son of Abdulkerim and the acting Wombai; and Zubairu, a son of Mallam Musa who as yet had held no important territorial office but who had nevertheless been nominated by Madaki Ali as the Mallawa candidate, and was neither committed to Sidi's segment nor Abubakar's. These three princes were escorted to Sokoto by the Galadiman Zazzau, Adamu. Of the three, two were unsuitable for immediate succession: Yero, because his father was the ruler just deposed; Zubairu, because he had not yet held territorial title and was therefore ineligible for immediate succession. Rank was a structural principle of equal status to descent in the succession and dynastic organization alike. In effect, therefore, Sokoto only had the choice between appointing the Katsinawa Wombai Sambo or selecting someone not nominated by the electoral council of Zaria. The Sultan had no wish to adopt the latter course; he would have gained little from so doing, and could lose much. The Sultan wanted a relatively stable political system in Zaria, with a kingship weakened by strong opposition. The Katsinawa were already well represented in office, and they were also due for a further period of rule. But as a dynasty they were much less formidable than either the Mallawa or Bornawa, both of whom had already suffered through depositions. Sambo was therefore selected to succeed Abdullahi, and he was formally crowned at the Sultan's court.

At the same time the suzerain laid down certain conditions of his kingship. To nullify Yero's opposition to his father's deposition, Sokoto instructed Sambo to replace Yero by another Bornawa Madaki. Sambo was also instructed to appoint the unsuccessful Mallawa candidate, Zubairu, to the office of Wombai, left vacant by his own accession, and also to retain the acting Mallawa Dan Galadima. In this way Sokoto appropriated powers to redistribute the three senior royal offices of Zaria at the same time as it decided the kingship, and this new power was used to distribute key offices among the new king's dynastic rivals. It is possible that Sokoto intended to develop a system of rotating offices linked with the kingship, in order to limit the dynastic conflict and weaken the throne. In the kingdom of Nupe there was already such a system.[1]

Sambo had to obey the letter of these instructions, while departing from their spirit in order to preserve his authority. He gladly dismissed Yero from the Madakiship, replacing him by Anu, a son of Yamusa, who was at this date far too old to be an effective war-leader or rival. Sambo may also have been relieved at the age of the Wombai appointed by Sokoto. He sought to strengthen

[1] See Nadel, 1942, pp. 88–103.

himself further by appointing one of his brothers, Babagana, to the position of Magajin Gari, and another to the title of Iya. His maternal kinsman was appointed Turaki Karami in place of the Bornawa official, and his son, Tsoho, was given the office of Makama Karami. The Bornawa Sarkin Ruwa, Yaji, the son of Abdullahi, was dismissed from office, and a Habe client of Sambo's by the name of Suleimanu was appointed instead.

When Zubairu died shortly after, the Mallawa retained the office of Wombai, Sambo appointing Nuhu, the son of Sidi, to that title. After Nuhu's death, another Mallawa prince, Yaro Muhammadu, Abubakar's son, was appointed. Yaro Muhammadu in turn was succeeded first by Muhammadu, the son of Sidi, and then by Aliyu, another of Sidi's sons. By these Mallawa appointments Sambo attempted to increase the rivalry (*hura wuta*) between the segments of Sidi and Abubakar, which his father, Abdulkerim, had initiated. On the death of the Dan Galadima Bamurna, Sambo appointed Gabdo, Madaki Ali's son, at Sokoto's request. Sambo also dismissed his Bornawa rivals from the offices of Shentali and Sa'i which Abdullahi had given them, and returned the title of Fagaci to the family of Sirajo, its first non-eunuch holder. Sada was dismissed from his two judicial offices of Salenke and Alkali, and the old judicial structure was restored. Sambo then dismissed Abdullahi's client, Adamu, from the office of Galadima, and appointed his own Habe supporter, the Sarkin Ruwa, Suleimanu.

Sambo's reallocation of office was guided by his need for strong and loyal supporters in all those positions which Sokoto left at his disposal; and while allocating the offices of Wombai, Madaki, and Dan Galadima in accordance with Sokoto's instructions, he tried to give his dynastic rivals as little advantage as possible by unsuitable selections.

Like his predecessors, Sambo came to the throne within a context which limited his freedom of action. The instructions from Sokoto which limited his control of appointments were the most important restrictions of all. Both his opponents, the Mallawa and the Bornawa, besides holding certain key offices under the protection of Sokoto, had much greater resources, experience, and prestige than he. His dynasty, which supported him solidly, was his principal resource. By his reallocations of office Sambo sought to maximize the value of the resources he commanded while minimizing those of his opponents; and, the necessities of government being what they were in Zaria, he can neither be criticized for adopting this policy nor for inefficiency in its application.

None the less, Sambo overlooked one feature which for all its novelty was now fundamental. This was the distribution of key offices among dynastic rivals. Its effect was to segment the administrative structure by political divisions; this political segmentation itself brought the administration directly into the political system and so eliminated its former monocratic organization. Appointment of political rivals to administrative office severely weakened the king's authority by reducing his political power. After the new distribution of office effected by Sokoto, the king was no longer an autocrat but *primus inter pares*, although traditional administrative and political patterns persisted.

Sambo's error lay in ignoring this basic change and in seeking to restore the monocracy by reducing the power of his rivals in office while maximizing his own. Within the Zaria political system this objective had for long been the structural precondition of effective kingship. But under the new conditions the king's attempt to dominate the administration simply intensified the political competition established by the distribution of office and accelerated the development of cleavages and political alignments within the administration itself. Despite his ingenious appointments, Sambo was neither able to reduce his official rivals to impotence nor to re-establish an absolute rule. To produce these conditions, Sambo had first to create new units of power and to bind them to his interest by strong political ties. To create these new units of power was itself a difficult problem; but to ensure their loyalty and control in these conditions may well have been impossible.

Sambo sought to achieve these objects by investing his Habe client, Suleimanu, with two offices and by placing the capital under his control. As Suleimanu was a Habe without other backing, the king expected to exercise indirect control over both his titles. Given the age and political impotence of his Bornawa Madaki and Mallawa Wombai, Sambo expected that, with the combined offices of Sarkin Ruwa and Galadima at his direction, he would now have a sufficient superiority to give him autocratic control, that is, the power to decide policy independently according to his own needs, and the authority to implement such decisions without stay. However, the king shortly found that he was dependent on his client. The combination of two offices had indeed created a new unit of power, and its inclusion within a system of political competition emphasized the political values and power of the unusual administrative authority vested in this client. After Suleimanu had consolidated his control over the offices of Sarkin Ruwa and Galadima, Sambo found that he could make no further appointments or dismissals without his Galadima's approval. When the Makama Babba, Mai-dauda, died, the Galadima obstructed further appointments to that office, and claimed that the fiefs of Makama Babba should properly be attached to his own, since he was the ruler's deputy, and being also the ruler's client, his power increased the king's. Thus Suleimanu continually exploited his position within this politically divided administration, and increased his own power by bargains with the king, while Sambo instead of increasing his own power found himself increasingly dependent. It is said that Suleimanu prevented Sambo from appointing his kinsmen to four offices which fell vacant consecutively. Some of these offices the Galadima persuaded the king to allot to his own clients; others Suleimanu decided to keep vacant, while attaching their fiefs to his own administration, although the fiefs of vacant titles should properly be administered by the king. 'Na yi taguwa da ita.' ('I have wrapped the office around myself like a robe.') Most important of all, Suleimanu had control of the capital as a fief. Sambo found that he was no longer the master in his own house. He therefore took what steps he could to reverse the balance of power and reassert his own supremacy. When Zubairu, the old Mallawa Wombai died, Sambo, being instructed to appoint further Mallawa to that office, chose Nuhu, the son of Sidi, who was younger and more aggressive. He gave the new Wombai a military command, although traditionally the Wombai had only supervised the reserve of spare horses for the cavalry.

Sambo was looking about for other offices which could be strengthened against the Galadima, who was at this time without doubt the most powerful man in the kingdom. Since the distribution of offices now depended on the Galadima's assent, and the Galadima now administered several vacant titles, for which clients competed, Suleimanu's clients now exceeded the king's in number and importance. None the less, Nuhu's appointment and investment with command stirred Suleimanu into action. He saw that by similar appointments the king could reduce his own power, and might yet acquire sufficient strength to attempt his dismissal from office. As a Habe, Suleimanu lacked any ethnic commitment to the maintenance of Fulani rule; and his present pre-eminence corresponded directly with Fulani weakness, born of their dynastic divisions, both within the administration and outside it. Present conditions seemed propitious if he attempted to seize the throne. But realizing that the Fulani of Zaria would combine to defend their dominion against such a challenge, and that they would also receive support from Fulani in nearby states, Suleimanu decided to recruit foreign allies—in this case, the Ningi.

Haruna, the reigning Ningi chief, was the son of the Habe Mallam Hamza, who had fled from Tsokuwa in Kano when Mommon Sani was king of Zazzau. Like Suleimanu, Haruna was a Muhammadan and a Habe. Both were hostile to Fulani rule. Both stood to gain by its overthrow. It was accordingly arranged that Haruna would mass the Ningi and wait at Yakasai, an old Habe town to the north-east of Zaria city, which was administered by the Galadima. Sambo was due to leave Zaria city on his annual visit of homage to Sokoto, and Suleimanu undertook to inform Haruna when the king had set out. Haruna was to attack Sambo's party just outside the city, kill the king, and seize the tribute to Sokoto. The Galadima, who as deputy remained in the city, administered the capital as a fief, and acted during the king's absence, would then seize the throne. Unfortunately for the plotters, Haruna's final letter arranging the details was by error delivered to Sambo himself after the latter had reached Tukur Tukur, just outside the walls of Zaria. Sambo guessed the remaining details and immediately withdrew to the capital; but the Ningi attacked before the king's entourage had reached safety, and the withdrawal turned into flight. Wombai Nuhu, who showed Mallawa chivalry in defence of his king, was killed at the gates of Zaria, and some of the tribute intended for Sokoto fell into Haruna's hands. In his chagrin at the failure of his main objective, the Ningi chief devastated the area around Zaria city, and is said to have taken 5,000 of Sambo's subjects to slavery or execution.

To Sambo the lesson was bitter; and his dynastic rivals were now especially critical of him, since Suleimanu could never have challenged Fulani rule if Sambo had not initially made this possible by his illegitimate allocation of office and power. The increased disloyalty of his rivals in office further weakened the king in his efforts to deal with the Galadima, while the latter's Habe status and bold attempt won him further support among the Habe of Zaria, whose resentment of Fulani rule increased with their heavy taxation and exclusion from senior office. In these circumstances Sambo found that he could take no direct action against Suleimanu. He lacked the necessary support. The two obvious courses, dismissal of Suleimanu, or reduction of the fiefs he controlled, were not possible without more power and authority than the king now possessed. Sambo feared that if he ordered Suleimanu's dismissal, the Galadima was sufficiently strong to object and could not be compelled to obey. Since the capital was Suleimanu's fief, he was very well placed to revolt if driven to do so. Evidently the king felt that he could not count on his dynastic opponents in or out of office for loyalty or effective support in such a situation.

Another Mallawa prince, Yaro Muhammadu, the son of Abubakar, was given the office of Wombai. Sambo then reconsidered Bornawa tenure of the Madakiship. So long as the Bornawa held this office, he could not entrust important military commands to his Madaki. Because of this, he could neither discipline nor dismiss his Galadima. The offices of Madaki and Galadima had always been counter-balanced, and the authority and power concentrated within them were unparalleled. In the Fulani system of government the Madaki's office had been pre-eminent under the king by reason of its military role; and the frequency with which kings appointed their sons to this position indicates the value attached to it. But when Sambo divested his Bornawa rival of the Madaki's command, he thereby upset the balance of power and left the office of Galadima without its counterpoise.[1] It was this disbalance which had permitted and stimulated Suleimanu to appropriate yet more power by vetoing Sambo's proposals to fill vacant titles and by attaching their fiefs to himself despite the king's opposition. Sambo concluded that by restoring to the Madaki's office its former power, Suleimanu's would be reduced; but before he dared to do this the king had to replace the Bornawa Madaki by someone of undoubted loyalty; and Sambo's experience with Suleimanu had warned him against dependence on clients.

---

[1] In separating the Madaki title and its military command to reduce the power of his Bornawa rival who held that office, Sambo may have had Sidi in mind. After appointing a Bornawa prince to the Madakiship, Sidi sent the army out of Zaria under his own brother. Although Sambo dared not repeat Sidi's illegitimate allocation of command, he did deprive the Madaki of military power, transferring this to the Wombai and Iya.

Under these circumstances the ancient Bornawa Madaki Anu was duly charged with selling some of the horses which were permanently attached to that title for the cavalry. It seems hardly likely that any Madaki would do such a thing; he would certainly know that the horses were official and not personal property, and that their alienation would lead to immediate dismissal, since the cavalry was critically important in the army of Zaria. None the less, Anu was formally charged with this offence and, after a trial, he was dismissed. Sambo may have felt that this precaution was necessary to divert the anger of the Sultan, who had reserved the Madaki positions for Bornawa. Sambo then appointed his kinsman Tsoho, the son of Jamo, as Madaki; and after Tsoho's death he gave the title to his own son, Lawal.

These appointments exacerbated dynastic tensions within the administration and outside it, and this increased opposition itself reduced the value of the new appointments to the king. In effect Sambo's intention of overpowering his Galadima with the restored Madakiship was thereby nullified. The Bornawa had lost heavily in the Ningi enslavement of the population round about Zaria. The dismissed Madaki Anu himself had had nine children enslaved by the Ningi. The blame for these losses fell squarely on Sambo; and his method of replacing Anu, through the instrumentality of the courts, was regarded as at once a repudiation of his agreement with Sokoto and a maladministration of justice. The king's failure to punish or dismiss his Galadima for the attempted revolt and ambush contrasted so sharply with his treatment of Anu that this new move merely increased disaffection and hostility. Under these circumstances Sambo feared revolts from two quarters: from the Galadima, who had already shown his ambition and his impunity; and also from rival dynasties who saw their hereditary dominion threatened by internal and external enemies whom Sambo could not resist.

News that Haruna had devastated the environs of Zaria city spread the story of Zaria's weakness far and wide. Dan Barahiya, the Habe ruler of Maradi, to the north of Katsina, decided to invade Zazzau. He marched through Katsina along its border with Kano, and entered Zaria along the same route as Mallam Musa, capturing Kudan, an important market-town in the Northern districts. Many of the townsfolk were enslaved. Meanwhile, the Ningi penetrations into the south and centre of Zaria reached as far as Kacia. The Ningi came annually during the dry season, and struck where they were not expected. Sambo had to divide and distribute his forces to deal simultaneously with these Ningi attacks, with the Maradawa, and with his internal rivals, the Galadima and the dynasties.

The king sought to repair the losses caused by Haruna's invasion through increased slave-raiding. To this end he led attacks on the Kadara of Libere, the Kagoro of Malagum, and the Gwari of Romi near Gwagwada; but in each case he had no success and lost reputation. Zaria's obvious weakness now encouraged her southern vassals to reassert their independence. Keffi and Kwotto again began fighting one another. Their war was over before Sambo was able to intervene; but with the support of Sokoto he fined the two vassals for fighting one another. The fines were paid in slaves, to help restore the Zaria slave-population.

The king's political and military weakness were interdependent. He was militarily weak because he was politically weak, as the head of an administration which was politically divided; and his military weakness itself prevented him taking action to eliminate his opponents from office and restore autocratic rule. He now made one last attempt to concentrate sufficient power in his own hands to give him control of his kingdom. The small force stationed at Kacia was increased until it was an effective standing army, and its slave-commander, the Sarkin Yamma, Yawa, was given new powers to administer his headquarters through its local chief.

This new disposition had several objectives: to protect the south and centre of Zaria against further Ningi attacks; to police the caravan routes and secure regular slave supplies through tribute and raids; to increase the military strength of the king, by adding this new standing army to those forces controlled by his son, the Madaki; and last but not least, to discourage rebellious movements in the capital, by maintaining a strong reserve force at a striking distance of 130 miles, under a commander whose slave status made him fully dependent on the king. Being unable to remove the capital from the Galadima's control, Sambo sought to restrain Suleimanu by creating this new force which stood at a distance ready to strike in defence of the throne. Since his son, the Madaki, resided in Zaria city, which was the Galadima's fief, the cavalry command which he held had not enabled Sambo to dominate the Galadima as he had hoped. By placing his new force away from the capital, Sambo next sought to nullify Suleimanu's strategic advantage. The best the king could now hope for was to forestall further moves against his person by the Galadima.

In this situation the kingdom was virtually defenceless. The Maradawa returned and recaptured Kudan.[1] The Ningi continued to ravage eastern Zaria annually, attacking Dan Alhaji, Soba, and towns near Makarfi; their captives included free Muhammadans as well as non-Muhammadan slaves. Sambo was impotent against these attacks. In the south the Habe of Abuja were raiding the caravan routes freely, but it was essential for Sambo to preserve his army under the slave, Yawa, as a safeguard against trouble at Zaria from his external or internal foes. His continued impotence against the invaders further antagonized the king's dynastic rivals, and other leading Fulani lineages, who suffered or feared losses. Complaints were made to Sokoto and finally, in 1890, the Sultan intervened, deposing Sambo on grounds of his inability to defend the state.

Sambo's deposition was popular in Zaria; but his failure was ultimately due to the conditions in which he had been appointed. He had been placed in charge of an administration deliberately constructed by Sokoto so as to weaken the kingship and increase its own ascendancy. From his accession the king's administration was disunited and politically divided. Yet if Sambo was to rule according to the traditions of Fulani Zazzau, it was essential that he should exercise an absolute control over his administrative staff; if sympathy with the ruler did not make them loyal, then fear of his power should.

The history of Sambo's reign is a history of his unsuccessful attempts to create the conditions in which he could dominate the administration. Each attempt further weakened the king's position. By investing his Habe client with excessive power, the king placed himself in a dependent position, and indirectly stimulated his client to entertain rebellious designs. Despite its failure he could not punish the Galadima's rebellion. Subsequently the king made two attempts to strengthen himself against his client, firstly, by making his son the Madaki, and then by creating a standing army

---

[1] It is said that their leader, Dan Barahiya, was searching for a woman of Kudan whom he specially wanted. He found her on his second capture of the town and removed her to Maradi as his concubine; she bore him a child, and was released after his death, returning to Kudan with this unconfirmed report of Dan Barahiya's love.

under a slave captain; but these dispositions dispersed the military forces of the state so widely that it was powerless to resist its attackers or dismiss his rivals; and this in turn led to the king's deposition.

Sambo had failed to protect the kingdom by trying to restore the kingship to its former commanding position; but he had been successful in preserving this kingship for the Fulani, and his deposition gave Sokoto a chance to reverse the disastrous policy which had infested the administrative structure of Zaria with political divisions, and broken down those clear distinctions between politics and administration which the Fulani of Zaria had developed and maintained as essential for their government with its competing dynasties. Although in theory under Sambo the throne enjoyed much the same authority as before, its power was so greatly reduced that its authority was often ineffective. The distinctions between power and authority and their interconnections are revealed most clearly by Sambo's reign.

(m) Yero, 1890–97

Sambo's deposition following on complaints from Zaria won widespread approval among the ruling Fulani. The electoral council of Zaria selected Yero as the leading Bornawa candidate. Lawal, Sambo's Madaki and son, was the leading Katsinawa candidate, and Sa'adu, who had succeeded to the office of Wombai, but whose father had not held the throne, was the leading Mallawa candidate. Lawal was unsuitable to succeed his father whose deposition had left the throne vacant; and the Mallawa candidate was also ineligible for the throne as his father had not ruled Zaria. This left only Yero, on whom the Sultan conferred the kingship, crowning him in Sokoto where the final selection was made. Sokoto took this opportunity to reverse its previous ruling about the Madaki and Dan Galadima offices, allowing the new king to fill them as he pleased; but the office of Wombai was once more reserved for Mallawa. In this way the Sultan sought to strengthen the king of Zaria against his Galadima, without allowing him to become strong enough to challenge his own ascendancy. With a disunited administration, no king of Zaria could claim autonomy, since his rivals in office would regard this as a move towards unilineal absolutism and react accordingly.·

Yero's first problem was to recover for the kingship all the powers it had lost to the Galadima Suleimanu. To this end he sought to fill all available offices with his closest supporters, namely, his lineage kin. He dismissed Lawal, Sambo's son, from the office of Madaki, and appointed his own son, Kwassau. Other Katsinawa were also dismissed from the offices of Magajin Gari, Makama Karami, Turaki Karami, and Iya, which they held under Sambo, and their places were taken by the new king's lineage kin. A Bornawa Dallatu was appointed; and Yero also appointed the great-grandson of Iya Atiku, a Bornawa, to the office of Dan Madami, thereby interrupting its quasi-hereditary transmission. Another kinsman, the grandson of Hamada's sister, was given the office of Shentali; and Yero gave his daughter's son the office of Sarkin Ruwa. The king appointed Ci-gari, the brother of his new Sarkin Ruwa, to the office of Makama Babba which Galadima Suleimanu had previously stopped Sambo from filling. These appointments to the titles of Sarkin Ruwa and Makama Babba from the king's kinsmen were direct challenges to the Galadima Suleimanu; and in making both appointments the king enlisted the support of another Fulani lineage as well as his dynasty. Suleimanu had to give in, and the fiefs belonging to these titles were turned over to Yero's loyal supporters. The Galadima found his former sway reduced; and only the fiefs properly attached to the title of Galadima were now under his control. None the less, Yero made no direct move to dismiss Suleimanu, probably fearing that such action might lead to his rebellion, which in its beleaguered position the state could not risk. So the Galadima continued in office, while the Bornawa ruler and his Madaki concentrated on rebuilding Bornawa power by war and other means.

Yero had twice lost his inheritance by his father's depositions from the throne. On Abdullahi's reappointment, his attempts to recover the estate he had lost by his first deposition were frustrated by Sokoto. Later when Abdullahi was again deposed, his second estate had also been shared between Sambo and the Sultan of Sokoto. It is true that Yero had himself received one-half of Sambo's estate, being appointed after Sambo's deposition. But he still regarded those persons who were beneficiaries of his father's depositions as holding property which formed a legitimate part of his own inheritance; and it seems that he was determined to punish the holders of such property, even if he could not formally recover possession.

Yero also decided to overawe the population with displays of royal strength. By demonstrating the force at the King's disposal, he hoped to discourage the disloyal hopes of revolt which Suleimanu had stimulated. He acquired a monopoly of the local trade in firearms, now available at Lokoja as trade goods from the Royal Niger Company. Slave detachments were trained in the use of these weapons; and these *'yan bindiga* (musketeers) were organized in squads under slave-captains. These squads were stationed near the king's palace in the city as a reserve against the Galadima and any Ningi or other raiders, but they were also well suited to short, rapid thrusts.

It is said that Yero made a practice of sending out these squads of slave-riflemen to despoil those persons whom he regarded as having portions of his inheritance; but the *'yan bindiga* did not confine their attention to such persons alone, and the population, uncertain of the king's complicity, had little redress against their *wasau* (despoiling of citizens' homes and property). Besides those whom the king might regard as having his estate, other persons suspected of disaffection were also visited by *'yan bindiga*; and these squads were also despatched to enforce the prompt payment of taxes, which were raised again. Yero increased the number and variety of occupational taxes by appointing officials such as the Sarkin Rafi (chief of streams and marshes) to collect agricultural taxes as well. Such marsh-crops as tobacco, cassava, onions, sugar-cane, or indigo were now liable to tax; but the system of collection allowed tax to be demanded of persons who no longer cultivated these crops, although they may formerly have done so; and the use of *'yan bindiga* to enforce payment deprived the population of opportunities for protest. These rifle squads sent out each contained about a hundred men, under slave-captains with such titles as Sarkin Ciyawa (Chief of grass),[1] Sarkin Magudantai (Chief of the young slave boys), and Sarkin Bindiga, who was in charge of them all. Yero terrified the population with this new instrument, and the Mallawa, who had benefited from the distribution of Abdullahi's estate and had contested its return through their leader, the Madaki Ali, suffered especially.

These new slave rifle squads also reduced Yero's dependence

---

[1] The significance of this title is its allusion to the king as the horse, following a well-known Hausa proverb. Thus this slave-captain brings grass for the horse to eat.

on the army stationed at Kacia, since through them he was now too strong to be challenged at Zaria. He was therefore free to reduce the force allocated to the Sarkin Yamma at Kacia, and to make a more effective use of his army. Thus Yero reduced the power of his dynastic rivals, of the Galadima and of the Sarkin Yamma, by the means of the same instruments with which he terrified the population. Without doubt, the kingship had recovered its autocratic power, but the cost was considerable. To recover supremacy it had developed an oppressive administration based on the illegitimate use of force and creating dangerous extensions of political rivalry.

The increasing disequilibrium of the governmental system under Sambo had consisted in the progressive political segmentation of the administration, with corresponding reduction of kingly power. This had now given place to a disequilibrium of the opposite kind, in which force was the basis of the overwhelming power now concentrated in the throne, and this force was being used to crush the king's rivals and terrify his subjects. The trend was clearly towards a unilineal absolutism, the prerequisites of which were twofold: firstly, the elimination of Sokoto's control; and secondly, the elimination of rival dynasties as political opponents. *Wasau*, once begun, could not easily be halted. If the Mallawa were to succeed after Yero, the population expected that they would retaliate with the same weapon as Yero had used against them. Such alternate plundering could not continue for long without producing open conflict. Either the tridynastic system with its prohibition of force in political competition would break down and give way to monodynastic autocracy; or further intervention by Sokoto would be necessary to restore or preserve the traditional structure.

At this point, certain differences between the principal political actors of Zaria in the treatment of their rivals may be mentioned; these differences indicate the conventional limits of political rivalry, and apart from the contrast which they represent they are also relevant to the understanding of *wasau* as developed by Yero. The property of rivals out of office was exempt from any state levies, as mentioned before; but death-duties at set rates were levied on the properties of those persons who died in office, including the rulers; kings deposed by the Sultan formed a separate category. These rules were common ground, but otherwise Bornawa and Mallawa treated officials dismissed from office differently; and as they were mainly responsible for dismissing one another, these differences exacerbated their political rivalry. The Mallawa are said to have followed a practice of distributing wealth and property among their supporters appointed to office, and to have retained as much of the property of the officials whom they dismissed from office as they conveniently could. The Bornawa in contrast are said to have allowed persons dismissed from office to retain half of the property acquired during tenure of office, but they did not usually distribute largesse among their appointees. It seems that some of the largesse distributed by Mallawa kings among their appointees may have come from the estates of persons dismissed from the offices to which the persons receiving such property were then appointed. In such a case the Mallawa interpretation of property distributions after dismissal could be summarized as a division of the estate of the displaced official between his successor in office and the king. This was similar to Sokoto's practice regarding the estate of deposed kings. In contrast the Bornawa interpretation allowed little to the next incumbent of the office, but treated the displaced official more liberally. It is understandable that Bornawa would resent their treatment on being dismissed from office by Mallawa, since they themselves were wont to treat Mallawa more liberally on dismissal. It is thus possible that the distribution of Abdullahi's estate on his first deposition may have decided the Bornawa dynasty to increase future confiscations of its rivals' property. Under Yero, this took the form of *wasau*.

This little detail illustrates some of the ideological points at issue between Mallawa and Bornawa; these ideological differences played an important part in their dynastic rivalry. In a sense, these two dynasties offered somewhat different patterns of rule, and to some extent their relative strength reflected the appeal of the system each advocated. But within the context of dynastic competition for a rotating kingship under Sokoto's supervision, these ideological differences between the Mallawa and Bornawa received less emphasis and development than might otherwise have occurred.

Yero also engaged in extensive slave-raiding, and tried to restore the control over his southern dominions which had been lost during Sambo's reign. He gave his brother, Makama Ja'afaru, power to lead an expedition against the Kadara of Girku; Ja'afaru returned with most of the women and children of this town. Yero himself attacked the Pitti and Rukuba tribes on the western scarp of the Jos Plateau at the borders of Lere. He failed to conquer them, but seems to have made them pay tribute. The Kadara of Rimau and Kuchinda near Kajuru were likewise attacked; but at Rimau, where his kinsman the Shentali was killed, Yero suffered a repulse; and the Kadara of Kuchinda and Ma'avelli escaped under cover of darkness.

Yero suffered a major defeat at Abuja which he attacked in 1893, on the advice of his Ma'aji Kau, who lived and ruled at Jere in Kagarko, and had been pressed by Abuja to become their vassal and pay tribute. It is said that Yero assaulted Abuja with over 2,000 cavalrymen, and was repulsed by the Habe of Abuja at little cost.[1] The Fulani of Zaria, on the other hand, lost heavily in this attack, and many office-holders were among the slain. Fulani rationalize the defeat as their punishment for disobedience. They say Musa had forbidden the Fulani of Zaria to attack the Habe after Makau had retreated to Zuba, and had prophesied that if the Fulani of Zaria disobeyed this order, they would suffer heavily. Yero died at Majeriri near Keffi after a raid on the Amawa tribe nearby.

Yero seems to have expected that his successor in office would be a rival, and that the new ruler would retaliate his own practice of *wasau*. To protect his estate, he gave his eldest son, the Madaki Kwassau, the *rinji* at Ibada which he built for his slaves before dying. On his death in 1897, Yero left Zaria stronger externally than he had found it, but internally just as unstable.

(n) Kwassau, 1897-1903

Yero's death again revealed the power of Galadima Suleimanu. When they heard that the Waziri of Sokoto would come to Zaria city to select and crown the next king, the Fulani of Zaria feared that Suleimanu was planning to seize the throne. This new method of settling the succession was attributed to Suleimanu's persuasion, since, as Galadima, he was head of the electoral council and was thus in charge of local arrangements for the succession. The electoral council selected three candidates, namely Kwassau, Yero's son and Madaki; Lawal, who was Sambo's son and who had also held the office of Madaki; and a Mallawa candidate, Muhammadu, who besides being blind with age was also deaf and

---

[1] See Hassan and Shu'aibu, 1952—*A Chronicle of Abuja*, p. 205. Also, Temple, 1919, p. 518.

dumb. Suleimanu expected that Kwassau would be disqualified, since the Sultan had always tried to rotate the kingship among the dynasties. He also hoped that Lawal's failure as Madaki under Sambo would be held against him. He hoped that the Waziri's choice would fall on the Mallawa candidate, especially since this dynasty had not held the throne for long. In such an event the government of the country would really be in the Galadima's hands, since Muhammadu was physically incapacitated, while the Galadima who administered the capital, was the king's official deputy (*Mukkadas*) and also held the principal office of state. Suleimanu therefore set out to persuade the Waziri to make the Mallawa Muhammadu king.

The Fulani of Zaria saw that in effect the only real choice they had was between the Madaki Kwassau and the Habe Galadima Suleimanu. Of all these candidates for the throne, only Kwassau, who now commanded the squads of *'yan bindiga* formed by his father, was a match for the Galadima. On Suleimanu's advice the Wazirin Sokoto decided to appoint the Mallawa mute to the throne; the Fulani of Zaria had already made their preparations and now closed ranks behind Kwassau. Their infantry, cavalry, and riflemen were stationed within and outside the city. According to some accounts, the king of Kano had also sent contingents of cavalry to Kwassau's assistance.[1]

In this situation, Kwassau informed the Waziri of Sokoto bluntly that if he was not appointed king peacefully he would seize the throne by force. The Waziri found that the Fulani of Zaria were already in arms with Kwassau against him, and also that many Mallawa were supporting their rival Kwassau, to prevent the Habe Galadima from ruling through a Mallawa puppet. The Waziri was overawed, and despite the Galadima's insistence he duly crowned Kwassau king, to avoid a war between Zaria and Sokoto. Thus Zaria finally achieved control of its own succession; and so too for the first time since Hamada's short reign, two kings were consecutively appointed from the same dynasty. This was also the first occasion on which the succession had been decided by a direct appeal to force.

[1] See Edgar, 1924, Vol. 1, pp. 198–202. In 1891–92 there had been a bitter accession war in Kano, and in part this had involved the question of internal autonomy; the new rulers of Kano were now ready to aid the Fulani of Zaria to settle their succession problem as they wished, and if necessary in opposition to Sokoto.

Yet even after his triumph, Kwassau dared take no direct action against Suleimanu. The new king appointed his eldest son, Kindi Ibrahim, to the Madaki's office made vacant by his own promotion. He appointed other kinsmen to such offices as became vacant during his reign, namely, the titles of Dallatu, Iya, Sarkin Ruwa, Makama Karami, and Turaki Karami. The king's kin also held the offices of Dan Madami and Dan Galadima. On Sokoto's demand the Mallawa retained the title of Wombai, Aliyu, the son of Sidi Abdulkadiri, now holding this office. The Katsinawa, discredited by their relations with Galadima Suleimanu, were in a deep eclipse.

Kwassau maintained his father's heavy taxation, together with the *'yan bindiga*. It is said that he continued to practise *wasau*, although he owed his succession to widespread Fulani support. Under Kwassau, the internal security of Zazzau rapidly worsened, as *'yan-pila* (armed horsemen) from Maradi and Kontagora raided rural Zaria, taking many settlers swiftly into slavery. It is perhaps just possible that these *'yan-pila* were occasionally confused with Kwassau's slave-squads. In the south-east the Katab tribes rebelled, refusing to pay the tribute, which had now risen to a hundred slaves per annum. Kwassau marched against them, refusing to take prisoners. He then attacked the Gwari of Ligau, and sent his brother the Iya Zubairu against the Kadara of central Zaria.

By this time the newly established Fulani kingdom of Kontagora, which lay to the south-west of Zazzau, had expanded to the borders of Zaria. The Kontagora dynasty were members of the lineage of the Sultans of Sokoto and were directly descended from the Shehu. The first Sarkin Kontagora (king of Kontagora) had taken the title of Sarkin Sudan (chief of the Sudan) formerly held by his father, a Sultan of Sokoto. The rulers of Kontagora were thus in a special relation with Sokoto. Ibrahim Ngwamatse, the reigning chief of Kontagora, may therefore have been acting under the advice of the Sultan, or officiously on his behalf, when he invaded the kingdom of Zaria in 1899, after overpowering the small Habe chiefdom of Birnin Gwari, which occupied an ambiguous position between Katsina and Zaria. It is possible that Ngwamatse's invasion of Zaria was intended to punish Kwassau and the local Fulani for setting aside the Sultan's authority and forcing the Waziri to crown Kwassau. On his part Kwassau could not risk an open breach with Sokoto by waging war with Kontagora. Such a course would strengthen the Habe Galadima and would reduce support for the throne. It would almost certainly lead to Kwassau's deposition, which Zaria could not risk now. On the other hand, Kwassau could not allow Kontagora to raid and lay waste his territory with impunity.

In 1901 the king resolved this dilemma by inviting Captain (later Lord Lugard) to send British troops to stop Ngwamatse's slave-raiding in Zaria. In 1900 the British had passed through Zaria on their way to Kano, and by the end of the following year, on Kwassau's invitation, there was a British garrison at Zaria. But in 1902 Kwassau was removed from the throne by his guests, and in 1903 he was deposed.

(o) *Some Observations*

In this chapter I have tried to combine a systematic review of the factors and processes which produced the Fulani government of Zaria during the last century with a chronological account of the events by which this development occurred. A formal attempt to analyse these historical data is given later, but some general comments on this narrative may be made here.

Firstly, the preceding chronicle deals mainly with the issues of succession, the allocation of office, the competition for promotion, and autonomy or dependence. These recurrent issues dominate. the account, and such administrative matters as taxation, war, or legal reforms receive less attention. This difference of emphasis reflects the difference between these two sets of facts we have just distinguished, and illustrates their relative significance in a history of development and change. The history of governmental change in Fulani Zaria is largely a record of political action, centred on the succession, and incorporating the struggles over autonomy with Sokoto, and over various forms of autocracy. The administrative changes which took place during these years were either the consequences of these political developments or of a purely instrumental character, which once reported, require little comment. Thus the difference of emphasis in this record corresponds to the distinction already laid down between political and administrative action.

In its omissions as well as its contents, this chronicle also supplies essential information on the character and development of the Fulani government in the last century. It shows how the lack of established promotional ladders within the official structure was clearly due to the rapid turnover of office among the supporters of the different dynasties who succeeded one another with increasing rapidity. The peripheral position of such quasi-hereditary titles as Cikum, Magaji Jisambo, Rubu, etc., is indicated by the infrequency of their mention. The record shows how the factors and conditions which governed the development of the Fulani kingdom as a whole, governed the relations between its parts also; for example, relations between the kingship, the dynasties, and the new order of household officials. The record also shows how and why the legal and religious offices came to lose their initial significance so quickly and thoroughly.

From this history of Zazzau we can see that its government was not simply feudal, but combined a variety of elements, the differences between which are only obscured by the use of vague and general categories. The chronicle shows that by 1863 the basic outlines of this system of government were already established, and that thereafter the Fulani faced serious problems in their efforts to maintain this system through a series of crises which expressed disequilibria. The record also emphasizes how historical accidents may affect development. What form of government would have developed had Jaye survived Yamusa, or had Haruna's letter to Suleimanu not been handed to Sambo, it is futile to guess. As the last forty years of Fulani rule show clearly, the struggle between the tendencies towards unilineal absolutism and a controlled kingship at Zaria was sharp and continuous. This suggests that at any moment the system actually operating reflected a special balance of forces produced by its history which continued to govern the rate, direction, and character of future change within the limits set by changing distributions of force on the one hand and historical accident on the other. This in turn suggests that the series of changes through which this system went themselves form a system which can be analysed as a unit of interconnected parts. An attempt at this analysis will be made later.

Finally, this chronicle directs attention to certain problems of historiography which are important to anthropologists in two ways. Firstly, a developed historiography enables anthropologists to study change; secondly, such study raises important questions about the adequacy of conventional historical data. The materials on which we have been drawing consist mainly of records of title-holders, their promotions, dismissals, appointments, inter-marriages, kinship relations, fiefs, powers, and the like. For a system composed primarily of offices distributed among patri-lineal groups, the adequacy of such materials may not be seriously contested. In the present record the question of their accuracy is more important. An interpretation based on inaccurate materials can rarely fail to mislead. But here we have two factors which assist us; firstly, there is the consistency of these field-data, the simple retention of which itself indicates their significance; and secondly, their relations form a coherent logical system, not com-pletely closed it is true, in view of Sokoto's position, but none the less coherent for that. The consistency and coherence of political developments in Fulani Zaria is most apparent from a detailed chronological record. Thematic treatment of such data would cer-tainly obscure important relations on which the chronological con-nections of changing situations focus attention. For example our chronicle shows that, although no two rulers of Zaria occupied an identical situation *vis-à-vis* Sokoto, their supporters, their rivals, or their subordinates, they had in common so many political objectives, problems, and techniques that their differing histories require detailed comparative studies of the rulers' contexts and yield further understanding of the development and operation of the system as a whole. Thus there is much to be said for the adop-tion by anthropologists of a chronological approach to history based on situational analysis. Such an approach emphasizes pre-cisely those qualities of interdependence and interrelation with which the anthropologist is best fitted to deal.

6

ZARIA UNDER THE BRITISH
1900-50

To understand the government of Zaria in 1950, we must know the history of its development under British rule. I shall therefore conclude this chronicle of Zaria with a history of these events.

1. THE ARRIVAL OF THE BRITISH

During the nineteenth century, the British had established contact with Northern Nigeria through a series of gallant explorers who risked their lives to map the course of the Niger. But as the details of their discoveries became widely known, interest in the Western Sudan grew quickly, stimulated alike by prospects of trade and by the determination to stamp out Muhammadan slave-raiding and slavery throughout this area. When France and Germany revealed their interest in Africa, the British redoubled their efforts in Hausaland, and under such leaders as Sir George Goldie of the Royal Niger Company, and Frederick Lugard, they won the race for a treaty with the Sultan of Sokoto which excluded their European rivals from this region.[1]

In 1897 British forces of the Royal Niger Company, under the command of Sir George Goldie, overpowered the Fulani kingdom of Nupe and overawed its neighbour, Ilorin. Three years later the charter of the Royal Niger Company was cancelled by Parliament, and the Protectorate of Northern Nigeria was established with Captain (later Lord) Lugard as High Commissioner. At first the Fulani of Northern Nigeria did not understand the differences between the Protectorate Government and the Royal Niger Company's Administration. To the Fulani both units were governmental agencies set up by the British, and they were naturally opposed to European political penetration and control of the

---

[1] For an excellent summary of British exploration and penetration of Hausaland, see Burns, 1929, pp. 75-96, 147-04.

north. Moreover, the Muslim Fulani disapproved of Christians. In addition, Lugard and the British were determined to suppress slave-raiding, war, and slavery in Northern Nigeria. The stated aims of the British were the pacification and commercial development of the Northern Protectorate; but despite their superiority of arms, their small numbers, susceptibility to tropical diseases, and unfamiliarity with the country, gave an impression of weakness and tended to encourage armed opposition. Although there was already a treaty between the Sultan of Sokoto and the representatives of the British, it is clear that this treaty meant different things to the parties concerned. To the British the treaty established their influence throughout the Sultan's territories, to the exclusion of French or German interests. The Sultan probably regarded the treaty as an alliance which promised protection against other European powers and perhaps against local revolts.

In 1900 Lugard deposed the ruler of Nupe whom Goldie had reinstated three years earlier when Bida was first sacked. The new ruler or Emir of Nupe owed his throne directly to Lugard and was appointed by means of a letter which obliged him to obey the Protectorate Government, to rule justly, and to suppress slave-raiding. In the same year Lugard also captured and deposed Ngwamatse, the king of Kontagora, who had been ravaging Zaria. Lugard then asked the Sultan of Sokoto to nominate a new ruler for Kontagora. The Sultan refused to do so, and Lugard prepared for hostilities with Sokoto. Lugard had acted inconsistently by asking the Sultan to nominate Ngwamatse's successor, after he had himself appointed the new Emir of Nupe without consulting Sokoto.[1] His actions in these two cases obscured the procedure of appointment. It is possible that Lugard wished the Sultan to nominate new rulers, while reserving to himself the power of confirming their appointment on his own conditions. In such a case the new rulers would owe allegiance to the Sultan as well as Lugard, and these loyalties were likely to conflict. But in appointing the Emir of Nupe directly, Lugard had emphasized that he personally expected the new ruler's allegiance, and the Sultan had been ignored. Under these conditions the nature and locus of suzerainty were obscured, and relations of allegiance became ambiguous in content, direction, and form.

When the British forces arrived in Northern Nigeria the Fulani

[1] See Burns, *op. cit.*, pp. 170–1.

empire was in an unusually unstable condition. The king of Kano, Aliyu, had recently seized his throne in direct opposition to Sokoto; shortly after this he had sent troops to Zaria to assist Kwassau against Sokoto. The important kingdom of Bauchi was likewise in difficulties, and faced tribal revolts, together with invasions led by a religious fanatic from the neighbouring kingdom of Misau. The Maradawa had inflicted severe damage on Katsina, and the army of Kontagora was ravaging western Zaria despite the rule which forbade war between vassals.

Within Zaria, the political order had deteriorated rapidly. The new practice of *wasau* seemed likely to promote armed conflict, and Kwassau's forcible seizure of the throne had set the precedent for disintegration. By their support of Kwassau's accession, the Fulani of Zaria had indirectly repudiated the authority of Sokoto; and many felt that this was the reason for Kontagora's attack. Kwassau's invitation to the British to garrison and defend his kingdom may thus have been his way of trying to throw back Kontagora's forces, while avoiding a war with Sokoto. But British intervention in Zaria led to the capture of the king of Kontagora, and this hastened the inevitable clash of force between the British and Sokoto.

The Sultan of Sokoto had steadfastly refused to recognize the British Protectorate of Northern Nigeria. The British were meanwhile establishing their Protectorate by military means. They had defeated the Fulani of Yola, the ruler of Bauchi, and the religious fanatic from Misau before the Sultan of Sokoto finally declared war against them. 'Between us and you there are no dealings except as between Mussulmans and Unbelievers, War, as God Almighty has enjoined on us.'[1] Lugard then overpowered Kano and Sokoto and deposed their rulers. He confirmed the new rulers nominated by the electors of Kano and Sokoto on carefully explained conditions of appointment. These events of 1902–03 established the British Protectorate on the basis of superior British force.

Zaria had been involved in the struggle indirectly, but was not an active participant. Their rights of garrison at Zaria had allowed the British to use Zaria as a base for mobilizing their troops to attack Kano and Sokoto. The British garrison at Zaria overawed Kwassau. Farther south the British forces had moved to Keffi after clearing the nearby country of brigands and raiders, and had cap-

[1] Burns, *op. cit.,* p. 175.

tured Abuja, which was their stronghold. Kwassau sided with
Sokoto and Kano in their opposition to Lugard, but could not aid
them directly with troops. Instead he instructed his vassal at Keffi
to oppose the British. In consequence, Captain Maloney, who commanded the British detachment at Keffi, was killed by order of the
Magajin Keffi, and the latter then fled northwards through Zaria
to Kano. The British felt that the ruler of Zaria was responsible
for Maloney's death and the Magaji's escape. Kwassau was therefore removed from Zaria city in September 1902, and for six
months the Habe Galadima Suleimanu was in charge of the kingdom. At the same time the British removed the chiefdoms of
Keffi, Kwotto, Jema'a, and Doma from the control of the ruler of
Zaria, and established them under separate provincial administration. By removing its southern vassals the British intended to
punish Zaria for the murder of Captain Maloney.

In March 1902 the Protectorate Government had established a
Provincial Administration at Zaria with Captain Abadie as Resident in charge. The provincial boundaries of Zaria in 1902 were
much wider than they now are, and initially the Province contained
two divisions, the lesser having its headquarters at Wushishi, the
larger being based on Zaria city. A tax on caravans was immediately instituted as a symbol of British administrative intentions;
but there was little chance for administrative reorganization immediately. Military and police action to suppress opposition and
slave-raiding had first priority. Although the British had not conquered Zaria, they had overpowered its suzerain, and they had
incorporated the kingdom in their system of Provincial Administration. Their initial acts were evidence of their superior force, and
on this basis they rested their claim to superior status. In the three
years since their arrival the British had reduced the dominions
under the king of Zazzau, removed the king from office, and deposed him after a delay of six months. Such actions were clearly
political; they expressed the new distribution of power between
the British and the Fulani of Zaria and Sokoto.

By the establishment of the Protectorate of Northern Nigeria,
and by his rapid and extensive conquests, Lugard had incorporated the state of Zaria within a political unit far greater than the
empire of Sokoto to which it had formerly belonged. Although the
rulers of this new protectorate were Christians from Europe, and
its largest units were Fulani-ruled Muhammadan kingdoms, it also

contained Kanuri Muhammadans in Bornu, and large non-Islamic populations whom the Fulani and Kanuri had formerly raided for slaves. Within the Protectorate, the former Fulani empire continued to occupy a dominant position. Its size and prestige made it essential for the British to win and keep its support in order to maintain effective rule. Lugard understood this condition clearly. To reassure the Fulani of his friendly intentions, he reinstated the Toronkawa king of Kontagora, and he again asked the Sultan to nominate successors to those thrones which were formerly subordinate to Sokoto, and which were now vacant through deposition or war. Thus the Sultan, on the advice of the electoral council of Zaria, nominated Aliyu, the son of Sidi, the acting Wombai, to fill Kwassau's place on the throne; and Bornawa rule again gave way to the Mallawa.

2. ALIYU, 1903–20

(a) The British and the Fulani

Aliyu owed his nomination to Sokoto, his confirmation and appointment to the British. The terms on which he was appointed emphasized his subordination to the British Administration especially with regard to war, raids, the sale of slaves, and slavery. Thus the new king had dual loyalties to the British and Sokoto. He had also inherited loyalties to the system of dynastic rule in Zaria, and in particular to his own dynasty, the Mallawa. His problem was to restore and maintain the political system of Fulani Zaria, within the context of its changing relations with Sokoto and the British, and within a context of major administrative and political change. Restoration of the traditional autocratic kingship seemed essential in view of the continuing dynastic competition. In the context of this competition, an autocratic kingship had always been the precondition of effective rule, and absolutism was even more necessary in this changing situation to safeguard the government's form and maintain its adaptability.

However, as a ruler appointed by the British, Aliyu was charged with the preservation of law and order, and under the Native Authority Proclamation, No. 2 of 1907, he was empowered to enforce obedience to his orders through the native (Muhammadan) courts. By this ordinance, dismissals from office were brought under the jurisdiction of the Muhammadan courts; and administrative offence was regarded as a ground for dismissals from office. This ordinance restated the principles which had led to the institution of an administrative court at Zaria under the Wali. The new king could not at once foresee the full implications of the British measure; but after the first years of his reign, Aliyu found that his freedom to dismiss officials or to keep them in office was limited by this new judicial power. In effect, officials supported by the king could be dismissed from office if they were found guilty of maladministration, which was defined as disobedience to British instructions. At the same time, officials of whom the king wished to be rid, could retain office, if they were not found guilty of any such offences, whether by commission or omission. Thus the authority of the ruler was defined and limited by the laws of the British Administration which had appointed him; but the essence of traditional kingship had been its overwhelming power, and its administrative unaccountability at law.

The British enforced and interpreted this Native Authority Proclamation by a burst of depositions and imprisonments in the early years of their rule, and thereby obliged the Muhammadan Judiciary to decide issues in which the king was vitally interested. This made the power of the kingship formally dependent on the whims of his judge or the technicalities of law. For reasons already given, the Fulani rulers of Zaria could not tamely accept such a redefinition of their position. They could neither acquiesce in the new distinctions established under the law between the king's power and authority nor, accept the new relations which this law laid down between the king and Alkali. In the new context different ideas of kingship made conflicts inevitable, and it was many years before the king's role and status were clearly defined.

Kingship stood between the British Protectorate Government and the administration of the native state. It was responsible to the British for public order, tax-collection, for the administration of justice, and for the execution of policy decisions. Decisions on such questions as the prohibition against raiding and sale of slaves, or the reorganization of administrative boundaries, the British reserved for themselves. Other questions were decided in association with the head of the Native Administration, by discussions between the British Resident and/or Divisional Officer and the local ruler, who was the recognized Native Authority.[1] Yet other decisions could

[1] For discussion of these terms, see Ch. 7, Section 2 (a) below.

be taken by the native ruler himself with British support; but various matters for which the native rulers were responsible were also supervised by the British Provincial Administrations through whom these rulers communicated with the Protectorate Government. The resulting ambiguities in relations between local rulers and the British administration could not be resolved except through political action of one sort or another, since the precise definition of their powers and duties was itself only possible through political bargaining and the exercise of political power.

After their initial attempt to resist the British by force, the Fulani had quickly learnt the futility of further attempts. The Sultan of Sokoto and the king of Gwandu had both been deposed in quick succession, together with other important Fulani rulers such as the kings of Yola, Bauchi, Kano, Katsina, Hadejia, Kontagora, Nupe, Katagum, and Zaria. The Fulani thereafter ceased to resist the British by force, and actively co-operated in the establishment of British rule, especially perhaps because the British ratified their political domination over the Habe and other peoples formerly conquered by their ancestors, without interfering with their religion in any way.

An event which tested Fulani loyalty to the British occurred in 1906, when a religious fanatic proclaimed himself Mahdi at Satiru, a village near the capital of Sokoto. Lugard feared a widespread religious outbreak against the British. But the ruling Fulani supported the British attack on Satiru with cavalry, although they had not been asked to do so. The British suffered the first reverse of their northern campaigns during their initial attack on the rebels of Satiru; but the Fulani rulers remained loyal during the following month, while another force was gathered which put down the revolt. Besides its Madhist elements and aims, the Satiru incident was partly a revolt against the Sultan of Sokoto and partly against the British. Suppression of this revolt showed the Fulani that the British would support their rule; and it also showed the British that the Fulani would support theirs. Thus the revolt at Satiru changed relations between the British and the ruling Fulani from superordination based on force to a near parity based on common interests. Relations of British dominance and Fulani submission which had been established by their military conflict, changed in this new situation.

To the British the Satiru incident clearly demonstrated their dependence on Fulani support; and in his Political Memoranda, which gave detailed instructions about the forms and aims of the British Administration, besides stressing this fact, Lugard devoted special attention to the cultivation and increase of Fulani loyalties and political parity. Provincial Residents and Divisional Officers were expressly forbidden to give orders or commands to the Fulani rulers, and were charged with advisory roles. This system of rule was carefully elaborated by Lugard and was expounded more generally in his later publications under the name of 'Indirect Rule'.[1] Its name emphasizes the collaboration and interdependence of the British and Native Administrations, but this in turn depended upon their satisfactory political relations.

Political relations between the British and the Fulani had various features and foci; but after the Satiru rebellion of 1906 there was a tacit agreement between them to avoid the direct use of force. This tacit prohibition of force itself improved the position of the Fulani *vis-à-vis* the British; but it also marked the end of British conquest and the beginning of British consolidation. The Fulani could rely on British guns and bayonets to suppress resistance to their rule. The British desired to avoid further fighting with the Fulani empire, and this served to limit political pressures on these states; in addition the British need for Fulani assistance in the administration of the conquered areas further increased the bargaining power of the rulers of these states.

Thus the assumption that Lugard's conquest established a simple relation of dominance-submission between British and Fulani is misleading. The relation established in the process of consolidation emphasized Anglo-Fulani interdependence in the government of the Protectorate; and this interdependence itself expressed the relative needs and power of the British and Fulani governments. Relations between these two units remained indefinite in many important particulars, and their development was left open to the future play of power. From this point of view indirect rule was a method of political association; to this was attached a code which defined what should not be done or allowed but which did not specify precisely the purposes and objectives of the British Protectorate. Fulani assumed that the British knew what they wished to do and that the British would try to enact their wishes. In the Fulani view the role of the British was

[1] Cf. Lugard, 1910 and 1918. Also Lugard, 1926.

to institute change, while that of the Fulani rulers was to limit it.

Thus the Fulani empire continued as a unit within the British Protectorate of Northern Nigeria. After the British conquest this unit lacked precise, formal status; but Lugard's frequent appeals to the Sultan for nominees to chiefdoms such as Zaria or Kontagora emphasized the fact that the British conquest had not abolished the system of relations already holding between Sokoto and other states of the empire. The individual states of this Fulani empire found that their imperial relations and membership increased their status and power *vis-à-vis* the British. A unit with the size, organization, and religious basis of the Fulani empire could not be treated lightly by the conquerors, however effective the military force at their control. Indeed, the empire's irreplaceability, and the administrative difficulties which would follow from its dissolution, were considerations which had led Lugard to support and maintain it.

In Zaria, relations between the king and the British reflected this general context. At Zaria the native ruler faced the British Administration directly in his regular consultations with the British Resident and Divisional Officer; but the king was also in contact with the British indirectly, through his membership in the empire of Sokoto, and through his subordinate, the Judge of Zaria. These various elements and references made for a complex relationship, the definition of which also required time.

(b) Appointments to Office

Aliyu's first commitment was clearly to put his own house in order. He began by dismissing the Alkali, ostensibly for intriguing against him.[1] The Alkali had been an elector of Zaria, and had held office under the previous régime. After his removal, Aliyu set about securing the dismissal of Galadima Suleimanu. Suleimanu had

---

[1] Aliyu's use of intrigue as a charge is worthy of note. It was new—there having hitherto been no necessity for a formal charge; but it expressed the old political principles which governed tenure of office clearly. The Alkali and the Galadima were successively dismissed on the charge of intrigue. It seems unlikely that the Alkali could have nourished political ambitions. It is possible that the Alkali was dismissed for failure to assist Aliyu in removing the Galadima. Under the new judicial system the Alkali's aid in this matter may have seemed essential to Aliyu and risky to the judge. But hesitancy or opposition in a subordinate were equally disloyal; hence perhaps the charge of intrigue. Alternatively, the Alkali may have been a client of Suleimanu, whose removal was desirable before action was taken against the Galadima.

ruled Zaria as a sovereign during the six months' interregnum which preceded Aliyu's appointment. He had maintained his dominating position at Zaria under Sambo, Yero, and Kwassau alike. Apparently he regarded himself as irremovable, and is reported to have lifted his hand to strike Aliyu after the latter's appointment as king. Aliyu reported to the British Resident that Suleimanu was intriguing for his overthrow and, with British support, Suleimanu was dismissed. Thus Aliyu eliminated a powerful opponent and laid open the way for restoring the autocratic kingship, within the indefinite limits consistent with British supervision.

Aliyu next dismissed Kwassau's son, Ibrahim, from the office of Madaki, appointing his own eldest son, Sa'idu. Another of the ruler's sons, Yero, replaced Suleimanu as Galadima; and Mallawa were also appointed to the offices of Wombai, Dan Galadima, Wali, and Iya. Bornawa were also eliminated from the offices of Shentali, Magajin Gari, Chikum, Makama Karami, Dallatu, and Sarkin Ruwa. Aliyu conferred these offices on the Fulani Zamfara, the Toronkawa, and other Mallawa clients.

Such wholesale redistribution of office did not pass without British notice and action. Either the British failed to perceive the reasons for this wholesale elimination of Bornawa officials or they refused to accept them. Many of the dismissed office-holders had not been accused of any administrative offence. The British regarded administrative efficiency and uprightness as the essential condition governing tenure of office. Under British pressure Aliyu was compelled to reappoint Ibrahim and Zubairu, two of Kwassau's sons whom he had dismissed from the offices of Madaki and Iya. This action won Bornawa support for British rule. The two princes were given less important positions. Ibrahim became Dan Madami, and Zubairu was made Sarkin Ruwa. To the princes these transfers on reappointment were really demotions; but demotions had not been a feature of Fulani rule during the previous century, since dismissal from office by the king had not been subject to review or revision; and such reappointments really marked a serious curtailment of kingly power to redistribute office. This practice first developed under British supervision.

The British were not content with securing the reappointment of officials dismissed by the king without proof of offence. They were also responsible for having the king's kin and supporters dismissed from key positions. In 1915 Aliyu's son, Sa'idu, was dismissed from the office of Madaki for embezzling the *jangali* (cattle-tax). Yero, another son, whom Aliyu had first appointed as Galadima, and had then moved over to the position of Makama Karami, replaced Sa'idu as Madaki in the following year; but Yero was also dismissed for maladministration in 1918; and before he could reappoint his son Sa'idu as Madaki, Aliyu had to secure British approval, and in the end on reappointment Sa'idu was only given a ward of Zaria town to administer. These British actions further increased Bornawa support for their administration.

It is unthinkable that a Fulani ruler of Zaria in the nineteenth century would ever dismiss his own sons from the position of Madaki; or that he should limit the scope and authority of that office to the administration of a ward of Zaria town. It would also be unthinkable for such a ruler to acquiesce in the appointment of dynastic rivals to the Madakiship; Sambo's dismissal of Anu in contradiction to orders from Sokoto illustrates this point. But with the pacification the significance of the Madakiship was changing. Although Aliyu could not immediately perceive this, the Madakin Zazzau had long ago led his last cavalry charge. Nor did the Madaki's pre-eminence among fief-holders continue for long. None the less, history had linked the title of Madaki to the succession of Zaria too intimately for the king to allow it to slip from the hands of his sons. For this reason Aliyu had dismissed Kwassau's son from the office, installing his own. Even after the British dismissed his two sons from this office consecutively, the king still sought to keep the title for them, although its powers were greatly reduced.

Apart from the king's kinsmen, several persons whom he had appointed to office were dismissed during his reign for peculation, maladministration, or on other grounds. These dismissals express British pressure. At the same time, by their administrative reforms, the British were effectively changing and reorganizing the structure and functions of the native official system in Zaria. By the end of Aliyu's reign, the nineteenth-century Fulani system of administration had been radically changed. The *Provincial Gazette*, compiled by Mr. E. J. Arnett, who was himself a Resident of Zaria during this period, gives the detail of this reorganization, and the changes which were then introduced.[1]

[1] Arnett, 1920. The following summary of developments at Zaria between 1903 and 1920 draws heavily on Arnett's *Gazetteer* for administrative details.

(c) Territorial Reorganization

A token caravan-tax had been instituted in 1902. In the following year a British military force was sent against Gadas and other
towns of north-eastern Zaria which had refused to pay this tax,
and the use of *jekadu* was prohibited by the British. *Jekadu* had
traditionally acted as agents of fief-holders resident in Zaria and
were charged to collect tax from the fiefs concerned. On the prohibition of *jekadu* the community chiefs were held responsible for
collection of tax; but after a breakdown in tax-collection had
revealed the ineffectiveness of these village chiefs, the British
restored the *jekadu* for a few years. However, the implication of
this early prohibition of *jekadu* became clear in 1905, when the
first fief-holder was removed from Zaria city and was sent to live
in his fief as a District Head in charge of an administrative district.
By the end of 1907 the kingdom (which was classified by the
British as a 'First-class Emirate') had been divided into thirty-two
such districts, of which three, Kajuru, Kauru, and Chawai already
had resident Habe chiefs of vassal status, the chief of Chawai being himself traditionally a vassal of the vassal chief of Kauru. Each
of these new districts was administered by a titled District Head,
whom the Emir appointed and the British confirmed. Thus the old
system of territorial administration by which officials resident at
Zaria had administered a variety of scattered fiefs was abolished;
and with this territorial system formally went the institution of
jekadanci which belonged to it.

This change in the system of territorial administration sharply
reduced the number of fief-holding offices at the king's disposal.
This reduction itself increased the intensity of competitions for the
surviving offices. Moreover, it was itself a precedent for further
reductions, through which the administrative costs and territorial
organization would be progressively rationalized. Several of the
titles which lapsed at this *gunduma* (redistribution of fiefs) were
already offices traditionally attached to special lineages and filled
in a quasi-hereditary fashion. Such positions were peculiarly
vulnerable to official reductions, being peripheral to the system of
competition for office among the Fulani within the capital. By 1920
the number of territorial districts had been further reduced to
twenty-seven, five of which, Kauru, Kajuru, Chawai, Kagarko, and
Lere, were hereditary vassal states. Since then, the number of ad-

ministrative districts has been progressively reduced, and by 1950 there were only seventeen. Each reduction has been accompanied by a corresponding reduction of administrative costs and by a corresponding increase in the effectiveness of the Emir's supervision. But each reduction has also meant an increase in the intensity of the political competition for the remaining territorial offices, and a corresponding reduction in the numbers of princes qualified by experience of territorial administration to contest the royal succession.

At the same time that the fiefs were transformed into territorial districts, the British Administration sought to transform fief-holders into salaried officers of the Native Administration, and further to transform this administration itself from a ruling into a controlled bureaucracy. The old system of tax-collection was abolished, and, after surveys to assess income-levels and former revenues, the *haraji* (land-tax), and *Jangali* (cattle-tax) took their place. Unauthorized forced labour and forced levies were both forbidden. Silver and copper coins were brought in to replace the cowrie currency, which was being bought up at a set rate. It was gradually established that tax was payable only in the form of the new currency.

From the date at which the Province of Zaria had been established, the Protectorate Government had claimed a share of the revenues collected by the Native Authority. When the new territorial system was introduced in 1907, the resident District Chiefs were allowed to retain between 20 and 25 per cent. of the tax which they collected, while the Protectorate Government claimed 50 per cent., and the remainder was left to the Emir and his central officials. In 1910 this measure was followed by the establishment of a Native Treasury, or Beit-el-Mal, after which the Emir and his central officials were paid monthly salaries instead of percentages of the tax as before. For the time, District Chiefs and Village Heads were allowed to retain minor shares of the tax which they collected. By 1912 the two new taxes, *haraji* and *jangali*, had completely replaced the old system of taxation in the Muhammadan districts of the emirate, and such tithes as *zakka* no longer formed part of the official revenue. In the following year the District Chiefs were given monthly salaries in lieu of shares of tax. Shortly after this the village headmen also lost their share of tax in return for small salaries. These changes in the conditions and terms of their employment were accompanied by the dismissal of several District Chiefs on British insistence for embezzlement, peculation, and the like. The institution of salaries and the prohibition of unauthorized levies, commissions, and forced labour, were immediate and far-reaching changes in their position which aroused the opposition of these territorial chiefs. Thus in the last years of Aliyu's reign there was a sudden increase in the number of District Chiefs dismissed from office for actions which had the sanction of local tradition, but which were now defined as offences under the new system.

In 1916, each resident District Chief was assigned a clerk, who was trained and paid by the Native Treasury in Zaria. The clerk's duty was to assist in the compilation of district records and statistics, and in official correspondence. In 1917 each District Head also received a paid messenger, and two *dogarai* (native policemen) as further additions to the district staff. The nucleus of an effective District Administration was thereby established throughout the kingdom, and District revenues accordingly increased.

(d) The New Judicial System

The British also reorganized and expanded the native judicial system. On the *gunduma* of 1907 the Alkali or Chief Judge had been given a small district near Zaria, in order to reduce his economic dependence on the Emir. At their arrival the British found three courts in Zaria city, the king's, the Alkali's, and the Salenke's. The Salenke had also acted as a travelling judge and dealt with legal issues which arose on campaigns. Appeal lay from the Salenke's court to the Alkali's, and from the latter to the king's court. The king's court dealt with land and boundary disputes, and also with issues arising from relations between his Muhammadan and non-Muhammadan subjects. Only the king's court could order capital punishment. Outside Zaria city there were courts presided over by *Alkalai* (s. *Alkali*, judge) at Kagarko, Lere, Jema'a, and Kauru. These were all vassal states, and their judges were appointed locally. Other vassal states such as Fatika, Kajuru, Keffi, and Kwotto did not then have *Alkalai* presiding over their courts.

Shortly after their establishment of Zaria Province, the British established a new Alkali's court at Wushishi, which was the second Divisional Headquarters of the new Province. This Alkali had powers of levying fines up to £1, which was then equivalent to about 30,000 cowries. Fines were to be paid in the new currency. In 1905 the British established other native courts under Alkalai at Paiko, Birnin Gwari, and Kacia. Of these only the court at Kacia fell directly within the kingdom of Zaria. But in 1910 four more courts were established at Soba, Rigachikum, Anchau, and Fatika, all of which lay in Zaria. With these increases in the number of courts there was an immediate increase in the annual number of native court cases, and also in the number of registered self-redemptions by slaves.[1] Court revenues showed corresponding increases, and so did the number of convictions. By 1912 it was necessary to build a larger prison in Zaria city to accommodate this increase of convicts. The new prison was built where Abubakar, the baMalle king of Zaria, had formerly had his home. New court-houses were also built, and the number of district courts continued to increase until 1919 when there were seventeen native courts within the kingdom. Effectively, this meant that there were two Alkali's courts for every three rural districts. With the continuing reduction in the number of territorial districts, as opportunities arose for their amalgamation, the British have since been able to establish a native court in each district of the emirate and to give them identical boundaries. Thus by 1950 the number of Alkalai in Zaria Emirate equalled the number of District Chiefs. The progress towards this equivalence in the numbers of senior territorial and judicial officials has been accompanied by an enormous increase in the administrative and political significance of the native judiciary. For several years the judicial establishment was the largest single unit or department of government in Zaria, except for the territorial administration which remained directly under the king.

Moreover, this progressive increase in the size of the judiciary has taken place together with an increase in its independence, power, and authority. In consequence, one of the most fundamental changes in the native government which has occurred under British rule consists in the new relations which have developed between the kingship and the judiciary, with the latter's growth in size and jurisdiction. From the first, the British made it plain that the native courts would adjudicate issues arising under the new regulations and laws promulgated by the Native Authority or the

---

[1] Under Lugard's Slavery Proclamation slaves were empowered to register their self-redemptions in Native Courts. See Burns, *op. cit.*, p. 187.

Protectorate Government, as well as the Muslim *shari'a*. Thus, under Lugard's Slavery Proclamation of 1901, all persons born after April 1st of that year were free; and slaves who wished to assert their freedom were empowered to claim it through the courts. By the beginning of 1912, 3,349 slaves had secured their freedom through the courts of Zaria. By the end of 1919, this number had risen to 9,472, the increase of 6,123 developing during the period when the new courts were being established in Zaria. Besides these Protectorate orders, the new courts enforced local administrative regulations. Thus rules made in 1916 by the Native Administration to control contagious cattle disease were referred to the native courts for enforcement. In the following year native court rules were promulgated to prohibit touting and to improve the quality of locally grown cotton. At this point, the Emir asserted that such rules were only enforceable in his court and by his judicial council. There were then seventeen Alkali's courts in the kingdom, and the Emir was quite rightly disturbed at the prospect of becoming politically dependent on these courts.

This prospect of political dependence arose at two levels. The Chief Alkali of Zaria had rights to hear appeals from the new district courts and to review their decisions. Secondly, he selected the persons suitable for appointment as judges of these courts. Thus the Chief Alkali could distribute judicial appointments and he could also protect his appointees by supporting their decisions, since the District Officer or European Magistrate supervising the Alkali's court, was rarely expert in Muhammadan law. Moreover, by his right to review the decisions of district courts, the Chief Alkali could systematically undermine the competence of judges whom he wished to replace, and he could also recommend their dismissal. Although such recommendations required the Emir's approval, the Emir could rarely reject them. Thus the king's control of his judiciary depended on his control of its most senior office, that of the Chief Alkali.

Indeed, the king's increasing dependence on his judiciary was emphasized by his failure to prevent dismissals from and re-appointments to territorial office consequent on judicial decisions. To retain supporters in office, and exclude his rivals, the Emir had to control his judiciary, and also to limit communication between his subjects and the British District Officers. Without this control, the ruler could neither maintain his supporters in office nor exclude his enemies. Aliyu recognized clearly that he could not rule as an autocrat without this control.

(e) The King and the Chief Judge

Lugard's political memoranda, which defined the relations between the British rulers and the Muhammadan emirates, gave very precise instructions about the behaviour of British administrative officials in relation to the native population.[1] Lugard was anxious not to alienate the ruling Fulani who dominated the Northern Protectorate. He also was well aware that if the population of these kingdoms were free to protest injustice and maladministration directly to the provincial officials, it would at the least create mutual distrust between Fulani and British, and could lead to wholesale dismissals of native officials, which might make administration itself extremely difficult. In consequence, relations between the British administrative staff and the *talakawa* or Hausa commoners were subject to strict regulations. According to this code, it was improper for British administrative officers to discuss or hear complaints from natives of the emirates privately. Some representative of the local chief should also be present; normally this would either be one of the chief's official and salaried messengers, or a native policeman, or the chief himself, or one of his unpaid agents. In effect, this meant that a Divisional Officer always had some escort or agent of the Native Authority with him to observe his dealings with natives. The Divisional Officer neither gave orders nor payment to the natives directly, but did so through their recognized and properly constituted authorities. In effect, this meant that orders could be attributed to the British Administration which they did not originate, and without their knowledge. It also meant that payments by the members of the British Administration could be withheld from those to whom they were due. Lugard's rules effectively frustrated the desires of malcontents, legitimate or other, to seek redress directly from or through the British, and thereby fulfilled his aim of preserving the local dominance of recognized native authorities.

However, this code of behaviour for British administrative officials did not protect officers of the Native Administration against discovery and punishment for malpractices traceable by written records; and the unfamiliarity of these native officials with ac-

[1] See Lugard, 1910 and 1918.

counting and with administration by written records made them specially prone to this category of offences, and peculiarly vulnerable to its investigation. Such issues at first tended to take the form of charges of embezzlement, peculation, or misappropriation of funds, and had a fairly common form. The official accused had to clear himself in a native or British court in the face of written and other evidence supporting the charge.

For the ruler these trials emphasized the judge's power, as well as the importance of keeping careful records. The unfamiliarity of native officials with records was only paralleled by their unfamiliarity with those conceptions of official accountability at law which the British had introduced. To control and protect his administrative staff, the ruler had therefore to control his judiciary. Moreover, the loyalty of his officials corresponded with the ruler's power to protect them from dismissal and punishment; and as the history of Fulani government in the nineteenth century emphasizes, the officials appointed by an Emir were specially chosen for their loyalty to his cause and his régime. In brief, political loyalties structured the traditional Fulani government; and these loyalties were directly threatened by the British rule that gave jurisdiction over administrative issues to the native Alkalai.

Such transfers of function to the Alkalai involved transfers of power also; if the Emir failed to limit the authority of his Chief Alkali, he would become dependent on the latter for the maintenance of his administration, especially since the responsibility of subordinate judges to the Chief Alkali protected them from direct dismissal by the Emir. In such a situation, the Emir had to reduce the power of his Chief Alkali in order to rule his emirate. This need was made more urgent by the fact that he had to face attacks by his dynastic rivals on his officials, and on himself as the gazetted Native Authority. In such a context of hereditary rivalry it was equally important that the Emir should retain control of his judiciary and that he should preserve it from the influence of his rivals or from those ambitions which its new position under the British reorganization tended to encourage.

By his actions Aliyu showed how clearly he recognized the changes in his situation. In 1917 he insisted that only the Emir's court had jurisdiction over cases arising under regulations of the Native Administration. These regulations (*dokoki*) differ from Muhammadan law (*shari'a*) in a variety of ways. Firstly, they are secular in origin and focus, whereas Islamic law is not, being an instrument for the pursuit of the good life by the Faithful. Secondly, these *dokoki* are administrative, revocable, often time-limited, indefinitely expandable, and of alien inspiration. With considerable foresight the Emir rejected British proposals to give the Alkalai jurisdiction over such issues, the full scope of which he could not foresee. Thus the Alkali's court was limited to the application of the *shari'a*; while the Emir had jurisdiction over the new administrative regulations (*dokoki*), land, boundaries, and over issues between Moslems and non-Moslems.

Aliyu employed other and more effective means to limit and reduce the rising power of the Chief Judge. He had opened his reign by dismissing the Alkalin Zazzau from office. In 1916 he promoted the then Chief Alkali Abdullahi (also called Mallam Bako) from the Chief Judgeship to the advisory office of Waziri, which was revived for this occasion with British support. Abdullahi's successor in the office of Chief Alkali died shortly after Aliyu's reign had ended. Aliyu had shown how the Emir's power to 'promote' the Chief Judge could be used to limit the latter's power. The Chief Judgeship thereafter ceased to be a life-tenure appointment, and its holder became subject to dismissal and 'promotion' alike.

During the nineteenth century, a total of ten appointments had been made to the Chief Judgeship of Zazzau, only two of which had been interrupted by dismissals. Of these Sada's dismissal by Sambo from the conjoint offices of Alkali and Salenke was clearly political. In the other case, Balingimi, Mallam Musa's first Alkali, asked Musa to let him resign because of old age. On no occasion was there any promotion from the position of Alkali throughout this period. It is thus clear that during the last century the office of Chief Judge was normally a life-long appointment. In view of the history of nineteenth-century Fulani Zaria, there can be no greater evidence of the political insignificance of an office than its allocation on a life-tenure basis. Such tenure implied that successive kings who were political rivals would have no cause to interfere with the tenure or administration of such offices; and this tolerance defined office as non-political. The combined political insignificance and life-tenure of the Chief Judgeship in nineteenth-century Zaria contrasts directly with the insecurity in the tenure of the Chief Judgeship and its increased political and administrative significance at Zaria during the present century. In the first fifty years of British rule, eight persons have held the office of Chief Judge, of whom three died in office. Another three were 'promoted' out of this strategic position, while two were simply dismissed by the king. Clearly, the great increase in the power of the Chief Judgeship under British rule has been associated with corresponding insecurity in the tenure of that office.

In 1910 Aliyu revived the office of Waziri which had remained vacant since the reign of his father, Sidi, in 1860. Aliyu may have done so to honour his father and to emphasize the continuity of Mallawa power by re-establishing this office last used by Sidi, or he may have intended an indirect taunt at Sokoto and at Abubakar's segment of the Mallawa alike. But in reviving the Waziriship, Aliyu had the full approval of the British, who felt that he needed a regular council with a chief councillor or vizier, and the British may even have suggested this appointment. Aliyu first appointed his Turaki Karami Ahmadu to the position of Waziri. In the next year the British formally recognized the new Waziri as the 'principal adviser to the Emir', and established a new Judicial Council consisting of the Waziri, the Alkali, the Ma'aji, or treasurer, and the Madauci, with the Emir as its head.

The British intended that this new unit would act as a Native Council of State; and their description of this cabinet, whose composition they decided, as a Judicial Council illustrates equally the British conception of the functions of a Native Council of State, and their misconception of the form and functions which a council of state would have in such a polity as Fulani Zaria. For the rest of his reign Aliyu had two councils, this Judicial Council and another, composed of his close kinsmen and certain office-holding clients, with which he discussed political affairs. The British Administration wanted the Council of State to act as the senior unit of the controlled bureaucracy they were trying to develop; and for this reason they wished it to contain officials versed in the new bureaucratic skills. By including the Treasurer and the Madauci, who were his clients, in this new Judicial Council, Aliyu satisfied the wishes of the British and also ensured that he would dominate the official council and be able to use it to sanction decisions arrived at privately. The Madauci was at this time in charge of Zaria city, Aliyu having learnt the dangers of allowing powerful officials of electoral status to control the administration of the capital. But before the British had had time to interfere with this by reorganizing the city administration and returning it to the office of the Galadima, Aliyu had taken further steps to alter the composition of his Judicial Council by 'promoting' Waziri Ahmadu to the position of Makama Karami, by moving his Chief Alkali out of that office into the position of Waziri, and by making another appointment to the position of Chief Judge.

By transferring Ahmadu from the office of Waziri to that of Mukama Karami, Aliyu revealed his opinion of the Waziriship and his recognition that its holder lacked power. Despite its seniority on the advisory council, this office had no executive functions other than temporary commissions granted by the king. On the other hand, its advisory role and status could be used to increase its holder's power and possibly to embarrass the king. The king was aware of this possibility and, in consequence, tenure of the Waziriship, like that of the Chief Alkali, became correspondingly insecure.

Within the traditional political system of Fulani Zazzau, which was at this time very much a reality, there was really no room for an office of principal adviser to the ruler. Such advice could not depart from the ruler's ends, since the maintenance of his rule and increase of his power were unalterable ends for the monarch. Advice was only possible on questions about the means for realizing given ends. Yet unsolicited advice was politically risky and could easily be mistaken for political pressure. Moreover, recurrent differences between the Emir and his principal adviser about the means to realize given ends of policy could only discredit that adviser with the king. Since only the king knew fully his own reactions to and opinions of the individual participants in his régime, and since the authority and power of these persons were critical elements in the context of policy decisions, only the ruler could really decide such questions. In such a system any adviser with the tactlessness to differ frequently from the ruler about appropriate means invited the suspicion that he also differed covertly about ends; the mere suspicion of this would nullify the adviser's effectiveness and hasten his downfall. This being the case it is not surprising that the office of principal adviser at Zaria has tended to be insecure as well as ineffective. In the system of dynastic competition, the king's most suitable advisers were his closest kin.

None the less, Aliyu and the Emirs of Zaria who came after him were quick to appreciate the relief from over-powerful Chief Judges with which the Waziriship provided them. They rapidly developed a practice of appointing the Chief Judge to the Waziri-ship, thereby separating him from his protected judicial position with its indirect power over the executive, and its opportunity to influence or upset matters of interest to the king. Such loss of power by individual Alkalai through promotion to the office of Waziri was often followed by loss of that office also; in this way the king could deal with a judge who threatened to become his political rival.

By changing his Chief Alkalai, the king also tried to keep the judiciary from usurping executive functions. Such usurpation could develop in either of two ways: by applying the *Shari'a* to 'test cases', which bore on the king's powers and authority over such matters as land-suits and the like; or by applying the *Shari'a* and its interpretations to the regulations promulgated by the Native Authority. In the words of a British official, there has been 'progressive encroachment of the Native Judiciary in land matters and the corresponding weakening in such matters of the Native Authority'.[1]

An important feature of the Chief Judge's position is its effective control over the appointment of other judges.[2] In fact, the district judges enjoy a greater security of official tenure than their chief, for the reason that their offices are politically secondary. District judges can only be dismissed for incompetence or dishonesty, and on the Chief Judge's recommendations. Needless to say, such recommendations are infrequently made, since the power of the Chief Judge depends on the loyalty of his subordinate judges; and such loyalty in turn involves mutual obligations, of which protec-tion in office is one. What the Chief Judge can and does do, quite systematically, is to use his power of appointment to fill such judgeships as become vacant during his term of office with persons who, besides being qualified by learning for such positions, are bound to him by ties of loyalty and especially by kinship. In 1950 the incidence of lineage relations in these judicial appointments was greater than in those controlled by the ruler.

The persons whom a Chief Alkali is most likely to appoint to subordinate judgeships are his close kin, especially his agnatic kin.

[1] Cole, 1949, p. 33.
[2] The present tense here refers to the period 1910–1950.

In consequence a rivalry for the control of the senior judgeship and its subordinate appointments has arisen between legal lineages which provides a striking contemporary parallel to the rivalry of dynasties for the throne during the last century. This rivalry between legal lineages for the control of subordinate judgeships allows the ruler to control the judiciary by occasionally changing the Chief Judge. His transfer reduces the power and solidarity of the department as a whole; and this reduction of power and solidarity is reflected in the initial isolation of the newly appointed Chief Judge. In their dealings with the Native Judiciary the rulers of Zaria in this century are simply following the practice of rotating office among competing lineages developed by the Sultans of Sokoto a hundred years earlier.

When a Chief Judge has filled several subordinate judgeships with his own kinsmen, his power is at its height, and he can reckon on several supporters in any legal dispute. Moreover, these subordinate judges, who are his kin, train other of his kinsmen as their assistants, and these assistants are thus qualified for promotion to such judgeships as fall vacant by death or dismissal. At such a time the king normally 'promotes' his chief judge, or secures his dismissal through the good offices of his Waziri. The Waziri, as a member of a rival legal lineage, may be sympathetic to the removal of his successor for reasons of lineage rivalry as well as on political grounds. The ruler is then free to appoint as Chief Judge one of the present district judges who combines a reputation for legal learning, and lack of kin within the judiciary, with the relation of personal clientage. The new Chief Judge finds on his appointment that several judges are against his promotion, and that kinship is the basis of their solidarity. To the degree that the new Chief Judge lacks the support of his subordinate judges, he is dependent on the king. To remedy this, as occasion arises, the new Chief Judge also fills junior judgeships with his own kinsmen; and when he has a sufficient number of kin in the judiciary, he is in his turn a potential rival of the king, and will then be either dismissed or promoted out of his office. In the long as well as the short run, such patterns of development allow the ruler to administer the government as an effective autocracy; but at any moment of time the particular distribution of power between the king and his Chief Judge is in process of change; and such continuous change in the relative power of king and Chief Judge implies their political interdependence and their solidarity in relation to the British Administration.

(*f*) *Other Changes*

We can now continue with the chronicle of developments under British rule. In the account of the government of Zaria in 1950 which follows, the significance of the changes just discussed will become increasingly evident.

The British were interested in rationalizing and developing the native administration and the native economy. To rationalize the administration, records were essential, and for this the Roman script was more suitable than the Islamic. Schools were established, firstly at Kano and, after 1914, at Zaria. Hausa boys were taught to read and write Hausa in Roman script. Such pupils later provided the staff for the central and district treasuries, for the judiciary, and other departments of the Native Administration. Over the next few years the number of schools and pupils increased steadily; so did the number of Native Administration employees trained in these schools. Initially, however, most of the pupils were drawn from leading lineages of the Fulani states in which these schools were located. Consequently, although new skills were acquired and exercised by the governing personnel of these emirates, the groups from which these persons were drawn remained as before, and so did the methods by which personnel were recruited to the Native Administration. Merit or ability assessed in terms of literacy and other European techniques was by no means a necessary or sufficient condition for employment in the Native Administration, even in 1950.

The initial economic changes made by the British were political in focus and form. The three major changes were effected by pacification, prohibition of the sale of slaves, and by proclamations permitting slaves to assert their freedom. Reduction in the incidence of taxation and other mandatory payments was part of the British administrative reorganization and increased the proportion of income retained by the peasants, but diminished that available to the nobility. The British quickly discovered that cotton could be grown commercially in Northern Zaria, and from 1911 they were concerned to improve the quality of local cotton, to establish a ginnery, and to develop cotton as a cash-crop. New varieties of sugar-cane were introduced; attempts were made to improve the

breed of cattle; and roads, railways, bridges, telegraphs and tele-
phones were established as rapidly as possible to service the
developing economy.

The great merit of Lugard's approach to the problem of slavery
in Northern Nigeria was its combination of gradualism and firm-
ness. The proclamation which permitted slaves to assert their
freedom also permitted masters to retain as slaves those who did
not.[1] By 1920 less than 10,000 slaves had registered their freedom
in the courts of Zaria. During this gradual transition from a
society based on slavery to one lacking that legal status, slave-
owners were able to secure income from their loyal slaves which,
despite its progressive diminution, maintained their style of living.

Lugard's method of suppressing slavery gave the slave-owners a
number of years in which to think out an answer to this problem of
the vanishing slave. To the Fulani the answer was clear. The ex-
slave should not be allowed to vanish. On this basis, aristocrats
asserted their rights to the land formerly attached to their *rumada*.
Ex-slaves working such land remained under the authority of its
owner (*iyayen giji*) and were indebted to him for rent which they
paid in kind (*gallan gona, aron gona*). In other words persons were
thereafter controlled indirectly through property in land. This
system of control still persists in Zaria, but its bases and objectives
are of necessity hidden from the British, who consequently find the
logic behind the system of land tenure in Zaria somewhat obscure
and puzzling.[2] However, income from other sources became increasingly available as income from slavery diminished.

3. DALLATU, 1920-24

In 1920 the Emir, Aliyu, was deposed by the British for various
reasons, including illicit slave-dealing, and was accordingly removed from the province. The electors of Zaria were consulted,
and the British appointed Dallatu, the son of Yero and the brother
of Kwassau, as the next Emir. Dallatu was of the Bornawa dynasty
and had held the title of Magajin Gari on Aliyu's accession. Aliyu
had immediately taken steps to dismiss him from office, but he had
been reinstated as Magajin Gari under pressure by the British

---

[1] See Burns, 1929, p. 187.
[2] Cole, 1949, pp. 32 ff. For a discussion of these see Ch. 7 below, Section 1,
(*g*) and (*h*).

Administration, who refused to accept Aliyu's reasons for dismissing him. This was the first time that anyone had been promoted to the throne from the office of Magajin Gari. Such an appointment implied that future rulers might also be promoted from offices which had not hitherto provided Zaria with kings.

Dallatu found M. Bako (Abdullahi) holding the office of Waziri, and a number of Mallawa holding titles of royal rank. He concentrated on eliminating the Mallawa from office, beginning with the imprisonment of Aliyu's son, Madaki Sa'idu, on another charge of tax-embezzlement, and also dismissing the Mallawa Wombai, Mamman Gabdo, the Iya Abdullahi, the Wali Haliru, together with other kinsmen and clients of the last ruler. Several of these dismissals took the form of charges concerning collection or returns of tax. How true or false they were is here irrelevant. The important thing about such charges is their timing. During his reign, a ruler sought to protect his nominees in office from such charges, and would only press them against officials he wished to dismiss. As pointed out above, the ruler's ability to protect his appointees was the condition of their solidarity and loyalty. Without effective protection against charges of maladministration by the ruler it would be foolhardy for persons either to seek or to accept office. But on his accession the same ruler took care to press charges against his rivals and their supporters, and thus to secure their dismissal from office; and his ability to secure their removal was a precondition of his power. Such charges were acceptable to the British as a ground for dismissal; and the British, somewhat inconsistently, were also prepared to allow the ruler a freer hand with office-holders of non-royal lineages, some of whom could be dismissed without prior legal process. Such inconsistency by the British naturally confused the Emir, and encouraged him to dismiss dynastic opponents without proper legal process, thereby stimulating British pressure for their reinstatement.

Dallatu followed up his dismissals by appointing his own supporters and kin to office. His son Abdu was given the Madakiship; and after Abdu's untimely death, another son, Shehu, succeeded to the position. Dallatu's appointment of his own son to the Madaki position shows that, like Aliyu, he continued to regard this office as the senior royal office, that is, the one which entailed likeliest promotion to the throne. The Madaki title has indeed retained its prestige and precedence of rank among the titles of Zaria; but its functions have been greatly reduced consequent on the administrative reorganization effected by the British; and it no longer exercised a supreme power under the kingship as formerly. Dallatu gave another son the office of Wali, and another kinsman replaced Mamman Gabdo as Wombai. He also appointed certain Katsinawa to office, and thereby sought to enlist their support for his régime. But Dallatu's time was short. In 1924 he died, and was replaced by Ibrahim, the son of Kwassau.

4. IBRAHIM, 1924–36

(a) Succession and the Dynasties

Ibrahim like Dallatu belonged to the Bornawa dynasty. His accession to the throne was thus an important departure from the traditional system of rotating succession. During the last century the rule had been developed that successive kings should be drawn from different dynasties as a practical defence against mono-dynastic absolutism, and this rule had been applied as consistently as possible. Ibrahim's appointment to succeed Dallatu showed that the British were either unaware of the traditional rules of succession or that they felt that the Bornawa were entitled by the brevity of Dallatu's reign to another innings; or that they had no intention of observing the traditional rules.

Ibrahim's accession had other peculiar features. He was promoted to the throne from the relatively minor office of Dan Madami, which had never before supplied a king, and which in consequence of his accession occupies an ambiguous position in the classification of royal and non-royal ranks. In deciding to appoint Ibrahim, it also appears that the British Administration acted without consulting Sokoto. These conditions indicated that important changes in the succession rules of Zaria were under way; however, any changes in the system of succession implied further changes for the kingship and the political system of the state as a whole.

Ibrahim's accession has one other far-reaching implication. Ibrahim was Kwassau's son; and Kwassau and Dallatu were brothers. Kwassau and Dallatu had both held the kingship, and each had appointed his own sons to office during his reign. In consequence there were now two rival segments of Bornawa interested in the succession, namely, those sons of Kwassau and

Dallatu who had held or were holding office. The development of these Bornawa segments was stimulated by the British innovation of successive appointments from the Bornawa dynasty. Although subsequent appointments to the throne remained uncertain, the precedent of Ibrahim's accession suggested that the Bornawa at the least had a chance of supplying the next Emir. Despite the British supervision which limited the development and overt expression of this competition between Ibrahim's issue and Dallatu's, its emergence is recognizable evidence of intradynastic segmentation consequent on the appointment of brothers to the kingship. There is a clear parallel between the Bornawa segments derived from Kwassau and Dallatu and the Mallawa segmentation under Sidi Abdulkadiri and Abubakar. Under the rules of nineteenth-century succession in Zaria, it had been rare for sons of a common father to hold kingship. The selection of one son had virtually implied elimination of the others; and if this initially stimulated fraternal competition, it also stimulated solidary relations between the king's brothers and himself after his accession, especially since further competition for the throne between their descendants was also ruled out under the principle that only persons themselves directly descended from a former king were eligible to succeed. The British, by appointing Ibrahim as Dallatu's successor, had seriously weakened the force of these restrictive regulations; and Ibrahim's appointment effectively promoted the growth of segmentation within the Bornawa by emphasizing the competition between the descendants of Kwassau and Dallatu.

The development of political segmentation within a dynasty involves major changes in the dynastic structure. In place of the progressive differentiation of the lineage by royal descent lines of dissimilar political status over the generations, such new developments involve a more symmetrical segmentary contraposition within the lineage itself, and it implies replication at each succeeding generation. Inevitably, as the new structure grows, it would include descent lines, differentiated by generation remove from the throne *if* the succession remained closed to all persons whose fathers had not held the throne. In the diagram attached, the structural changes implicit in the new succession practice are represented on this proviso. It will be observed that if such developments are systematic and regulated by successive appointments to the throne from the same dynasty, they would merely reproduce

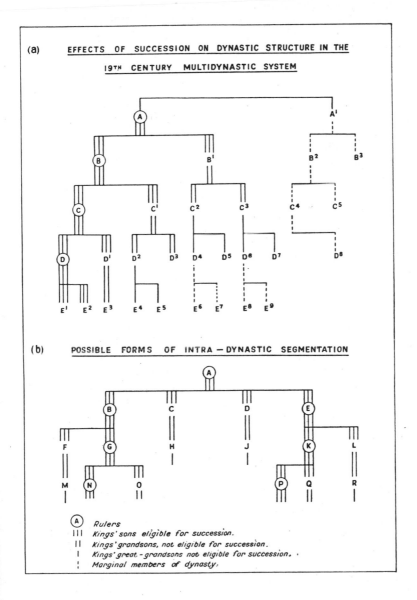

(a) EFFECTS OF SUCCESSION ON DYNASTIC STRUCTURE IN THE 19TH CENTURY MULTIDYNASTIC SYSTEM

(b) POSSIBLE FORMS OF INTRA – DYNASTIC SEGMENTATION

(A) Rulers
||| Kings' sons eligible for succession.
|| Kings' grandsons, not eligible for succession.
| Kings' great-grandsons not eligible for succession.
¦ Marginal members of dynasty.

the pattern of nineteenth-century multidynastic competition, with
segments of the same dynasty taking the place of dynasties formerly
distinguished by descent. In other words, unless there were further
changes in succession patterns, or in the political system as a
whole, the political segmentation within a single dynasty which
monopolized the succession would be basically similar to the
traditional multidynastic system in its structure and function. The
form and function of the segments of the Suleibawa dynasty which
monopolized the throne of Kano during the last century provides
evidence in support of this view. The competition of these Suleibawa segments eventually expressed itself in the bitter civil war of
1891–92 for the throne of Kano. It is thus possible that the simple
reservation of the throne for one of the several dynasties will not
entirely change or abolish the system of political competition
already established. While the political units change, political
forms and functions may still persist. However, such continuity of
function and form would depend in this case on retention of all
rules and practices governing the traditional succession.

(b) Ibrahim and His Officials

Ibrahim's appointment to the throne merely opened the way for
the developments we have been discussing by stimulating an
intra-Bornawa rivalry. It did not of itself institutionalize such a
system, although Bornawa realignments reflecting these possibilities followed immediately. By their supervision the British also
limited the ruler's freedom to reallocate office. Dallatu's son,
Shehu, retained the office of Madaki, and another of the late king's
sons continued to act as Wali. Ibrahim moved his brother,
Zubairu, whose son, Usuman, had been appointed Wombai by
Dallatu, from the position of Dan Galadima to that of Sarkin
Ruwa. This was clearly a demotion, and reflected Ibrahim's desire
to reduce Zubairu's chances of the succession, thereby also, under
the traditional succession rules, disqualifying Zubairu's son, the
acting Wombai. The ruler then appointed his own son, also called
Zubairu, to the office of Dan Madami which had become vacant in
consequence of his accession. Under British pressure, he reinstated the Mallawa Abdullahi in the office of Iya, from which
Dallatu had dismissed him on grounds which the British regarded
as unsatisfactory. The British also disapproved of the Mallawa
Mamman Gabdo's dismissal from the office of Wombai by Dallatu,

but they were unable to secure his reappointment by Ibrahim. Ibrahim appointed his brother, Hayatu, to the title of Galadima; and another brother, Sambo, succeeded Zubairu in the office of Sarkin Ruwa, on the latter's dismissal. With British support, Ja'afaru, a grandson of Sarkin Zazzau Yero, whose father, Mallam Ishiaku, had held no office, was appointed as Katuka. But the most significant appointments effected by Ibrahim involved the two most significant offices of the state, the Chief Judgeship and the new office of Waziri.

Mallam Bako still held the office of Waziri on Ibrahim's accession, but he died shortly afterwards, and Ibrahim then appointed Yusufu, of the Katsinawa 'yan Doto, as Waziri, promoting him from the office of Turaki Karami. During these years the Chief Alkali was Yakubu, a Kanuri kinsman of the vassal chief of Kajuru, who had been appointed by Dallatu. Yakubu appointed his kinsmen to judgeships as these became available; and on his death the ruler appointed a judge of different lineage, but soon had to dismiss him. Yakubu's brother, Umoru, was then appointed Chief Judge. Umoru continued the policy of appointing his own kinsmen to available judgeships, and soon this family held seven judgeships. At this point, Ibrahim promoted Umoru to the position of Waziri which had been made vacant by Yusufu's dismissal. Muhammadu Lawal, of the Katsinawa 'yan Doto, was then appointed Chief Alkali. Lawal was Waziri Yusufu's half-brother. Thus when the Katsinawa 'yan Doto held the Waziri office, their rivals, the Habe of Kajuru, dominated the judiciary; and when the Habe of Kajuru held the Waziriship, the 'yan Doto dominated the judiciary.

The new Chief Alkali was a son of the Alkalin Kasuwa, the judge of the market in Zaria city. He followed the practice of his predecessor in office by appointing his kin to judgeships. In this way, the power of Waziri Umoru over the judiciary progressively declined, while that of the Katsinawa 'yan Doto increased. With his judiciary divided in this manner the king was politically dominant, and could protect his territorial officials fully.

Rivalry between different segments of the Bornawa which began with Ibrahim's appointment weakened him in various ways. The ruler could not longer rely on the wholehearted loyalty of his own dynasty in his struggle with their common rivals. But this struggle continued and was exacerbated by British interference in the kingdom's internal affairs, in consequence of which the ruler's power to dismiss his political opponents from office was severely limited. In addition to these sources of potential opposition, the ruler had further to ensure that the judiciary remained politically impotent.

Ibrahim was also involved in continuous negotiations with the British Administration on many different kinds of issues, and their supervision of his régime was an outstanding threat to its security. In his dealings with the British, the ruler especially needed the assistance of his judiciary and judicial council. By pleading Islamic law, many innovations of an undesirable character could be effectively frustrated, since the British were seriously concerned not to interfere with or undermine the native religion. Moreover, as charges against administrative officials were initially tried in native courts, it was important that these courts should favour the king's interest firstly against those of his rivals and secondly against the British. To mollify the judiciary for their loss of power, Ibrahim allowed the Alkali's courts to hear cases involving claims to land.

(c) The Development of Technical Departments

During Ibrahim's reign the British Administration took their next major step in their development of the government of the emirate. Their initial concern had been to rationalize and systematize the territorial, judicial, and financial organization of the Fulani emirates, and to secure or enforce conformity of the Fulani rulers in their new role as a controlled bureaucracy. Meanwhile, important changes had taken place in the local economy, and formal education of a western type had been introduced. These western institutions had been introduced by 1915, and there followed a lull of nearly fifteen years, during which the new type of economy continued to develop, and the schools released their first graduates. During this period the British were occupied with campaigns in the Cameroons to the east of Nigeria against the Germans and with other problems related to the first World War. By the middle of Ibrahim's reign, when the British in Nigeria were ready to introduce further changes into these governments, the economies and revenues of the Fulani emirates were able to accommodate them.

This second wave of changes aimed at the establishment or expansion of technical departments of the Native Administration. In Zaria, the new departments established at that time included Forestry, Sanitation and Health, a Sleeping Sickness service, a Veterinary service, Agriculture, and Public Works, in that order. A Department of Prisons had been established during Aliyu's reign following the judicial reorganization, but together with the native police force, this remained under the Emir's control. Other departments of Education and Marketing were added in the following reign.

The new departments were placed under the Emir's control. He appointed their heads, and the head of each department was largely responsible for the recruitment, control, discipline, and promotion of his subordinate staff. Emphasis was placed by the British officers who supervised and guided these native departments on their technical functions and performance. The British regarded these new departments as necessary instruments for further development of the government, population, and economy of the emirate. The extension and reorganization of these technical services was thus guided by opportunity, as well as by purely technical considerations; but their expansion was progressive and cumulative. By 1950 each territorial district had, beside its District Chief and its Alkali, a Galadiman Daji (Forestry officer), a Mallamin Gona (Agricultural officer), a Sarkin Shanu (Veterinary officer), and a number of teachers (Mallaman Makaranta), together with a warder (Yari), scribes, District Treasury officials, police, an Alkali and judicial assessors.

This progressive expansion of the Native Administration involved a corresponding increase of the number of offices at the king's disposal. Likewise the heads of these new departments found that the number of offices at their own disposal were continually increasing. Following traditional practices and patterns current in the judiciary, appointments to these new offices were given to kinsmen and clients of those controlling their allocation. Thus the king appointed one of his kinsmen Yarin Zazzau (Chief Warder), and another was placed in charge of the reorganized police force with the title of Wakilin 'Yan Doka, over the head of the Sarkin Dogarai (Police Superintendent) who was a *bawan Sarki* (royal slave). The Turaki became Head of Public Works, and the Mardanni was Head of the Agricultural Department.

In their internal organization each of these new departments tended to repeat the system of territorial administration, and most of these departments distributed most of their staff among the territorial districts. These new departmental heads also exercised considerable power to appoint their supporters to the new offices. Although the king was not dependent on these new departments to anything like the same degree to which he was dependent on the judiciary, whose legal decisions affected his position and policy, he was careful to allocate departmental headships to his loyal kinsmen and strong supporters; and he also applied the technique of promotions into territorial and other offices to interrupt the tenure of departmental headship and to forestall or disperse accumulations of power by their heads. At the same time the king was concerned to protect his departmental heads from dismissal or punishment on charges of maladministration supported by the British. The departmental heads in turn sought to protect their loyal subordinates, kinsmen, and clients, and to increase their own political standing and chances of promotion.

Thus the traditional objectives and practices of political and administrative action penetrated the new departments from the moment of their establishment. In consequence, the technical standards and intentions of the British Administration which introduced these departments have been substantially frustrated. Experience of Western education was no guarantee of suitability for these new appointments. From the beginning the recruitment of pupils for the new schools had been restricted by birth. Political solidarities and pressures remained the decisive condition for recruitment or retention of office, whether new or old.

In this situation, control of the judiciary by the king became increasingly urgent to protect this rapidly expanding administrative staff. Ibrahim was able to offer appointments within these new structures to kinsmen of his judges, and he could occasionally give such persons senior territorial office, thereby linking the judiciary to the executive and committing the former to the maintenance of the latter. Put crudely, by appointing his Alkali's kin to territorial or departmental office, the king took hostages whose security depended on the Alkali's co-operative behaviour. This device was developed considerably by Ibrahim's successor.

The establishment and progressive expansion of these technical departments more than made up for the number of offices which had been put in abeyance by territorial reorganization in the initial years of British rule. The Fulani compensated by introduction of these new offices were inclined to support many other administrative innovations by the British, so long as these did not directly challenge the principles of their political life. Such a sudden increase in the number of official employments multiplied the chances of successful political clientage, and thereby increased the participation of aristocratic Fulani whose traditional tenure of certain titles had been interrupted by the elimination of fiefs. Moreover, the number of new departmental offices was great enough to accommodate many literates of non-aristocratic descent.

These departmental offices are of special interest in their combination of occupational and territorial functions. They recall the old occupational orders in the specificity of their technical interests, and they also mirror the new territorial offices in their territorial distribution. They have therefore been easily accommodated to the prevailing concepts of *sarauta* (office) which involved title, rank, political clientage, administrative responsibility, compounds, remuneration, promotional careers, and the like. In a sense these departmental offices have been regarded by the Hausa-Fulani as superior substitutes for the occupational order which had been eliminated by the tax rationalization of 1907. In local opinion they rank midway between these old occupational offices and the territorial titles to which the departmental heads are sometimes promoted. It is not surprising therefore that many of the technical officials regard their roles as combining the functions of territorial administration with those of the old occupational tax-collectors. The generality of this view corresponds to the intermediate prestige rating of these departmental offices. Even though these departmental offices are functionally quite different from the occupational order of Habe officials, and though their heads and executive officers are generally Fulani nobles, they continue to receive less prestige than territorial titles.

The Emir Ibrahim took the opportunity of these administrative innovations to create two new titles of his own, the Wakilin Yamma (Warden of the West) and the Wakilin Gabas (Warden of the East).[1] These positions were allocated to aristocrats, including per-

[1] These titles are neat examples of continuity and change occurring together. The title of Wakilin Yamma derives from the slave-title of Sarkin Yamma in Fulani Zazzau, as that does from the free title of Barden Yamma in Habe Zazzau (see Ch. 3, Section 1). The title of Wakilin Gabas likewise derives from the Fulani slave-title of Bajimin Gabas, which in turn derives from the

sons of royal rank, and they were placed immediately under the Galadima, who was once again in charge of the administration of the capital. The Galadima's district was thereby divided into two portions which were placed directly under these new officials, and in this way the Galadima's opportunities to influence events at the capital and appropriate power was reduced.[1] Ibrahim's Galadima, Hayatu, was the king's half-brother, and was himself a candidate for succession. Ibrahim's attempt to reduce his brother's power reflects the increasing internal division of the Bornawa referred to above.

5. JA'AFARU, 1936–

(a) The Changing Succession

On Ibrahim's death the British consulted the traditional electors of Zaria, who were at this time the Limamin Juma'a, the Alkali, and the Waziri. This council duly presented a list of acceptable candidates. The British Administration then appointed Mallam Ja'afaru, the acting Katuka, who was not mentioned in the list according to my informants. Thus in this appointment the British neither consulted Sokoto, nor followed the decision of the electoral council of Zazzau.

Ja'afaru had been excluded from the list of acceptable candidates because his father, Mallam Ishi'aku, had not held the throne. Under the traditional rules of succession, only sons of kings were eligible to become kings. Ja'afaru was a grandson (*jika*) of Yero, but under this rule he was not eligible. It is said that for this reason

Habe title of Madakin Gabas. These different appellations have similar reference, namely, Wardens of the West and East respectively; but the titles concerned differed in their function, rank-organization, and promotional connections. They were also allocated among persons of differing status-condition. Yet, despite these and other differences, the continuity of the reference of this title is clear. This capacity to combine change and continuity is the special virtue of a system of titled offices.

[1] This recent administrative subdivision of the capital is curiously similar to that which Mallam Hassan reports for the capital of Abuja in the last century; but this parallelism of form does not connote historical connection. Rather it reveals the formal convergences which develop on purely functional grounds. Ibrahim's administrative division of Zaria city was an attempt to solve the problem posed fifty years earlier by the Galadima Suleimanu. Its formal parallelism with the Habe arrangements is therefore historically fortuitous, although functionally identical. This instance is one of many which emphasizes the necessity of combining formal and functional analyses of all elements which form the data of diachronic studies. Having identified formal parallels it is necessary to examine the functions, relations, and history of each to establish their historical connection and its character. See preceding footnote.

the electoral council did not consider the possibility of his succession.

Ja'afaru's appointment from the position of Katuka was the third successive appointment to the throne by the British from offices which had not previously supplied Zaria with any kings. By these appointments the British had increased the number of territorial offices which were regarded as qualifying their holders for promotion to the throne; and on this change in their status each of these offices was transferred to the royal ranks, and was thereafter allocated to members of the ruler's dynasty. This continuing increase in the numbers of royal offices took place at the expense of the very small number of territorial offices held by non-royals.

Ja'afaru's promotion to the throne was the third successive appointment from the Bornawa dynasty. This completely broke with the traditional prohibition against consecutive appointments from the same dynasty. Thus the appointments of Ibrahim and Ja'afaru each marked a stage in the transformation of the monarchy and the political system from a system of competition between several dynasties to a qualified monodynastic autocracy. It is unlikely that the British were fully aware that these successive appointments from a single dynasty involved the radical transformation of the native political system through its most important and vulnerable organ, the kingship. We cannot say whether the British deliberately intended to change the multidynastic monarchy to a monodynastic one by these appointments; but by appointing a *jika* (grandson) to succeed Ibrahim they introduced another change with uncertain implications.

Tenure of territorial office has traditionally been regarded as an essential qualification of persons eligible by birth for promotion to the throne. Traditionally, and up to the present, kings have tried to exclude their rivals from territorial office in order to control the administration. Undue retention of the kingship by one dynasty is accompanied by reduction of the number of eligible persons in others who have had the opportunity to qualify for the succession by the exercise of territorial office. The Suleibawa, after Audusallami's death, failed to secure further appointments to the throne because of exclusion from territorial office by their more powerful rivals. A similar position has recently developed among the Katsinawa and Mallawa consequent on serial appointments to the throne from the Bornawa dynasty.

There are now only seventeen territorial offices in Zaria, of which in 1950 three were held by vassals and eight by the king's kin. Hitherto, appointments to the throne by the British have followed the traditional pattern in requiring tenure of territorial office as a qualification for eligibility. The large number of new departmental offices have not yet been recognized as qualifications for ultimate promotion. At the same time the British have introduced a most important restriction. Under British rule, no territorial official otherwise eligible by birth for the kingship who has been dismissed from office on valid grounds has ever continued to be eligible for the throne. In effect this means that the only eligible candidates for kingship are those persons of royal rank who actually hold territorial office on the death of the previous ruler. For reasons already familiar it is extremely unlikely that many of the late ruler's rivals will be found in such positions. This effectively means that as further appointments are made from one dynasty, the chances of other dynasties filling the throne are correspondingly reduced. Such progressive reduction in the political status of rival dynasties involves redefinition of royalty and of kingship itself. These redefinitions cannot be effected by legislation, their development either requires a sudden revolution or a gradual change over long periods of time; but, despite their extra-legal character, they are not the less effective and important for the system of government as a whole.

During the last century the kings of Zaria had dismissed their rivals without enquiry into their administrative conduct. Such dismissals did not disqualify persons otherwise eligible for the succession to the throne. These dismissals were the recognized consequences of political competition, and several rulers of Zaria during the last century had some personal experience of dismissals from territorial office.

In contrast with this traditional pattern, the British have sought to make the retention of or dismissal from office contingent on strictly administrative performance; and they have consistently exercised their powers of supervision to secure the reinstatement of officials who have been dismissed purely on account of political rivalry. The reappointment of the baMalle Mamman Gabdo to the office of Magajin Gari under Mallam Ja'afaru is the latest example of British insistence on administrative performance as the sole ground for dismissal from office. The British have also insisted that no officials of whose dismissals they have approved may be reappointed to senior office. On the other hand, by appointing Ja'afaru the British have widened the range of eligible successors by dropping the rule that only the sons of kings can succeed. Even so, unless tenure of departmental headship comes to be regarded as qualification for promotion to the throne, the changes which have taken place under the British involve a notable reduction in the number and categories of claimants eligible for the succession; and this reduction has developed along with substantial uncertainties about the rules, form, and direction of the succession itself.

(b) Official Appointments

In consequence of these successive appointments from within it, the Bornawa dynasty has been structurally changed. The segmentary contraposition of Kwassau's and Dallatu's descendants has only been deepened by Ja'afaru's appointment. In 1950 the ruler had no heirs, and he had not been regarded even by his own kin as eligible for promotion to the throne. During his reign, the descendants of Ibrahim, Dallatu, and Kwassau, who were already holding office, continued to compete with one another for the succession. Ja'afaru did not interfere with his predecessor's appointments, except to dismiss the latter's son, Zubairu, from the title of Dan Madami, and to appoint another of Ibrahim's sons, Umoru, in his stead. This dismissal may have been due to British influence; but it is regarded by the Hausa-Fulani as a step taken by Ja'afaru to eliminate a rival, although the latter was also a lineage kinsman. Ja'afaru also appointed his brother, Suleimanu, to the office of Katuka, but otherwise he has consistently sought to avoid appointing Bornawa to district headships. Instead he has filled these offices with his affinal or matrilateral kin or with royal clients. In consequence, the ruler's solidarity with his own lineage is relatively low, and the Bornawa lineage remains divided into two competing groups descended from Kwassau and Dallatu respectively.

Ja'afaru's accession took place while Umoru was still Waziri. Muhammadu Lawal was then the Chief Alkali. Waziri Umoru died in 1938, and the Waziriship was left vacant by Ja'afaru for several years. During this time Muhammadu Lawal, as Chief Alkali, continued to appoint his 'Yan Doto kinsmen to such subordinate judgeships as became available, and thus reduced the power of the Kajuru Habe within the judiciary. By 1950 the Chief Alkali had appointed four members of his lineage as judges, while another four of these offices were held by the Kajuru Habe. The remaining seven subordinate judgeships were filled by persons drawn from as many lineages. Ja'afaru relied heavily on the support of the 'Yan Doto Alkali in his dealings with his rivals as well as with the British. He appointed a close kinsman of the Chief Alkali to the territorial title of Sarkin Fada, and other kinsmen of the Chief Judge were given office in the new departments. These relatives of the Chief Alkali were really hostages held in office by the king. But by 1950 the Chief Alkali had attained a political eminence under the Emir which made his promotion out of that position advisable. He was at this time quite widely recognized as the most powerful man in the kingdom after the Emir, and was far more powerful than the Madaki, Dallatu's son, who was regarded as one of the Emir's rivals. To reduce the power of the Chief Alkali, the ruler should promote him into the position of Waziri which had been carefully kept vacant. In this advisory position the ex-chief Alkali would retain prestige and lose power; and the king should make a new appointment to the Chief Judgeship from another lineage. This happened in 1952.

7

THE GOVERNMENT OF ZARIA IN 1950

I. THE POLITICAL SOCIETY

(a) Unity and Diversity

CONTEMPORARY Zaria is a heterogeneous unit.[1] Its population can be classified by religion, as Christian, Muhammadan, and 'pagan'; or by ethnicity, as European, Fulani, Habe, Southern Nigerian (mainly Ibo and Yoruba), and 'pagans' (*arna*); by language or by culture. Differences between the urban and rural populations are also important, and these categories are themselves further divisible.

The emirate contains two important towns: the old city of Zaria with its three new suburbs, the Sabon Gari or 'New Town' which was built for Southern Nigerians; the 'barriki' or European reservation; and Tudun Wada, which has a population of Northerners from other emirates and districts.

Fifty miles to the south lies Kaduna, a new town established by Lugard as the administrative capital of Northern Nigeria, and now like Zaria, a flourishing railway centre. At Kaduna there are three main settlements, the European township, the Sabon Gari or Native Town, which is subdivided among Northern and Southern Nigerians, and the garrison, which contains troops drawn from various ethnic groups.

Among the rural population of Zaria, settlement patterns vary, and the Hausa, the nomad Fulani, and pagan tribes such as the Katab have widely differing forms of settlement. Even among themselves the Hausa distinguish several types of settlement by population size and social characteristics. Thus the population of a district capital has a more complex social and economic differentiation than that of a village or a hamlet. In addition, Hausa settlements in the Northern Hausa half of the emirate differ in their form and function from Hausa enclaves in pagan country to the south and west. Hausa themselves emphasize these rural-urban

[1] Throughout this chapter the ethnographic present is 1950.

differences, and these conditions are occasionally cited in pleas for divorce.

In the following discussion we shall try to define the political society of Zaria, to determine its present (1950) limits, its membership, organization, and character. We must therefore begin by describing the population which is identified with the emirate as a political unit, and which owes no direct or immediate allegiance to any other political unit either as the arbiter of its internal affairs or as its representative in dealings with external bodies.

The overwhelming majority of the population which is identified with the emirate in these ways are local Muhammadan Fulani and Hausa. In addition there are local Fulani nomads, who are by no means fully Muhammadanized, and the pagan Habe or Maguzawa, who are scattered in small settlements throughout Northern Zaria. For racial, linguistic, historical, and cultural reasons, these nomad Fulani and pagan Habe have considerable attachment to the emirate and recognize the territorial jurisdiction of its government. The nomad Fulani share important elements of race, origin, language, interest in cattle, history, and culture with their settled cousins who rule Zaria. The pagan and Muhammadan Habe also have common origin, language, agricultural interests, cults of spirit-possession, technology, and historical associations. But the communities of culture and history just referred to are balanced by dissimilarities; and these differences of culture, history, and racial purity divide the loyalties of nomad and settled Fulani on the one hand, and those of pagan and Muhammadan Habe on the other. Thus these pagan Habe and nomad Fulani recognize a loyalty to the emirate which is neither immediate nor exclusive but is clearly conditional and indirect. These pagan Habe and Fulani nomads owe their immediate loyalties to their lineage-heads and local headmen, the Fulani *ardo*, and the Maguzawa Sarkin Arna (chief of the pagans). Their residential segregation supports this ethnocentric political organization and authority structure. Beyond their own local group, both the pagan Habe and Fulani nomads recognize ties of a more direct and compelling character with their fellow tribesmen than those which bind them to the Muhammadan Hausa-Fulani of Zaria. Thus the nomad Fulani and pagan Habe cannot be regarded as full members of the political society of Zaria, although they are closely linked to it. These two groups are none the less included by the Muhammadans within the ethnic stratification of the emirate. Among the Muhammadans, the settled Muhammadan Fulani (*Fulanin gida*) have the highest status, and the nomad Fulani rank below them, but in a marginal position as befits their nomadic character and indirect affiliations. Next come the Muhammadan Habe, and last of all the pagan Habe or Maguzawa, who are looked down upon by their Islamic cousins for their attachment to ancient 'superstitions' (*tsafi*), and for their tribal organization.

(b) Resident Aliens

The population which identifies itself with the emirate regards itself as the heirs of the history of Zazzau, and distinguishes itself from four other population groups within the province. Firstly, there are the Europeans (*Turawa*), the majority of whom are British, and who are sometimes referred to en masse simply as Christians (*Nasara*). In 1950 the great majority of the Europeans in Zaria Province were government officials. These officials were concentrated at Kaduna and Zaria city. The Provincial Administration was located at Zaria, and there were also many European missionaries, commercial and Railway personnel near the old city. Christian missions were not allowed to prosyletize among the Muhammadans, and these missionaries were settled either in the Sabon Gari among Yoruba and Ibo Christians, or at Wusasa, where by request of the Native Authority of Zaria they ran a leper colony in addition to their hospital and schools.

Kaduna is the capital of the Northern Region of Nigeria, and is the headquarters for the Regional Administration. Consequently the majority of Europeans resident there are government personnel who are not concerned directly with the administration of Zaria Province. Many of the Europeans living at Kaduna were military men and their families, mainly officers of the three battalions and other field units stationed there. Kaduna also contained some Europeans who were engaged in commerce, together with a number of missionaries who were interested in the pagan populations to the east and south.

Relations between the emirate population and the local Europeans are either administrative or economic. Administrative relations between these two groups are channelled through the Native and Provincial administrations; in this system there is little room for individual association except between the senior personnel of the counterposed units. In contrast, economic relationships are direct and dyadic. Many Hausa are employed as house staff by Europeans, and many others are engaged in trade with European firms. These interracial employment and commercial relations were highly segmental and specific. Many Europeans cannot speak fluent Hausa, and few Hausa can speak fluent English.[1] Mutual ignorance or misunderstanding infests their specific individual associations even when economic transactions are involved. In their administrative relations with Europeans Hausa enjoy more real equality than in their economic contacts; and European ignorance or misunderstanding of the details of their culture and society has often been politically serviceable to Hausa; but apart from the Emir and his possible successors, individually and in the aggregate, Europeans generally have the higher status.

In their relations with the 'pagans' of the province, the Muhammadans are dominant. The bulk of this pagan population are subjects of the Emir, and are ruled indirectly through their own chiefs and councils by Hausa or Fulani District Chiefs. These pagans (*arna*) are divided into some thirty tribes, three of which, the Kagoro, Jaba, and Moroa, occupy independent districts under their own chiefs. Kagoro, Jaba, and Moroa have been recognized by the Regional Government as separate Native Authorities, and are supervised by the British Provincial Administration directly. However, administrative estimates for these lesser Native Authorities were calculated together with that of the emirate and the small chiefdom of Birnin Gwari in a single annual budget for the Native Administration of Zaria Province. Thus for budget purposes these independent districts are linked directly to the emirate; they also share common technical departments and services. But politically they remain distinct from the emirate, with separate internal administration.

The Emirate of Zaria has been gazetted as a first-class chiefdom by the Regional Government. Its Native Authority, the Emir, exercises judicial powers which include capital sentences, although these require British approval before execution. Hausa refer to the Emir as a '*Sarkin Yanka*' (a chief with power to pass capital sentence). The four other Native Authorities of Zaria Province,

---

[1] For convenience and brevity I refer to the Muhammadan Habe and Fulani of Zaria emirate as a unit by the general term 'Hausa'. More Hausa now speak English.

namely Birnin Gwari, Kagoro, Moroa, and Jaba are third-class chiefdoms with considerably less judicial and administrative prerogatives, political influence, population, revenue, area, wealth, and importance. Although the emirate population accords a higher status to these independent pagan populations than to tribesmen incorporated within the kingdom, as pagans they still rank lower than any stratum within Hausa society itself.

Relations between the emirate Muhammadans and the Southern Nigerians who are settled at Zaria or Kaduna differ in their content and form from those between Hausa and pagans. These Southern Nigerians are themselves ethnically divided into rival groups of Yoruba and Ibo. Many Yoruba have accepted Islam, but very few Ibo have done so; and although these converts are still not regarded as one of themselves by the Hausa-Fulani, they are distinguished individually from the non-Muhammadan Southerners. Between the Muhammadan Northerner and the non-Muhammadan Southerner there is mutual hostility and suspicion. Southerners living in Zaria emirate have to obey the Native Authority of Zaria and its officials; but within the Sabon Gari these Southerners are administered by their own tribal headmen. Their subordinate status as unwanted immigrants is continually made clear to them; but educationally and technically these Southerners are on average far ahead of the Northern Muhammadans, especially in their familiarity with European techniques, methods, and organization. For this reason they generally enjoy higher individual cash incomes than do Hausa, and they also have the support of their European employers. The Ibo and Yoruba artisans of Zaria are regarded by the Hausa as belonging to the Southern Regions of Nigeria, which are the rivals of the Northern Provinces in the contest for Federal Nigerian power. The outburst of violence against the Ibo of Sabon Gari at Kano in 1953 indicates a degree of Hausa hostility to these Southerners which is paralleled in Zaria also.

(c) The Nature and Expression of Political Personality

Thus, within Zaria Province, the population identified with the emirate is distinguished by its contraposition with the Europeans who dominate the province in administration and commerce; with the Ibo and Yoruba who represent the economic and political rivals of the Muhammadan Hausa; and with the pagans within and outside the kingdom, over whom the Hausa maintain or seek domination. By the several contradistinctions within this context, the emirate population is defined as a separate political society; but that society is itself highly stratified and segmented.

Only adult males are recognized as legal persons under Muhammadan law. In 1950 the emirate contained just under 150,000 adult males in a registered population of 536,000. Of these 150,000 male adults, 124,000 were taxpayers, the remainder being aged, blind, or lepers. At first glance it may seem that the payment of *haraji*, the land-tax which is really a capitation-tax, provides an index of a man's political standing; but this index is not unambiguous. Many adult males who do not pay tax are politically active, and sometimes the evasion or non-payment of tax is itself a clue to their political activities. Many others who do pay tax have indirect relations with the Native Administration, and are political minors. As long as a man's sons live with him, he remains responsible for them to the local officials, even though they may be registered taxpayers. He pays their tax to the Ward or Village Head who collects it, and instructions from the Native Administration for his sons are relayed through him. The Ward or Village Head cannot deal directly with a man's resident dependants, who are thereby defined as political minors. A chief or other official may also have clients (*barori*) living in or near his compound for whom he pays a nominal tax, say 6s. a year. These men, although politically active, are dependants and agents of the chief. Politically, their status is very similar to that of true minors, although their position is quite different from that of the resident sons of a compound head. These instances illustrate the Hausa distinction between legal and political personality; the latter is defined by direct dyadic relations of citizenship and authority between the native officials and their subjects, dependants being excluded. Those full-grown men whose relations with the state are mediated through other persons, including the chief, are therefore political minors, however active they may be.

These differences of political maturity and minority are assumed and expressed in the structure of clientage relations. Among the Hausa a compound head is politically mature in the sense that he deals directly with his local ward or village chief, but normally he is also a client or dependant of some more powerful person, through whom he deals indirectly with the local chief or the latter's superiors. The compound head's patron is equally likely to be a client of

MAP C
Map of Zaria Town, 1936.

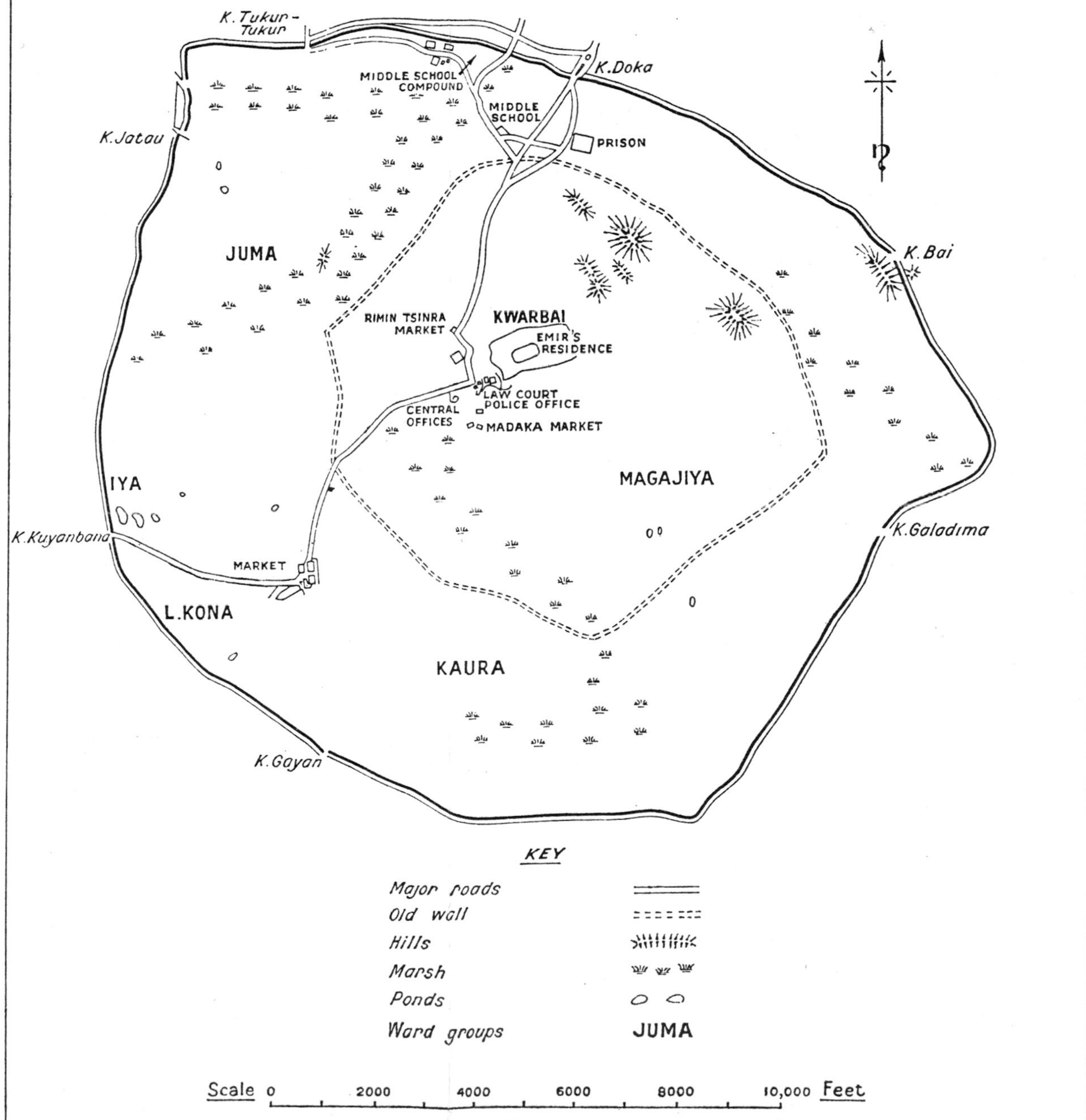

K. Tukur-Tukur

MIDDLE SCHOOL COMPOUND

K. Doka

MIDDLE SCHOOL

K. Jatau

PRISON

JUMA

K. Bai

RIMIN TSINRA MARKET

KWARBAI

EMIR'S RESIDENCE

LAW COURT

POLICE OFFICE

CENTRAL OFFICES

MADAKA MARKET

MAGAJIYA

IYA

K. Kuyanbana

MARKET

K. Galadima

L. KONA

KAURA

K. Gayan

KEY

Major roads

Old wall

Hills

Marsh

Ponds

Ward groups   JUMA

Scale 0   2000   4000   6000   8000   10,000 Feet

some yet more powerful person, through whom he seeks to deal with his rivals of comparable status, and with those officials whose activities bear on his immediate interests. At the top of this pyramid of clientage is the Emir, who is explicitly identified with the state under the Native Authority Ordinance.[1] '*L'état, c'est moi*,' is the constitutive principle of the emirate; and, this being the case, its official hierarchic administrative structure is paralleled and combined with a hierarchy of unofficial clientage, through which political personalities which are formally of equal and independent status develop concrete differences of content, influence, or dependence, according to their individual positions in the pyramid of power.

The competing leaders of groups of clients carry with them the political fortunes of their supporters, as well as those of their own kin. The client whose patron fails to secure office is at a disadvantage compared with him whose patron succeeds; and the more important the office secured by the patron, the higher the political status of the client. In such a system, the commoner without a patron is not merely a deviant but also a rebel, since he admits of no personal allegiance; and such an individual occupies a disadvantageous position in this society. The fact that some people nowadays avoid entering into clientage is frequently mentioned by Hausa and Fulani as an indication of individual over-ambition, disloyalty, and of social disorganization through change. But these social isolates are few in number, and are especially likely to emigrate. Ties of clientage identify individuals who are members of the political society of the emirate, and the boundaries of this political society are defined by the limits within which the population is organized by clientage. Nor should this be cause for surprise, since clientage is the characteristic medium for expression of Hausa political relations, and the limits of a political society are limits between populations organized within distinct systems of political relations.

At the apex of this pyramid of political relations the Emir, as the most powerful member of his dynasty, heads the largest structure (*kunjiya*—loosely organized group) of clients. Each of the ruler's powerful kinsmen heads another such structure, and his dynastic opponents are also supported by similar groupings. Non-participation in this segmentary system of political relations offers no

[1] See below, Section 2 (*a*).

guarantee of political neutrality, but surrenders available protection and prospects of benefit without corresponding securities. A person who is politically isolated has little chance to protect himself or his dependants against officials except by attempts at direct appeal to the British. Through the operation of clientage, politically active commoners rarely need to seek redress through appeals to the British; and, by its operation, clientage reduces their opportunity to do so, since the client's duties include informing his patron of all local developments which affect the latter's welfare. In this way the client protects his lord from rivals and malcontents, and by maintaining the lord's power he furthers his own interests and is himself protected. This feature of clientage is institutionalized by office-holders, who control elaborate communication systems which focus on the Emir's court and the Provincial Administration at the capital, and have agents in all local units subordinate to them. The agents of such communications structures are known as *'yan labari* (reporters); and officials are well aware that the Emir controls the most highly developed communications system within his dominions.

(d) Vassalage in Zaria

In its territorial organization also, this political society has a repetitive hierarchical pattern. The emirate is divided into districts, each of which is divided into village areas, and the great majority of these are further subdivided into wards, hamlets, and the like. Rivalry obtains between wards of a village, between village areas in a district, and between districts in an emirate. Boundary disputes generally express these rivalries. Such rivalry may be purely local and communal in character, but it may also reflect the competing aspirations of administrative officials such as Ward Heads, Village Chiefs, or their seniors.

In certain cases the local organization departs from this reduplicative hierarchic model. These deviations arise from the incorporation of former vassal states as local units within the kingdom. Such incorporation has followed two lines. Some former vassal states, namely Kajuru, Kauru, and Kagarko, have been accorded district status, and within them the District Chiefship remains hereditary within the vassal lineage. Unavoidably the boundaries of these new districts depart to some extent from the traditional boundaries of the vassal states which form their political and administrative basis; but in delimiting these vassal districts the principle of compensation has been followed, so that in overall area these districts are approximately equal to the original vassal states. None the less, in consequence of these boundary changes, districts based on former vassal states contain fairly large populations which neither owed traditional allegiance to the vassal chief who presently rules them, nor have any official redress against his administration other than appeal to the British. This relative lack of redress reflects continuity of the vassal status of these District Heads and also the fact that the populations placed under them are mostly pagans. The Emir does not like to interfere in the relations between his District Heads of traditional vassal status and their pagan subjects. Consequently, the administration of districts based on former vassal chieftainships differs in many ways from that of purely appointive district chieftainship.

The former vassal states of Fatika and Lere were too small to be given separate district status. During the progressive reorganization of district boundaries, these two vassal states have become classified as village areas within larger districts. They differ from all other village areas in the emirate in certain important ways. The chiefs of Lere and Fatika are hereditary, they still have their *tambari* or other insignia of vassal status, and each of them controls several village areas besides that to which he is directly appointed. Although villages formerly ruled by these vassal chiefs have been accorded an administrative status equal to that of their former lord and are formally quite independent of him, the traditional pattern of their political relations continues. The chiefs of Lere and Fatika really rule distinct sub-districts within their present districts, and these sub-districts correspond to their traditional domains. In both these districts the relative statuses of the District Head and of the village chief whose vassalage persists *sub-rosa* depend directly on the position which the District Head occupies in relation to the royal succession. The chief of Lere District in 1950 was Wali Umaru, a son of Dallatu and a likely candidate for the throne. In the district of Giwa, which includes Fatika, the District Head at that date was Fagaci Muhammadu, a descendant of Mallam Musa's Katuka Sabulu and a client of the king. The vassal chief of Fatika therefore enjoyed a higher political status within Giwa District than did the vassal chief of Lere under the Wali. These two vassal chiefs with the official status of village heads still rule their former dominions and are always consulted by the District Heads before the appointment of village chiefs traditionally subordinate to them. They both retain rights of immediate access to the Emir and each still had his own *kofa* (door) in Zaria city. Fatika to-day retains those rights to the fief within the capital which were given to its rulers before the Fulani conquest. It is a fine point whether the village chief of Fatika had a higher real status than his District Head, and whether he still enjoys the independent political status which was his by vassalship. Of the two, the District Head has far greater power and wealth, but his office is appointive, and his issue are unable to succeed him directly, while the vassal chief has a continuing hereditary status based on his continuing vassalage. Such unofficial persistence of vassalage within the kingdom has its parallel in the unofficial persistence of the vassal relations between Zaria and Sokoto, despite the British conquest and supervision.

In the territorial system of Zaria the position of Chawai is unique. The Chawai are a pagan tribe located in the extreme south-eastern corner of Zaria, who have adopted many elements from Hausa culture.[1] During the last century the Chawai were administered by a vassal of the Sarkin Kauru, who was himself a vassal of Zaria. The ruler of Chawai had the title of Wakili (deputy), and lived in the tribal area. The Chawai number about 15,000 and are culturally distinct from the Katab and Kurama on their frontiers. It has therefore been administratively convenient to retain the office of Wakilin Chawai and to treat this tribe as a sub-district of Zangon Katab, the district ruled by Katuka.

(e) Relations with Sokoto

Zaria's suzerainty of Keffi, Kwotto, Jema'a, and Doma has been discontinued by their incorporation under separate Provincial administrations, but Zaria's vassalage to Sokoto persists, and the Sultan is still recognized as the lord of the Emir of Zaria. According to Zaria informants, in 1949 the Sultan of Sokoto instructed his vassal, the Emir of Bauchi, to remove the Emir of Zaria's staff of office, which symbolized his appointment by the British Administration. Shortly afterwards, the Emir of Zaria sent his client and private secretary, the Madauci, on a tour to Sokoto and other

---

[1] For accounts of the Chawai, Katab, and neighbouring tribes, see Meek, 1931, (2), Vol. 2, pp. 1–219.

Fulani capitals. When the representatives of the Southern and Western Regions of Nigeria met later that year to discuss proposals for a Federal Nigerian constitution, the Emir of Zaria, speaking on behalf of the Muhammadan North, faced them with a blunt demand for 50 per cent. of the seats in the Federal Legislature as the condition of Northern participation. This demand was a complete surprise to the British officials as well as to the Southern representatives. The Emir based his demand on the argument that a 50 per cent. vote was essential to protect the Muhammadan religion of Northerners against legislation by the Federal Parliament; but in fact, approximately one-third of the population of Northern Nigeria are not Muhammadan. The real function of this demand was to reintegrate the Fulani empire politically, and to give it the commanding position within the federal legislature which it already had in the Northern one.

When this new constitution had been introduced, the Sultan's kinsman the Sardauna of Sokoto, was elected as leader of the Northern political party, and Prime Minister of the Northern Assembly. The Sardauna is popularly regarded as a likely Sultan of Sokoto; and it is not unlikely, that, should the elective system which the British introduced in 1950 continue, the leadership of the Northern legislature and political party will be identified and will tend to become a hereditary office of the Toronkawa lineage of Sokoto, as was the case with the traditional office of Waziri (vizier).

Another revealing expression of Zaria's continued allegiance to the Fulani empire occurred when the telephone line between Zaria and Sokoto was opened in 1951. The Residents of both provinces were present at the formal opening, during which the rulers of Zaria and Sokoto spoke to each other. The ruler of Zaria addressed the Sultan as his suzerain openly, and referred to the bond between Sokoto and Zaria as the latter's vassalage.

Development of the Federal and Regional legislatures has restored the Sokoto empire and renewed its vitality, since there is no other unit by which the Muhammadans and their rulers can so effectively defend their society against Yoruba and Ibo Southerners, and against the attacks of disaffected Northerners, pagan or Muslim. By uniting under their Sultan, the emirs are able to dominate the Northern elections and legislature without difficulty; and by securing 50 per cent. of the seats in the federal legislature they expect to control that also. It goes without saying that the Emir of

Zaria could not have dared to make his demand on behalf of the North without the Sultan's foreknowledge and consent. In the same way that vassalage within the emirate of Zaria is not officially recognized, there is likewise to-day no official recognition of the vassalage between Zaria and Sokoto. But perhaps this is hardly necessary; ever since the establishment of the Northern House of Chiefs, the Fulani emirs have acted in unity under Sokoto; and even such formerly independent Muhammadan chiefdoms as Habe Abuja have been forced by this situation to follow the Fulani lead in order to avoid isolation. By concerted action within the new legislatures, the Fulani rulers have also been able to contain proposals which seemed to strike at the roots of their power;[1] and as a unit they have recently been able to recover much of the influence they lost in Lugard's early years. But the Muhammadans of Northern Nigeria can only develop such unified political action against British pressure towards democracy, and against Southern competition for federal dominance, within the traditional framework of the Sokoto empire. Thus by no paradox, British efforts at liberalizing and democratizing these Northern emirates have stimulated the restoration of active solidarities and imperial relations among the ruling Fulani, and within the next few years we may witness an open restoration of the Fulani empire.

(*f*) *The Stratification of Free Persons*

Within the Muhammadans of the emirate the principal division is between Fulani and others. The bulk of these non-Fulani are Habe, or are classified as such by the Fulani, who use the term 'Habe' to distinguish their Muhammadan subjects from others. Tuaregs (Buzaye), Kanuri, or Northerners of Arab descent are also distinguished from these Habe by the use of special terms. Possibly, the bulk of the Habe of Zaria are descended from slaves, but the acculturation of slaves to Hausa-Fulani society has been such that their incorporation as Habe has entailed far less change in the content of Hausa culture than in the structure of Hausa society.

Divisions among the Fulani of contemporary Zaria tend to follow those laid down in the last century. The Fulani are stratified in terms of their traditional and current associations with govern-

---

[1] Cf. *Gaskiya Ta Fi Kwabo* (Hausa vernacular newspaper), No. 413, of 23rd August, 1950, p. 1. Report of speech by Malam Abubakar Tafawa Bolewa in Northern House of Representatives.

ment and power. Dynasties form the uppermost layer; and at any moment the ruler's dynasty has the greatest power and prestige of any. A rung below the dynasties come such important lineages as the Toronkawa Gidadawa or the Katsinawa 'yan Doto. Such lineages as the Shanonawa, which occupied assured positions of power during the last century but which have since lost them, now occupy a lower position, which corresponds with their political fortunes under British rule. Other official lineages, such as the legal lineage of the Haben Kajuru, rank below the leading Fulani on ethnic grounds, although their political prominence ensures them high prestige. Within any of these noble lineages, moreover, relative status corresponds to the prospects and present political positions of the persons concerned, and to the ranks held by their aganatic ancestors. The general character of this differentiation has already been discussed.

As a rule few Habe now hold high office in Zaria except those whose ancestors have been incorporated in the ruling class since the early days of the conquest under Musa. In 1950 the acting Fagaci belonged to a Habe lineage which had such a history. Within their villages Habe village chiefs naturally have the highest individual status; but where semi-nomadic Fulani (*Agwai*) have settled in Hausa village areas they maintain an exclusive settlement and unity under their own Ardo (head), who deals with the Hausa village chief, and may also deal with the District Head direct.

Settled Fulani are not well represented among the craftsmen or small traders of Zaria; although they frequently pursue such occupations they are rarely classified by Habe in occupational terms, and they are less heavily dependent on craft and trade for their income than are other persons of moderate means. The stratification of individuals and their families in terms of occupational class is especially developed among the Habe, who are the bulk of the craftsmen and small traders of Zaria, and who lack lineage segmentation and political office. Essentially, this Habe system of classification assumes occupational inheritance and is inherently static. Habe recognize that it is imprecise and ascriptive. It nevertheless corresponds with a prestige scale which they use for one another in rural areas. In this prestige scale, mallams have the highest status of any occupational class, and the butchers, hunters, eulogists, blacksmiths, and tanners have very low status. Cloth-workers, such as weavers and dyers, have a middle position, together with silversmiths, commission agents, and farmers. The position of merchants in this scheme varies according to their type, wealth, and political connections. Many craftsmen or farmers also engage in trade; and some of these persons are more properly classified as traders (*'yan kasuwa*) than as farmers or craftsmen. The rich merchant (*attajiri*) with a large trade turnover comes near the head of the Habe prestige hierarchy, and exercises important economic influence. Often, such wealthy merchants seek to raise their status by pilgrimage to Mecca. But the poor mallam who has made his pilgrimage on foot or by lorry has greater religious prestige than the merchant who went by aeroplane, since the mallam's effort is the more meritorious, and is itself an act of faith.

Prestige distributions based on occupation hold within limits set by such factors as income levels, kinship and marriage relations, age, and the legal status of a person's ancestors as free or slave. Where such differences of ancestral status obtain, the occupational rankings referred to above do not always hold. Two weavers descended from slave and free parents would differ in status accordingly, despite other factors; a butcher of free descent, despite the low status of his occupation, may occupy a position in the local prestige scale approximately equivalent to that of a weaver descended from slaves.

People's behaviour further affects their status and prestige ranking. The instance of meritorious pilgrimage which has just been given illustrates this. So does an individual's mode of marriage. Hausa practise degrees of wife-seclusion, varying from complete purdah (*kulle*) to its opposite, which is discredited by its name—*auren jahilai* (the marriage of the ignorant)—for imputed religious unorthodoxy. Two persons of similar descent and occupational class who practise different forms of marriage are differentiated in the prestige scale accordingly.

An even more important type of relation which affects a person's status and prestige is clientage. As pointed out above, the client whose patron is successful in the quest for office, often has clients of his own, on whose behalf he seeks to exercise influence with his powerful patron. By fortunate relations of clientage, an individual may himself obtain political office, and thereby social mobility. Personal power corresponds with an individual's position in the structure of clientage relations which hold between and within the official and non-official sectors of the society as a political system.

Although clientage is an exclusive relation, it may be changed or renewed as occasion warrants; and the client's capacity for independent political action and upward mobility alike may be a result of his ability to change patrons opportunely.

(g) The Position of Ex-slaves

Despite clientage, marriage, occupational mobility, fortune, and meritorious religious action, the Hausa system of status distribution remains primarily ascriptive. Moreover, the essential distinction here is between persons whose ancestors were free and those descended from slaves. This distinction is emphasized more heavily than that between the freeborn and the freedmen, since in the fifty years after Lugard's Slavery Proclamation, most freedmen have died. The slave-owners of Zaria, who were Habe as well as Fulani, naturally disapproved Lugard's prohibition of slave-raiding and slave-dealing.[1] At their depositions, Kwassau and Aliyu, the first two emirs under British rule, both had charges of slave-dealing against them. Yet less than 10,000 slaves registered their self-redemption or freedom in the courts of Zaria during the first twenty years of British rule; and the emphasis which Hausa place on free or slave parental status indicates that the freedom which Lugard conferred on children born of slave-parents after 1st April, 1901, has nevertheless been qualified by the fact of their slave parentage.

Hausa society no longer contains an explicit status of slavery (*bauta*; slave = *bawa*, f. *baiwa*; pl. *bayi*); but Hausa emphasize the status of a person's parents and grandparents. The children of slaves are described as *dimajai* (s. *dimajo* literally, issue of a slave); and the children of *diamjai* are described as *matankara* (literally, grandchildren of slaves). Traditionally, the *dimajo* was inalienable; and under British rule all sale of slaves has been forbidden. The *dimajo* traditionally lived on his master's *rinji*, and shared in certain of the ceremonial exchanges (*biki*) of his owner's family (*iyayen giji*); he laboured on the master's farm and received food and housing in return, his marriage was arranged by his master; he was from birth incorporated in the Muhammadan population, and addressed his master as father (*baba*); his master's children, real and classificatory, were his siblings (*'yanuwa*), and some of

---

[1] See Smith, M. G., 1954, for a comparison of slavery and its abolition in Hausaland and the British West Indies.

them were his joking relations. Although not a full member of his master's family, still less an independent legal or political person, the *dimajo* was a member of the master's *kunjiya* (group of dependants), and benefited thereby. Facial marks indicated the slave status of *dimajai* as well as captives.[1] These facial marks are no longer common; but in many other respects the old *dimajai* relation persists between slave-owners and the issue of their former slaves. The emphasis which Hausa place on parental status as slave or free has the function of maintaining these *dimajai* relations. This emphasis does not contradict Lugard's rule that persons born after 1st April, 1900, are free, but simply ignores it, and it also modifies the effect of self-redemption by slaves.

Thus, although there may be very few slaves in contemporary Zaria, except for the *dogarai* (native police) or slave-officials who benefit considerably from the slave-status which they voluntarily maintain, there are a great many sons and daughters of slaves, and probably many more *matankara*. Either such persons seek to repudiate their ascribed positions and avoid recognition, in which case they frequently move elsewhere as strangers (*baki*); or they accept their situation and accommodate themselves to it as best they can. By birth they are subordinated to the heirs and family of their parent's master. If accepted voluntarily and maintained cheerfully, this subordinate relation offers the *dimajai* or *matankara* as much personal security as the political influence of their *iyayen giji* (owner's family) can afford. But such protection is neither vicarious or altruistic. By protecting their *dimajai* from undue interference, the owner and his kin are concerned to preserve and enjoy their property.

The *dimajo* expresses his cheerful acceptance of his position by regular participation in kinship exchanges (*biki*) with his *iyayen giji*. He should attend their weddings and the naming ceremonies of their children, and should contribute to the alms distributed on the death of members of their family. In addition the *dimajo* should greet his *iyayen giji* with gifts at the various Muhammadan festivals; and he should remember to send them part of his annual tithe of grain (*zakka*). These exchanges are unequal, and the *dimajo* or *matankara* frequently receives less than he gives. Besides these gifts, the issue of slaves have to provide their *iyayen giji*

---

[1] For a first-hand account of Hausa slavery, see Mary F. Smith, 1954, pp. 40–3, 46 ff., 68 ff., 119–20, 122, 128, etc.

with annual payments of grain in lieu of rent for the use of their farm land and compound sites. These payments are known as *aron gona* or *gallan gona* (dues for the loan of a farm). They are commonly increased by addition of the Koranic tithe known as *zakka*. They point to the fact that the land worked by those *matankara* or *dimajai* who remain at their owner's *rinji* belongs to the owner by right of initial clearance, as well as by direct alloca- tion from former rulers of the kingdom or village area when the *rinji* was established. Inheritance of land rights by the family of the *iyayen giji* is therefore sanctioned by the power of the king or chief over matters involving land. Since land-suits are decided by the king and his local chiefs, the original allocations of land for *rumada* are difficult to contest or revoke. This is one point of sub- stance behind the royal jurisdiction over land-suits.

When *dimajai* or *matankara* desire to escape their *iyayen giji*, they usually move away from the *rinji*, often to another emirate, as strangers. However, such migration from one emirate to another is less frequent than might be expected, due to certain aspects and conditions of Hausa marriage, which must now be discussed. Hausa classify any adult who has no spouse as a wastrel or prostitute (*karuwa*), irrespective of sex. A single woman of repro- ductive years must seek shelter with some practising prostitute, because there is nowhere else for her to live. Her kin will not receive her since her single condition is an explicit rejection of their authority and her own minority status. The wifeless man on his part has to find some master or patron who will provide him with regular food and shelter. The servitude implied by this rela- tion is an abject admission of individual failure and worthlessness (*banza*); but the alternative is outrageous, since it is virtually taboo for a Hausa man to prepare his own food (*abinci*).[1] Indeed, the time spent by a man in preparing his own food (*tuwo*) would be time lost from his farming, trade, or craft; and this time-loss, if recurrent, would soon leave him with no food to prepare. In

---

[1] *Abinci* (food) refers mainly to *tuwo* (grain porridge) and *miya* (stew), which is the standard daily meal of the Hausa. Snacks, cakes, sweetmeats, and other light refreshments are sold in all Hausa communities, and are classified as *marmari* (snacks). Married persons and bachelors alike buy snacks; but snacks are not regarded as food; and custom has made the daily meal of *tuwo* essential to individual well-being. *Tuwo* fills, snacks do not, but men neither prepare *tuwo* nor snacks. Hausa division of labour by sex rests on the distinction be- tween the complementary roles of male and female. Men provide the materials for food, women prepare it. Hence the Hausa emphasis on marriage.

consequence, for social and economic reasons, Hausa men seek to keep at least one wife, and preferably more, since pregnancy, divorce, death, or withdrawal to her kinsfolk (*biko*), leaves the man who has only one wife in much the same position as the man with none. Help from one's daughters is of course unavailable to men, since these daughters marry at the age of about fourteen years, and thereafter remain with their husbands. The only safeguard for wifeless men is for them to live with some kinsman, their father or brother, whose wife will then cook for the household. Yet even such a situation underlines the dependence of the wifeless male on his married kinsman, and this is expressed by unequal distributions of prestige as well as the grain they cultivate jointly. In consequence, Hausa men try to avoid these situations by marrying and establishing their own households.

Many Hausa men find it difficult to finance their own marriage. These arrangements are costly and substantial presents must be given to the lady and her parents. Moreover, in such affairs, there is a high risk that the lady or her parents will break their contract if it suits them to do so, and the suitor will then lack redress, unless he can produce evidence of payments which is satisfactory to the local court. But maintenance of his marriage is more difficult for a man than its arrangement. Among the Hausa divorce is both frequent and easy, and the general male desire for two wives apiece to safeguard them against dependence on one mate is itself a factor in maintaining the high rates of divorce. A woman collects from her prospective husband the money she needs to repay portions of the bridewealth to the husband she is leaving, and then asks the court for a divorce. If after resuming her freedom, she no longer wishes to marry her former suitor, she can repudiate the engagement without fear that he can enforce payment, since this can only be done through the court, which is more likely to fine her suitor for disrupting her former marriage than to support his claim for repayment.

For *matankara* and *dimajai* who wish to escape their servitude, these and other aspects of Hausa marriage present serious obstacles. Unless the man's wife is also of slave descent, and shares his desire to escape her own masters by moving the distance necessary to ensure anonymity, migration seriously endangers his marriage; and in the event of divorce after such migration, the *dimajo* will find himself in severe difficulties in his attempt to get another wife. He will then have to compete with men already established in their own homes who are known to the local women and linked to them by kinship and other ties which are of considerable importance in mate-selection among the Hausa. The *dimajo* whose migration has left him wifeless may therefore return to his former home to seek another wife with the aid of his kin; or he may try his fortune in the area of his settlement, in which case he usually becomes the menial client of some locally important person, receiving food and shelter in return for his services, and hoping that in due course fortune or his patron will give him a wife.

The alternative to long-distance movements is for the *dimajo* to move away from the *rinji* on to nearby uncleared land. This also has its difficulties. A new compound must be built, and the new land must be cleared and cultivated for more than a year before the *dimajo* is fully able to establish his new household.[1] Such preparations cannot be executed in secret. The *iyayen giji* cannot fail to know, and may take effective action to halt these designs. The *iyayen giji* can simply deny the disaffected *dimajo* further use of the land on which his crops are presently growing. In practice, this means that the *dimajo* must then make special efforts to complete his preparations before the following agricultural season. It is difficult for the *dimajo* or *matankara* to remain in the *rinji* while refusing to pay the *aron gona* or *gallan gona* required by the *iyayen giji*, if the latter are powerful.

The following cases illustrate how this indirect control of *dimajai* through rights in land worked in 1950. In the first case, slaves living at the *rinji* of an important Fulani lineage were ordered to leave the village, unless they immediately presented the overdue *galla*. They were opposed to doing so, but had to give in. They were then compelled to observe the other conditions characteristic of relations between *dimajai* and their owners. In the second case, a *dimajo* claimed a piece of land in a *rinji* near a district headquarters which a member of the *iyayen giji's* family desired for his farm. The *dimajo's* claim rested on the fact that his father and elder brothers had actually cleared and worked this land for a number of years, and the *dimajo* argued that although the land was

---

[1] Hausa first plant a catch-crop of cotton or sweet potatoes on virgin land, to break in the soil. These catch-crops give low yields; but the following crops are full bearing. Thus it is more than a year before a farmer can rely on cleared land for his domestic grain supplies.

now fallow, he intended to cultivate it. This case went to the local *Alkali*, who awarded the land to the *dimajo*. No question of *galla* or ownership was involved; this was simply a conflict of claims between the *iyayen giji* and the *dimajo* for use of the land. Being marsh, the disputed plot was specially valuable, and its use was keenly contested. The third case involves a *rinji* belonging to one of the royal lineages. Its *ubangiji* (owner) was resident, and its population, apart from the owner's immediate family, were mainly of slave descent. Relations between the owner and his *dimajai* had continued along traditional lines. European agricultural officers persuaded some of these *dimajai* to accept ploughs and cattle and to take up mixed farming. The plough increased their acreage considerably, and they were then given more fallow. To improve yields the mixed farmers made a practice of manuring their farms regularly, and they were thereby enabled to farm the same plots beyond the normal number of years. The *ubangiji* felt that his mixed farmers were gradually establishing rights to the land they farmed, and decided to prevent this. He announced a redistribution of farm-plots among the people of his village, which even a village chief has no power to make. By this redistribution the mixed farmers were given further tired and fallow farm lands, and the *ubangiji* took their manured land for his own farm. In despair or protest some of these farmers surrendered their ploughs, and in due course attempts were made to secure redress on their behalf. The *ubangiji*, although belonging to a different dynasty from the ruler, is said to have visited him and explained the issue, pointing out that the interests of all the *iyayen giji* of Zazzau, including the ruler's dynasty, were identical with his own, and were equally threatened by the introduction of mixed farming and similar practices. The Native Authority took no action to secure the return of their former farm lands to these mixed farmers. Nor did the protesting mixed farmers leave the *rinji*.

It is necessary to describe these conditions and sanctions of the *dimajo* relationship for various reasons. Unless one understands the basis of the *ubangiji*'s power, it is difficult to appreciate the extent to which servitude continued in Zaria fifty years after proclamations intended to eliminate slavery; and it is also difficult to appreciate the form which this servitude had taken; yet, according to my noble informants, '*Kowanne gari yana da iyayen gijinsa, ko ba shi da sarauta*' (Every settlement has its owner, even if the latter has no title); or again, in discussing relations between masters and *dimajai* in contemporary Zaria, *'Har gobe, za a yi'* (Until tomorrow, i.e. for ever, this will remain). Of course, the *dimajai* are no longer slave-born, and their owners recognize this; *dimajai* are merely persons descended from slaves, who, although not slave-born, inherit some of their parents' servitude. In the words of one *uban giji*, 'If you buy a hen and a rooster in the market and they have chickens, to whom do the chickens belong?' (*'In ka tafi kasuwa, ka sayo zakara da kaza, sai su haifu, 'ya'yansu na wanne ne?*). This piece of rhetoric must be related to the remark that 'each settlement has its owner,' whose identity is well known. It is quite clear that the ascription of personal status, on the basis of parental condition as slave or free, has provided a form under which large numbers of Hausa continue in a servitude defined so as to differentiate it from the slavery from which it derives. No one can reasonably object to the description of persons descended from slaves as children or grandchildren of slaves; and, so long as the present custom relating to land remains in force, no power of the British Administration will be able to interpose between the *iyayen giji* and those persons who, although not slaves, are descended from slaves, and who thereby inherit certain of their parents' obligations and disabilities, although they are technically free. This is how important slave-owners accommodated themselves to the problem posed by British anti-slavery legislation.

(h) Clientage and the Political Society

By considering the present position of the ex-slave the persistence of traditional patterns of territorial organization can be readily appreciated; and further light is also thrown on the significance of clientage in the definition and organization of the political society of Zaria. Traditional patterns of territorial organization have not been changed as radically as might at first appear. Fiefs have been replaced by districts, and village areas are now the recognized units of local administration; but *rumada* have not been eliminated and may continue indefinitely. *Iyayen giji* who are powerful enough to insist on their rights, and those who are less powerful but reside in their settlements, maintain their *rumada* with little change. The sanctions which governed relations between *dimajai* and their owners have altered from physical force to political power and law. In the present circumstances it is usual for descendants of slaves to seek relations of clientage with the owners of their parents; and when *dimajai* seek to escape their servitude by flight, they are often driven into the more menial forms of clientage in the areas to which they move. The *iyayen giji* with *dimajai* or *matankara* clients either have patrons who protect their enjoyment of property rights or are themselves also patrons of free persons many of whom will have client *dimajai* of their own.

Clientage is thus coterminous with Hausa political society, and is accordingly almost as complex; this complexity expresses the multifunctional character of the institution. In some situations clientage is candidly political, and its focus is office; or it may be directly economic, balancing work and reward. In other situations its functions are covert, and are not immediately evident. Among these obscurer types of clientage, those which express relations between *dimajai* and *iyayen giji* are important. The institution of clientage provides a medium for gradual and agreed change in relations between slave-owner and ex-slave by integrating these categories within the wider political system.

Clientage also incorporates such differentiating factors as ethnicity, occupational status, lineage, and rural-urban distinctions, and defines the boundaries of the political society of Zaria emirate in functional terms. Clientage which crosses the emirate boundaries has a specific and segmental character, but within the emirate their relations embody power, property, status, and quasi-kinship. The clientage relations which Muhammadan Hausa and Fulani of Zaria have with one another do not apply to Maguzawa, Yoruba, Ibo, European, or other ethnic groups. By its functions, content, and form, clientage differentiates the members of the political society from outsiders; and it thereby expresses the structure of political relations in the emirate. Direct links between this political society and others such as Sokoto are accordingly expressed in this idiom also.

It is difficult to over-estimate the significance of this institution in the political organization of Zaria; but its incidence may be guessed from the following figures. The registered population of Zaria emirate, 1948–49, was 55·5 per cent. Muhammadan Hausa-Fulani; in 1950 the emirate contained 124,300 registered tax-payers, of whom about 72,000 would thus be Hausa-Fulani. Assuming on other evidence that there are 1·1 tax payers per domestic unit among the Hausa, then one in every fifty Hausa

TERRITORIAL TITLES

THE KING

(a) Royals	(b) Clients	Order of Mallams	Senior Departmental Officers	The King's Servants
MADAKI	(i) Hereditary†	LIMAMIN JUMA'A*	MA'AJI (Treasury)	MAHARI (In charge of the Palace)
WOMBAI	MAKAMA BABBA	LIMAMIN KONA	S. RUWA (Emir's Office)	
MAKAMA II	S. KAJURU	MAGATAKARDA	TURAKI (Works)	S. TAMBARI
MAGAJIN GARI	S. KAURU	S. MALLAMAI	SARKIN SHANNU	S. LAIMA
IYA			(Veterinary)	S. FIGINI
WALI	(ii) Non-hereditary	*Judicial Order*	SARKIN DAJI (Forestry)	S. BUSA
DALLATU	FAGACI	ALKALIN ALKALAI*	MARDANNI (Agriculture)	S. KAKAKI
DAN MADAMI	SARKIN FADA	(Chief Judge)	GALADIMAN MAGANI	MADAKIN TAUSHE
KATUKA	S'AI		(Medical)	S. ZAGI
GALADIMA*		(a) City Judges	SARKIN TSABTA	SHAMAKI
DAN GALADIMA	† Titles held by dynasties of former vassal-states.	SALENKE	(Sanitation)	MAJIDADI
		ALKALIN KASUWA	WAKILIN YANDOKA	
		ALKALIN TUDUN WADA	(Police)	
			WAKILIN MAKARANTA	
		(b) District Judges	(Schools)	
		ALKALIN LERE		
		„ ZANGON KATAB	YARI (Prisons)	
			MADAUCI (The Emir's Private Secretary)	
		„ KACIA		
		„ KAGARKO		
		„ KADUNA		
		„ RIGACIKUM		
		„ GIWA		
		„ MAKARFI		
		„ IKARA		
		„ KUBAU		
		„ SOBA		
		„ KAURU		

STATE ORGANIZATION IN ZARIA 1950

* = electors

S = Sarki = Chief (of)

compounds contains a native official, almost all of whom have several clients each.

2. THE ADMINISTRATION OF ZARIA IN 1950

(a) The Statutory Basis

In 1950 the Zaria Native Authority was governed by the Native Authority Ordinance, No. 17 of 1943, which vests the power of appointment in the Governor of Nigeria. In Zaria emirate the Native Authority directly recognized by the Governor of Nigeria is the Emir. The Native Administration are the staff recruited by the Emir to assist him in the administration of the state. Hausa aptly describe members of the Native Administration as *ma'aikatan sarki* (employees of the Emir), thereby emphasizing their salaried status and also their direct responsibility to the Emir. This Native Administration is indirectly sanctioned by the ordinance which establishes the Native Administration as the instrument of that Authority, who is responsible to the British Governor through the British Provincial staff for the proper and efficient conduct of the Native Administration.[1]

Under the 1943 Ordinance the primary duty of the Native Authority, i.e. the Emir, is to maintain 'order and good government' within his domain. To this end, the Native Authority has powers to arrest suspected offenders and to supervise the execution of judicial sentences passed in its courts. The Native Authority also has power to issue orders and regulations (*dokoki*) on matters affecting the welfare of the community, in so far as these orders are not 'repugnant to morality and justice'. The Resident, who heads the British Provincial Administration, also has powers to issue such orders, in the event that the Native Authority refuses to do so, and orders of the Resident must be obeyed in the same way as orders of the Native Authority. Initially, the 1943 Ordinance made little reference to the Native Treasuries, either as regards revenue or expenditure. The amending Ordinance, No. 4 of 1948, formally recognized the power of a Native Authority to levy rates for the upkeep of public services and utilities; but no powers of changing taxes or raising taxation directly have been allocated to the Native

---

[1] See Hailey, 1951, Part 3, Vol. 3, West Africa, pp. 1–22, 45–50, 63–98; also *ibid.*, Part 4, Vol. 4, A General Survey of the System of Native Administration: see also Niven, 1937 and 1950.

Authority under either of these ordinances. Another amendment to the 1943 Ordinance recognizes the power of the Native Authority to make rules modifying native law and custom in issues dealing with land.

Under the Direct Taxation Ordinance of 1940, the Native Authority must consult with the Provincial Administration annually to decide on the form and incidence of tax, and the Provincial Administration assists in preparing its estimates for the Native Authority. In Zaria, the principal taxes in 1950 were the capitation-tax (*haraji*), and the cattle-tax (*jangali*). Rates varied, the wealthier districts being assessed more heavily than others. A small portion of these direct revenues was paid by the Native Treasury into regional funds; and in return, the Native Authority received certain grants from the Regional Treasury. In 1950, the Regional Treasury of Northern Nigeria was financed partly by a share of the indirect taxation on imports and exports which enter or leave Nigeria, partly by direct revenues of its own, especially licence, income-tax, and the like, partly by funds made available under various colonial development and welfare schemes.

Subject to the Governor's approval, the Native Authority is empowered to issue orders on a variety of specific issues, such as the prevention of disease, control of trade, the maintenance of peace, and the administration of such rapidly developing new towns as Kaduna. Where such new settlements have been gazetted as Townships, power to issue byelaws is vested in the Local Authority of the Township, until Native Authority rules governing these matters have been made. Further, the Native Authority has powers under the Ordinance of 1943 to organize its own police force.

In 1950 the judicial organization and functions of Native Authorities in Nigeria were still governed by the Native Courts Ordinance No. 44 of 1933, as amended by Order in Council No. 1 of 1945, and Ordinance No. 36 of 1948. Under these ordinances, native courts are established and constituted on warrants issued by the British Administration. These courts exercise jurisdiction over persons who recognize the Native Authority to which these courts are attached as their representative head or ruler. Native courts administer native laws and custom, 'except in so far as this is repugnant to morality and justice', and under recent amendments they have also been empowered to administer certain statutory law, particularly those statutes which deal with criminal offences. Capital sentences from these courts require approval by the Governor before they may be executed, and corporal punishment has to be confirmed by the Native Authority. No lawyers may take part in disputes heard by native courts, but the Provincial Administration has the right to review their cases. Native courts are of four grades, with diminishing power, and rights of appeal or review are vested in the superior grades of native courts. Provision is made for a Final Native Court of Appeal constituted as occasion arises by the Provincial Resident, and normally in Zaria this appeal court embodies members of the Emir's judicial council. An alternative arrangement is for the appeal to be transferred to a Magistrate's Court, and so to the Supreme Court in which lawyers may appear.

These Ordinances and Orders in Council provide the legal framework within which the Native Authority, the Native Judiciary, and the Native Administration function. The ordinances do not define the relations between these different units, nor do they define the precise content of their activities. Having application to the colony of Nigeria as a whole, these ordinances are specially intended to be flexible and general in their character, and they apply throughout the colony despite its diversity of conditions and cultures. It is therefore necessary to supplement this summary of the legal basis of Native Administration in Zaria by details of its actual organization. Many of these details have already been related. In the present summary, such familiar features will only be mentioned, but others which have not as yet been discussed may require more comment.

(b) The Territorial Organization

We can conveniently discuss the administrative structure of Zaria under three headings: namely, the territorial system which provides a basis for the legal and departmental administration; the fiscal administration; and the conditions of employment within the N.A. The territorial organization is the main principle of administrative integration. The emirate contains seventeen districts including the capital, each of which has its own Alkali and departmental attachments. The head of each district also has certain officials on his own district staff. These district officials include the *magatakarda* (scribe), and messengers. With their aid, the District Chief administers his area through village chiefs, each of whom has subordinate ward-heads and other assistants in his village area. As a rule at least one member from each technical department of the Native Administration is attached to each district. The District Chief also has two or three Native Authority policemen at his headquarters, and a warder is in charge of the district prison. Minor sentences are served at this gaol under the warder's supervision. The local police are controlled by the District Head, who employs them to execute the Alkali's requests, or to apprehend criminals. Each district capital also has an unpaid *iman* (*liman*, priest), and villages within the area also have their own *imams*.

Departmental officers attached to a district are under dual control. They receive instructions from their departmental chiefs at the capital; they inform the District Head of these instructions, and he then decides on the details of their execution. The departmental official is responsible to his departmental head for the technical aspects of his office, and to the District Chief for its local administration. Similarly, the Alkali has to make a monthly return of his judicial issues to his senior, the Chief Alkali of Zaria; he also has to consult the District Chief in all cases which involve imprisonment, arrest, or other executive action. The Alkali has no executive staff at his command, and often relays his summonses for witnesses and the like through the District Head.

The latter is likewise responsible for recruiting labour as required for road maintenance, repair to buildings, etc. This he does with the assistance of his village chiefs. The District Head is further responsible for the proper conduct of a variety of activities which also have technical, departmental origin or reference. Thus he may be called on to supervise the distribution of superior seed, where new crop varieties are under development; or to select or approve the siting of wells, schools, missions, and the like; or on behalf of the Native Authority he may have to purchase grain at harvest for use in hospitals, schools, prisons, and other institutions. He is likewise responsible for making annual returns of population from his district, classifying them in terms of sex, occupation, adult, or other status, and the like. These population returns provide a basis for the annual calculation of the capitation tax by the Central Administration.

Each departmental official in a district, including Alkali, reports to his departmental head on the local execution of orders, and the District Head also makes reports to the Central Administration. The District Head's reports are both routine and occasional.

Routine reports required from the district give returns of the population, livestock, etc., and details of tax-collection. Occasional reports from the district on specific problems may also be requested.

Technical officers of the Nigerian Government, who are responsible for the guidance and supervision of the various departments of the Native Administration, are usually stationed at the emirate's capital. On their visits to rural areas they communicate directly with the local District Head, whenever his assistance is required or it is necessary to inform him of their activities. Normally, departmental officials attached to a district receive written instructions from their departmental heads, who are also Hausa-Fulani; they may also be summoned to the capital by the departmental head for discussions with him or for further instructions by the European specialists who co-operate with their department. Officials of the Provincial Administration may visit districts after duly informing the Emir of their intended routes; this information is passed on by the Emir to the District Heads concerned; on entering each district, the British Officer reports his arrival to its chief, and he will be escorted by the latter's messengers and agents, so long as he remains in the area. If the British Administrative Officer wishes to visit one of the village areas of a rural district, he first informs the District Chief; a date is then set, the village chief is informed, and if he is unable to go himself, the District Chief sends one of his own men to escort the British official. Thus communication between the population of a district and the Provincial Administration is effectively controlled by the District Head.

The District Head has powers to appoint village chiefs within his area, although the Emir's approval is also necessary; but village chiefs cannot now be dismissed without legal proof of their maladministration. Heads of districts within which Fulani herdsmen have settled for some years administer these groups through their own *ardo* (headmen), who are held responsible for law and order within the nomad camps (*ruga*), and who also collect the *jangali* due from their *ruga* in return for a commission (*ushira*). Their nomadic character and lineage organization has hitherto frustrated the introduction of salaries among these Fulani headmen. Pagan tribes within a district are administered under chiefs appointed by the District Head, and often have their own native courts exercising very minor powers, which administer tribal

TABLE II

BUDGET OF DISTRICT X, 1948–49

District Revenue	£	s.	d.
1. General-tax (*haraji*)	5,080	18	9
2. Cattle-tax (*jangali*)	5	7	6
3. Native courts	169	19	5
4. Other	–	–	–
	£5,256	5	8

District Expenditure[1]

	£	s.	d.
1. Central Administration	–	–	–
2. District Administration	637	1	8
3. Village Administration	390	0	0
4. Judicial staff	217	0	0
5. Transport of specie	2	2	0
6. Police staff	344	0	0
7. (1) Warder	27	0	0
(3) Prisoners' necessities		6	0
(4) Prisoners' rations	6	4	6
8. (2) Stationery		4	3
(3) Telegrams		2	0
(12) Transport of staff	2	13	0
(14) Vehicle allowance	34	17	6
9. (2) Maintenance of buildings	75	7	8
(4) Maintenance of N.A. roads	27	1	6
10. Veterinary staff	61	13	4
11. (1) Education staff	394	1	8
(2) Elementary school equipment	4	13	10
13(*a*). (1) Medical staff	113	16	8
(2) Transport of drugs		15	10
(3) Maintenance of pauper patients		1	6
(5) Minor dispensary equipment		13	0
(9) Dispensary labour	48	0	0
13(*b*). Health and Sanitation staff	83	6	8
14. (1) Agricultural staff	353	1	8
(3) Cotton markets, labour to build	34	12	6
15. (1) Forestry staff	91	5	0
(2) Fire protection	5	1	10
(4) Fuel plantation	6	13	0
16. (1) Beef production scheme	150	0	0
(3) Forest regeneration	6	2	0

Recurrent expenditure £3,217 18 7

Non-recurrent expenditure

	£	s.	d.
(*a*) Foodstuffs purchased for the Native Authority	281	11	6
(*b*) Advances to officials, etc.	828	3	11

Total Expenditure £4,227 14. 0   £1,009 15 5

[1] Expenditure is itemized here under headings used in Native Administration accounts.

customs and law through benches composed of their own village chiefs (*magadai*). Except for the Wakilin Chawai, the kingdom of Zaria contains no tribe administered directly by a single official. Indeed, by stimulating rivalries between chiefs of the same or different tribes, the District Head effectively maintains and increases his power over all the tribes in his area. The District Head cannot legislate on tribal matters; but he can issue certain orders, which if disobeyed are enforceable at law under the wide range of offences known as *kin umurni* (disobedience). Moreover, the Emir can and does legislate to prohibit certain tribal institutions such as secondary marriage, and to introduce other practices, such as *idda*, of Islamic origin.[1] The District Chief can also nullify decisions of tribal courts by refusing to enforce them.

(c) Fiscal Forms and Content

To illustrate the character of District Administration, I attach an account of the revenue and expenditure of one of the districts of Zaria. The budget refers to the Native Authority financial year 1948–49, when this district had a registered population of 28,496, of whom less than 2,000 were non-Muhammadans, mainly Maguzawa and Gwari. There were then approximately 6,800 taxpayers and 25 village units in the district.

This district budget should be studied in relation to the annual estimates for the emirate as a whole. To illustrate the emirate budget, I have chosen the financial year 1949–50, when the emirate had a registered population of *c.* 520,000 people, of whom approximately 124,000 were taxpayers. The Native Administration estimates are prepared by the British Provincial staff and Central Administration of Zaria emirate for the province as a whole. The Zaria Native Treasury serves the independent districts of Birnin Gwari, Jaba, Moroa, and Kagoro as well as the emirate. In 1949–50 these four districts contained a total registered population of 57,400, of whom about 11,500 were taxpayers. To estimate emirate revenues and expenditures we must accordingly reduce these provincial totals by a like proportion. The ratio of emirate staff to the total staff paid by the Provincial N.A. Treasury can be assumed to correspond with these population ratios for the emirate and the province. In the summary of provincial expenditure I have therefore included details of the total staff paid by the N.A. Treasury

[1] See Smith, M. G., 1953.

TABLE III

ZARIA NATIVE ADMINISTRATION ACCOUNTS 1949–50
ZARIA PROVINCE

A. Summary of Revenue[1]

		£
1.	General-tax (*haraji*)	87,365
2.	Cattle-tax (*jangali*)	11,970
3.	Native courts	6,150
4.	Interest on investments	1,320
5.	Miscellaneous	21,895
1–5.	Local revenue	£128,700
6.	Grants, etc., from regional funds	15,675
7.	Grants, etc., from other sources	70
		£142,737
8.	Commercial undertakings	13,750
9.	Grants—capital works	3,771
	Total revenue	£160,258

Distribution of Taxes	Haraji	Jangali
	£	£
To Regional Government	3,349	1,330
To Zaria N.A.	87,365	11,970
Total direct taxes	£90,714	£13,300

[1] Figures taken from *Native Administration Estimates, Zaria Province*, 1950–51, p. 2.

and the numbers actually employed within the emirate under each head of expenditure.

Certain points in these district and provincial accounts merit attention. Firstly, the two budgets correspond formally, differences between them reflecting the greater complexity and scope of the central administration, and its direct relations with external sources of funds, such as the Regional Government. The emirate is also charged with administration of commerical and development schemes, and enjoys certain resources, such as interest on invested reserves, which are lacking at the district level. Excluding these features, it is obvious that the district administrations are modest replicas of the central administration, and that district staffs now discharge the same functions as the central administration. These functions are broadly divisible into territorial administration which involves the judiciary, the police, prisons, tax-collection, treasury and audit, the last being carried out by European staff of the Nigerian Government; and development administra-

TABLE III—*continued*

B. *Summary of Expenditure,* 1949–50 [1]

	Per cent.	Item	Total £	Personal Emoluments £	Total Provincial Staff†	Emirate Staff‡ only
I.	4·4	Central Administration	5,975	5,945	42	36
2.	8·1	District ,,	10,838	10,838	129	113
3.	5·6	Village ,,	7,430	7,430	378	320
4.	5·0	Judicial	6,808	6,768	69	₄52
5.	1·6	Treasury	2,174	1,684	15	15
6.	12·8	Police	17,183	15,662	311	250
7.	5·5	Prisons	7,357	3,837	85	65
8.	5·4	Miscellaneous	7,200	950	20	20
9.	15·4	Works, recurrent (P.W.D.)	20,672	5,152	51	51
10.	2·6	Veterinary	3,468	2,938	46	40
11.	11·6	Education	15,731	9,381	132	103
12.	0·1	Survey	250	—	—	—
13.	12·6	Medical and Health*	16,918	4,908	80	67
14.	3·7	Agriculture	5,004	3,104	60	50
15.	3·8	Forestry	5,178	3,428	54	48
16.	0·6	Pensions, etc.	745	—	—	—
17.	1·3	District Councils Fund	1,650	—	—	—
	100		£134,580	£82,025	1,486	1,230
18.		Trade and Industry	13,230	1,765	20	20
19.	(P.W.D.)	Works Extraordinary	26,240	—	—	—
		TOTALS	£174,050	£83,790	1,506	1,250

[1] Figures from *Native Administration Estimates, Zaria Province,* 1949–50.

NOTES: * Medical and Health. These are really two separate departments, and are separately budgeted for in N.A. estimates. In 1949–50 the Provincial N.A. Medical staff was 33, of whom 28 worked in the emirate. The Provincial N.A. Health staff was then 47, of whom 39 worked in the emirate. The overwhelming majority of N.A. personnel working in the emirate are recruited from its population.

† Total Provincial staff = All staff paid by Zaria N.A. Treasury. Unpaid staff are not included. Some Provincial staff working outside the emirate are recruited from within it.

‡ Emirate staff only = Staff working within the emirate and paid from Zaria N.A. funds. These figures are estimates, based on field work, and on the analysis of the Provincial N.A. accounts. It is unlikely that they are over-estimates of the personnel employed in the emirate.

tion, which involves the departments of education, public works, medicine and health, agriculture, forestry, veterinary work, and commercial undertakings. The order in which these technical departments were historically established corresponds with the order in which their several expenditures are listed in the provincial estimates.

The important point that these estimates emphasize is the administrative scale and complexity of the emirate. Altogether, approximately 1,250 persons were employed on salaries by the Native Authority of Zaria emirate in 1950. Many others also participated regularly in the Native Administration who were not on this official pay list. Using calculations of local household incomes in Muhammadan Zaria, the budgeted expenditure of this emirate administration represents about two per cent. of the annual cash income of the population, and about one per cent. of their gross annual incomes in cash and kind.[1] Despite this low incidence of taxation, the emirate administration disburses considerable funds. It is by far the largest employer of labour within the emirate, and its organization is correspondingly complex. Little of the N.A. expenditure is directed towards 'welfare' in its current sense. In the District Budget, Item 13(a) (3) shows a figure of 1s. 6d. for the 'maintenance of pauper patients'; and items 7(3 and 4) show a total of £6 10s. 6d. spent on prisoners' necessities and rations. In the provincial estimates this level of detail is not given; but £1,650, or 1·5 per cent. of total expenditure, is allocated to district council funds, mainly for approved development and welfare schemes; and another £745 is allocated for pensions. It is therefore correct to describe the administration of Zaria in 1950 as focused on development and the maintenance of order.

Another noteworthy feature of this emirate budget is the size of the new development departments and enterprises. By European standards they are quite modest adventures, and their funds are also modest by comparison with the emirate revenue, but by comparison with similar activities in other Native Administrations of Africa these enterprises and departments are substantial undertakings and their funds form a fair portion of the surplus income of the emirate. Works recurrent (Item 9 of the provincial expenditure) and Works extraordinary (Item 19) together total over £46,000, or about 30 per cent. of the gross annual expenditure of the provincial treasury.

Of the 1,250 employees of the Zaria emirate administration, 499 are members of the development departments budgeted between Items 8 (Miscellaneous) and 18 (trade and industry). Excluding Education, which employs over 100 persons, these departments average about 40 emirate officials apiece. With this number of subordinate staff, each native departmental head is clearly im-

[1] See Smith, M. G., 1955.

portant. His importance is not merely administrative, but has political aspects also. Departmental votes for 'personal emoluments' reveal the approximate financial equality of their respective staffs, and also the approximately equal status of the new departments. In certain departments, such as Agriculture, Public Works, Education, Medicine and Health, or Trade and Industry, personal emoluments form a lower portion of total expenditure than in others, such as Veterinary and Forestry expenditures, where salaries account for the greater portion of departmental outlay. But on average the ratio of total outlay which goes to pay staff in these new departments is considerably below that of the older and more prestigious departments specially charged with the maintenance of law and order, collection of tax and the like. On the other hand, these new departments disburse larger sums for purposes of development.

(d) The Character of Administrative Relations

One of the most revealing items in the account of provincial expenditure is No. 16, the vote for 'Pensions, etc.', which amounts to £745. Virtually, such a small allocation for pensions implies that appointments to the Native Administration are either lifelong or non-pensionable. Either or both of these inferences raises further questions about the terms and conditions of recruitment and employment in the Native Administration. I was not able to discover a code of administrative regulations applying to employees of the Native Authority in 1950; it is doubtful whether such a code existed, and also whether it could either be established or enforced. General or Standing Orders which define the relations and obligations of Nigerian Government officials can have no parallel in a Native Administration established under any chief whose appointment as sole Native Authority inevitably defines him as an autocrat. Administrative autocracy is incompatible with codes which limit the autocrat's power over his subordinate staff, and which defines relations between administrative officials in fixed terms. The character of employment conditions under the Zaria Native Authority is decisive for the characterization of its administrative staff. None the less, given the autocratic relations between the Native Authority and the Native Administration (ma' aikatan Sarki), it is academic to ask whether employment by the Native Authority is pensionable or life-long.

By their supervision the British seek to protect senior staff of the
Native Administration against arbitrary dismissals from office by
the Native Authority. In this way they seek to limit the ruler's
power over his senior officials, and the British have been effective
in protecting officials on various occasions. But it is doubtful
whether British supervision has had equal success in securing the
dismissal of officials who are either incompetent or unscrupulous
in their use of office. In such issues the Emir, with assistance from
his judiciary, can offer considerable protection to his subordinates
if he wishes. In effect, therefore, the conditions of appointment, employment, promotion, transfer, and dismissal which
define relations between Native Administration and the Native
authority, are subject to *ad hoc* political action which involves the
British Administration, the Native Authority, and the native
courts. Such *ad hoc* political action is limited to the decision of the
individual cases which promote it, as in the instances already
cited. Since a code regulating relations between officials of the
Native Administration and the Native Authority is incompatible
with the statutory basis on which that Authority is itself established, this *ad hoc* political action is the best that the British can
do. In effect, British supervision of the Native Administration is
thus a permanent political issue entailing vigilance by Provincial
Officers and Emir alike.

Since there are no defined procedures and codes governing the
relations and behaviour of Native Administration staff, there can
be no codes which govern their recruitment or dismissal. Recruitment indeed continues on traditional lines and emphasizes political
loyalty to the immediate superior in office. Thus in 1950 the sole
Mallawa District Chief had an unusual number of Mallawa territorial and departmental officials stationed in his district. The
Mallawa departmental heads of N.A. Medical and Health Departments, who were rivals for promotion to territorial office, and for
the leadership of the Mallawa dynasty, each had an unusual
complement of kinsmen within his department. Other departmental and territorial officials behaved similarly. The simplest
way to illustrate contemporary patterns of recruitment to office is
to classify the officials in various departments of the N.A. by
ethnic status, lineage, affiliation, and school experience.

The following table requires few comments. Of the 529
Northerners employed by the Zaria Native Administration in 1945

TABLE IV

ETHNIC, KINSHIP, AND EDUCATIONAL STATUS OF NATIVE ADMINISTRATION EMPLOYEES—ZARIA, 1945[1]

Dept.	Fulani Lineages						Total Fulani	Non-Fulani	South Nigerians	Ex-N.A. Schoolboys	Total
	(B)	(M)	(K)	(T)	(YD)	Other					
1. Emir's office	6	2	1	1	—	1	11	14	—	3	25
2. District Chiefs	8	1	1	—	1	3	14	3	—	9	17
District Staff (Admin.)	22	3	18	2	1	20	66	30	3	12	99
3. Judicial staff	15	3	5	—	13	7	43	12	7	1	62
4. Ward heads, etc.	12	2	4	1	1	5	25	—	—	3	25
5. Treasury	2	1	—	—	—	5	8	6	—	12	14
6. Zaria Prison	1	1	1	—	—	1	4	1	—	4	5
7. Public Works	9	1	1	4	—	3	18	32	35	7	85
8. Dispensaries	6	—	1	—	1	—	8	4	—	1	12
9. Health	2	2	5	1	1	8	19	19	13	22	51
10. Agriculture	8	2	4	2	—	7	23	9	1	5	33
11. Veterinary	2	—	5	3	1	11	22	5	—	—	27
12. Forestry	18	6	5	1	1	7	38	12	—	—	50
13. Education	9	4	5	3	2	21	44	39	—	83	83
TOTALS	120	28	56	18	22	99	343	186	59	162	588

B = Bornawa.　　M = Mallawa　　K = Katsinawa　　T = Toronkawa
YD = 'yan Doto (The Chief Judge's lineage)
[1] Village chiefs and policemen are not included.

who have been classified above, 343, or 64 per cent., are Fulani, and 205, or 39 per cent., belong to one or other of the three principal dynasties. At this date 120, or 22 per cent., of the 529 Northerners employed by the N.A. were members of the ruler's dynasty; and their principal supporters, the Katsinawa had 57 members, or 11 per cent. There were only 28 Mallawa in the 529 Northerners classified above, a ratio of 5·6 per cent. The Mallawa are the chief rivals of the Bornawa. Between 1945 and 1950 the Mallawa increased their numbers in the N.A., in consequence of Mallawa promotion to headship of the Medical and Health departments. In 1945 other leading Fulani lineages between them held 138, or 26 per cent. of these 529 N.A. positions, while non-Fulani Northerners held 186 positions, or 36 per cent. Most of these non-Fulani Northerners employed by the Zaria N.A. were Muhammadan Habe; and in 1948 the political society of the emirate contained 252,000 Habe as compared with 54,000 Fulani. These figures show that the Fulani receive preference over the non-Fulani as regards employment by the Zaria N.A.; that the dynastic Fulani receive preference over other Fulani; and that the members of the ruling dynasty receive preference over their dynastic rivals. The composition of the Zaria judicial staff at this date repeats the patterns by which office is distributed among the dynasties. Of the 65 Northerners in the emirate judicial staff in 1945, 13 were members of the lineage of the then Chief Judge, and of the 12 non-Fulani occupying judicial office, 10 were members of the Haben Kajuru lineage which had formerly held the office of Chief Judge. The 7 Southern Nigerians on the N.A. judicial staff were members of courts situated in the new settlements outside Kaduna and Zaria, and dealt with the affairs of the Southern populations living there.

The preceding table also informs us about the educational status of Northerners on the Zaria N.A. staff. Of these 529 Northern employees, 162, or 31 per cent., had attended the new N.A. schools which teach Roman script. It is likely that this sample contains other persons who were able to read and write Hausa in Roman script, although they did not attend these schools; but their inclusion would not alter the proportion just given by very much. Moreover, one-half of the 162 ex-schoolboys in this sample of N.A. employees were themselves engaged in the emirate education departments as teachers; and all N.A. teachers listed in Table IV were literate in Roman script. To assess the educational background of the N.A. staff not directly engaged in education accurately, we must therefore exclude the teachers. On this basis we find that, of the remaining 446 N.A. employees, only 79, or 18 per cent., have attended N.A. schools.

Clearly British expectations that the literate population of school-leavers would provide the Native Administration with most of its staff have not been fulfilled. The figures just quoted indicate otherwise; but the cause is not a shortage of pupils. In 1948 the schools of Zaria N.A. contained over 1,300 boys. Even if the percentage of literate N.A. staff was doubled to allow for those employees literate in Roman script who had not attended N.A. schools, it is clear that in 1945 familiarity with Roman script was neither a necessary nor a sufficient condition for appointment to the Native Administration. Despite certain changes, this was the position in 1950 also. Set beside our information on kinship and ethnic status presented above, these figures on the educational background of N.A. staff reveal the extent to which non-technical factors govern appointments to N.A. offices, and they further imply that such factors influence behaviour within the Native Administration, especially with respect to the conditions of employment, promotion, transfer, dismissal, and public conduct as well as other intra-administrative relations. Briefly, these non-technical factors reflect political relations and have political significance.

One further point requires attention. Relations between the officials of the Native Administration and the subjects of the Emir are as poorly defined and regulated as are relations between these officials and the Emir himself. This is especially true with regard to the new technical staff. The subject population (*talakawa*) are very often quite ignorant of the powers and duties of these new officials; and since these duties and powers are subject to technical considerations and goals, they are also frequently subject to redefinition and change, so that information about the rights, functions, and authority of these officials has to be kept up-to-date by continuous enquiry. The commoners' ignorance of these matters is coupled with their incapacity to take effective action against officials of any department who act *ultra vires*; in short, *talakawa* are largely defenceless against N.A. officials. By virtue of these conditions the new technical offices have become progressively assimilated to the traditional concept of *sarauta*, and are now offices exercising mandatory powers. The commoner who rejects an official's command invites trial for *kin umurci* in the Alkali's court; and commoners expect that in such an issue the court will favour the official against them. *Talakawa* see *masu-sarauta* (office-holders) as sharing common interests which are contraposed to their own; they also recognize those political solidarities of N.A. officials which have been indicated in Table IV. These solidarities are not merely ethnic. Kinship, marriage, clientage, and other ties bind officials together, and provide the bases for their corporate solidarity and action against *talakawa* who dispute their authority and power. Officials of the new departments are thus in structural contraposition with the subject population, and the latter's ignorance of the precise details of these new official functions provides tempting opportunities for administrative malpractice of various sorts. Through such practices these new officials display their power and assimilate their new *sarauta* to the traditional official structure and forms of rule.

Commoners have a longer acquaintance with the powers and functions of territorial chiefs at both the village and district level. But these powers and functions are also subject to change and redefinition by decisions and regulations of the Native Authority; and territorial chiefs, especially District Heads, suffer in local esteem from decisions taken in Zaria by which they have to abide, and from the principle of part-payment or under-payment for labour on N.A. roads, buildings, and the like to which they are thus committed (see Item 9 in the District Budget, *supra*). Commoners engaged on these works receive some payment, but at local rates these payments are inadequate for the work done, and they are not distributed among the persons who carried out the work in any uniform fashion. In consequence local suspicion attaches to the District Head or other official entrusted with these payments. Yet often the District Head or other official may have been specially scrupulous in paying out all monies allocated for these purposes. The fact is that the monies are insufficient; that their amount is not known to the *talakawa*, and that it also varies in relation to the work done by time and place. Territorial and other officials who have to make these inadequate payments occupy an unenviable position. However, to District Chiefs, misunderstanding and hostility promoted by such underpayments have the useful function of recurrently reminding their subjects that the contemporary government of Zaria is not based on consent but on power. For this reason such chiefs make little effort to inform their subjects about these or other details of their administration.

Local rulers have no need to inform commoners about governmental policy, or to discuss their administrative objectives and methods with the people. Indeed, the commoners' ignorance of these matters expresses their dependent political status and subject role. It also emphasizes that the officials of the N.A. are not the people's servants but their rulers. Lack of communication between officials and the Hausa public about official aims and procedure serves to redefine relations between these two groups in political terms. Thus administrative office has a political expression as well as political basis and mode of recruitment.

3. THE POLITICAL SYSTEM OF ZARIA IN 1950

The three features which are critical for an analysis of the political system of Zaria in 1950 are its limits, its form, and its character. I shall discuss each of these in turn.

(a) The Boundaries of this System

During 1950 preparations were actively under way for the establishment of a Federal Nigerian Government on the basis of universal suffrage. There were frequent discussions between the chiefs and leaders of the various regions about the allocation of seats in the federal legislature, and about other constitutional issues. These matters were also discussed by the chiefs and leaders of the Northern region meeting separately. Within Zaria emirate the proposed changes and the elections which would establish the regional and federal legislature were continually being publicized, and information was distributed by rediffusion, by newspaper, and by individual contacts. Change was imminent, its preparation was afoot, and the British and Native Administrations were alike committed to such change.

There was a branch of the *Jam'iyyar Mutanen Arewa* (Northern People's Congress) at Zaria, and its local head was the Native Chief of Works, the Turaki Aliyu, a member of the local branch of the Toronkawa lineage descended from Mallam Musa's daughter and Dan Fodio's Waziri Gidado. This *Jam'iyya* was then reorganizing to become the dominant political party of the Muhammadan North; and within the region its only opposition then came from another party known as the Northern Elements' Progressive Union, which had its headquarters in Kano city and demanded radical reforms in the northern emirates. Each of the two southern regions also had a regional political party, that in the east being led by Dr. Azikiwe, and that in the west by Chief Awolowo. The eastern party stood for the Ibo interests, that in the western provinces for Yoruba interests, and the *Jam'iyyar Mutanen Arewa* for the interests of the Muhammadan North. Thus in 1950 the parties of each region were mobilizing their forces to fight the coming elections on regional lines.

The emirate of Zaria was clearly involved in this developing system of federal political relations; and the lead which the Emir of Zaria gave to the Northern members of the consultative as-

sembly which was summoned in 1950 to consider the federal
('MacPherson') constitution demonstrates the Emir's awareness
of Zaria's position. The British Administration were also involved
in this emerging system of federal politics, being concerned to
secure its establishment and supervise its operation. The Yoruba
and Ibo with whom Zaria now had to deal on a federal level were
distinguished from the Muhammadan North by culture, region,
language, and political party organization. Within Northern
Nigeria the dominant political idea and unit was that of the Fulani
empire of Sokoto. This offered a powerful centre around which
Muhammadans could rally, and it also had a history and organization capable of directing these Muhammadan forces to their
greatest effect. Indeed, the great majority of Northern Muhammadans, and some states in the western region also, were former
tributary members of this Fulani empire. In the closing months of
1950 the Sultan of Sokoto formally assumed the mantle of Northern leadership with his call for voluntary donations to a fund to
equip the North to meet the challenge of new responsibilities. This
fund, known as *Kurdin Taimakon Arewa* (Money to help the
North), soon amounted to more than £40,000, although non-
Muhammadans contributed little and the normal individual
contribution was only threepence. In this emerging system of
federal politics Zaria was directly attached to the Fulani empire,
and through this empire the emirate was associated with other
Northern Muhammadan states, such as Abuja, in opposition to
the Yoruba and Ibo of the South.

At this time the emirate was thus engaged in relations with the
British Administration on three levels, locally, regionally, and
federally. In the regional and federal contexts, the emirate by
virtue of its membership in the Fulani empire was able to face the
British Administration on more or less equal terms. To illustrate
the measure and significance of this equality, one example may
suffice. In 1950 charges were being made quite openly that the
Native Administrations in the Northern emirates were corrupt.[1]
The British Administration was disturbed by such allegations.
Finally, the Northern House of Chiefs established a committee to
consider such malpractices. The conclusion reached by this committee revealed a wisdom like unto Solomon's. They decided that

[1] See *Gaskiya Ta Fi Kwabo* (Hausa Vernacular Newspaper), No. 415 of 23rd
August, 1950.

henceforward punishment for bribery and other similar forms of corruption should fall equally on all parties involved. Thus he who offers the bribe and he who takes it would suffer alike. This ruling put an end to further complaints of official corruption, and was heralded in Britain as a fundamental attempt by the Northern rulers at self-reform. This decision illustrates the power of the Fulani chiefs in 1952, and the extent to which they had recovered the ground lost to the British Administration in the early years when the Protectorate was established. Thus in 1950 Zaria faced the British Administration at the regional level as one of the states led by Sokoto, and through this political association the Emir was able to influence and limit British political supervision of emirate affairs.

Despite its persisting vassalage, in 1950 the emirate of Zaria formed an independent unit within the Fulani dominions, sub-ordinate to the authority and leadership of Sokoto, but internally autonomous. The Sultan no longer received annual tribute from Zaria; nor did he have the right to appoint or dethrone its rulers; nor did they have to render annual homage by visits to Sokoto. These conditions of vassalage had lapsed under British rule, with-out the relation itself falling into abeyance. In much the same way, the vassals of Zaria no longer make formal allegiance in the traditional manner, though the relations and status of vassalage persist; the autonomy of these vassals within Zaria has been respected as far as possible. Where a former vassal state has been incorporated within one of the emirate districts as a village area, it is part of the emirate in substance as well as in form; but where a former vassal state now constitutes a separate district, its dis-tinctness and vassalage persist together; and such a unit, although formally a part of the kingdom, is highly autonomous in its internal affairs. Put otherwise, the Emir of Zaria does not hold himself responsible for the government of such vassal districts, nor for the selection and protection of their chiefs, nor do his subjects hold him fully responsible for conditions in these vassal states.

Thus vassalage remains important among the external relations of the emirate. The effect of British supervision has been to modify its form and content, but in the same way that vassalage differenti-ates Zaria from its suzerain, Sokoto, it also defines Kauru, Kajuru, and Kagarko as outside the true political society of Zaria emirate. The conditions of membership in the political society of Zaria have already been discussed at length. Only those persons whose relations to the constituted authorities are immediate, exclusive, and direct are full members of this political society. Dependants of these persons are also members of Zaria society but they have the political status of minors. In short, only Hausa-speaking Muhammadans really belong to the political society of the emirate. Pagan tribes under emirate rule are subject populations, and are not full citizens of the state. Membership in the political society of the emirate involves an exclusive identification with the emirate as a unit, with its history, its rulers and form of rule, and with its future. This identification is neither vicarious nor merely psychological. Political indentification is expressed by participation within the political system of the society which forms the emirate; and such participation is characteristically expressed by clientage, by serfdom, or by kinship and marriage relations.

The variety of political roles which these relations of solidarity or subordination support and require include chieftainship, official membership of the Native Administration, unofficial agency and communication by *'yan labari* or *jekadu*, agency (*fadanci*), serfdom, and the like. Such political action has as its object the maintenance and increase of the actor's power and influence. The structure of political action is therefore segmentary and involves competition between individuals, lineages, or other rival groups to secure or retain power and office by all the means at their disposal. Kinship, marriage, and clientage are the main principles through which persons of free parentage are brought into this system, at both the community and emirate levels; the assimilation of serfdom to clientage provides the basis for the participation of those descended from slaves.

(b) The Political Structure

Before proceeding to discuss the political system of Zaria in 1950, it is necessary to reconsider its relation to the British Administration. If the term 'Native Administration' is taken literally, it would mean that the emirate of Zaria is not a political unit at all but merely an administrative district. Likewise, the British Administration would be classifiable as a non-political and purely administrative organization. Actually, Lugard, who established British rule in the region, and who was primarily responsible for defining the form and character of its British Administration, consistently distinguishes between the 'political officers' of the Protectorate Government, whose duty it was to administer, and the technical or departmental staff, who were engaged on such projects as education or railways, and were subject to direction by the political officers. In this way Lugard clearly recognized that the Protectorate Government was a *political administration*, the instrument used for such purposes being the 'administrative' staff, particularly the British staff in charge of Provincial Administration.

To describe the Native Administration of Zaria as part of the native political system does not, of course, exclude its classification as an administrative structure. As we have seen, an administrative organization may have prominent political elements and functions. Accordingly, questions about the extent and significance of political elements and functions in the Native Administration of Zaria are questions of fact. To answer these questions we must have detailed knowledge, firstly about the relations between the Native Administration and its British supervisors, and secondly about the relations among the members of the Native Administration, and between that administration and the population it administers.

Relations between the British and the Native Administration pivot on the Emir of Zaria. His opposite number, the Resident of Zaria, is assisted by a staff of Divisional Officers, and reports to the Lieutenant-Governor of the Northern Provinces. The Emir has a formal council to assist him, but he need not report to his subjects. As Native Authority, he heads the Native Administration, which is directly responsible to him, and not to the British officials who supervise it. In such a situation, the Emir's power to control his Native Administration clearly corresponds with his power to limit British control. This simply means that the Emir's control over his administration increases *pro rata* with the ineffectiveness or intermittency of British attempts to supervise and control this administration. In this structural context the Emir is therefore compelled to try to limit the effectiveness of British supervision. Such action by the Emir is *ipso facto* political action. It mobilizes personnel and resources within one organization against those of another. The relation is clearly segmentary, despite its formally hierarchic character. This being the case, it must be conceded that the Native Administration operates under the Emir as a political unit in its dealings with the British Provincial Administration. At the regional level the emirate also confronts the British Regional Administration as part of a wider political unit, the Fulani empire. At the still more inclusive level of the Nigerian Federation, the emirate, in association with other units of the Muhammadan North, and especially as a member of the dominant Northern unit under Sokoto, confronts the representatives of Southern Nigeria in the competition for control of federal policy and fortunes. At each of these levels the political relations in which the emirate is engaged involve the contraposition of competing units. But it is only at the Provincial level that the emirate meets the British Administration alone and face to face.

The extent to which Native Administration can be regarded as overtly and effectively political depends in part on its freedom from British control. Freedom from such control can be tested in certain ways. Essentially, effective British control or supervision implies close correspondence between the performance of the Native Administration and its goals as set by the British.[1] For example, annual population returns are required of this administration for purposes of tax-assessment. If the Native Administration is effectively administered or controlled by British supervisors, or if it has fully absorbed their aims and methods, then these official returns of population should correspond to the actual population in the area. The British have always insisted strongly on accurate returns of population and tax from their earliest days in Northern Nigeria.[2] Yet in 1950–51 the registered population of Zaria emirate was reported to be less than 540,000 persons, whereas the Nigerian census of 1951 revealed a population well over 750,000. Clearly, the performance of the Native Administration in this case corresponds neither with the reality nor with British expectations and requirements. This example is all the more revealing since the British have for long been concerned with the apparent failure of population in these Fulani emirates to increase in accordance with their expectations. During 1929–30, an elaborate investigation was conducted into the reasons for low Hausa fertility. Diet was blamed, on the curious ground that rats fed with Hausa staples tended to lose their powers of reproduction.[3] Actually, Hausa are

---

[1] Lugard, 1918; also Cameron, 1934; also Hailey, 1937, *passim.*
[2] See Colonial Reports, Northern Nigeria, No. 377 of 1901; 437 of 1903; 594 of 1907–8. Also Lugard, 1926.
[3] McCulloch, 1929–30.

highly fertile, and despite an appalling rate of infant mortality, the population appears to increase by 2·5 per cent. per annum.[1] However, this increase has not been fully registered, perhaps because village headmen and others charged with its registration are able to increase their income by collecting and keeping tax from a substantial portion of unregistered persons. These village chiefs are underpaid (about 15s. or £1 per month being their average salary in Zaria in 1950), and this, coupled with inadequate supervision and some encouragement from their superiors, may have inclined them to reward themselves by under-representing the population of their areas on the scale indicated by the figures. Field work fully bears out this explanation.

This instance of population under-representation indicates the sort of relations which hold on the one hand among the Native Administration staff, and between that Administration and the emirate population on the other, as well as relations between the N.A. and the Provincial Administration. The relations between the N.A. and the emirate population illustrated by this case are clearly political in so far as they are *ultra vires* or consist of deliberate failure to perform official duty. The sorts of relation among members of the territorial administration which these facts imply are also political, having their foci and expression in solidarity, protection, and tribute. This instance further indicates the degree to which the Native Administration has eluded control by the Provincial Administration; yet to the extent that it is not controlled by the British, the Native Administration must be regarded as ruling independently, within limits indicated by its own caution and the strength of its political opponents.

Bearing this in mind, we can now discuss the form of this political system. As of 1950 the political system of Zaria clearly involved the British Administration, which was in structural contraposition to the Native Administration under the Emir, these two units being engaged in a structurally fixed competition for control and power. In some ways the relation of Zaria to the British in 1950 resembled that with Sokoto in 1870; but there are many important differences. None the less, the British Administration formed an important element in the system of political relations which centred on the Emir. This system also involved the Native Administration and the Native Judiciary. In this context the

[1] See Smith, M. G., 1955, Appendix 1.

Native Administration was at once the Emir's instrument and his prize. Through his official staff the Emir took such action as his political relation with the British seemed to require; and one of the major objectives of action by the Emir was the protection and control of that Native Administration itself.

In his efforts to contain British supervision and to retain or increase his control of the Native Administration, the Emir had to take the Native Judiciary into account. They occupied a strategic position, and one which might seem invulnerable. Appointed on the recommendation of the Senior Judge, the judiciary exercised jurisdiction over issues involving the Emir's administrative staff. The British normally hesitated to dispute the verdicts of these native courts, since reversal of these verdicts would tend to undermine the authority of such courts in native eyes, while appeals which repeated the decisions of such courts would serve little purpose. Moreover, if the court's decision was based on the Koranic oath, there was really no point in a retrial. Thus the native courts could exercise influence on both the British and Native Administrations by the way in which they decided cases involving native administrative staff. Although appeals lay from these courts to that of the Emir, for various reasons the Emir can not regularly exculpate officials in his own courts, nor can he therein directly incriminate those whom he desires to ruin. Appeal to the Emir's court is therefore reserved for specially important cases, and the stock method of trial in these situations is to administer the Koranic oath, perjury being held to be punishable by Allah rather than the Emir.

The Native Judiciary poses a political problem for the Emir because of its capacity to assist him in preserving the Native Administration from British interference, or to undermine his own control of this Native Administration by its decisions. In order that the Emir should protect and control the Native Administration effectively and enjoy security in his relations with the British, he must therefore control the Native Judiciary.

To the Emir, control of the judiciary is only essential when issues of administrative or political import arise. For the bulk of their legal administration the native courts need fear no interference from the Emir. But issues do arise from time to time in which the Emir's position and power are involved, and in these situations the security of his control over his subordinate staff is identified with the latter's security. When such cases develop, the Emir and the Chief Alkali confront each other.

The Emir's principal resources in his dealings with the Chief Judge are his powers of appointment and promotion. By promoting the Chief Judge the Emir can remove him from office and render all his kinsmen who hold judgeships insecure. Moreover, by promoting the Chief Judge into a purely advisory role, or into territorial office, the Emir places the Chief Judge directly under his own control, and can punish the judge's obstinacy by dismissal or other means. By the same measure the Emir frees himself to appoint a more co-operative official as Chief Judge, and in this way he can then transfer control of judicial appointments to lineage rivals of the former Chief Judge. Finally, by promoting the Chief Judge from office, the Emir deprives him of power, the loss of which is probably itself the greatest personal blow of all. In addition, the Emir may also appoint kinsmen of the Chief Judge to lucrative and important office (See Table IV, *supra*). Such appointments influence the Chief Judge to comply with the Emir's wishes in administrative issues, partly because of the increased identification it establishes between the Native Administration and the Native Judiciary, partly because it discourages the Chief Judge from actions which may endanger the political prospects of his own kin. In any event, despite the great prominence of the Chief Judge, and his control over the Native Judiciary, his position *vis-à-vis* the Emir neither permits of parity of power nor open opposition. By the device of promotion, the Emir is able to divide and rule the Native Judiciary, simply by rotating the office of Chief Judge among the leading legal lineages and by allowing the Chief Judge to give office to his kin.

In fact the Chief Judge heads a segmented judicial structure, and its division between his kin and supporters, and his lineage rivals and their allies, weakens his capacity to resist the Emir in issues of interest to the latter. A co-operative association with the ruler, therefore, offers the Chief Judge far more than the opposite. By co-operating with the Emir the Chief Judge maintains his own position, and this in turn gives him opportunities for the appointment and promotion of kin, for the exercise of judicial and other power, for mutually profitable co-operation with the king, for canvassing his own interests and those of his kinsmen and friends, and especially for effective participation in those affairs of state which centre on relations between the Emir, the British Administration, and the Native Judiciary.

Thus in 1950 the political system of Zaria consisted of the Emir and his administrative subordinates, the Native Judiciary and the British Administration. In this system, the Emir, with the assistance of his judiciary, sought to protect the Native Administration and native political system from interference and control by the British Administration. In this undertaking the essential measure of an Emir's success is the number of his opponents and supporters who have suffered dismissal from office during his reign. By such a test there could be no doubt that in 1950 the Emir of Zaria was fully in charge of the situation. His promotion of the Chief Alkali to the advisory office of Waziri two years later, indicates that he was equally well aware of the basis on which his control rested, and was determined to maintain this control independently.

However, in 1950 the political system of Zaria emirate did not consist solely in relations between the Emir, the Native Judiciary and the British Administration. This system of political relations had itself been preceded by another, of which the Emir was the conscious heir, and this older system also persisted. This older political system was constituted by the rival dynasties, their various clients, and relations between them. In 1950 as before this dynastic rivalry was focused on the distribution of office, especially on the supreme office with its power of allocating subordinate offices. The Native Administration being appointed by the Native Authority as the agency of a statutorily constituted autocrat, its insulation from political factors and influences in this situation was impossible and incompatible with its statutory base; in consequence in its composition the Native Administration reflected the conditions of this traditional dynastic rivalry. The extent to which it did so in 1945 has already been indicated in the preceding analysis of the central staff of the Zaria N.A. The Emir's structurally inescapable need for monocratic authority over his administrative staff itself arises from his position within this political system of rival dynasties. As the figures already given indicate, the present dynasty has sought to win support for its régime from one of its former rivals, the Katsinawa, by liberal appointments to office, while excluding its most important opponents, the Mallawa.

By 1950 the Bornawa dynasty had already held the kingship

without a break for thirty years. At that time there were only two dynastic rivals of the Bornawa who held territorial office, and neither of these persons were directly descended from former rulers. Time had so far advanced its erosion of the Emir's dynastic rivals, by the elimination of their leading candidates, and by the virtual exclusion of their members from senior territorial office. Despite British aims and intentions, and the revisions of succession rules and procedure under British supervision, the traditional system of multidynastic competition had partly been replaced by one of monodynastic autocracy; and within the ruling dynasty rival segments descended from Kwassau and Dalhatu respectively were becoming progressively estranged. Thus the old patterns of political competition and segmentation were continuing, despite the changing constitution and character of the segments themselves.

In this situation the Emir was as much concerned to scrutinize the loyalties of his kinsmen as the behaviour of his dynastic rivals. Of the eight District Heads appointed to non-hereditary office by M. Ja'afaru between 1936 and 1950, one was his brother, and another, the Dan Madami Umoru, who was a son of Ibrahim, M. Ja'afaru's predecessor, was appointed after his own brother had been dismissed from that office; another District Head belonged to the rival Katsinawa dynasty, while the other five appointed by this ruler were of non-royal lineage. In part these distributions of office among non-kinsmen may be traced to the Emir's lack of male issue, but in part they reflect the rivalries already current among Bornawa, and their opposition to his accession.

The native political system in 1950 was thus quite complex. Its pivot and basic principle was the kingship, and it depended on this institution for its unity. On one level the Emir was engaged in political relations with the British and the Native Judiciary simultaneously; on another, with his dynastic rivals; on yet a third, with his own kinsmen in and out of office. He was also bound to the Native Administration by political ties. Through his control of this administration the Emir was able to keep rivals weak by excluding them from office, to limit British intervention in the affairs of his emirate, and to reduce the power of the Native Judiciary. Moreover, it was through this Native Administration that the Emir ruled his subjects, official and other. His powers of appointment, transfer, promotion, and dismissal effectively allowed the ruler to control his subordinate administrative staff. With the Emir's consent, his senior officials exercised a similar power over their districts or departments, but it has always been recognized that the Emir has the ultimate right and power to distribute departmental and territorial office alike. Needless to say, for the most part, the ruler is directly concerned only with the most senior positions in such structures. Those to whom he entrusts departments or districts are persons in whose loyalty he has confidence. These individuals enjoy the Emir's support in the administration of their offices, and have little to fear from his supervision, so long as their political solidarities persist. In this situation clientage is stimulated and expressed by office.

As indicated above, appointment in the Native Administration is not governed by merit or technical qualifications, but by ties of loyalty in a situation of political rivalry where the stakes are considerable. Consequently, in much the same way that the Emir appoints his own supporters and kin to office, or the Chief Judge appoints his kinsmen to judgeships, so do the departmental and territorial chiefs allocate office on bases of personal loyalty and solidarity to themselves. Once appointments to office had been made on such grounds, the exercise of office is thereafter conditioned by the system of hierarchic solidarities. In such a structure the subordinate expects protection and possible promotion from his superior, while the latter in return expects loyalty and obedience from his client. In effect, political relations ramify throughout the administrative organization, and political factors saturate its technical and non-technical positions alike. Many of these political relations have purely internal reference and functions; others refer to the context of British supervision, and to the Emir's responsibilities and needs in this situation; yet others refer to the relations between this administration and the population over which it rules.

(c) The Character of Politics in Zaria

If relations between the Native Administration and the population of the emirate are purely administrative, they must necessarily conform to the definition of official functions and duties. As far as possible there should include no official sins of omission or commission. To the extent that the Native Administration departs from this pattern in its relations with the native population, then relations between these two categories of persons become correspondingly political. Moreover, to the extent that the Native Administration has political relations with the population which it administers, and is not subject to any external agency such as the British Administration, then these relations themselves indicate the degree to which the N.A. is a ruling bureaucracy. Yet, the extent to which this N.A. rules the emirate population politically is the measure of its independence from effective control by the British; and this in turn is the measure of the Emir's effective power.

Bearing these points in mind, we may consider a few cases which simultaneously illustrate the character of relations between the Native Administration on the one hand and the population of the emirate on the other; between the Emir and his Native Administration; and between the Emir, the N.A., and the British. The following examples will also reveal some of the various factors and situations involved in Native Administration. In the case of the under-registration of population, already mentioned, the effect has been seriously to deprive the Native Treasury, if not the native officials, of revenue. It is also quite likely that the under-reporting of persons liable to pay *haraji* is matched by under-reporting of cattle for which *jangali* is due. Another illustration consists simply in the maintenance of the prohibited systems of *jekadu* and levies of foodstuffs from the local population. Another example consists in the use of forced labour on the farm of a certain District Head, on one occasion over 150 persons being mobilized as a body. The close connection between territorial and judicial officials in settling disputes is also worth mention. In one instance, appeals were made to a District Head to secure a favourable decision from the local court, and gifts formed a prominent part of the appeal. Formally, of course, there is a clear division between executive and judicial offices and functions; but operationally this need not be so. Another case involved the Native Treasury of Zaria Province, which is also the emirate Treasury. Funds paid out by this Treasury are drawn from a reserve account which the Nigerian Government keeps at a certain level. Native Treasury balances and accounts are subject to frequent audit by British Divisional Officers. In 1950 it was discovered that out of a reserve of about £44,000 which the Zaria Treasury had with the Nigerian Govern-

ment, some £20,000-odd were missing and could not be traced.[1]
Two Ibo clerks in the Native Public Works Department, who had
absconded, were later held responsible for this loss, and were
brought to trial and sentenced. The perpetuation of serfdom
through the device of controlling land which has already been
discussed provides another illuminating example of relations between the people and their rulers. Another case occurred in 1950
at the first elections in Zaria city of delegates from Zaria Province
to the Regional Assembly of Northern Nigeria. Voting for this
election began in the villages, each village selecting one or more
representatives, who then met at the District Headquarters to
elect one or more Representatives from the District. These District
representatives duly met at the capital to elect four delegates from
Zaria Province to the Northern House of Representatives. This
Northern House of Representatives would in turn select a certain
number of members to sit in the federal legislature. It is reported
that on the eve of the provincial elections, the Emir of Zaria
gathered his District Chiefs and instructed them how their detachments were to vote on the morrow. Certain delegates who were
taking part in these provincial elections, having received these
instructions, made a public declaration of the matter at the place
of election to the assembly on the following day in the presence of
the Resident of Zaria. It is reported that the Resident emphasized
the freedom of voters to exercise their vote as they pleased; but it
is also reported that the results of these provincial elections conformed exactly with the orders issued.[2] A similar experience was
reported to the acting Colonial Secretary, Mr. Oliver Lyttelton,
by a delegation from the Northern Elements' Progressive Union
which visited London for the specific purpose of complaining
about the manner in which these elections had been held at Kano.
Later in 1951 when this Party held a meeting in one of the Hausa
districts of Zaria emirate, thirty-seven persons who attended the
meeting were arrested and imprisoned by the District Head for
attending a political meeting without permission to do so. Thus the
rulers of Zaria distinguish between freedom to speak, which they
may accept, and freedom to listen, which they may not.

[1] See *Gaskiya Ta Fi Kwabo* (Hausa Vernacular Newspaper), No. 48 of 13th
September, 1950, p. 1.
[2] These facts were reported to the writer in letters from two persons who took
part in these provincial elections. As these individuals do not know one another,
collusion is unlikely.

These examples could be multiplied; but they are probably sufficient to show that in 1950 the Native Administration ruled the population of the emirate without much fear of effective British supervision. They simultaneously illustrate the character of relations between the members of the Native Administration and the Emir, and also between this Native Administration and the emirate population. Such relations clearly demonstrate that in 1950 the Native Administration of Zaria emirate was an effective ruling bureaucracy. The incapacity of the subject population of the emirate to complain directly to British officials in Zaria was itself largely due to the rules established by the British Administration to govern its relations with the Northern emirates; but lacking direct protection from the British, the population of the emirates remained defenceless against office-holders, except in so far as individual relations of clientage were able to offer protection, relief, or assistance.

It is now possible to describe the government of Zaria emirate in 1950 as an autocracy ineffectively supervised by the British. Within this government, the Native Administration acted as a ruling bureaucracy, and was itself an object of political competition between rivals for office, and an instrument of political administration. The bureaucratic character of this structure is too obvious to need further comment; so is its ruling power, which was delegated through a hierarchy of officials under the Emir, each official exercising such power as his political and administrative position permitted or warranted, without the system revealing any tendencies towards disintegration. None the less, although the administration was saturated with political factors, motivations, and relations, it was merely one political structure and unit in a system of such structures, and was therefore neither coterminous with the native political system nor an exact replica of the latter. In this administration many political functions and relations were identified with administrative office, and administrative office was itself largely political, without producing an exact or consistent equation of the two modes of action. In 1950 the Native Administration was in fact part of a wider political system which was then in a rapid process of change.

At one and the same time a variety of changes were under way in Zaria. New segmentary political structures were developing within the Native Judiciary. Changes in the traditional system of multidynastic competition for the throne were already far ad-vanced; and it then seemed possible that in future the emirate would be ruled by one dynasty, the Bornawa, which was itself developing internal segmentation as a reflex of these changes. The Native Administration occupied a curious position in this persist-ing system of multidynastic political competition, since it was both the object and means of this competition, and its character and composition revealed the decisive impact of this historic rivalry. Yet this rivalry itself was changing, and besides the old dynasties, there were now new segments competing for ascendancy within the Bornawa.

Over this structure the Emir ruled like an autocrat. Under the Native Authority Ordinance of 1943, he was by statute as well as by fact an autocrat. But his power was not absolute. Rivals within his dynasty and in other dynasties competed for power with him as well as with one another. Other units of power with which he had to deal included his own Native Judiciary, and the British Provincial Administration. Beyond his frontiers, the Fulani em-pire offered support and assistance, but also enjoined vassalage, and was unlikely to tolerate an unqualified hereditary absolutism at Zaria. Moreover, political relations with the Yoruba and Ibo of Southern Nigeria were becoming increasingly important.

To guess the future of this system would be hazardous in the extreme. Perhaps the most important single element in its im-mediate development remains the succession. Until the death of Mallam Ja'afaru it must remain quite uncertain whether the tri-dynastic system will continue as the dominant political system of the emirate, or whether a hereditary monarchy with a single dynasty will be fully established. If the provincial elections of 1950 are any indication, it seems unlikely that the Emirs of Zaria will lose much power in consequence of recent democratic reforms. The resumption of relations with Sokoto which has already taken place suggests that after the Northern Region has resumed full control of its destiny, restoration of the Fulani empire and Zaria's vassalage are both likely. Any significant penetration of these Muhammadan emirates by Southern politicians, whether Ibo or Yoruba, is clearly out of the question for many years to come; and it is doubtful whether radical movements can continue long in the North, once the British have withdrawn.

That power which the Fulani emirs had informally appropriated from the British under the system of Indirect Rule, is now being formally transferred to them through newer and increasingly liberal constitutions, which ironically permit the revival of those political forms which belong to the heyday of empire. The vitality of the Fulani political system has been amply proved by its persistence over the fifty years of British rule; and so has its flexibility and adaptability. Instead of the unstable, unqualified absolutism of Yero and Kwassau, in 1950 there was an effective limited absolutism which showed signs of considerable stability, and in which power exercised by officials over the population corresponded with their positions within the hierarchy of power and office at every level. It is unlikely that this quality of the régime will change significantly in the near future without considerable pressure, but it is conceivable that it may change substantially over long periods of time.

8

GOVERNMENT AND STRUCTURAL CHANGE

I. INTRODUCTION

IN the preceding chapters we have given successive accounts of the systems of government in Abuja, in Fulani Zazzau of 1865, and in the emirate of Zaria in 1950. The history of Zaria from 1804 to 1950 has also been related. These data distinguish three clearly differentiated systems of government as stages in a continuous process of change and development. In this chapter we shall try to see whether these processes of change exhibit any regularities of a structural kind. To find such a structural order we must try to reduce all the phases and forms of change in the government of Zazzau to a single framework of recurrent relations. The sort of order we shall be seeking must hold for minute and specific sequences of change, as well as for the general, inclusive process. If these processes of governmental change do have a common structure, then this will apply at all levels and spans of the total sequence.

These three systems are indeed a very small number from which to work out a generalized framework for the analysis of governmental change; yet there are certain factors in our favour. Firstly, we have already analysed all three forms of government in terms of a single conceptual system, and consequently do not have to cope with ambiguities or differences in definitions, categories, or concepts. Secondly, it is likely that the analysis of changes within a single continuous process, the details and stages of which are adequately documented, may well avoid the difficulties which beset comparative studies of change in unrelated or dissimilar systems. Thirdly, we shall start with a theory of government which has already proved helpful, and the utility of which we can test further by applying it to the analysis of change. Fourthly, and perhaps most important, our task is greatly simplified by certain uniformities among the governments and societies of Habe, Fulani, and Anglo-Fulani Zazzau.

These uniformities are all structural, and they define the context of these governmental systems. During all stages of the developments under study, relations between the agents of government and the rest of the society have been strictly authoritarian. The ideology of these systems of government also remained unchanged, since the Muslim political theory, law, and religion which furnished these kingdoms with guides, principles, and models were profoundly conservative.

In all three successive stages of Zaria society, moreover, the status structure remained unchanged. There was an important reversal of status relations between the Fulani and the Habe after 1804, it is true; but this neither altered the character of the status system nor modified the status span. The system of stratification remained formally as before, despite the changed positions of the Habe and Fulani within it.

The arrival of the British in Zaria after 1900 did introduce a new ethnic group and a new status element; but the British were not incorporated into Zaria society and remained outside the Hausa-Fulani status system. Like the Ibo and Yoruba who followed them northwards, the British became an important element in the new political and economic context of Zaria. Differences between the Hausa-Fulani of Zaria on the one hand, and the British, Ibo or Yoruba immigrants on the other, are expressed as well by separation of residence, legal administration, language and religion, as by dress, etiquette, deferential behaviour, and differences in the status systems of these ethnic groups themselves.

The profound differences in the governments of Habe, Fulani, and Anglo-Fulani Zaria already described have therefore developed independently of any major changes either in the status system of the society itself or in the character of the relation between rulers and ruled. Thus theories or analyses of governmental change do not always presuppose or entail corresponding theories or analyses of other social changes. A society may remain unchanged, and the relations between government and the rest of the society may be also unchanged; but the system of government may none the less change significantly. We cannot therefore agree with such writers as Marx who hold that governmental change is always a function of other social and economic changes. Government and society are quite distinct systems, although they are interrelated; and we should gain very little indeed by undertaking to analyse the governmental changes of Zazzau within the wider framework of social change. Clearly, the isolation of governmental change for analysis, independent of wider social change, presents us with a developmental sequence of the simplest kind open to study; and this relative simplicity is a major advantage in analyzing the history of Zazzau.

In the limits of their political systems also, the Habe and subsequent Fulani governments of Zazzau exhibit uniformity. All three governments had external suzerains. The overlords of Habe Zazzau were the rulers of Bornu; Fulani Zazzau was a unit in the empire of Sokoto. More recently Zaria has been governed under British supervision. In all these cases the relations of vassalage and supervision were external ones, marking the limits of the political unit of Zaria. However, a contrast in the vassalage of Habe and Fulani Zazzau reflects the differences in the internal organization of the two governments. The monodynastic Habe system, with its constitutional checks on royal power, offered little room or cause for intervention by the suzerain: but the multidynastic Fulani system with its correlated rotation of power did generate an intense rivalry which required vigilant supervision by the overlords. Thus the difference in the activities of the suzerains of Habe and Fulani Zazzau reflects differences in the governmental systems of these two states. As such, these differences are functional rather than formal, and in both cases the vassal state represents a unit for separate analysis. This conclusion also applies to Fulani Zaria under British supervision. We have seen that the effectiveness of British supervision declined as the internal solidarity of the native government increased.

Relations between suzerain and vassal are external political relations, the qualities of which vary with the political conditions of these two units. Vassalage marks the limits of the political units thereby associated. The three states of Zazzau now under study were therefore units of the same kind, and had limits of similar form.

2. DIACHRONIC THEORY AND METHOD

To differentiate units within a system of government, the analytically critical distinctions have been found in those between political and administrative relations and actions. By means of these distinctions, any system of government can be formally analysed into political and administrative sub-systems, each of which will contain units having similar or different roles and statuses. When we speak of the form of a system of government, we therefore refer to the arrangement and interrelations of its political and administrative structures. Changes in governmental form thus involve changes in the structure and relation of these political and administrative sub-systems.

As a totality, any government also has certain primary functions, for example legal administration, preservation of public order, defence, and the collection of revenue. Each of these governmental functions involves a certain set of activities. These activities are normally distributed among different units within the system. This body of activities forms an important part of the content or substance of the governmental system; but it is never the whole of this content, and its distribution is an aspect of the system's form. The substantive aspect of any unit of a governmental system consists in its governmental activities and functions; but the formal aspect of such a unit consists in its relations to other units of the political and administrative sub-systems of the government. In short, the structural continuity of the governmental system is equivalent to the continuity of these relations between its various parts.

The stability of these structural relations is thus a precondition of the maintenance of the system. But these relations are affected by such important secondary functions as the recruitment, reward, promotion, control, training and supervision of personnel, the organization of which is directly related to the prevailing allocations of power and authority within the system. Accordingly, these internal relations form a constant focus of political attention. Unless the secondary functions just mentioned are carefully distributed and co-ordinated, the unity and continuity of the system must remain problematic; if their distribution changes, the form of the system changes correspondingly; and the diversity of possible ways in which these functions can be organized means that governmental systems are correspondingly diverse and are correspondingly liable to change under the pressures they generate within themselves, even without any alteration in the span of governmental functions, or in the relation between government and the rest of the society.

In our analysis we must therefore distinguish the formal and substantive aspects of governmental change; and since the redistribution of functions or powers can only be effected by the exercise of political power, we must recognize that the basis of governmental organization or change is the system or power relations. Thus changes in the form of the system will be mediated through political action, and will normally follow changes in the modes or distribution of political power within it.

(a) A Common Frame of Reference

Our first task is to list those features of the Habe constitution which have persisted from 1804 to 1950 despite other change. In listing these features it is useful to set them in what will be shown to be the order of their logical priority. In this order, the persistent features are as follows:

(1) Status differentiation.
(2) Offices differentiated as perpetual statuses.
(3) Differentiation of office by status conditions of eligibility.
(4) Kingship as the most senior of such offices.
(5) Rank organization of offices.
(6) Role differentiation of offices.
(7) Organization of offices with similar status qualifications in exclusive promotional series.

However they are phrased, these conceptions would seem to cover the principal features of the Habe constitution which persisted throughout the government of Fulani Zaria. But these categories and their interrelations are purely formal. Thus, kingship is derivable from the categories which precede it as the most senior of an hierarchic series of differentiated offices. The persistence of these formal categories does not exclude changes of their content within the systems under study. Thus status differentiation in nineteenth-century Zaria included a reversal of previous Habe-Fulani status relations which was fundamental to the entire process of governmental change. Likewise, the statement that offices in all these systems were differentiated by role is purely formal. It does not indicate that the old Habe distinctions between military and civil roles were largely abandoned by the Fulani, who substituted as role differentials the administration of particular fiefs, and assimilated the formerly distinct military and civil divisions of officials within a common code of administrative duties. Neither does it indicate that military organization lapsed under the British while new forms of role differentiation developed. Such variations of content are all consistent with the persistence of the general forms distinguished above; and if, remaining at our present level of generality, we now list those features of the old Habe constitution which underwent change in this century and the last, and rank them in an order of precedence, we get the following result:

(1) Changes in the content of the system of status differentiation.

(2) Changes in the system of offices.

(3) Changes in the status qualifications governing eligibility for various offices.

(4) Changes in the content of kingship and in its relation to subordinate offices.

(5) Changes in the rank organization of offices.

(6) Changes in the role differentiation of offices.

(7) Changes in the promotional organization of offices.

This list, of course, simply repeats the earlier list of persistent categories, as it logically must; but the sum of the substantive redefinitions to which these formal concepts were subject amounted to a major structural reorganization of the governmental system, first under the Fulani and later under the British. In other words, the seven formal categories constitute the irreducible minimum definition of the general type of government to which the systems of Abuja, Fulani Zazzau, and Anglo-Fulani Zazzau all belong, and the limits within which they differ.

(b) *Logical Priority and Change*

We set out to search for a structure in the processes by which governmental change has developed at Zaria. By the structure of a process, we mean the way in which the parts or sequences of that process are arranged, that is, the order which regulates the process itself. Since we are seeking a structure which will hold for the smallest as well as the most inclusive sequence of change, the relations between the elements which constitute this structure must be logically necessary ones. Only if these relations are governed by logical necessities can the conditions just mentioned occur. Moreover, the processes under study are not purely repetitive. Our analysis deals directly with change. Thus the only possible structure of the kind we seek is an order the elements of which are arranged in a fixed line of succession. The only possible basis for such a fixed succession is logical necessity, and the only basis for such logically necessary succession among the categories themselves is that of formal priority. By this I mean the condition in which successive concepts of a series cannot be formulated without assuming those which precede them. A series of categories or concepts governed by such relations is arranged in an *order of logical priority.*

Priority may be empirical or logical. As applied to change, empirical priority denotes an order of occurrence of events, and refers directly to actual entities. Logical priority on the other hand connotes an order of succession among concepts or categories. Thus to apply a system of categories arranged in an order of logical priority to an empirical sequence, the latter must be conceptualized in terms of its relevant formal categories, and these must then be examined for necessary relations.

By virtue of its logical structure, the revision and redefinition of a system of categories arranged in an order of logical priority can only proceed by a sequence which repeats the order of logical relations holding among the categories themselves. Moreover, the revision of any single category in such a system presupposes certain changes in the content of the categories which precede it. In consequence, the order in which categories change will be identical with that in which the system as a whole undergoes revision. Thus the order of logical priority is the order by which change of necessity proceeds at all levels of the system. This follows from the fact that in such a system change always involves some form of conceptual revision and redefinition; and since subsequent concepts of the logically successive series assume those which precede them, their revision or reformulation cannot occur independently of the concepts which they assume. Thus the order of logical priority among the formal categories of a given system will be the structure by which the change of that system proceeds.

(c) The Logical Structure of the Common Forms

We have already defined the common elements of the governments under study by means of seven concepts, arranged in an order of precedence, which is also their order of logical priority. To demonstrate the relation of logical priority among these categories is simple. We need only consider whether any category in the series can be formulated without assuming those which precede it. Thus office presupposes status differentiation, since office is only one type of differentiated status. Official hierarchies in turn presuppose office, but kingship does not presuppose an official hierarchy. These official hierarchies also presuppose the status differentiation of offices and involve some system of rank-orders, while promotional arrangements also presuppose official rank-orders and their differentiation by status and role qualifications. Each of these notions is literally inconceivable without assuming those concepts ranked before them in the series as logically prior. Moreover, since the revision of such a series proceeds through the redefinition of its component categories, and since this redefinition is itself governed by the fixed order of logical relations holding between these categories, it follows that the orders of changed and persistent forms in both transformations of the government of Zazzau will be identical, as are the categories themselves, and that both will have an identical order of arrangement.

An important condition of any conceptual system informed by logical priority is that successive concepts decrease in the generality of their reference and in their implications for the system as a whole. This decreasing generality of dependent concepts is matched by their increasing complexity and specificity; and in part this increase is due to the manifold relations which hold between subsequent concepts and all those which precede them. To illustrate the point, we may contrast the extreme specificity and complexity of the notion of an official promotional series with the extreme generality of the notion of differentiated status. Official promotional series presuppose concepts of office and of rank-orders; but the idea of differentiated status neither presupposes nor entails any other concept as a precondition. There are many societies which operate systems of differentiated status without having the concept of office. In short, the subsequent concepts in a logically successive series assume but are not directly entailed by those which precede them. The process by which subsequent concepts of such a series are developed from antecedent ones is eductive and 'evolutionary' rather than deductive or deterministic. These latter categories give explicit expression to possibilities latent in those which precede them. Conversely these earlier categories are implicit in those which follow after; but consistency rather than necessity governs the development of the subsequent concepts; and inconsistency indicates either that a self-defeating process of change is under way, or that the system includes formally incompatible elements and is accordingly unstable.

From this it also follows that the development of later concepts is progressively circumscribed as we move from the beginning of the series to its end. For this reason, changes in subsequent concepts are more easily effected than changes in those which precede them. Changes in subsequent categories have progressively less consequence for the system as a whole than do changes in their antecedents. Thus the initial categories of any series arranged in an order of logical priority are the most basic to the structure of the system concerned, as well as the most generalized. Subsequent concepts become progressively more specific and less fundamental. Changes in the basic initial categories of such a system will thus evoke or entail changes throughout the system as a whole, and they are for that reason the slowest and most difficult to develop, although for this reason also they are likely to be among the foremost targets of programmes for change.

We now have a tool with which to tackle the analysis of governmental changes at Zaria. If our system of categories is truly governed by logical priority and does correctly define the form common to all three governmental systems, then the processes and stages by which change occurred should correspond exactly with the order of logical succession holding among the categories which define these governmental systems. Conversely, where attempts at change failed and were not institutionalized, they should either be formally incompatible with the categories which constitute the system or with the order of priority which governs and regulates change. We shall quite soon test these propositions; but we must first determine the nature of the relation between changes of content and changes of form.

(d) Simultaneous and Successive Change

The preceding discussion implies that all change in the form of a governmental system will develop in a single order; since this order is governed by principles of logical priority which define the relations of constitutive forms. Formal change is therefore always sequential, and the order of such change is fixed and irreversible, being logically necessary. However, in addition to changes of form we have to deal with changes of content. Besides necessarily successive change, we have to analyse simultaneous developments. To distinguish these patterns of change and to understand their parts in the total process, we must examine the complex of changes which are said to occur in functional relations.

In current usage to say that a functional relation exists between two or more elements or processes in a condition of change may mean one of several things. Firstly, it may denote an explicitly functional relation between the units or events, such that their order of change is reversible, symmetrical, and always simultaneous. Secondly, it may denote an implicitly functional relation, marked by simultaneous changes of two or more units concerned due to common 'causal' processes. Thirdly, it may mean that there is a constant asymmetrical relation between the items, as shown by actual events or logical necessity, such that changes in one are always followed by changes in the other.

Asymmetrical relations with a logical basis will always be governed by logical priority, and will thus involve changes of form. Recurrent sequences of asymmetrical character show that the units which undergo such change are categories related to one another by logical priority. Thus all 'functional' changes which develop in irreversible orders are governed by logical priorities and involve sequences of formal change.

Simultaneous changes which arise as effects of other antecedent developments may or may not be governed by asymmetrical relations. If such changes are in fact an empirically asymmetrical series, then their basis will also be a set of categories arranged in an order of logical priority. If such series are reversible and asymmetrical then the complex of units or events to which they refer will be linked by explicitly functional relations and will change simultaneously.

In short, the application of concepts of logical succession to the complex of 'functional' changes enables us to distinguish asymmetrical and symmetrical series, and to define the first class as changes of form. The second type of change will therefore be changes of content or substance, in the senses defined above. We shall return to this distinction later; but before attempting to analyse the earlier governmental transformation at Zaria, it is worth pointing out that the application of the concept of logical priority to the total complex of changes allows us to distinguish and isolate all changes of structure in the system under study for analysis by reference to the formal categories which serve to define the system.

The objects of such an analysis are threefold: firstly, it is essential to determine whether all changes in the form of the system did actually develop in the order corresponding with the logical relations among the categories which define their constitutive forms; secondly, we must seek to determine the conditions which governed all unsuccessful attempts at change, meaning thereby changes which, although initiated, failed to persist as elements of the system, and were not institutionalized; thirdly, we must seek to determine the conditions by which substantive change develops, and their relations to changes of form. In the following section I shall make a fairly detailed analysis of the first governmental transformation, and will deal with these points systematically. To avoid repetition, the second transformation will then be discussed more summarily.

3. THE FIRST TRANSFORMATION, 1804–1900

(a) Logic and Historical Change

The principal changes in the constitution of Zaria which developed during the last century can be summarized in haphazard order as follows: dynastic multiplication and coexistence; changes in the pattern of succession; changes in the status qualifications for office, and in official roles; changes in the political and administrative implications and capacities of office, most notably of course in the kingship; changes in the rank-organization of offices; assimilation of functions among traditionally diverse types of office; insulation of the official structure from the segmentary political competition of the dynasties; changes in the modes of paying officials; the development of a new cadre of occupational tax-collectors of Habe status; the appropriation of despotic authority by the king under the supervision of Sokoto. The inclusiveness of this list can be checked by reference to Chapters 4 and 5.

As our account of the processes by which the earlier Habe constitution was changed under the Fulani has already shown, the emergence of the four competing dynasties was the most important single factor governing the entire process of constitutional change. Yet this development in its formal aspect was only a redefinition of royalty, which is merely one in a system of differentiated statuses. However, the revision of this category involved further redefinitions of hereditary rights in the succession and of eligibility for the throne.

The progressive increase in the allocation of important office to noble Fulani, and the corresponding exclusion of Habe from such positions together redefined the status of Habe and Fulani in relation to the government of Zaria. This revision involved further redefinitions of the status qualifications governing eligibility for offices of various types. The creation of an order of occupational tax-collectors staffed by Habe in the middle of the last century marked the end of these status redefinitions.

Our preceding discussion showed that the early and more fundamental categories of an order arranged in logical priority are less easily changed than others, since their revision has profound implications for the system as a whole. It took the Fulani of Zaria nearly eighty years to work out a new definition of royalty, and in this process, which was marked by severe tension throughout, they developed three dynasties and rejected a fourth. At each critical stage in this redefinition of royalty and in the development of this multidynastic system, other elements of the government were also changed; and of these dependent changes, the progressive revision of Habe-Fulani status relations was only one among many. Indeed, the progressive appropriation of important office by the Fulani was regulated by the development of the multidynastic system, which emerged from the redefinition of royalty. As we have seen, the new ruler was obliged to recruit his officials among loyal supporters from his own dynasty and from other important Fulani lineages. In consequence, Habe chances of high office were reduced progressively.

Less important changes aroused less resistance and took far less

time to develop. Thus Musa redefined the status of official mallams to include the administration of fiefs, but not captaincy in
war; and Yamusa redefined that of the royal women to exclude
them from the system of office. Neither of these changes evoked
resistance, and both were effected by simple exercise of the ruler's
power.

Other changes, such as the assimilation of functions traditionally
allocated to different offices, or the reorganization of official rank-
orders in accordance with the new system of status differentiation
and qualifications for office, developed by stages which followed
developments redefining the conditions of royalty and ethnic status.
The degrees of change evident in dependent categories at any time
must be consistent with the stage thus far reached in the revision
of the categories on which they depend.

The reorganization of official rank-orders thus proceeded
primarily through the king's appointment of his own kinsmen to
offices previously held by persons of non-royal status, whether
freemen, eunuchs, or slaves. This process continued throughout
the century, varying in its details and intensity with the political
positions of differing rulers. In consequence the Fulani neither
developed a clear promotional arrangement of offices nor maintained the old Habe promotional systems. Other changes in the
distribution of office which resulted from this progressive increase
in the number of royal officials included the appointment of free
clients to new offices or to offices formerly held by eunuchs, by
women of the royal house, or even by slaves. It may seem that the
processes by which the Fulani transformed the structure of the
Habe official system included many instances of simultaneous
changes linked by explicitly functional relations. A more detailed
examination will show that this is not the case. For example, the
revision of Habe rank-orders presupposed revision of the system
of status differentiation and of the status qualifications for offices
of various types. The simultaneity of these developments is only
apparent. At any particular moment those formal changes which
had already occurred presupposed others without which they could
not develop. Thus changes in the official system just mentioned
were all dependent on the revision of royalty status, and on changes
in the old relations between the kingship and other elements in the
governmental system. For instance, Yamusa's accession to the
throne preceded the transfer of the Madaki's office from the client

to the royal ranks. It expressed a redefinition of the status of royalty, a redefinition of kingship and eligibility for that office, and especially of the relation between the throne and other governmental units, official or dynastic.

Even where formal changes are expressed simultaneously, a careful analysis of their development shows that the order of logical succession among the categories concerned underlies such apparent simultaneity. Thus the tool appropriate for this analysis is the concept of logical priority. To illustrate this briefly, we may consider the appointment of slave-generals to administer fiefs. Such appointments apparently involved simultaneous changes in the status qualifications for fief-holding office, the addition of a new rank-order, and some revision of the previous official structure as a whole. In fact, these slave-appointments presupposed redefined relations between the king, his officials, and other units of government. The distribution of office among the politically effective status-groups had already been revised, together with the official rank-orders, and the distribution of official functions. This sequence eventually gave rise to the appointment of slave fief-holders before it concluded with the king's deposition and the restoration of the previous system. Historically, the first appointments of slave-generals were made by Abdullahi in 1876–80, and preceded by some years their investiture as fief-holders; but this investiture itself only expressed the degree to which relations between the ruler and his officials had changed since Abdullahi's reign. In short, the appearance of simultaneous formal changes is quite illusory. Changes of form develop successively and in a constant order.

Of the ten or twelve modes of change listed haphazardly at the start of this section, the multiplication of dynasties and the changed succession patterns are clearly determinant; yet both these changes themselves presuppose redefinitions of royalty, of the kingship and of its relation to the rest of the system, of the status conditions governing eligibility for the throne and for offices of various types, and of the rank-organization of offices. In turn, as we know, the emergence of several dynasties and changes in succession patterns initiated further revisions of the rank-orders and status conditions of office, of their relation to the throne, and of official roles. The revisions of slave offices just discussed are simply one instance of these secondary changes. The important point to grasp is that the order in which the formal categories of the Habe constitution changed under the Fulani of Zaria corresponds exactly with that of the logical succession in which these categories are arranged. Thus the internal order of the process by which the form of the system changed historically is the same as the order of logical priority among its categorical forms.

(b) The Problem of Substantive Change

To infer changes of content from a structural analysis of changing forms, we need an adequate structural analysis of governmental systems. Given this, we can try to combine the preceding theory of structural change with the analysis of government as a synchronic system to determine probable changes of content corresponding to known changes of form.

The passage from a synchronic to a diachronic analysis of government involves one especially important transposition, the logical basis of which is explained below. By this transposition, the formal categories of the synchronic system become the substantive categories of the diachronic process and of diachronic analysis. Thus, in our analysis of government as a synchronic system, the primary formal categories are the political and administrative systems, while the substantive categories consist of governmental activities and tasks. But in the analysis of governmental change at Zaria, these political and administrative structures form the content of the system which undergoes change, and the structure of the diachronic process is the fixed order of logically necessary relations which regulates the change of constitutive forms.

We have already seen that the content of a system changes by relations which are simultaneous, reciprocal, and transitive, whereas changes of form do not. In the processes of formal change a fixed and necessary order is fundamental; but simultaneity and explicitly functional relations are equally fundamental to the development of substantive change. It is partly for this reason that the formal categories of synchronic systems become the substantive categories of diachronic processes. Since the content of any synchronic system is organized functionally, explicit functional relations will govern the substantive change which occurs in that system. By comparing the substantive aspects of the Habe and Fulani constitutions and by examining the way in which these contrasts developed, we shall find that they did so by means of changes which occurred in explicitly functional relations. These changes simultaneously redefined the content of the political and administrative sub-systems of the government, the functions of office, the modes of official reward, and the conditions of official appointment, tenure, and promotion. Moreover, at any point in the total span of change the substantive organization of the Fulani government differed from that of the Habe in a degree which corresponds exactly with the revision of Habe constitutional forms already achieved.

To lay bare the specific relational structure of these substantive changes, we must therefore re-examine the processes by which the categorical forms of the Habe constitution were revised and re-defined. We must accordingly begin with the redefinitions of royalty and ethnic status, the development of the new dynastic system, the dual development of multidynastic competition for the throne and of new succession rules, and the increasing dynastic appropriations of office.

All the substantive changes which developed in the constitution of Zaria under the Fulani involved redefinitions and redistributions of power and authority within the governmental system. Thus official functions were assimilated, official roles were revised, a new cadre of occupational tax-collectors was established, the council procedure of Habe Zazzau was abandoned, and the Habe political system based on certain rank-orders was replaced by a new pattern of dynastic competition which flourished outside the administration. The king appropriated despotic authority, but the succession went to his rivals, the modes of official remuneration and the functions of office were also changed, and Habe promotional arrangements lapsed entirely.

According to our general theory of government, any change in the specific administrative and political relations of office is equivalent to a change in the structure of the governmental system. Such structural change redefines the boundaries, constitution, and interrelations of the political and administrative sectors of government. They are accordingly changes in the substance of the system.

It is clear also that the switch from the Habe political system of contraposed official orders to the Fulani system of discrete political and official sectors involved simultaneous changes of a symmetrical character. Thus, as dynastic competition developed under the

Fulani, dynastic rivals and their supporters were excluded from office. The relation between these two developments was symmetrical and transitive. Similarly, as the kingship increased its despotic power, so did the officials lose their influence on policy formation; and these developments, like the other substantive changes, were also simultaneous and reciprocal. The end result of the processes of political competition and formal change under the Fulani was a government which lacked the Habe distinctions between administrative and political office, or those between military and civil administration, between officials differentiated systematically by reference to rank, by modes of remuneration, status conditions, and promotional careers. All the changes just listed were changes of substance which developed simultaneously within limits set by the changes which had already occurred in the form of the system. For this reason the Fulani never developed a fixed promotional system, since it was incompatible with the continuing development of their political system, as well as with its form.

The necessary consistency of substantive and formal changes in a system will hardly cause wonder. In so far as a system is indeed an integrated unit composed of interdependent parts, the consistency of these elements is the basic condition of its operation and continuity. Incompatibilities of function and form denote corresponding instabilities in the system which further changes must either reduce, replace, or intensify. The mere continuity of a system as a whole throughout a process of extensive change is therefore evidence of the congruence and synchronization of its formal and substantive development. In effect, such systems are instances of moving equilibria.

(c) *The Analysis of Exceptional Cases*

Thus far we have been discussing the main stream of change and development at Zaria, and we have confined our attention to those changes which entered into the final form of the governmental system, that is, to changes which became institutional. However, not all changes which arose in Zaria had such successful careers. Many changes were initiated which failed to persist. Many other developments seem to have become arrested in mid-stream, or at all events to have left little mark on the main trend of change, although persisting anomalously within the total fabric. In a later section we shall consider those changes which failed to win acceptance. In this one I shall discuss those changes which persisted but were somewhat exceptional.

There are four exceptional cases of this second kind in the history of Fulani Zaria. Under Musa, official mallams were placed in charge of fiefs, and some of these mallams, such as the Limam, were given considerable administrative powers. Yamusa reduced the fiefs controlled by these official mallams, but otherwise upheld Musa's reform. Throughout the rest of the nineteenth century the position of these official mallams remained unchanged. This sequence therefore began with a partial assimilation of mallam to other offices of the government, and stopped with a partial reversal of this initial change. Neither the initial nor subsequent change promoted any further changes in the mallams' offices. Mallamships remained distinct from other fief-holding offices, since only mallams were eligible for them, and they did not involve captaincy in war. In short, Musa's reforms redefined official mallamships to include the administration of fiefs only, and Yamusa's changes in no way altered this.

Another series of contrary changes involved the order of household officials. Musa began by transforming the old Habe household order quite radically. Several offices were allowed to lapse. Others were removed from the royal household and were placed in charge of fiefs, being assimilated to the formerly distinct public orders in their territorial and military administrative roles. Musa also revised the council organization of Zaria in ways which abolished the political influence of the household order. In consequence there was at first no order of household officials under the Fulani. None the less, by the end of the century we find a new household order, by far the greater portion of which were military captains charged with protection of the king and control of his own forces. These new household offices lacked fiefs and had no role in the royal council such as their Habe counterparts formerly enjoyed. In short, developments affecting the household order were in certain respects quite contrary to one another. None the less, these developments occurred in an order which corresponds with the main sequence of formal change.

Musa sought to replace the Habe council by another mainly composed of mallams, in order to give more effect to the Islamic reforms he desired. However, conditions in Zaria changed rapidly after Musa's death, and, in the context of dynastic rivalry and competition for the throne, subsequent rulers increasingly felt the need for a body of household officials bound to them by special ties and charged with their protection. The new order of household officials grew up gradually as a result of the basic changes in political structure which arose with the multidynastic system. But loyalty to the rulers being prerequisite for this new order, and the rulers being drawn from different dynasties, these officials were accordingly attached to the throne rather than to the kings as individuals, and many retained office under successive sovereigns who were political rivals. Lacking fiefs, they were fully dependent on the king for support and reward. In short, both the abolition of the old Habe order of household officials and the emergence of the new Fulani order were consistent with the changing political conditions in which they occurred.

The quasi-hereditary order of fief-holding clients provides yet another case of unusual development. Some of these officials lived in their fiefs. All had hereditary claims on particular offices. In some respects they resembled vassals more closely than they did other fief-holders; but they also shared many conditions with other fief-holders. Thus they had no independent legal jurisdiction, nor could they lead military expeditions without the king's commission. Moreover, these offices were not hereditary within a lineage as were vassalships. No lineage had hereditary rights to any of these offices, but only a claim. Normally at least two lineages held equal claims to each such office. Often they were appointed alternately. The insignia of fully hereditary chieftainship, such as kettledrums (*tambari*), were never allotted to these officers. As we have seen, they represent special adjustments to the problems of territorial administration which arose after the expansion of the Fulani kingdom into areas peopled by large tribes with quite different institutions. The tendency of these hereditary fief-holding offices towards independent vassalship was arrested by the need for maintaining the state as an integral unit. Under prevailing conditions of dynastic competition, their recognition as vassals would have promoted fragmentation of Zaria. None the less, the special problems of territorial administration which faced Fulani Zazzau required corresponding adjustments, and these offices were the result.

The creation of the Habe occupational order, already mentioned, is the last anomaly. The institution of this order initiated no further

political change, but it did express the new status relations existing between Fulani and Habe. The occupational order was purely
bureaucratic, and its creation by the king in a single exercise of his
power expressed as well his own changed relation to the state as
that of the Habe. We have already shown how this development
was governed by changes in the definition of royalty and in the
political organization of the state.

The four cases of exceptional character just discussed arose in
response to the special patterns of political development at Zaria,
and they can only be understood by reference to those changes
which had already occurred. Like other formal developments, they
were governed by logical priorities and by the need for consistency
with more basic parts of the system.

4. THREE LAWS OF STRUCTURAL CHANGE

(a) The Law of Differential Resistance

One measure of the relative ease with which changes occur is the
duration of the processes of change. Another is the type and intensity of the action focused on such change. We can combine
these measures in the concept of *resistance*. Changes of different
kinds encounter differing degrees of resistance, and develop
through processes of different type and duration. Thus mallams
and slave-generals were put in charge of fiefs, women were removed from the territorial administration, and a new order of
occupational tax-collectors was instituted by single unilateral
actions of the ruler. On the other hand, the redefinitions of royalty
and of Habe-Fulani status relations took several generations to
become explicit, and so did the constitutional revision which
resulted in separation of the multidynastic political system from
the official structure. The reconstitution of the free household
order was governed by these latter developments and belonged to
this general process. Because of these developments the quasi-
hereditary clients never achieved vassal status, but continued as a
specialized group within the order of free fief-holding officials.

We can summarize the conditions which governed the variable
developments of these and other governmental changes at Zaria in
general terms as a law of differential resistance which regulates
structural change.

(i) *Resistance to changes in the form of a system varies directly with their significance for the persistence of the system in its current form.*

One corollary is important. *Specifically administrative changes in a system of government evoke less resistance than do specifically political changes.* We can rephrase this corollary as follows: *changes initiated on the basis of authority and focused on its reallocation evoke less resistance than changes initiated on the basis of power and focused on its redistribution.* Thus changes in the administrative system are more simply effected than changes in the political system, since the latter has greater significance for the persistence of the government as a unit of a particular form.

Applied to the cases we have just been discussing, this means that the allocation of territorial fiefs to mallams or slave-generals, and the creation of new orders of household officials or occupational tax-collectors were all instances of changes in the administrative system effected by exercise of the king's authority. In contrast, the redefinition of royalty and kingship and the reconstitution of the government on new political bases were all changes of a political character, marked by processes of long duration and intense action among many persons. We already know that these political developments often brought the Fulani of Zaria to the brink of civil war.

In such a case as that of the quasi-hereditary fief-holders, the political structure of Fulani Zazzau ruled out their transformation into vassals, but required their presence as a special group of territorial administrators. No Fulani ruler of Zaria could accord these officials the status of independent vassals without the consensus of rival dynasties having an equal hereditary claim on the kingdom, nor could such action be contemplated without the consent of the Sultan of Sokoto and the support of the other official orders of Zaria. The grant or cancellation of vassal status was a specifically political act involving a transfer of power as well as a change in the system of territorial administration; and the ruler, although temporarily invested with despotic powers, lacked the independence necessary to legitimize such change. The kingdom belonged to other dynasties as well as the ruler's; and he would almost certainly be succeeded by a rival. Vassalship was not in the ruler's power either to confer or to abrogate; and shortly after Sidi Abdulkardiri did abolish the vassalship of Durum, he was duly deposed.

It is also instructive to apply the law of differential resistance to the cycle of events which issued in the creation of slave fief-holders. As related above, this cycle began when the rulers of Sokoto attempted to change the political system of Fulani Zaria by appointing the ruler's dynastic rivals, on his accession, to certain key offices. By these appointments, Sokoto deliberately sought to redefine the status of kingship and its relation to the rest of the governmental system. Only the Sultan by virtue of his position could attempt to initiate so important a change and in such abruptly unilateral fashion. But initiation is not accomplishment, and authority can neither initiate nor control political change. The instability of the Fulani government was never so marked as during this experiment; and the creation of slave fief-holders was simply the ruler's last attempt to reassert control. In the end Sokoto recognized the failure of its attempt to effect this change in the political system of Zaria, deposed the king, and restored the previous system as nearly as it could.

All units in a system of government cannot occupy identical roles or positions. Some will be concerned with policy more than others. In any administrative system, some hierarchical structure is also unavoidable, and if this hierarchy is complete, then the highest office will inevitably combine administrative and political functions. In such governmental systems the critical position of these supreme offices makes them the outstanding target of programmes aimed at change, and the most powerful agencies through which structural change actually develops. They provide the system with its most powerful and sensitive fulcra. However, since the condition of the highest office has profound implications for the system as a whole, it evokes the most continuous, intensive, and varied political action within it.

The stability of an administration and its effectiveness depend on the maintenance of those political conditions in which its authority was defined and allocated. Changes in political structure accordingly have wider implications for changes in the government as a whole than do purely administrative developments. In consequence, changes in political organization evoke greater resistance and proceed less directly than do changes in the administrative system. The degree to which an overtly administrative change provokes resistance is the measure of its political significance, direct or otherwise.

In his administrative capacity as head of the state, the Fulani king could enact administrative change by simple fiat; but the political changes which redefined the conditions of royalty and kingship developed only through intense struggles in ways which none of the protagonists could control or foresee. As Musa's appointments to office show clearly, the course of future political developments was then quite unsuspected. Yamusa also had no idea that he would be succeeded by the founder of a third dynasty. Such data suggest that fundamental changes in a political system arise indirectly as the effects of political action within the system itself. We shall return to this point later, after reviewing those changes at Zaria which failed to persist and were not institutionalized.

(b) Diachronic Irrationality

During an initial analysis of the processes by which a system has changed, we do not need to pay much attention to those attempts at change which were unsuccessful, in the sense that the innovations or revisions aimed at were not institutionalized. Such failures are none the less quite important, and they require explanation by the same principles which govern other processes of structural change.

Viewed diachronically, these unsuccessful attempts at change seem somehow 'irrational'. Their irrationality, such as it is, consists in the failure to achieve their objectives. However, there are various forms and conditions of such irrationality, and failures alone do not exhaust the entire body of irrational developments. We can distinguish certain 'successful' changes or developments as formally irrational, in the sense that they repeat or multiply an established form without promoting further structural change. In Fulani Zaria the development of four dynasties is an instance of such formal irrationality, since two would have been quite sufficient for the operation of a multidynastic system of this type. Indeed, of these four dynasties, one held the kingship on only one occasion and another twice, while the two which remain provided Zaria with nine of the twelve kings who ruled it during the last century. The formal irrationality of this multidynastic system is therefore shown by the tendency towards simplicity in its operation.

Whereas only 'successful' developments provide examples of formal irrationality, all 'unsuccessful' attempts at change are substantively irrational, and owe their failure to this common condition. Developments are substantively irrational when the content of changes which they seek to promote is inconsistent with the structure of the system of which they are intended to be part, or when the mode of their development is incompatible with the order by which change actually proceeds. Thus attempts to effect changes of form by means of substantive changes are quite as irrational as are attempts to effect changes of substance incompatible with current forms. Yet since all instances of self-defeating attempts at change are substantively irrational, they require a careful analysis to determine the precise conditions which governed their failure. Such analyses also illuminate the structure of the process of change, and amplify our understanding of it.

(c) Substantive Irrationality in Fulani Zazzau

There were several substantively irrational attempts at change in Fulani Zazzau during the last century. Sidi's attempt to restructure the system of political relations by his unfortunate bargain with Hamada provides an early example, and this eventually led to Sidi's deposition after splitting his own dynasty. Essentially, this agreement sought to effect a political change by administrative means; but the political changes at which it aimed could neither be effected by such means, nor by agreements between any two principals of the political contest. The consensus of all persons having an equal status and claim was also required, and even Sidi's half-brother Abubakar repudiated the agreement, protesting to Sokoto until Sidi was deposed. In sum, the agreement between Sidi and Hamada was incompatible with current political conditions at Zaria; and it also sought to promote certain structural changes, namely, redefinitions of the kingship, by means of substantive change, namely, by redistributions of power and authority.

Sokoto's attempt to redefine the kingship by simultaneously appointing members of rival dynasties to important offices provides another case of failure to change the political system of Zazzau. The multidynastic system and the rotating monocratic administration, which had developed together, were mutually consistent. When Sokoto tried to replace this rotating monocracy by a system of joint administration, leaving the dynastic system unchanged, a series of disruptive developments ensued which ended in the reversal of this policy by Sokoto. The government of Zazzau having developed the structure it had, thereafter functioned in a particular manner. The basis of this structure being the political system, administrative change could neither transform it, nor could it take effect in so far as it was incompatible with political conditions. Like Sidi, Sokoto had tried to effect a formal revision by means of substantive change, and both attempts proved to be dismal failures.

Most of the substantively irrational developments in Fulani Zaria relate to the system of offices. Yamusa created the office of Wali to enforce an administrative code which could not actually be enforced without the agreement of dynastic rivals. Later Sidi revived the office of Waziri, which Musa, his father, had first established at Zaria. Like Musa, Sidi intended his Waziri to be his chief administrative subordinate; but the political conditions of Sidi's reign differed widely from those of Musa's, and the Waziriship under Sidi was just as ineffective as the Waliship instituted by Yamusa, and it lapsed at Zaria when Sidi was deposed. Under the conditions of multidynastic competition, neither could the ruler transfer his own reserve power to a subordinate official, nor could such officials supervise the administration without this overriding power. These two official innovations were therefore substantively irrational; but whereas the office of Waziri formally lapsed, the office of Wali simply became yet another *sarauta*, functionally identical with those it was intended to supervise.

In the last century, three Fulani kings of Zaria appointed persons to hold two offices simultaneously. Abdulkerim, the first Katsinawa ruler, gave his kinsman Jamo the offices of Sa'i and of Magajin Gari; Sambo, the second Katsinawa ruler, appointed his client Suleimanu to the offices of Sarkin Ruwa and of Galadima; Abdullahi on his reappointment as king of Zaria gave Sada the two judicial offices of Salenke and of Alkali simultaneously. Abdulkerim and Sambo were politically so weak that they sought by these means to strengthen themselves, and in Sambo's case the experiment was quite disastrous. Abdullahi on the other hand was interested in recovering the estate he had lost on his earlier deposition, and accordingly he vested the two judgeships in the hands of a loyal client. However, in all cases, the rulers who next succeeded immediately reversed these appointments and restored the system of exclusive office. In fact, such dual appointments were incompatible with the conception of office on which the government of Zaria was based. As we have seen, by definition office (*sarauta*) is a perpetual and exclusive status in a system of such statuses. The combination of offices is thus inconsistent with this structure, and for that reason no dual appointments were ever ratified by the successor of the ruler who made them.

Sidi's allocation of authority without office to his kinsmen Nuhu and Ali represent another type of development of this kind, since it was incompatible with the definition of office on which the government of Zaria was based. Such *ad hoc* commissions could find no place in a system of territorial and military administration through offices, and after Sidi's deposition his example was never repeated.

The last important focus of substantively irrational action in Fulani Zaria, and the one with the longest history, is the relation of vassalage to Sokoto. Successive kings of Zaria struggled to reduce Sokoto's authority, to win independence for Zaria, and to extinguish the content of vassalage while retaining the form. Yet the multidynastic system of which they were the heirs fostered external supervision and depended on Sokoto for its maintenance. In their struggle for internal autonomy the Fulani of Zaria were only courting their own disaster; but since their own dynastic organization made unity impossible, their efforts to win autonomy were happily doomed to failure. These movements were thus irrational in the sense that they presupposed certain changes in the local political system before they could become effective. They were also inconsistent with that system in its current form.

(d) The Law of Self-contradiction in Change

In every case the unsuccessful innovations we have just reviewed sought to establish new political and administrative relations and forms in advance of certain changes in the political system which their successful development presupposed. Even the struggle for internal autonomy was in essence an attempt to transform a political relation into an administrative one. All these unsuccessful attempts at change came to grief because the dynastic competition continued and could not be abolished unless the dynasties and the Fulani political system were also abolished. We can summarize the basic condition which governed all these unsuccessful developments as the law of self-contradiction in change:

(ii) *Resistance to changes in the content of a system varies according to their significance for the maintenance of the current structure.*

As a corollary we can say simply, *attempts to change the form of a system by changing its content are self-defeating.*

As has been shown, changes of substance develop through explicitly functional relations which express themselves in simultaneous and symmetrical patterns of development. Changes of structure occur in a fixed and necessary order of succession which is that of logical priority among the categories undergoing change. It is therefore not possible to produce formal change by means of substantive change. Moreover, the only sorts of substantive change which are likely to persist and become institutionalized are those which are consistent with the current political forms. We have already seen how structural change actually develops through progressive redefinition of the categories which give the system its form.

The attempts by Sidi and Sokoto to limit dynastic rivalry, and by Yamusa and Sidi to develop a supervisory subordinate office, however laudable their aim, were irrational in their method, since they preceded the structural changes which they presupposed. Despite their administrative form, all these unsuccessful innovations had direct political implications and premises. Their institutionalization presupposed major transformations of the total system of government. For this reason such changes could not be institutionalized solely by administrative action. The form of a system limits the range and development of its content.

(e) *The Law of Structural Drift*

The two preceding laws may well apply to other systems besides government which undergo change, although they have been developed in an analysis of governmental change only. The more general application of these laws seems probable since they deal with general relations of structure and function in social systems which undergo change. Since structure and function are the most general categories of social analysis, the most general laws of social dynamics will naturally define their relations in the condition of change. If we have an accurate idea of these general relations we can apply them to the study of changes in particular systems such as government, kinship, or economy.

The corollary of the first law distinguishes administrative and political change according to their significance and resistance. The corollary of the second law holds that the form of a system cannot be changed by attempts to alter its content. We have just examined several attempts of this sort, and found such action self-defeating. These cases provide a revealing contrast with the successfully instituted administrative changes discussed earlier, and also with the general processes of basic political change. They also differ sharply from the cases of exceptional character discussed above.

By applying the two laws already formulated to all these instances of change, the successful, the unsuccessful, and the partial or arrested developments, we emerge with the following conclusions:

(1) Purely administrative action is action focused on substantive changes within limits consistent with the political structure of the governmental system.

(2) Purely political action is action which redefines the formal categories of this system directly.

(3) Actions intended to redefine the formal categories of the system by administrative means are substantively irrational.

(4) Unilateral attempts to redefine the formal categories of a system by one of its members can only succeed if they reconstitute the basic categories by purely political means.

We can summarize these four propositions in the following law of structural drift.

(iii) *Given stability in its context, the structure of a governmental system changes as a function of the political action it generates internally.*

As a corollary we can say that *the rate and type of change in a governmental system corresponds to the type and intensity of the pressure which its operation focuses on the revision of the formal categories on which its structure is based.*

Even in revolutions, the pressures which generate structural change arise as by-products of conditions of the competition for positions to control policy. In consequence, the process of structural change is never fully controllable by any members of the political system undergoing such change. Planned programmes of change are by definition administrative, and thus cannot promote the structural changes which they sometimes seek. We have already discussed several instances of this kind which occurred at Zaria.

Unilateral political actions designed to reshape a constitution are also incapable of realizing their designated goals, since the

political system at which they are directed involves a distribution
of power among its members, and never remains under the control of one agent indefinitely. The concept of total political power
leads many to believe that dictators and despots are able to determine structural change; but this is mistaken. Power, being relative,
can never be total; and being a quality of a system in change, it
can neither by static nor perpetual. This simple exercise of such
unchallenged dominance promotes developments unplanned by
the ruler. The form of a political system changes as a consequence
of the political actions within it, and such action can never be
unilateral. In consequence, political systems change by a process
of structural drift.

5. THE SECOND TRANSFORMATION, 1900-50

The administrative reorganization of Zaria under the British has
already been summarized. In view of the foregoing analysis, we
shall now be principally concerned with changes in the native
political system. These political changes were revisions of the
categories which defined the structure of the previous system. The
main changes are listed summarily below:

(1) There has been a progressive but incomplete redefinition of
the concept of royalty by successive appointments from one
dynasty.

(2) The status of kingship and its relation to other governmental units has been redefined.

(3) The status of certain official mallams has been revised.

(4) The status of slave-officials has been revised.

(5) The order of military household-officials disappeared as a
unit after the kingship lost its military power.

(6) Official roles, rank-orders, and promotional arrangements
were revised to conform to the foregoing changes.

Our preceding account of the government of Zaria in 1950
describes the content of these formal changes. In the present
context we are concerned only with the structure of the process by
which they developed. We have already seen that the formal categories which define the governmental systems of Abuja and nineteenth-century Zaria apply also to the government of Anglo-
Fulani Zaria in 1950. Thus, despite changes in the content or the

specific reference of these formal categories, they denote the structural principles on which the governmental system of 1950 was based, and the structural type to which it belonged.

We have already seen that the form of a governmental system changes by political processes which redefine its basic categories, and that these revisions follow the order of logical relations among the categories undergoing change. The strains evoked by these processes of revision vary with their significance for the persistence of the total system in its current form.

Bearing these points in mind, it is clear that the two most important changes which occurred at Zaria under the British are the redefinitions of royalty and kingship. These revisions began with Kwassau's appeal for British help against Kontagora, included his own deposition and that of his immediate successor, and ended in the effectual exclusion of all but one dynasty from the succession, after the rules which traditionally governed this succession had also been changed. These revisions of royalty and the kingship provide the context within which the status of the legal mallams has also been transformed.

As noted earlier, in 1950 these legal mallams were drawn mainly from two lineages which competed for control of the judiciary. This competition has many parallels with the dynastic competition, and with the lineage competitions for certain quasi-hereditary client offices, which took place at Zaria during the last century. However, since the object of this new intra-departmental rivalry, namely the senior judgeship, was subordinate to the throne, the form and intensity of this judicial rivalry varied with the conditions of kingship and dynastic competition, so that its significance in the political changes since 1900 is not immediately apparent.

With the British revisions of kingship, the gradual entrenchment of one dynasty on the throne and the virtual elimination of others as effective rivals, relations between the king and his judiciary have also changed, and the new lineage rivalry for judicial office promoted by the throne is an essential feature of these changed relations and of the judiciary's new position in the political system of 1950. At that time the territorial and legal administrations of Zaria supported one another, and their interrelations reflected the distributions of power within the state. Kingship linked and controlled both these sub-systems, and the judiciary could not compete politically with the throne, firstly because the ruler had control of its senior appointment, and secondly because the mallams were not eligible for the royal succession. By periodically reversing the distributions of power within the judiciary, the king was able to control the department effectively.

This new judiciary was established under British political pressure as part of their revision of the kingship and of its relation to the rest of the governmental system. The redefinition of kingship included also a new system of territorial administration, the reorganization of old departments, such as the Treasury, and the eventual development of new ones, such as Forestry, Health, or Education. To improve legal administration, a system of district courts was established under a supreme court at the capital which was empowered to hear appeals and to deal with certain types of administrative offence. These formal revisions had many substantive implications, some of which involved simultaneous changes in the judicial functions of the king and his legal mallams. The head of this new judiciary was given decisive influence over appointments within his department, and thus became the most powerful subordinate official of the state.

In 1950 the British Administration was the most important single element in the political context of Zaria. The native political system at that time consisted of two unequal segments, namely, the judiciary under the senior judge, and the territorial and other departmental units under the throne. Within this new political system an older segmentary order of multidynastic competition persisted. This traditional system of dynastic competition was the centre and source of resistance to the British redefinitions of kingship, and to the administrative reorganization of the state. However, in this century, as in the last, the rivalry of these dynasties allowed the suzerain of Zaria a fair degree of initiative. Thus the British have gradually revised the old concept of royalty by changing the patterns of succession, and they have also revised the form of kingship in the ways related above. Since the throne is the central organ of all these interlocking systems of political relations, its revision has been the essential precondition of any structural change. Thus the new, more heterogeneous system could develop no faster than the revision of the old. For nearly forty years the British blueprint for the government of Zaria waited on changes in the traditional political forms without which it could not take effect; and even in 1950, as we have seen, the British governmental model did not function as it should, owing to the persistence of basic elements from the old political structure.

We can illustrate these abstractions by examining developments in Zaria since 1920. By that time the territorial and legal administration had been reorganized and was well understood by the native officials. New relations between the king and the Chief Judge on the one hand, and between the Chief Judge and his subordinates on the other, had alike developed, within the limits set by the changes already effected in the traditional multi-dynastic system; but the changes in this system presupposed others in the definitions of royalty and kingship.

Since the death of Dallatu in 1924, the chances for members of dynasties other than the Bornawa to become king have been reduced progressively by three consecutive Bornawa appointments, the two last of which both broke with traditional rules. The statuses of royalty and kingship have thus been progressively redefined, and the old political system of dynastic competition has been gradually transformed in this process. This transformation is, however, by no means complete, as the difference between the form and the reality of the government of Zaria in 1950 amply illustrates. Even a fourth consecutive Bornawa kingship could not constitute a final and unequivocal redefinition of royalty or entirely eliminate the multidynastic system; and such an appointment is rather unlikely. None the less, the Fulani concept of royalty assumes equal chances of promotion to the throne among royal lines; negligible chances of such promotion entail the loss of royal status, as has already happened with the Suleibawa dynasty at Zaria. Thus despite the incompleteness of the changeover from multidynastic rule towards a fully hereditary monarchy, and despite the probability that this drift may shortly be reversed, by 1950 the old political structure had changed profoundly, and the direction of change seemed likely to continue as long as current political conditions were maintained. In short, the royal successions since 1920 had effected a partial redefinition of royalty, which although far from final, exercised a profound influence on the rest of the constitution, and governed the rate and form of change within it.

Relations between Zaria and the British during these years were also changing and ambiguous. Initially defined as a relation between the British and the ruler as sole Native Authority, under the reorganization effected by the British, indirect relations between the Native Judiciary and the British Administration were also established. Had the Native Judiciary become truly independent of the Emir, these indirect relations with the British would have been politically significant, since native courts can try cases which involve native officials, and these courts could expect British support for just decisions. However, the Native Judiciary remained politically dependent on the ruler, who alone represented the state in its dealings with the British.

During their early years the British deposed two emirs of Zaria, revised the conditions of kingship, and sought to define their position as the new suzerains of Zaria clearly. Accordingly, relations between the British and Zaria became decisive for the maintenance or development of the native state. Hitherto Zaria's vassalage to Sokoto had been a relation between separate political units. After 1900, Zaria faced the British, who claimed superior authority but sought to exercise this as a political unit co-ordinate in status with the Zaria Native Authority, and tried to direct local developments by influencing policy decisions. In this latter role the British could not exercise the superior authority they claimed as suzerains.

The contrast with Zaria's traditional vassalage is clear. Relations between Zaria and Sokoto in the last century were clearly hierarchic; those between Zaria and the British were hierarchic in some contexts and segmentary in others. In effect, the rulers of Zaria opposed British reforms politically in so far as their traditional institutions seemed in danger. Since the traditional government was a principal target for British reforms, the rulers of Zaria strove to defend it as far as possible, and their success in that regard has already been shown.

In this context of political contraposition between the British and the Emir, the new judiciary acquired special significance. Whoever controlled this judiciary would dominate the political scene. The British as well as the king realized this, but they were careful not to deal directly with the Native Judiciary, although seeking to secure its independence from the throne. The king's recognition of the new position of the judiciary at first expressed itself in abrupt replacement of the senior judges; but as the old multidynastic competition gradually receded into the political background, and the ruler's security correspondingly increased, relations between the throne and the judiciary changed accordingly;

and it was mainly by means of these changes that the kingship was able to retain its old autocratic powers within the context of British supervision.

To recapitulate, during the last century there were eleven Alkalain Zazzau, only two of whom did not die in office. Between 1900 and 1924, when the traditional system of dynastic competition clearly dominated the government of Zaria, there were five appointments to the office of Chief Alkali. Of these, two ended in the Alkali's dismissal from office, and one in promotion to the revived office of Waziri, dismissal from which followed shortly after. During Ibrahim's reign, 1924 to 1936, when the traditional system of dynastic rivalry was still sufficiently recent and vigorous to dominate the government of Zaria, there were four Alkalain Zazzau. Of these one died in office, his successor was promoted to the Waziriship, the third was dismissed from office, and the last, who survived Ibrahim, retained the senior judgeship for nearly twenty years, until he too was promoted to become Waziri by Ibrahim's successor in 1953.

Tenure of the Chief Judgeship first became unstable in 1903 when Aliyu succeeded Kwassau and the British attempted to re-define kingship by creating an independent judiciary. The tenure of this office remained highly unstable until 1936, when the British appointed the third consecutive Emir from the Bornawa dynasty. During this period the long-defunct office of Waziri was filled intermittently by promotion from the Chief Judgeship, and the judiciary was neatly divided between two competing lineages, which held the senior judgeship alternately.

These changes and their duration can only be understood by reference to the gradual processes by which royalty and kingship were redefined, as the traditional political system grew into the new one. As initially planned by the British, the Chief Alkali's office was inconsistent with the prevailing definitions of royalty and kingship. The tenure of this senior judgeship was therefore highly unstable. However, with the decreasing significance of dynastic competition after the appointment of the third consecutive Bornawa ruler, the king's need for close supervision of the judiciary has also diminished, and with the throne's success in promoting lineage competitions among the judiciary, the power of the Chief Judgeship has declined sufficiently to permit its holders a fair security of tenure.

Administrative records show that until about 1930 there were frequent dismissals of senior officials in Zaria on charges of intrigue or maladministration. These dismissals sometimes conflicted with the norms of dynastic rule, although they were usually in accord with them. However, since 1930 such dismissals have become increasingly rare in Zaria, although my field studies in 1949–50 showed that the British had not succeeded in suppressing maladministration. So long as the judiciary seemed to threaten the throne politically, the tenure of senior judicial office remained unstable; but by the end of the long period of Bornawa rule the tenure of all senior offices, including the senior judgeship, had increased in security, and British supervision had become less effective.

The pivotal positions of royalty and the throne in this second transformation of government at Zaria will now be clear. The serial successions to kingship from one dynasty each marked a new stage in the progressive revision of royalty and kingship. At each of these stages, relations between the ruler, his judiciary, his senior officials and his British supervisors altered accordingly. By the end of this process the British had lost that decisive influence over local policy which was formerly theirs, though their technical functions had increased. By 1950 the solidarity of the Native Authority and the Native Administration, including the judiciary, was sufficiently great to ensure the preservation of traditional governmental forms and practice, in so far as these were consistent with the changes on which the new equilibrium was based.

In sum, this Anglo-Fulani government of 1950 had developed by progressive redefinitions of royalty, kingship, judicial office, and of relations between the native state and the British. This summary directs attention to the substantive irrationality of the British reforms at the period of their introduction. It also indicates that the Hausa-Fulani political system of 1950 differs as much from the British blueprints of 1900 as from the traditional Fulani system, and does so in consequence of the structural necessities which governed the historical processes by which this transformation occurred.

When the numerous departmental and other administrative changes introduced by the British are compared with the political changes we have just analysed, their structural marginality is apparent. Of themselves, these administrative innovations had no direct implications for political change, and indeed their effectiveness often presupposed certain political changes. The elimination of household and occupational official orders, or the redefinition of the slave order evoked no resistance, since they affected administrative structures only and had no political significance. Like the establishment of new departments, other than the legal department, these cases only restate the contrast between administrative changes which evoke little resistance and are marginal to the process of structural change, and the changes of a political system which develop indirectly, gradually, and under conditions of special strain.

9

CONCLUSION

OUR study has three principal interests: ethnology, method, and theory. The ethnological conclusions can be stated simply. We have shown that although the Fulani conquerors of Zazzau initially sought to preserve the Habe constitution so far as this was consistent with their religious and administrative ideas, they were constrained to abandon or alter many of the most distinctive and significant institutions of the Habe government under the pressures produced by their own internal political competition, and this process continued until the original structure had been thoroughly transformed. The most important changes to have taken place since 1900 under British supervision, at first seem administrative rather than political; closer study reveals that these administrative changes are less important than the unnoticed and unpremeditated changes which have restructured the native political system. The British in this century, like the Fulani in the last, have tried to preserve the traditional constitution in so far as it was consistent with their own moral and administrative ideas. None the less in both periods there were significant political changes, and the system of government was transformed.

As regards method, we have found certain types of historical materials essential for our analysis, others irrelevant. Field problems of historiography have been discussed in our opening scrutiny of the data and their sources.

One feature of our analytic method is worth special attention. This is its inherently comparative character. Our study is really an exercise in the application of the comparative method to the problems of diachronic analysis, despite the fact that the units compared are stages of a single developmental continuum. The application of comparative method to diachronic analysis presupposes initial study of the units concerned as isolated synchronic systems. The next stage is to make a detailed historical study of the processes of change, and then to develop a single set of categories which will define each of these systems. These categories will then provide the following analyses with a common logic and frame of reference.

The critical conceptions of a general theory of the system under study provide the basis for a comparative typology, the categories of which can be tested in diachronic analysis. Such categories permit the use of comparative methods in diachronic studies.

Diachronic analysis presupposes comparative methods. In such an analysis we begin by ignoring the specific processes of change, and seek to define the common and singular structural conditions of successive stages in the continuum, by their inductive comparison. Probably the method of analysis is more significant than the specific notions we have advanced about the process of change in governmental systems. Even so, the logical organization of the system of formal categories in a necessary and irreversible order is essential for any analysis which seeks to explore the structure or logic of change. Without such conceptual instruments we can neither identify the structure of change nor isolate and analyse its numerous incidental, anomalous, or irrational elements.

By this method of analysis we found three major categories of development: unplanned changes which were institutionalized; planned changes which were institutionalized; planned changes which failed to persist. By analysing these three types of development closely we were led to formulate three laws of structural change. The real test of any diachronic analysis is its ability to distinguish different sorts of development, and to explain their differing histories by a single set of general relations.

This study contains two adventures in theory. We began with a general theory of government which provided the conceptual framework for the analysis of the three governmental systems of Zazzau. In concluding we developed a theory of structural change by analysis of all the changes or attempts at change, which formed part of the processes by which these systems of government were transformed. Probably both these theories are unsatisfactory. However, any theory of structural change presupposes a general theory of the system undergoing such change.

The argument has been long and difficult. We have had to distinguish between government and society, and to define their mutual relations and limits; to examine the credentials of our data; to develop a working historiography for this type of study; to assess the comparability of the systems described by these data;

and then to analyse and compare them. Within the process of change we were forced to distinguish between harmony and disharmony. In addition, we have had to stress the distinction between substance and form, and between successive and simultaneous relations.

The complexity of this analysis reflects the complexity of the problem it deals with. We set out to search for a logic in change, a necessary structure within the processes by which development takes place. We have made an analysis of structural change. But such change also has its own structure, that is, the orderly relations of its parts and processes. We have therefore been concerned to determine the structure by which structural change proceeds.

APPENDIX A

THE CONSTITUTION OF THE HABE OF ZAZZAU[1]

1. *Rukuni* (Principal, i.e. first order chiefs)—Madawaki, Galadima, Wambai, Dallatu.

2. *Rawuna* (Turbanned, i.e. second order chiefs)—These are divided into two groups, those who follow (i.e. are subordinate to) the Madawaki, and those who follow (i.e. are subordinate to) the Galadima. Those following Madawaki are—Kuyambana, Sata, Garkuwa Babba, Makaba Babba (also referred to as Makama I, or Makama the Greater), Lifidi, Wagu, Shenagu; those following Galadima are—Iyan Bakin Kasuwa, Barwa, Sarkin Pawa, Wandiya and Dankekasau. (See Chart A.) There was also Sarkin Gayen, a stranger who followed Makau from Zaria. Formerly he was chief of a certain village (Gayen). Although he is not listed in any of the seven classes of Habe office-holders, he followed Galadima because he lived in Galadima's territory. So did the Dan Galadima (the king's chosen successor); although he was of royal descent, none the less he was under Galadima's orders.

3. *Fadawa* (Officers of the king's household)—include Sarkin Fada (chief of the palace) Jarmai, Barde, and Hauni. These also had their assistants, thus, Cincina, Jagaba, Bakon Bornu, Gwabare, Magayaki—all these followed Sarkin Fada. Ciritawa, Madakin Jarmai, Kacalla—these followed Jarmai. Durumi, Kangiwa, Barde the Lesser, Barden Maidaki, Garkuwa the Lesser, Magayakin Barde, Madakin Barde—all these followed Barde. Madakin Hauni and Barden Hauni followed Hauni.

4. In former times the king's eunuchs were—Makami Karami (also called Makama the Lesser), Ma'aji, Sarkin Ruwa, Turaki, Fagaci, Sarkin Zana. These are also called chiefs of the inner chamber. That is to say, in former times they alone among the officials could enter the king's sleeping-chamber.

5. These are the principal servants of the king—Sirdi, Shamaki, Madakin Gabas, Kunkeli, Sarkin Karma, Banaga, S. Bindiga (chief of the musketeers), S. Baka (chief of the archers) Magajin Kwa, S. Noma (chief of farming), Bikon Tambari, Magajin Nagaba, and Baroka.

6. Chiefs of the royal line—the Dan Galadima, the son of a chief, the Sarauniya, the daughter of a chief, and the Iya the 'mother' of the chief.

---

[1] Hassan, Sarkin Ruwa, and Shu'aibu, Mukaddamin Makaranta Bida. *Tarihi da Al'adun Habe na Abuja*, Gaskiya Corporation, Zaria, 1952, pp. 28–38. Bracketed comments to clarify passages are inserted by the present writer.

7. The chiefs of the (Koranic) scholars (*Mallamai*) were as follows—Magajin Mallam, Limam Juma'a, Salanke, and Magatakarda (the king's scribe).

When business was being discussed, chiefs of the first and second orders (*Rukuni* and *Rawuna*) would collect in the Council Chamber (known as the Entrance-hut of Zazzau) and hold council. No one else could enter except those. It was at this entrance-hut that all installations of these chiefs took place at night. When Kuyambana, or Sata, Iyan Bakin Kasuwa, the Sarauniya, or Iya (the queen mother) were appointed, there would be drumming on the *tambari* (the royal drums) for seven days. Among the household officials, only Sarkin Fada and Jarmai were installed at night, and then without any drumming on the *tambari*. At their installation only the *pampami* (the lesser of the royal horns) would be blown. So also for the remainder of the Turbanned chiefs, only the royal horns were blown, there was no drumming of *tambari*.

A LIST OF OFFICIALS AND THEIR WORK

Even now the majority of these titles are still filled at Abuja. When one title-holder dies, his successor is appointed. But only a few of these offices now carry their traditional duties, the remainder are retained mainly for tradition's sake; for however great the change of the times may be, it is not possible to abandon ancient institutions all at once. The majority of these old offices are now given to employees of the Native Authority, or to elders of the capital who care about public affairs. The following is an account of the duties of all these offices in former times.

(a) *Madawaki*. The Madawaki was next in importance after the king. He was greater than all other title-holders. For this reason he was greeted as 'Head of the Chiefs'. He commanded the cavalry and was in charge of military operations. He was in charge of that half of Abuja town east of the Wucicciri river. The king neither dismissed nor appointed any office-holder without asking Madawaki's consent. He also answered the king's speech on the (Muhammadan) festival days. When all the office-holders went to greet the king at his palace after the (Muhammadan) festival, they were obliged to wait until Madawaki came, then they followed him and went in. Together with him the other office-holders of the first order selected a new king, but if they (i.e. the other first order of officials) were of royal descent, then Madawaki called Kuyambana (instead) and the leading mallams to help him select a new king.

(b) *Galadima*. Formerly this office was held by one of the king's eunuchs. His main work was to administer the capital when the king went to war. He also officiated at the marriages and naming ceremonies of the king's children.

(c) *Wambai*. He officiated at naming ceremonies of the king's children and was one of the king's eunuchs also. He was responsible for the cesspits and the urinals of the king and women of the palace.

(d) *Dallatu*. He supervised arrangements for the war camps where he also deputized for Galadima.

2. The Turbanned Officials (i.e. the Second Order)

These offices were held by slaves or elders of the town.

(a) *Kuyambana*. The Madawaki's principal assistant.

(b) *Sata*. In charge of the king's servants. He also thatched the principal entrance-hut to the palace, and swept and weeded the palace door.

(c) *Garkuwa Babba*. His duty was to guard the war camp. He also helped the infantrymen dance with the king, for in those days if the king enjoyed the drumming, he would dance himself.

(d) *Makama the Greater*. He arranged the dispositions of the warriors and divided the booty. With the assistance of Wagu, Lifidi, Shenagu, and Dankekasau, he guarded the palace door on festival days, before the king came forth to the mosque, and also at the *Gani* festival (held to celebrate the birth of the prophet Mohammed).

(e) *Lifidi*. In charge of the 'yan lifida (the foot-soldiers wearing quilted cotton armour).

(f) *Wagu*. His duty was to guard the tombs of the kings, and to repair and watch over them. When the children of the royal line were being married he prepared the (masked dancer known as the) *Dodo* of Wagu.

(g) *Shenagu*. He made ropes for the king's horses.

The following turbanned officials followed Galadima:

(h) *Iyan Bakin Kasuwa*. His work was to supervise the markets of the capital and the villages.

(i) *Barwa*. He prepared the king's shelter at the war camp, and repaired any of his resting-places. He carried out the punishment on pregnant unmarried girls. He set them to grind and pound grain, and to carry out any similar tasks for their entire ward. When a new king was appointed, he bound leaves of the sheanut tree to his body and remained outside the hut in which the new king was isolated for seven days. It is he who teaches the new king the royal gait, so that he will not walk quickly, as he used to do when a commoner.

(j) *Sarkin Pawa* (chief of the butchers). He was responsible for the slaughter of cattle and other beasts in the market.

(k) *Wandiya*. When the king's daughters married he provided them with decorative plates.

(l) *Dankekasau*. He had to stand outside the palace door on one leg on festival days before the king set out for the prayer-ground. This was done so that if the king came forth disturbed in mind, when he saw Dankekasau, he would laugh, and forget the business that troubled him.

3. Fadawa (Officers of the King's Household)

(a) *Sarkin Fada* (chief of the King's household). He supervised the household and the behaviour of the household officials. He assisted Makama Babba in dividing the war booty; he would take away the king's share, and then give Makama Babba the Madawaki's share. Those who followed Sakin Fada are:

(b) *Cincina.* His work was to spy out the news of the country so that he would know who was plotting in rebellion.

(c) *Jagaba.* He went ahead of the more heavily armed foot-soldiers. He also arrived first at the camp before the king came.

(d) *Bakon Bornu.* The messenger to the king of Bornu.

(e) *Gwabare.* He was responsible for the thatching of all the huts in the king's palace. During the month of the Fast, he provided oil for the lamps which were lit in the entrance-hut where the king made the *Ashan* prayers. The king would reward him with a robe for this work at the end of the Fast.

(f) *Magayaki.* He assisted Jagaba.

(g) *Jarmai.* He commanded the reserve force on the battlefield. If the enemy overcame Madawaki's forces, he assisted them. He also gave the Sarkin Fada advice on household affairs. His followers were:

(h) *Ciritawa.* He carried Jarmai's shield.

(i) *Madakin Jarmai.* He assisted Jarmai.

(j) *Barde.* When the king planned to go anywhere, Barde went ahead to inspect the king's resting-place before his arrival. On campaigns he also went ahead to locate the enemy, then he returned to inform Madawaki. He assisted Sarkin Fada. His followers were:

(k) *Durumi.* He was responsible for marshalling the king's bodyguard about the king at the war camp. He also provided the wood and mat fences for the king's tent at the war camp.

(l) *Kangiwa* (elephant's head). He received all the beasts brought to the king by the hunters who killed them. The king used to give Kangiwa the head of every beast slain.

(m) *Barde the Lesser.* He supported Barde on campaigns.

(n) *Barden Maidaki.* His duty was thatching and building the hut of the king's senior wife, and also the carrying out of her commands.

(o) *Magayakin Barde.* An assistant of Barde.

(p) *Garkuwa the Lesser.* An assistant of Garkuwa Babba.

(q) *Madakin Barde.* An assistant of Barde. Also Barde's messenger to the king.

(r) *Hauni.* He deputized for Jarinai when the latter was absent. He also supervized the king's servants. He assisted Sarkin Fada with counsel. His followers are: (i) *Madakin Hauni* and (ii) *Barden Hauni.*

4. The King's Eunuchs, or Officials of the Inner Chamber

(a) *Makami Karami* (or Makama the Lesser). He was head of the officials of the Inner Chamber, and was the king's messenger to the Limamin Juma'a, the Magatakarda, the Sarauniya, Iya, the Garkuwa Babba.

(b) *Ma'aji.* He was treasurer of the throne, and also helped Makama the Lesser at the Palace.

(ç) *Turaki.* He was the king's messenger to the Madawaki and the Turbanned officials, and also to Salanke. He advised Makama the Lesser.

(d) *Sarkin Ruwa* (the Chief of the Waters). He was the king's messenger to the fishermen and was responsible for all matters pertaining to water. He also helped Makama the Lesser with advice.

(e) *Fagaci.* He was the messenger to Galadima, Dan Galadima, Sarkin Gayen, Magajin Dangi (literally, the head of the kinsfolk, the acting head of the royal lineage?). He also helped Makama the Lesser with advice.

(f) *Sarkin Zana* (chief of the enclosure). He was the king's messenger to the women of the palace. He disciplined the palace women and the young children of the king when they committed offences. He always remained in the palace, morning and night, until the time at which the king went to sleep, then he would lock the palace door. He looked after the king's store-rooms, and advised Makama the Lesser.

5. The Principal Servants of the King

(a) *Sirdi* (saddle). His work was to see to the king's harness and all other equipment for the king's horses.

(b) *Shamaki* (stables). His work was care of the king's horses.

(c) *Madakin Gabas.* He guarded the environs of the king's compound, and was in charge of the king's guinea-corn granaries.

(d) *Banaga.* His work was to clear river-courses, and to open roads on campaigns.

(e) *Sarkin Karma* (chief of the foot-soldiers). He would set fire to the enemies' villages on slave-raids.

(f) *Sarkin Bindiga* (chief of the musketeers). He commanded the infantry musketeers.

(g) *Sarkin Baka* (chief of the archers). He commanded the infantry archers.

(*h*) *Kunkeli.* He was in charge of the foot-soldiers with shields.

(*i*) *Magajin Kwa.* He was the king's barber-doctor.

(*j*) *Sarkin Noma.* He was overseer of the king's farms.

(*k*) *Bikon Tambari.* He was in charge of the royal drums (*tambari*).

(*l*) *Boroka.* She was the (king's) principal female messenger.

6. The Royal Office-holders

(*a*) *Dangaladima.* He was the king's chosen successor. (In a footnote to this remark, Mallam Hassan says 'but only one Dangaladima ever became king (at Abuja). He was Abu Kwaka.' (2) p. 34, footnote 1).)

(*b*) *Sarauniya.* She is the eldest daughter of (a ? the ?) king, and looked after the affairs of the king's daughters with regard to marriage. She also took charge of the king's wives when he was on a journey, and took charge with *Iya* in preparing the feasts for the *Gani* festival.

(*c*) *Iya.* One of the wives of the deceased king always holds this title, but not necessarily the reigning king's mother. She was in charge of the marriage arrangements of the deceased king's concubines.

7. The Chief Koranic Scholars

(*a*) *Limamin Juma'a.* He is the chief of all mallams (Koranic scholars). He makes the prayer over the corpse at the death of every commoner in the town. He takes service at the mosque on Fridays. He is among those who elect a new king.

(*b*) *Salanke.* He takes the service at the prayer-ground (i.e. on festival days), and makes the prayers over the corpse of every official. He is among those who elect the new king.

(*c*) *Magajin Mallam.* He was the representative of the king of Bornu, and he installed the new king.

(*d*) *Magatakarda.* He was the priest of the king's compound. He made the prayers over the king's dead attendants. On the day of the new year feast he would also foretell the events of the coming year.

The remaining officials were as follows:

Kacalla. A messenger to the king of Bornu.

Sarken Gayen. He was not among the Habe chiefs at Zaria. He was the chief of a certain village in the country near Zaria, and helped Galadima.

Abokin Sarki (the king's friend). He acts as the bridegroom's friend when the king marries.

Dogarai (the king's guard). Their work was to capture and discipline offenders, and to guard the town together with the warders.

'Yan Doka (police). They were in charge of prisoners and executed murderers. They also acted as public criers in the town.

COUNCIL PROCEDURE

Every morning the officials of the Inner Chamber went in to greet the king. If he had received any information necessitating counsel, the king would inform them and they would discuss it with him; when agreement was reached, they would all come forth together. In leaving the chamber, Makama the Lesser went in front, then Ma'aji, then Sarkin Ruwa, then Turaki, then Fagaci, then Sarkin Zana carrying a sword, then the king, then Baroka, the female messenger behind the king. They would proceed to the entrance-hut known as the hut of the Royal Drums.

When the king was ready to recline on his couch there, the chamber officials would spread out their robes wide, so as to hide him, that no one may see the king sitting down. When the king was settled, they went to their places and stayed there. Then Turaki would get up and approach the king, cover his mouth with the sleeve of his robe, and tell the king that Sarkin Fada had arrived and was waiting at the palace door. The king would tell Turaki to call him. Then Turaki would go to Sarkin Fada, cover his mouth with his sleeve, and announce that the king had come forth and ordered Sarkin Fada to approach. On this Sarkin Fada, Jarmai, Barde, and Hauni would go in to the king. When they came to the door of the hut of the royal drums the four of them would greet the king two or three times, and then enter and take their places.

When they were all settled, Makama the Lesser would tell Sarkin Fada the matter in question, and the advice they had given. Sarkin Fada would then ask Jarmai, Barde, and Hauni what they thought of Makama the Lesser's advice. If it seemed sound they would agree. If it did not seem sound, they would give their views as to how the matter should be handled. If Sarkin Fada thought that the problem could not be resolved without Madawaki, then the king would send Turaki to call Madawaki, Galadima, Wambai, and Dallatu. When they entered the council room, then all officials of the household and of the Inner Chamber went outside and left them alone with the king.

The king would explain the matter to them and say he wished them to discuss it thoroughly among themselves and advise how best it should be handled. They would then leave the king and proceed to the *Zauren Zazzau* (the entrance-hut of Zazzau) and after calling Kuyambana and telling him, they would collect all the Turbanned officials and discuss the matter with them. When the discussion was over, Madawaki would call Turaki and tell him what they had decided, and Turaki would go to inform the king.

If the king agreed with their advice, he dismissed them. If Sarkin

Fada and officials of his order also agreed with the advice, they accepted it, but if they disagreed with it, they would tell the king they rejected the proposal. Then the king and Madawaki would take counsel together how the matter might be handled without Sarkin Fada's disagreement. But if no compromise could be reached, the king would stop the dispute—that was that—no one had any further argument with the king, his command was obligatorily obeyed. Sometimes Madawaki would take counsel with Sarkin Fada secretly, so that their common proposals should not conflict in the council. . . .

. . . The king held council with the Sarauniya on matters concerning the daughters of the royal line; he held council with Iya on matters concerning the womenfolk of the palace. He took council with Dangaladima concerning the affairs of males of the royal line.

LAW

Formerly there was no Alkali (trained Muhammadan judge)[1], but complainants took their case before the king. The officials of the Inner Chambers and of the household were always with the king; anyone who had a complaint and came to the palace would find them together, and could bring his complaint. If the charge was not serious, for instance if there was no murder or wounding involved, the king decided the issue himself. But if a serious criminal offence was involved, the king would seek the advice of his leading mallams.

When a criminal was to be punished, the Turaki would tell the Dogarai (bodyguard) to capture and take him to the prisoners' ward. There were no jails then, but prisoners had their legs put in stocks and were detained in the entrance-hut. The warders would fetch food of all kinds that were being sold in the market, and prepare meals for the prisoners. To this day, there are two prison-chains at the prisoners' ward which were brought from Zaria long ago. One is 26 feet long, the other 19 feet. Murderers were bound with these chains. In former days the chains were also used in ritual. Apart from these, there is also another chain at Dada's compound, that is, the quarters of the guard (*dogarai*), and there is another at the Galadima's compound. Offenders who were fined were bound with this latter chain, and were detained until the money was paid. When an offender would not confess the truth, he was bound with the chain and tortured so that he would speak the truth, but prisoners sentenced to punishment were not tormented. A thief had his hand cut off; a murderer was executed by the executioner[2].

---

[1] Elsewhere M. Hassan notes the arrival of Mallam Umaru, the first Alkali at Abuja, in the reign of Abu Kwakwa, 1851–77 (see (1) pp. 17–18).

[2] Concerning execution, see *op. cit.* (1) pp. 12–13.

TERRITORIAL ADMINISTRATION

The important (hereditary, vassal) chiefs in the kingdom (of Abuja) were Sarkin Izom (the chief of Izom), Sarkin Kuta (the chief of Kuta), Sarkin Kawu, Sarkin Jiwa, Sarkin Kuje, Sarkin Abuci, Sarkin Zuba and Sarkin Gwazunu. Each of these (vassal) chiefs had his representative (*kofa*) inside Abuja town. Whatsoever happened in their territories, they would send their messengers to inform the king. Turaki was (the king's) representative to Sarkin Izom, Sarkin Ruwa was messenger to the chiefs of Kawu and Gawu. Fagaci was messenger to the chiefs of Kuta, Gwazunu, and Abuci. Galadima acted as go-between for Sarkin Jiwa; Wambai as go-between for Sarkin Kuje.

(Apart from this) the smaller districts (of the kingdom) were allocated among the king's *rukuni* (first order of chiefs), the Turbanned councillors, and the members of the royal house. Madawaki was in charge of the people of Kafin, Kagarko, Fanda and Tawari. (That is to say, these were Madawaki's fiefs.) Galadima was in charge of Guni and Gusoro. Uma'isha, Abaji, and Koton Karfe belonged to the king. The king's eunuchs came from the last two of the king's towns. Sarauniya administered Kurmin Gurmana, and Kabula (see map A).

TAXATION

Both the (hereditary vassal) chiefs and all other office-holders provided tribute of slaves and money. Each of the (vassal) chiefs gave the king one or more slaves and 100,000 cowries or more, one or more times a year. They also gave their agent one-tenth of the amount they gave to the king. Craftsmen also paid tribute with their products. (For example) the Kadara (pagans settled near Kuta) provided 100 mats for the king (each year) and gave the go-between ten. The people of Gawu gave the king 100 locally made black-and-white cloths, and their messenger ten. The people of Kawu provided 100 lumps of iron ore, and gave their messenger ten. And so too with all the remaining crafts.

Itinerant traders in cattle, horses, goats, sheep, natron, salt, onions, each gave some of their produce to the king. Those itinerant traders who were housed in Madawaki's ward would also give Madawaki his share, apart from what they gave the king. Those who stayed in Galadima's ward also gave Galadima his share apart from the king's. Besides all this, there were also the payments on installation in office. Both the Madawaki and the Galadima each gave one million cowries to the king. The other principal officials gave 200,000 cowries each, and the remainder of the officials gave what they could afford. Booty in war was given to the king and the Madawaki. Fulani nomads also paid cattle-tax; they paid 10,000 cowries for every head.[1]

The king had many obligations to the officials and the general populace. When a new Madawaki or Galadima was installed in office, the king would give each a bernous, a splendid robe, a large turban, a huge stallion and equipment for it. The Turbanned officials were given a gown and a turban each (hence their name). Other officials received a gown apiece only.

When any vassal chief or the chief of any village in Abuja kingdom sent news of raiders to the king, the latter would despatch warriors to help the defeat of the enemy. The king also provided his troops with horses, and rewarded any who had shown bravery in battle. When news of highway robbers or extortioners who distressed the common people was received, the king would order their capture and punishment.

The king also bought canoes from the Kakanda and placed them at the main rivers to ferry people across. He had bridges built over the smaller streams. He assisted destitute strangers and disabled persons, providing them with clothes, food or winding sheets, or arranged their marriages or naming ceremonies. He gave alms to those students who completed learning the Koran. Thus when a boy graduated from the Koran School he was taken before the king, who gave him an embroidered cap and gown, after he had tested the boy by asking him to read something written on his writing board.

In a letter written by M. Hassan on 26th July, 1952, the following replies are given to questions concerning the statuses of various orders of officials put by the present writer:

'(2). Household officials and the king's "servants"—the majority of the household officials were clients (i.e. freemen), but the king's "servants" were slaves.

(3) The principal servants of the king could not become household officials, they were a separate order of their own, but the household officials could be promoted. Thus Sarkin Fada could be promoted and become Madawaki. Similarly, the king's eunuchs could be promoted (i.e. chamber eunuchs). For example, I was formerly Sarkin Ruwa, but was recently promoted and became Makama the Lesser. After this I am eligible to become Galadima.

(4) Officials under the Galadima were clients, not slaves.

(5) Household officials and the king's slaves had no territorial fiefs. The whole country was theirs, as they appointed the other officials.

[1] Cowries were converted into currency at Zaria in 1900–10 at an average rate of $\frac{1}{2}d$. for 100.

(6) Magajin Dangi. This was an office of the order of mallams from the days of the Habe in Zaria. He was known as Magajin Dangi of the Habe so as to differentiate him from the Magajin Mallam of Bornu origin.'

———————

An undated manuscript by Masterton-Smith, an officer of the Nigerian Administration, ex. M.P. 36,002, called 'Abuja, the Heart of Nigeria', yielded further information, some of which, not given by M. Hassan's text, may be summarized here.

Of the four *rukuni* offices of Abuja, that of Madawaki was held by a nobleman or the king's son, while the offices of Galadima, Wambai, and Dallatu were held by eunuchs. (On the other hand, M. Hassan states that at Abuja the office of Madawaki was not held by members of the dynasty. Possibly Masterton-Smith may here be alluding to developments under British rule, or more probably M. Hassan is describing the traditional pre-1804 constitution, omitting to mention changes in the nineteenth century.) Of the offices subordinate directly to the Madawaki, Masterton-Smith lists the titles of Wagu and Sata as held by slaves, while the remainder, Kuyambana, Makama Babba, Garkuwa Babba, Lifidi, Shenagu, were held by nobles. The titles of Barwa and Bakon Bornu, directly subordinate to the Galadima and the Sarkin Fada respectively, were held by slaves. Masterton-Smith also includes the Magajin Dangi, head of the (? royal) lineage, among the order of mallams.[1]

Masterton-Smith, *op. cit.*, para. 17.

APPENDIX B

1. OFFICE-HOLDERS UNDER M. MUSA, 1804–21

(The Habe orders of rank are followed in these tables)

Title	Holder	Origin	Comments
	Musa, 1804–21		
SARKI		Mallawa	
Rukuni titles			
Madaki	(1) Makayo	Fulani Kwantambale	
	(2) Yamusa	Fulani-Bornawa	Sarkin Zazzau 1821–34.
Galadima	Dokaje	Fulani-Tofa	
Wombai	Fache	Habe	Slave
Dallatu	The younger brother of Katuku Sabulu	Habe-Kano	
Royal titles			
Magajiya	Inne (a woman)	Musa's daughter	Wife of Waziri Gidado.
Iya	Atu (a woman)	Musa's daughter	Wife of Limam Gabbo.
Mardanni	A'i (a woman)	Musa's daughter	
Dangaladima	Sidi Abdulkadiri	Musa's son	Sarkin Zazzau 1860.
Magajin Gari	Zakari	Musa's son	Dismissed by S.Z. Yamusa, 1821–34.
Rawuna titles			
Kuyambana	None		
Makama I	Sharubutu	Zaria Habe	Slave.
Wan'ya	N/K.*		

* N/K = Not Known.

Title	Holder	Origin	Comments
Danmadami	Yaje	Fulani-Kazaure.	
Iyan Kurama	Dan Hakurau	Habe.	
Jisambo	Inusa	Fulani-Wunti.	
Rubu	Dan Citta	Fulani-Yegwarnawa.	
Katuka	Sabulu	Habe-Kano.	
Ma'ajin Kacia	Jibir	Fulani-Kano.	
Sa'i	Abdulkerim	Fulani-Katsinawa	Sarkin Zazzau 1834–46.
Wali	None.		
Sarkin Mai	Anakuma	Habe	Administered Maguzawa.
Turaki II	None.		
Magajin Zakara	Abdusallami	Fulani-Zangon Aya.	
Mallams			
Waziri	Cafadu	Fulani-Gusau	Office usually vacant.
Alkali	(1) Balingimi	Fulani-Kano	Retired.
	(2) Manga	Fulani-Katsina.	
Limamin Juma'a	Gabdo	Fulani-'Yan Doto.	
Salanke	Sadi	Fulani-Shanonawa.	
Chamber officials			
Makama II	Abdusallami	Fulani-Suleibawa	Sarkin Zazzau 1860–63.
Turaki	Ba'idu	Habe-Zanfara	Slave, freed.
Fagaci }			
Sarkin Ruwa }			
Ma'aji		From Azben.	Said not to have been appointed.
Household officers			
Sarkin Fada	Yahaya		
Barde	(1) Damarugu	Habe-Kano.	
	(2) Dan Masada	Habe-Kano.	
Madauci	(1) Zonau	Habe	Slave.
	(2) Fadi	Fulani.	
Sarkin Yaki	Muhamman	Fulani-Katsina.	
	Maizabo	Fulani.	

2. OFFICE-HOLDERS UNDER YERO 1890–97

Title	Holder	Origin	Comments
SARKI	Yero	Bornawa	Formerly Madaki. Succeeded S.Z. Sambo (1881–90) of the Katsinawa dynasty.
Rukuni titles			
Madaki	Kwassau	Bornawa	New appointment. (Yero's son.)
Galadima	Suleimanu	Habe	Appointed by S.Z. Sambo.
Wombai	(1) Muhammadu	Mallawa	Appointed by Sokoto.
	(2) Aliyu	Mallawa	Appointed by Sokoto.
Dallatu	Umoru	Bornawa	New appointment.
Royal titles			
Magajiya	Title lapsed.		
Iya	(1) Fate	Bornawa	New appointment. Died.
	(2) Zubairu	Bornawa	New appointment.
Mardanni	Aliyu	Bornawa	New appointment.
Dangaladima	Sule Mai-turare	Bornawa	New appointment.
Magajin Gari	(1) Mai-kawari	Bornawa	Yero's son.
	(2) Dallatu	Bornawa	Yero's son. S. Zazzau 1920–24.
Rawuna titles			
Kuyambana	Mai-Roron Aiki	Fulani-Yegwamawa	New appointment.
Makama I	Ci-gari	Bornawa	New appointment.
Wan'ya	(1) Yero	Fulani-Gadidi	New appointment. Died.
	(2) Abubakar	Fulani-Gadidi	New appointment.
Iyan Kurama	None.		
Jisambo	Gidado	Fulani-Wunti	Son of Inusa.
Danmadami	Grandson of ex-Iya Atiku	Bornawa	New appointment.
Rubu	Mumuni	Fulani-Yegwamawa	Son of Dan Citta. New appointment.
Katuka	Dalhatu	Fulani-'Yan Doto	New appointment.
Ma'ajin Kacia	Kau	Fulani-Kano	Son of Jibir.
Sa'i	Audusallami	Fulani-Katsinawa	Son of Sa'i Habu. New appointment.

Title	Holder	Origin	Comments
Wali	(1) Dan Kakai	Fulani-Bornawa	Son of S.Z. Yamusa.
	(2) Muhammadu	Fulani-Torankawa Gidadawa	New appointment.
Sarkin Mai	Dabo	Habe-Likoro	
Turaki II	Dan Manga	Fulani-Bornawa.	
Magajin Zakara	(1) Zubairu	Fulani-Zangon Aya	Son of Audusallami. New appointment. Died.
	(2) M. Jamo	Fulani-Zangon Aya	Kin of Audusallami. Died.
	(3) Suleimanu	Fulani-Zangon Aya	Kin of Audusallami. Became Ward-head of Magajin Zakara Ward of Zaria City under British.
Mallams			
Waziri	None.		
Alkali	Gambo	Habe-Katsina	Son of previous Alkali.
Limamin Juma's	(1) Nasamu	Fulani-'Yan Doto	New appointment.
	(2) Sambo	Fulani-'Yan Doto.	
Salanke	(1) Wobe	Fulani-Shanono	New appointment. Died.
	(2) M. Iyel	Habe-Kajuru.	
Chamber officials			
Makama II	Ja'afaru	Fulani-Bornawa	New appointment. Died.
Turaki	(1) Aikinci	Habe	New appointment. Slave. Died.
	(2) Yakubu	Habe	New appointment. Son of Fagaci. Sirajo.
Fagaci	Hamza	Fulani-Katsina	New appointment.
Sarkin Ruwa	Mijin Mama	Fulani	New appointment. Husband of Yero's sister.
Sarkin Zana	Amshe	Fulani	New appointment (see text, Ch. 4).
Household officers			
Sarkin Fada	Sadi	Fulani-Katsina	Son of previous S. Fada.
Barde	Dabo	Fulani.	
Madauci	Bature	Habe	Slave. Son of Madauci Huguma.
War titles			
Sarkin Yaki	(1) Kwassau Dan Madina	N/K*	New appointment. Died.
	(2) Tanko	Fulani-Daura	New appointment.
Shentali	Shetu	Fulani	New appointment. Cognatic kinsman of Yero.

* N/K = Not Known.

3. OFFICE-HOLDERS UNDER M. JA'AFARU, 1936—

(Appointments up to 1950)

Title	Holder	Origin	Comments
SARKI	M. Ja'afaru	Fulani-Bornawa	Formerly Katuka.
Rakuni titles			
Madaki	Shehu	Fulani-Bornawa	Appointed by S.Z. Dalhatu.
Galadima	Hayatu	Fulani-Bornawa	Appointed by S.Z. Ibrahim.
Wombai	Usuman	Fulani-Bornawa	Appointed by S.Z. Dalhatu.
Dallatu	Muhammadu	Fulani-Bornawa	Appointed by S.Z. Ibrahim.
Royal titles			
Magajiya	Title lapsed.		
Iya	Aminu	Fulani-Katsinawa	New appointment.
Mardanni	Muhammadu Bawa	Azbinawa	New appointment. Promoted Makama II in 1950.
Dangaladima	Shehu	Fulani-Katsinawa	New appointment. Died 1950.
Magajin Gari	Mamman Gabdo	Fulani-Mallawa	Appointment said to be under British Administrative pressure.
Rawuna titles			
Kuyambana	Title lapsed.		
Makama I	Halidu	Habe-Kajuru	Appointed by Dalhatu at Administrative pressure.
Wan'ya	Title lapsed.		
Iyan Kurama	Title lapsed.		
Jisambo	Mazadu	Fulani	New appointment. No district attached.
Danmadami	Umoru	Fulani-Bornawa	New appointment.
Rubu	Title has lapsed.		
Katuka	Suleimanu	Fulani-Bornawa	New appointment. S.Z. Ja'afaru's brother.
Ma'ajin Kacia	Title lapsed.		
Sa'i	Muhammadu	Fulani	New appointment.
Sarkin Mai	Title lapsed.		

Title	Holder	Origin	Comments
Wali	Umoru	Fulani-Bornawa	Appointed by S.Z. Dalhatu.
Turaki II	Ali	Fulani-Torankawa Gidadawa	New appointment. Head of N.A. Public Works Department.
Magajin Zakara	N/K*	Fulani Zangon Aya	Wardhead in Zaria City.
Mallams			
Waziri	None appointed at 1950.		
Alkali	Muhammadu Lawal	Fulani-'Yan Doto	Appointed by S.Z. Ibrahim.
Limamin Juma'a	Muhamman	Habe, Limamin Kona's family	New appointment.
Salanke	Isma'ilu	Fulani-Katsina	New appointment. Descendant of Musa's Madauci.
Chamber officials			
Makama II	(1) Ladan	Fulani-Dan Durrori	New appointment. Died 1950.
	(2) Muhammadu Bawa	Azbinawa	New appointment. Formerly Mardanni.
Turaki	See Turaki II above.		
Fagaci	Muhammadu	Habe-Kano	New appointment. Grandson on Musa's Katuka Sabulu.
Sarkin Ruwa	(1) Sanusi	Habe	Promoted Ma'aji.
	(2) Sambo	Fulani-Bornawa.	New Appointment.
Ma'aji	(1) Ibrahim	Habe	Promoted to Madauci.
	(2) Sanusi	Habe	New appointment 1949.
Household officers			
Sarkin Fada	(1) Muhamman	Fulani-Suleibawa	New appointment. Died.
	(2) Sambo	Fulani-'Yan Doto	New appointment.
Barde	Title lapsed.		
Madauci	Ibrahim	Habe	New appointment. Formerly Ma'aji.
War titles			
Sarkin Yaki	Gidado	Fulani-Sokoto	S.Z. Aliyu's appointment. Formerly a District Head, but no functions in 1950, when Gidado died.

*N/K = Not Known.

APPENDIX C

STATE TITLES AND ASSOCIATED FIEFS UNDER FULANI RULE IN NINETEENTH-CENTURY ZAZZAU

Sarauta (Title)   *Garuruwan sarauta* (Fiefs)

Sarkin Zazzau   Gangara, Makarfi, Ruma, Kidandan (Fatika), (Lere 1) (Durum, post 1860), Kagarko, Bugai, Mangi, Kwoi, Dumbi, Awai, Dan Alhaji, (Dan Maliki), Hunkuyi, Gubuci, Kwari, Mayare.

TITLES FILLED MAINLY BY MEMBERS OF DYNASTIES

Madaki   Janjala near Kagarko, Keffi, Kwotto, Karigi, Bagaji, Jema'an Dororo, Yelwa, Kwassallo, Zaben Kudan, Gimba, (Kuzuntu) Ricifa, Madaci, Kuringa, (Fatika, 1890), Rigacikum.

Dan Galadima   Kasaya, (*Gwari*), (Durum, 1860), Koraukorau, Sherifa Ginta, Ashehu, Ibada, Turunku, Kakangi, Wusono, and Kwandoro near Abuja.

Wombai   Gwibi, Talata, (Kacia), *Jaba* of Kacia, Danayamaka, Sabon Gari, Bajimi, and Samban Gida.

Magajin Gari   Saulawa, Garun Gwunki, (Kuzuntu), Dan Mahawayi, Turawa, Rikoci, Dakaci, Auchan.

Makama Karami   Kahugu, Agunu, Kauru, Kajuru, Igabi, Juran Taba, Rubu (near Bikaratu).

Iya   Dan Dako, (Nassarawa 1), Sakadadi, Kauran Wali, Iyatawa, (Fatika 2).

Wali   Bikaratu, Juran Kari, Bakura, Rahama.

TITLES FILLED MAINLY BY *BARORI* (FREE CLIENTS)

Galadima   Aribi, Katugal, Kubaca (all near Kagarko); Lazuru, Tudai, *Amawa, Gure, Kadara, Kaje*, Zonkwa, Zabi, Haskiya, Parakwai, Amana, Kwarau, Ifira, Kangimi, Afaka, Rikoka, Birnin, Bawa.

Sarkin Fada   Kudan, Madobi, Doka, Bankanawa, Dan Dako.

Turaki Babba   Guga, Soba, Likora (on Kaduna River).

Turaki Karami   (Lere 2), (Durum 1), *Cawai*, Dan Damisa, Shimbir.

Sarkin Ruwa	Likoro, Kawu, Nasari, Girku, Damau, Kaban, Bomo, Cigo.
Dan Madami	Bassawa, Zuntu, Karshi.
Salenke	Tukur Tukur, Matarkaku, (Zaben Zaria, 1861–63).
Fagaci	Abaji, Wutana, Makwolo, Rikobi, (Nassarawa), Gimi.
Ma'aji II	Kunci, Kurmin Kaduna.
Mardanni	Mardanni
Makama Babba	Riawa, Marke.
Ma'aji I	(Kacia), Jere.
Dallatu	Anchau, Dambo, Sabon Birni.
Madauci	(Dan Maliki 2. Post 1900.)
Katuka	*Ikulu* and Gadagau.
Iyan Kurama	Dutsen Wai, Kudaru, Gaskora, Lewa, Sugau.
Wan'ya	Gwaraji, Togace, Kan Rafi—Gwagwada to Sarkin Pawa.
Sarkin Mai	Gadas. All *Maguzawa*.
Jisambo	Gwagwada, Kadi.
Magajin Zakara	Sheru near Nassarawa.
Cikum	Chikum, Dafako Gwari.
Waziri	No towns.
Sa'i	No towns. All *Bororo Fulani* in Zaria.
Hauni	Dan Wata.

MILITARY TITLES

(1) *Freemen*		*Slave Titles said to be without Fiefs*
Sarkin Yaki	None	
Barde	Paki, Dawaki	
Kuyambana	Luka	Sarkin Zana, until
Rubu	(1804–21, Ifira Dinki, Tanni, Keffin Bangoji), Moroa	1893
		Garkuwa
		Tafarki
		Wagu
		Shamaki
		Jagaba
		Kilishi
		Sarkin Dukawa
(2) *Slaves*		Barwa
Sarkin Yamma	(Kacia)	Sarkin Lifidi
Sarkin Yara	Dan Guzuri, Kacia town	Kwaramaza
Sarkin Ciyawa	Bogari	
Shentali	(Ruma), Gwanda, at Katari in Kacia	

RELIGIOUS AND JUDICIAL TITLES

Limamin Juma'a	(Maigana, Kinkiba, Marwa, Awai—gifts from Mallam Musa.) Zangon Aya, Gwada, Kufena, (Jema'an Dororo, 1804–21).
Limamin Kona	Kona, Matari.
Alkali	Wuzata.

VASSALS

Sarkin Kajuru	Kasar Bishini, Mai Ido, Kafayawa, Anguwan Sarkin Baka, Pambambe, (*Katab* 1), Kajuru, *Kacicere*.
Sarkin Kauru	Kauru, Buruma, Kaibi, *Kitimi*, Gidan Agam, Karko, (*Katab* and *Kamantan*—gifts from Kajuru).
Sarkin Fatika	Fatika, Rafin Taba, Galadimawa, A. Doka, Yakawadda, Murai, Butaro, Kaya, Yankore, Anguwan Gagara, Kushariki, Gahun, Kadage, Laban, Kurmin Mallo, Rago.
Sarkin Lere	Lere, Domawa, Sheni, Kayarda, Saminaka.
Sarkin Kagarko	Jere, Kagarko, Buba, Akote, Kabara, Kazaze, Kurmin Dangana, Kubo, Kuduri, Kasuru.
Magajin Keffi	Keffi.
Sarkin Kwotto	Kwotto.
Sarkin Jema'a	Jema'an Dororo, Sambon, Nok in Zaria Province.
Sarkin Doma	Doma.
Sarkin Bagaji	Bagaji (now in Keffi).

NOTE.—Bracketed names denote fiefs which appear to have been transferred between offices during the years 1840–1900. Italics denote tribal groups.

APPENDIX D

TAXES IN FULANI ZAZZAU, 1880–1900

1. Hoe-tax (*Kurdin galma*):
Towns east of Zaria	7,000 cowries per hoe
Towns south of Zaria	6,000 cowries per hoe
Towns west of Zaria	4,000 cowries per hoe
Towns north of Zaria	6,000 cowries per hoe
2. Cassava (*Kurdin rogo*) — 4,000 cowries per plot
3. Tobacco (*Kurdin taba*) — 2,000 cowries per plot
4. Onions (*Kurdin albassa*) — 2,500 cowries per plot
5. Sugar cane (*Kurdin kara*) — 8,000 cowries per plot
6. Indigo (*Kurdin shuni*) — 3,000 cowries per plot
7. Butchers (*Kurdin pawa*) — 5,000 cowries per man
8. Blacksmiths (*Kurdin kira*) — 7,000 cowries per man
9. Brokers (*Kurdin dillalai*) — 5,000 cowries per man
10. Dyers (*Kurdin korofi*) — 3,200 cowries per pit
11. Beekeepers (*Kurdin zuma*) — 3,000 cowries per man
12. Tobacco-grinders — 5,000 per man
13. Drummers (*Kurdin kida*) — 4,000 cowries per man
14. Bori dancers (*Kurdin Bori*) — 4,000 cowries per dancer
15. Cattle-tax (*jangali*)—nominally a tithe of the herds, but actually very much less.

In addition, *zakka* or tithe of the grain crops was paid by every farmer.

From: Arnett, E. J., 1920, *Gazetteer of Zaria Province, Northern Nigeria*, p. 16. Waterlow & Sons, London.

APPENDIX E (1)

Some official transfers in Fulani Zaria, 1804–1902

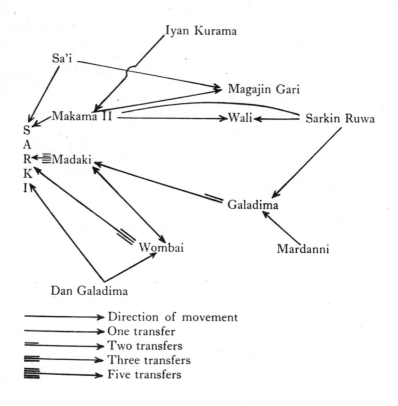

Direction of movement
One transfer
Two transfers
Three transfers
Five transfers

APPENDIX E (2)

Some official transfers in Zaria, 1903–50

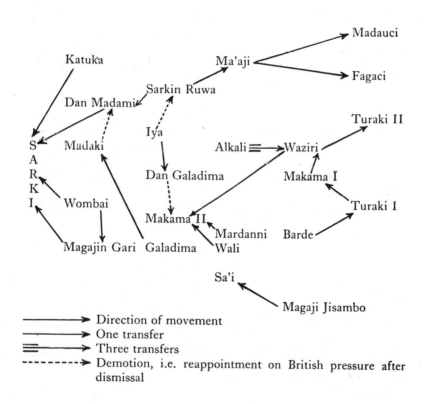

Direction of movement
One transfer
Three transfers
Demotion, i.e. reappointment on British pressure after dismissal

BIBLIOGRAPHY

ARNETT, E. J., 1909. 'A Hausa chronicle', *J. roy. Afr. Soc.*, vol. 9, pp. 161–7.
— 1920. *Gazetteer of Zaria Province*. London: Waterlow.
BARTH, H., 1857. *Travels and Discoveries in North and Central Africa*. London: Ward Lock. 2 vols. (1890 edition.)
BURNS, A. C., 1929. *History of Nigeria*. London: Allen & Unwin. (4th edition, 1948.)
CAMERON, Sir D., 1934. *Principles of Native Administration and their Application*. Lagos.
COLE, C. W., 1949. *Land Tenure in the Zaria Province of Nigeria*. Kaduna: Govt. Printer.
DENHAM, D., CLAPPERTON, H., and OUDNEY, W., 1826. *Narrative of Travels and Discoveries in Northern and Central Africa in the Years 1822, 1823, and 1824*. 2 vols. London: John Murray.
EDGAR, F., 1924. *Litafi na Tatsunyoyi na Hausa*. 3 vols. Lagos.
Gaskiya Ta Fi Kwabo (Hausa vernacular newspaper). Zaria: Gaskiya Corporation.
GREENBERG, J., 1946. *The Influence of Islam on a Sudanese Religion*. (American Ethnological Society Memoir No. 15.) New York: Augustin.
HAILEY, Lord, 1951. *Native Administration in the British African Territories*. 4 vols. London: H.M. Stationery Office.
— 1937. *An African Survey*. London: Oxford University Press for Royal Institute of International Affairs.
HASSAN, MALLAM (Sarkin Ruwa, Abuja), and SHU'AIBU (Mukaddamin Makaranta, Bida), 1952 (1). *Makau, Sarkin Zazzau na Habe*. 1952 (2). *Tarihi da Al'adun Habe na Abuja*. Zaria: Gaskiya Corporation.
HEATH, F., *transl.* 1952. *A Chronicle of Abuja*. Ibadan: University Press for Abuja Native Administration.
LUGARD, Sir FREDERICK (afterwards Lord Lugard), 1910 & 1918. *Political Memoranda*. Lagos.
LUGARD, Lord, 1926. *The Dual Mandate in British Tropical Africa*. London: Allen & Unwin.
McCULLOCH, W. E., 1929–30. 'The dietaries of the Hausa and town Fulani', *W. Afr. Med. J.*, vol. 3, pp. 8–22, 62–73.
MASTERTON-SMITH, n.d. *Abuja, the Heart of Nigeria*. Ex. M.P. 36002 (unpublished).
MEEK, C. K., 1931 (1). *A Sudanese Kingdom*. London: Kegan Paul, Trench, Trubner.

— 1931 (2). *Tribal Studies in Northern Nigeria*. 2 vols. London: Kegan Paul, Trench, Trubner.

NADEL, S. F., 1942. *A Black Byzantium*. London: Oxford University Press for International African Institute.

NIGERIA. *Native Administration Estimates, Zaria Province*, 1949–50, 1950–51.

NIGERIA, NORTHERN. *Colonial Reports*, 1901, 1903, 1907–8. London: H.M. Stationery Office.

NIVEN, C. R., 1937. *A Short History of Nigeria*. London: Longmans, Green.

— 1950. *How Nigeria is Governed*. London: Longmans, Green.

SMITH, MARY F., 1954. *Baba of Karo: a Woman of the Muslim Hausa*. London: Faber & Faber.

SMITH, M. G., 1953. 'Secondary marriage in Northern Nigeria', *Africa*, vol. 23, No. 4, pp. 298–323.

— 1954. 'Slavery and emancipation in two societies.' *Soc. & Econ. Stud.* (U.C.W.I., Mona, Jamaica, B.W.I.), vol. 3, Nos. 3 and 4, pp. 239–90.

— 1955. *The Economy of the Hausa Communities of Zaria*. London: H.M. Stationery Office.

— 1956. 'On segmentary lineage systems'. *J. roy. Anthrop. Inst.*, vol. 86, pt. 2, pp. 39–80.

STENNING, D. J., 1957. 'Transhumance, migratory drift, and migration: patterns of pastoral Fulani nomadism', *J. roy. Anthrop. Inst.*, vol. 87, pt. 1, pp. 56–73.

— 1959. *Savannah Nomads*. London: Oxford University Press for International African Institute.

STENTON, D. M., 1951. *English Society in the Early Middle Ages* (1066–1307). London: Penguin Books.

TEMPLE, O., 1919. *Notes on the Tribes, Provinces, Emirates and States of the Northern Provinces of Nigeria*. Cape Town: Argus Printing Co.

VON GRUNEBAUM, G. E., 1955. *Islam: Essays in the Nature and Growth of a Cultural Tradition* (Memoir No. 81). *Amer. Anthropologist*, vol. 57, pt. 2.

WEBER, M., 1947. *Theory of Social and Economic Organisation*. Trans. A. N. Henderson and Talcott Parsons. London: Hodge.

WITTFOGEL, KARL A., 1953. 'The ruling bureaucracy of oriental despotism: a phenomenon that paralysed Marx'. *Rev. Pol.*, vol. 15, pp. 350–9.

INDEX

SET BY HAZELL, WATSON AND VINEY, LTD.
AND REPRINTED LITHOGRAPHICALLY AT
THE UNIVERSITY PRESS, OXFORD
BY VIVIAN RIDLER
PRINTER TO THE UNIVERSITY